STUDY GUIDE

to accompany

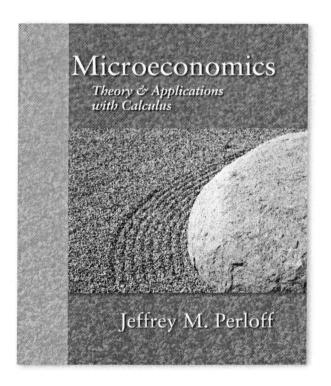

Microeconomics
Theory & Applications
with Calculus

Jeffrey M. Perloff

CHARLES MASON

University of Wyoming

LÉONIE STONE

State University of New York, Geneseo

PEARSON
Addison
Wesley

Boston San Francisco New York
London Toronto Sydney Tokyo Singapore Madrid
Mexico City Munich Paris Cape Town Hong Kong Montreal

ISBN-13   978-0-321-41234-8
ISBN-10   0-321-41234-6

2 3 4 5 6 OPM 10 09 08

Contents

Preface

This Study Guide to accompany *Microeconomics: Theory & Applications with Calculus*, by Jeffrey M. Perloff, has a simple purpose—to help you better understand microeconomics and earn a higher grade in your microeconomics class. The guide was written by two professors who regularly teach intermediate microeconomics. Léonie L. Stone, of the State University of New York–Genesco, wrote Chapters 1 through 10. Charles F. Mason of the University of Wyoming, wrote Chapters 11 through 19.

Each chapter (with minor exceptions) follows the same format and includes these sections:

- A Chapter Summary carefully recaps the material in *Microeconomics* and includes a list of Key Concepts and Formulas. This opening section is designed to be torn out of the Study Guide, inserted into your class notes, and studied over and over again as you prepare for exams.
- Next, an Application takes the concepts introduced in the chapter and applies them in a new way that goes beyond the examples used in the text. Often the Applications discuss historical or policy issues. In each case, the Application shows the power of the tools introduced in the chapter and helps you better understand these models.
- There are two to four Solved Problems in almost every chapter. Immediately below each of these problems is a step-by-step solution. These problems should serve as a model, showing you how to set up and solve the types of problems you may see on a test.
- The heart of each chapter is a collection of Practice Problems. Most chapters include about 20 of these, beginning with a few Multiple-Choice, Fill-in, and True-False-Ambiguous and Explain Why problems. More than half the Practice Problems are Short-Answer problems, most of which ask you to draw a figure or provide a numerical solution. Many of these Short-Answer problems come from tests and homework that we have used in our own classes.
- The Answers to Practice Problems come in the next section. You should always try to solve the Practice Problems before turning to the answers.
- The final section contains about ten Exercises. These are designed to be used as homework problems, and working through the Solved Problems and Practice Problems will prepare you well for them.

We sincerely hope that working through these Study Guide problems helps you succeed in learning microeconomics and earning a higher grade in your course.

Charles F. Mason
Léonie L. Stone

Chapter 1
Introduction

■ Chapter Summary

The purpose of this chapter and of the entire textbook is to teach you to think like an economist. Economists are unique in the way that they view the world and approach problems. The key assumption of economics (especially microeconomics) is that "individuals allocate their scarce resources so as to make themselves as well off as possible." This assumption is central to economics; there is an "economic way of thinking" that is different and distinct from the methods of other social sciences.

Microeconomics is the study of the allocation of scarce resources—how individual consumers and firms (producers) make decisions and how these many decisions interact. Economic resources are the factors of production available for producing goods. **Scarcity** exists when people want more than they can get with their limited resources. Scarcity implies that society must make **trade-offs**—that we must give up something to get more of another thing. For example, if I want to spend an hour sleeping, I cannot get it without giving up something else, such as an hour of studying.

Society faces three key trade-offs: **what** goods and services to produce, **how** to produce them, and **who** gets the goods and services. A **market** is an exchange mechanism (such as a physical structure or a computer network) that allows buyers to trade with sellers. In a market economy the three allocation outcomes (what, how, and who) reflect the interactions of independent decisions made by millions of individual consumers and firms. **Prices** link and coordinate the three sets of decisions. Prices influence the decisions of individual consumers and firms, and the interactions of these decisions by consumers, firms, and the government in turn determine prices. Most of the textbook is concerned with how prices are determined within a market and the conditions (number of buyers and sellers, amount of information available) that determine whether price is equal to the cost of production.

A **model** is a description of the relationship between two or more variables. Economic models begin with simplifying assumptions and then deduce the implications of these assumptions. Economic **theory** is the development and use of a model to test **hypotheses**, which are predictions about cause and effect. Economists test theories by checking whether the predictions of models are correct. A good theory is relatively simple to use and makes clear, testable predictions that are not refuted by evidence. If a model is too simple, its predictions may be incorrect. If a model is too complex, all of its predictions will be ambiguous and therefore untestable.

A key assumption in almost every microeconomic model is that individuals allocate their scarce resources so as to make themselves as well off as possible. This assumption of **maximizing subject to constraints** implies that consumers pick the bundles of goods that give them the greatest possible enjoyment, and that firms try to maximize their profits given limited resources and existing technology.

Individuals, firms, and governments use microeconomic models and predictions to make decisions. A scientific prediction is called a **positive** statement: a testable hypothesis about cause and effect. "Positive" does not mean that we are certain about the truth of the statement—it only indicates that we can test the statement's truth. A **normative** statement is a value judgment—a conclusion about whether something is good or bad. In making economic policies, economists use positive economics to predict what will happen if certain policies are adopted, and then use their beliefs and judgment to select which of the policies yields the best outcome. Economists are usually careful to separate their predictions from their judgments of right and wrong. This often requires careful use of language, such as when the economist points out that what many people call "needs" are actually only "wants."

■ Key Concepts and Formulas

- **Microeconomics:** the study of the allocation of scarce resources.
- **Scarcity:** the situation that arises when people want more than they can get with their limited resources.
- Trade-offs measure how much of one thing must be given up to get more of another thing.
- **Market:** an exchange mechanism that allows buyers to trade with sellers.
- Prices measure the trade-offs available in the marketplace and coordinate the independent decisions of consumers and producers.
- **Model:** a description of the relationship between two or more economic variables.
- **Theory:** the development and use of a model to test hypotheses, which are predictions about cause and effect.
- Economists assume that individuals exhibit **maximizing behavior**—that they allocate their scarce resources so as to make themselves as well off as possible.
- **Positive statement:** a testable hypothesis about cause and effect.
- **Normative statement:** a value judgment.

■ Application: Agreement among Economists

Stories about economists disagreeing among themselves are legendary. Yet economists insist that there is an "economic way of thinking" and speak about key assumptions that almost all economists hold.

Question: Do economists agree with each other on any important issues? If so, why do they agree on some issues and disagree on others?

Answer: As shown below, recent surveys show that economists actually agree about a lot of things, but that there are major disagreements on some fundamental issues. The results show that there is often more agreement on the subject we are now studying—microeconomics. This may be because most economists agree with the central assumption of microeconomics: that almost all individuals allocate their scarce resources so as to make themselves as well off as possible. This essential postulate leads to a number of clear predictions. Aggregation to the macroeconomic level involves feedback effects and hard-to-understand complications. This is probably what explains the lack of consensus on many key macroeconomic issues. In general, economists are more likely to disagree when (1) they disagree about the appropriate model to use, (2) they disagree about how to interpret data, and (3) they disagree about normative issues (i.e., what "should" be done).

Not everyone agrees with the central assumptions of microeconomics, however. A recent survey asked social scientists whether or not "individuals are rational utility-maximizers." Among economists, 70 percent agreed and only 13 percent disagreed. However, among political scientists, only 33 percent agreed, while 43 percent disagreed.

Microeconomic Propositions	Percent Agreeing
1. Pollution taxes or marketable pollution permits are a more economically efficient approach to pollution control than emission standards.	93
2. Tariffs and import quotas usually reduce general economic welfare.	93
3. A ceiling on rents reduces the quantity and quality of housing available.	93
4. Cash payments increase the welfare of recipients to a greater degree than do transfers-in-kind of equal dollar value.	84
5. The Social Security payroll tax is borne almost entirely by workers, not their employers.	83
6. A minimum wage increases unemployment among young and unskilled workers.	74
7. Economic evidence suggests that there are too many resources in American agriculture.	73

Macroeconomic Propositions	Percent Agreeing
1. An economy in short-run equilibrium at a real GNP below potential GNP has a self-correcting mechanism that will eventually return it to potential real GNP.	60
2. In the short run, a reduction in unemployment causes the inflation rate to increase.	48
3. The Federal Reserve should increase the money supply at a fixed rate.	44
4. The major source of macroeconomic disturbances is supply-side shocks.	40

Sources: Richard Alston, J. R. Kearl, and Michael Vaughan, "Is There Consensus among Economists in the 1990s?" *American Economic Review: Papers and Proceedings*, May 1992; Robert Whaples, "Is There Consensus among American Labor Economists?" *Journal of Labor Research*, Fall 1996; Dan Fuller and Doris Geide-Stevenson, "Consensus among Economists: Revisited," *Journal of Economic Education*, Fall 2003; Robert Whaples and Jac C. Heckelman, "Public Choice Economics: Where Is There Consensus?" *American Economist*, Spring 2005. "Are Public Choice Scholars Different?" *PS: Political Science and Politics*, forthcoming.

Note: "Percent Agreeing" sums those who "generally agree" and those who "agree with provisos."

■ Practice Problems

Multiple-Choice

1. Asking whether an increase in the minimum wage will decrease employment is
   a. a question of positive economics.
   b. a question of normative economics.
   c. neither a nor b.
   d. both a and b.

2. Which of the following is a positive statement? (More than one may be correct.)
   a. Intermediate microeconomics should be required of all economics majors to build a solid foundation in economic theory.
   b. When the price of a good goes up, people buy more of it.
   c. When the price of a good goes down, people buy more of it.
   d. Jeffrey Perloff was the first President of the United States.

True-False-Ambiguous and Explain Why

3. The government should spend more money on manned space missions.

4. Market prices are determined by large companies.

5. Economists' models generally predict that individuals allocate their scarce resources so as to make themselves as well off as possible.

6. Extremely wealthy people, such as Bill Gates, don't face scarcity.

Short-Answer

7. Most economic models assume that the goal of all firms is to maximize their profits all the time. This assumption, however, is obviously not correct, so the theories based on these models are not valid. How would an economist respond to this line of reasoning?

8. Dr. Mergatroid's theory is that the price of compact disks is determined by the workings of evil spirits. When the evil spirits are active, the price of a compact disk rises. When the evil spirits are at rest, the price of compact disks falls. Is this a useful theory? Why or why not?

9. You may have heard people use the term the "marriage market" to describe the process by which men and women find marriage partners. In what ways is the "marriage market" similar to the market for a service such as a haircut or day care? How does it differ?

10. How many economists does it take to screw in a light bulb?

■ Answers to Practice Problems

1. a. Positive statements are about cause and effect. Asking whether an increase in the minimum wage will reduce employment is a testable hypothesis that can, in principle, be demonstrated to be supported by empirical evidence (or not supported by evidence).

2. b, c, and d are positive statements—this is, testable hypotheses. Choice a is a value judgment, hence a normative statement.

3. Ambiguous. This is a normative ("should") question whose answer will depend on the values of the person answering the question. In answering, you will begin by discussing the trade-offs facing society. Resources are scarce, so spending more on manned space missions means that less can be spent on other things (including unmanned space missions). A maximizing individual will compare the benefits from spending more on manned space missions (e.g., the value of additional knowledge gained by the missions) versus the costs (e.g., higher taxes, lost lives). Princeton University economist Paul Krugman weighed these benefits and costs in the *New York Times* (February 4, 2003) following the explosion of the Columbia space shuttle. He pointed out that the additional costs of putting humans into space are substantial. The shuttle and International Space Station cost about $7 billion per year.

The benefits, he argues, are scant. Machines can carry out almost any research that humans can do in space—scientific observation and experiments or even mining asteroids—and at a much lower cost. He concluded that NASA should not spend additional money on manned space missions.

4. False. The price system is a decentralized mechanism by which the decisions of millions of consumers and millions of producers are coordinated. In later chapters, the extent to which large firms influence prices will be considered, but in any case, the decisions of consumers have a significant impact as well.

5. False. This is the most widely used assumption of economic models. It is not a prediction.

6. False. Scarcity is the situation that arises when people want more than they can get with their limited resources. Wants generally exceed resources, even for very wealthy people. Your time is scarce because you'd like to spend the next hour studying for an exam, catching up on your sleep, hanging out with your friends, and playing that addictive new video game, but you can't spend the hour doing all four of these things in the next 60 minutes. Because wealthy people also face time constraints and have lots of things they'd like to do, they face scarcity, too.

7. Because the world and the economy are so complex, all models must simplify. Thus, all models are subject to the criticism that their assumptions do not reflect reality. But we cannot throw out all models. If we did, we would have no way of testing theories or making predictions. If we are to act sensibly it is crucial that we predict the consequences of our actions before we make them. Instead, we accept the fact that assumptions do not perfectly reflect reality, and focus on the ability of a model to predict. If a model makes better predictions than any other model, then it will be accepted as valid (until a better model comes along). Economists generally use the assumption of profit maximizing firms because it has a great track record of making predictions that match the real world.

8. Most economists would reject Dr. Mergatroid's theory. Even if the theory is an accurate reflection of reality, it has an insurmountable problem: It is not testable. Unless there is a method of measuring the activity level of evil spirits, there is no way to make predictions using this theory and to show that its predictions are generally correct. In addition, economists have developed an alternative theory—the theory of supply and demand. If there were a way to measure the activity of evil spirits, then we would need to see if it made better predictions than the theory of supply and demand.

9. A market is an exchange mechanism that allows buyers to trade with sellers. There are all sorts of places (colleges, bars, church socials) and institutions (networks of friends, classified ads, dating services) that allow men and women to get together. In this sense, there is a marriage market. Men and women "shop around" (as Smokey Robinson put it in his classic Motown song) trying to find the best bargain in a spouse—exhibiting maximizing behavior. The marriage market is different from the market for another service because it is less clear who is buying and who is selling. Both parties seem to be "buying" and "selling." In addition, there is not usually an explicit price in the marriage market. However, there are contemporary societies and historical cases in which prices can be seen more clearly—for example, when one of the families pays the other a dowry.

10. How many economists does it take to screw in a light bulb?

    Economists' answers to this joke can be very "illuminating."

    a. None. If the light bulb needed to be screwed in, the market would have already done it. (In other words, economists have a lot of faith in the market's ability to get things done.)

    b. It depends on the wage rate. (In other words, economists think that prices—which include wages—are needed in just about any explanation involving people.)

c.   Seven, plus or minus ten (i.e., sometimes economic models' predictions are overly imprecise).

d.   Eight: one to screw it in and the others to hold everything else constant.

These jokes were lifted from *The Wharton Journal,* February 21, 1994 by Selena Maranijan, who also includes this zinger:

Q: Why did God create economists?

A: In order to make weather forecasters look good. (Ouch!)

Chapter 2
Supply and Demand

■ Chapter Summary

On a long-ago episode of *Saturday Night Live*, a comedian (Don Novello, a.k.a. Father Guido Sarducci) got up and gave a very brief lecture on economics. He held up one index finger and said "Supply." He held up the other index finger and said "Demand." Then he brought them together to form an X and concluded "Supply and Demand. That's it." And he was right; the two crossing curves, supply and demand, are the foundation of all economics, and a powerful tool for understanding the real world.

The **quantity demanded** is the amount of a good that consumers want to buy at a given price, holding constant all other factors that influence purchases. Other factors that influence purchases include *tastes, information, prices of other goods, income*, and *government rules and regulations*.

The **demand function** shows the mathematical relationship between the quantity demanded, the price of the product, and other factors that influence purchases. A **demand curve** plots the demand function, again holding constant other factors. Demand curves are always graphed with the price per unit on the vertical axis and the quantity (number of units per time period) on the horizontal axis. One of the most important findings of empirical economics is the **law of demand**: consumers demand more of a product when the price is lower, holding all else constant. The law of demand implies that demand curves slope downward, or that the derivative of quantity with respect to price is negative.

A change in the quantity demanded that is due to a change in price is called a **movement along the demand curve**. If some factor other than price causes a change in the quantity demanded at the old price, then there is a **shift in the demand curve** and it is necessary to draw a new demand curve. To find the demand curve for a group, simply add up the quantity that each individual consumer demands at each price.

The **quantity supplied** is the amount of a good that firms want to sell at a given price, holding constant all other factors that influence firms' supply decisions. Other factors that influence supply decisions include *costs of production, technology*, and *government rules and regulations*.

The **supply function** shows the relationship between the quantity supplied, the price of the product, and other factors that influence the number of units supplied. A **supply curve** shows the quantity supplied at each possible price, again holding constant other factors that influence supply decisions. Like demand curves, supply curves are graphed with the price per unit on the vertical axis and the quantity on the horizontal axis. Most supply curves for goods and services slope upward—when the price is higher, firms are willing to sell more.

A change in the quantity supplied by firms that is due to a change in price is referred to as a **movement along the supply curve**. If some factor other than price causes a change in the quantity supplied at the old price, then there is a **shift in the supply curve**. Among the factors that determine the position of a supply curve are costs of production, technology, the prices of other things that the firms could be making, and government rules and regulations. The total quantity supplied by an industry is found by adding together the quantity supplied by each firm at each price. One way in which governments can influence the total supply of a good on the market is by setting **quotas**, limits on the amount of a foreign-produced good that can be imported.

An **equilibrium** exists if no market participant wants to change its behavior. In a market, equilibrium occurs at the price and quantity where the demand curve and the supply curve intersect. Market forces— actions of consumers and firms—will drive the price and quantity to their equilibrium levels. If the price is initially lower than the equilibrium price, there will be **excess demand**; consumers will want to buy more than suppliers want to sell. Frustrated consumers will offer to pay firms more than the initial price, and/or firms, noticing these disappointed consumers, will raise their prices. Both actions will drive up the price toward the equilibrium. If the price is initially above the equilibrium price, there will be **excess supply**— the consumers will want to buy less than the suppliers want to sell. In order to sell all that they have made, firms will cut the price—rather than paying storage costs, letting the product spoil, or having it remain unsold. At the equilibrium price, firms are willing to sell exactly the quantity that consumers are willing to buy and no one has an incentive to pay more or cut the price. The equilibrium price is often called the *market clearing price*, because at that price there is neither excess supply nor excess demand.

Once an equilibrium is reached, it can persist indefinitely, but if a change in some determinant of supply or demand causes either (or both) curves to shift, the market will move to a new equilibrium. A shift of the demand curve causes a movement along the supply curve. A shift of the supply curve causes a movement along the demand curve.

Assuming that the demand curve slopes downward and that the supply curve slopes upward, the result of demand or supply curve shifts is predictable. Analysis of how variables such as price and quantity react to changes in *environmental* or *exogenous* variables is called **comparative statics**, comparing a static equilibrium to the new (static) equilibrium that results from the change.

When demand rises (shifts outward), the equilibrium price and quantity will rise. When demand falls (shifts inward), the equilibrium price and quantity fall. When supply falls (shifts inward), the equilibrium price will rise and equilibrium quantity will fall. When supply rises (shifts outward), the equilibrium price will fall and equilibrium quantity will rise. Both the size of the change in the environmental variable and the shape of supply and demand curves have an impact on the magnitude of the changes.

Elasticity measures the sensitivity of one variable to changes in another variable, or more precisely, elasticities measure the percentage change in one variable in response to a given percentage change in another variable. All elasticities take the form

$$E = \frac{percentage\ change\ in\ z}{percentage\ change\ in\ x} = \frac{\Delta z/z}{\Delta x/x} = \frac{\partial z}{\partial x}\frac{x}{z}$$

where the change in the variable on the bottom causes the change in the variable on top.

The **price elasticity of demand**, ε, measures the responsiveness of quantity demanded to a change in price and takes the form

$$\varepsilon = \frac{percentage\ change\ in\ quantity\ demanded}{percentage\ change\ in\ price} = \frac{\Delta Q/Q}{\Delta p/p} = \frac{\Delta Q}{\Delta p}\frac{p}{Q} = \frac{\partial Q}{\partial p}\frac{p}{Q}$$

where Q is the quantity demanded, and p is the price. Because demand curves slope downward, the elasticity of demand is always negative. If the elasticity of demand is between 0 and −1, then it is **inelastic** or unresponsive, since the percentage change in price generates a smaller percentage change in the quantity demanded. If the elasticity of demand is less than −1, then it is **elastic** or responsive, since the percentage change in price yields a larger percentage change in the quantity demanded.

The elasticity of demand varies along most demand curves. Two exceptions are a horizontal demand curve, which is **perfectly elastic** (the elasticity of demand is negative infinity) and a vertical demand curve, which is **perfectly inelastic**. A vertical demand curve has an elasticity of demand of zero—as the price rises, the quantity demanded does not change at all. Along a *linear* demand curve, demand is elastic above the midpoint, unitary at the midpoint, and inelastic below the midpoint. *Constant-elasticity* demand curves have the exponential form $Q = Ap^{\varepsilon}$.

Two other demand-side elasticities are the **income elasticity** of demand and the **cross-price elasticity** of demand. The income elasticity of demand is the percentage change in quantity demanded divided by the percentage change in income. Income elasticities may be positive (*normal* goods) or negative (*inferior* goods). The cross-price elasticity of demand is the percentage change in the quantity demanded divided by the percentage change in the price of some other good. Cross-price elasticities may be positive (*substitutes*), negative (*complements*), or zero (unrelated goods).

The **price elasticity of supply**, η, measures the response of quantity supplied due to a change in price. It takes the form

$$\eta = \frac{percentage\ change\ in\ quantity\ supplied}{percentage\ change\ in\ price} = \frac{\Delta Q/Q}{\Delta p/p} = \frac{\Delta Q}{\Delta p}\frac{p}{Q} = \frac{\partial Q}{\partial p}\frac{p}{Q}$$

where Q is the quantity supplied, and p is the price. The sign of the price elasticity of supply depends on the slope of the supply curve, which could be positive or negative. If a supply response is larger than the change in price (in terms of percentage change) it is said to be elastic ($\eta > 1$, in absolute value). If it is smaller ($\eta < 1$, in absolute value), it is inelastic. As with demand curves, supply curves can be perfectly elastic, perfectly inelastic, or have a constant elasticity of supply.

Demand elasticities depend crucially on the ability to find substitutes, which often varies with time. In general, there are more opportunities for substitution in the long run, so for most goods, demand is more elastic in the long run than in the short run. Likewise, almost all supply curves become more elastic over time, as firms have time to make major output adjustments by building new production facilities.

Government imposition of taxes affects market equilibrium. *Specific* or *unit* taxes are collected per unit of output sold. *Ad valorem* taxes are based on a percentage of total spending on the good. A tax that is levied on producers shifts the supply curve upward, and a tax that is levied on consumers shifts the demand curve downward. Both producers and consumers will generally pay part of the tax, no matter who is legally required to pay the tax.

For a specific tax, τ, imposed on producers, the shift in supply raises the market price and creates a wedge between the new price the consumers pay, p, and the new price the suppliers receive, $p - \tau$. The **incidence of the tax** is determined by the relative elasticities of supply and demand. The portion of a specific tax that falls on consumers equals $\eta/(\eta - \varepsilon)$, where η is the elasticity of supply and ε is the elasticity of demand. (Remember that the demand elasticity is a negative number.) Thus, if the demand elasticity is twice as big as the supply elasticity, the consumers will pay one-third of the tax. Whoever is more responsive (higher elasticity) is able to more easily respond to a higher price (by reducing quantity demanded or supplied) and thus pays less of the tax. If supply (demand) is perfectly inelastic, producers (consumers) will pay all of the tax. If supply (demand) perfectly elastic, producers (consumers) will end up paying none of the tax. Analysis of ad valorem taxes yields similar results.

A tax changes the market equilibrium price and quantity, but other government policies may prevent the market from reaching equilibrium. A **price ceiling** is a maximum price set by the government. If the ceiling is set below the market equilibrium, it will cause a **shortage** (a persistent excess demand)—if it is enforced and if buyers and sellers do not find a way to get around it. Shortages mean that sellers select buyers using some criterion other than who will pay the most, such as who stands in line the longest or who the seller likes the most. A **price floor** is a minimum price set by the government. If the floor is set above the market equilibrium price, it will cause excess supply. One example of this is unemployment caused by the minimum wage.

The supply and demand model is most applicable in *perfectly competitive markets*. In such markets, everyone is a price taker (when no consumer or firm can affect the market price); when firms sell identical products; when everyone is fully informed about the price and quality of goods; and when transactions costs are low. This model has proved to be appropriate and useful for understanding agricultural, financial, labor, construction, service, wholesale, retail, and other markets.

■ Key Concepts and Formulas

- A demand function is a mathematical relationship between the quantity demanded of a good, the price of the product, and other factors that influence purchases. A demand curve shows the amount of a good or service that consumers want to buy at each possible price.
- A supply function is a mathematical relationship between the quantity supplied of a good, the price of the product, and other factors that influence production. A supply curve shows the amount of a good or service that firms want to sell at each possible price.
- When only price changes, there is a movement along a demand (or supply) curve.
- Changes in factors other than the good's price can cause its demand (or supply) curve to shift.
- Market equilibrium occurs at the price and quantity where the supply curve and the demand curve intersect.
- The price elasticity of demand, ε, measures the responsiveness of quantity demanded, Q, due to a change in price, p.

$$\varepsilon = \frac{percentage\ change\ in\ quantity\ demanded}{percentage\ change\ in\ price} = \frac{\Delta Q/Q}{\Delta p/p} = \frac{\Delta Q}{\Delta p}\frac{p}{Q} = \frac{\partial Q}{\partial p}\frac{p}{Q}$$

- A response is elastic if the percentage change in one variable causes a percentage change in another variable that is larger in magnitude. It is inelastic if the percentage change in the second variable is smaller in magnitude.
- Elasticity of supply, η, measures the responsiveness of quantity supplied, Q, due to a change in price, p. $\eta = (\Delta Q/Q)/(\Delta p/p) = (\Delta Q/\Delta p)(p/Q) =$ (percentage change in quantity supplied)/(percentage change in price).
- Vertical demand and supply curves are perfectly inelastic (elasticity = 0). Horizontal demand and supply curves are perfectly elastic.
- The incidence of the tax is determined by the relative elasticities of supply, η, and demand, ε. The portion of a specific tax that falls on consumers equals $\eta/(\eta - \varepsilon)$.
- Price ceilings and floors do not shift demand or supply curves, but they can cause movements along these curves and block the market from reaching equilibrium.

■ Application: Incidence of the Social Security Tax

Question: Taxes are generally borne by both buyers and sellers. Why do economists think that the Social Security payroll tax is borne only by workers?

Answer: The incidence of a tax is determined by the relative elasticities of supply and demand. In the labor market, firms demand labor and workers supply it. For the workers to bear the entire tax, either the elasticity of demand must be almost infinite or the elasticity of supply must be approximately zero. Empirical evidence suggests that the elasticity of demand for labor averages somewhere around −1.0, while the elasticity of supply for labor is very close to zero, especially in the long run. (In a recent survey, 78 percent of labor economists agreed that "most adult men are on the vertical section of their labor supply curve." As women have increased their attachment to the labor market, estimates of their elasticity of labor supply have become very close to zero as well.)

The federal government collects an OASDI (Old Age, Survivors, Disability Insurance) tax on all labor market income below a maximum (which is indexed to inflation and was \$94,200 in the year 2006). This tax equals 12.4 percent of wages. Figure 2.1 shows the incidence of this tax. The tax shifts employer's labor demand curve down by 12.4 percent, from D to D_{SS}. Notice that D_{SS} is not parallel to D, but is always 12.4 percent below it. Because the labor supply curve, S, is approximately vertical, the wage falls from W_0 to $0.876W_0$. Even though the law states that half of the tax is to be paid by the worker and half by the employer, the invisible hand of the market works so that the worker effectively pays all the tax. Next time you get a paycheck, notice the amount listed under FICA (Federal Insurance Contribution Act). Doubling this amount will give a better estimate of the amount of Social Security taxes that you've paid (unless you are one of those people who actually does change hours of work in response to a change in wages).

Knowing who bears the Social Security tax is important for knowing how good your "investment" in the Social Security system is likely to be. For years, Social Security administrators argued that it was a great investment, because retirees have received so much more than they have paid into the system in taxes. Recently, many people have been convinced otherwise, after realizing that workers bear both halves of the tax. One recent set of estimates, which acknowledges the fact that workers bear the entire tax, reports that those retiring in 2050—this may be you—will earn returns of about 2 percent per year, while the most recent retirees will earn about 3 percent per year. (The rate of return will be even lower if Social Security tax rates are raised or if the normal retirement age is raised. Both of these seem likely, since the system is projected to run out of money otherwise. In addition, these rates are lower for those who earn more than average, higher for one-earner couples, and lower if you die early.) The 2 or 3 percent rate of return compares to the stock market's long-run rate of return, which is around 8 percent per year. In this case, knowing the incidence of the tax can have a profound impact on the popularity of a governmental program.

(See Ronald Ehrenberg and Robert Smith, *Modern Labor Economics,* ninth edition, Addison-Wesley-Longman, 2006, and 102–104; Robert Whaples, "Is There Consensus among American Labor Economists?" *Journal of Labor Research,* Fall 1996; and C. Eugene Steuerle and Jon Bakija, *Retooling Social Security for the 21st Century,* 1994, p. 290.)

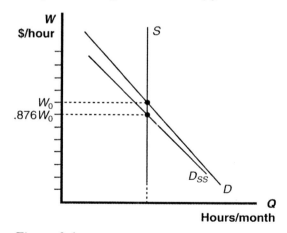

Figure 2.1

■ Application: Estimating the Effect of a Minimum Wage Increase on Teen Employment

Economists routinely predict that an increase in the minimum wage will *decrease* the employment of teenagers. They use a simple one-graph supply-and-demand model such as Figure 2.10 from the textbook. However, critics point out that employment among teens has actually *increased* in most years in which the minimum wage has been raised.

Question: Can the standard minimum wage story (which predicts decreasing employment of teens) be correct? Aren't its predictions failing? Can the model explain rising employment in years in which the minimum wage has been raised?

Answer: The standard minimum wage model predicts that *if nothing else changes*, an increase in the minimum wage will reduce the employment of low-wage workers (such as teens). Unfortunately the real world does not stand still. As we move from the year before the minimum wage increase to the year of the minimum wage increase, the minimum wage is not necessarily the only thing changing. Both the labor supply curve and the labor demand curve might shift as we go from one year to another. In fact, it would be unusual if both curves did not shift. Demographic changes routinely shift the teen labor supply curve, and the ups and downs of the economy routinely shift the demand for teen labor. Figure 2.2 shows the teen labor market in the years 2003 and 2004. In 2003 the equilibrium wage, w_{2003}, prevails. In 2004 the minimum wage is set at w_{min}. If all else remained the same, the model predicts that employment will fall from L_2 to L_1. However, because the economy is growing (as it usually does), the demand for labor shifts out from D_{2003} to D_{2004}. The model predicts that if the minimum wage was not raised to w_{min}, the wage would rise to w_{2004} and employment would rise to L_4. However, the minimum wage is higher than w_{2004}, so employment rises only to L_3. In this case, the minimum wage model predicts that employment will rise, but that it will rise by less than it would have if the minimum wage were not imposed. Thus, the standard textbook model can be modified slightly to explain what happens over time in a dynamic economy that more closely matches the real world. Shifting supply-and-demand curves imply that estimating the drop in employment due to a minimum wage increase is very tricky. Economists use multivariate regressions (which are briefly described in Appendix 2A) to control for other factors and isolate the impact of minimum wage increases.

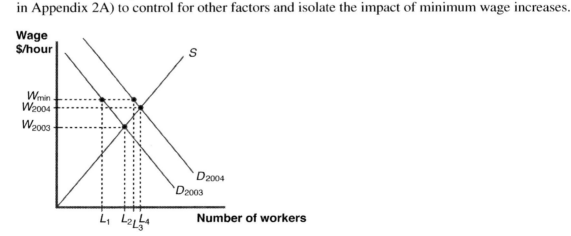

Figure 2.2

■ Solved Problems

1. The following problem gives the supply and demand for Spam in two different markets. Calculate the equilibrium price and quantity of Spam in each of the two markets, and graph the supply and demand curves in each case.

Case 1: Base camp at the bottom of Mount Everest (the highest mountain in the world)

$$Q_d = 100 - 2p$$
$$Q_s = 40 + p$$

where quantity is measured in cases of Spam per week and p is the price of a case of Spam in dollars.

Case 2: At the top of Mount Everest

$$Q_d = 100 - 2p$$
$$Q_s = -80 + p$$

Give an explanation for the difference between the two supply curves.

Case 1:

Step 1: Find the equilibrium price at the base camp by remembering that equilibrium requires that the price adjust to the point where quantity supplied, Q_s. equals quantity demanded, Q_d. Algebraically:

$$100 - 2p = 40 + p \quad \text{or}$$
$$60 = 3p \quad \quad \text{or}$$
$$20 = p$$

Step 2: Find the equilibrium quantity by plugging the equilibrium price into the quantity supplied or the quantity demanded equation. It is a good idea to plug the price into BOTH equations. The quantity will be the same in both equations. If it is not, then you've made a mistake.

$$Q_d = 100 - (2 \cdot 20) = 60$$
$$Q_s = 40 + 20 = 60$$

Step 3: To graph a linear equation, find two points on the line and connect the dots. For a demand curve, it is easiest to find the points along the vertical and horizontal axes. Along the horizontal axis the price is zero. Putting a price of zero into the equation for quantity demanded reveals that consumers will take 100 cases of Spam if the price is zero (i.e., they are giving Spam away for nothing). This is point A in Figure 2.3. Along the vertical axis the quantity demanded is zero. Set $Q_d = 0$ and solve for p. This tells the price at which consumers are no longer willing to buy Spam.

$$0 = 100 - 2p, \quad \text{so}$$

$p = \$50$ where the demand curve hits the vertical axis. This is point B in Figure 2.3.

Graphing the supply curve is a bit more difficult because supply curves usually only hit one axis.

However, we know the point where the supply curve intersects the demand curve, so we can hook up these two points.

Putting $p = 0$ into the quantity supplied equation shows that the supply curve hits the horizontal axis at 40. This is point C in Figure 2.3.

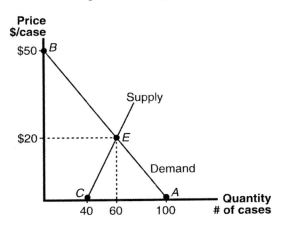

Figure 2.3

Finally, the supply and demand curves intersect where price is $20 and quantity is 60. This is point E in Figure 2.3.

One important note about supply and demand curves: They are often estimated to be linear, but the estimates are only reliable in the range of observation. These estimates are better in the range near where the market is or has been in the past, but at extremely high or low prices these estimates are not always reliable. Since no one has ever given Spam away for free or sold a case for $1, we don't really know how much Spam people would take or buy at these low prices. The bottom line is that the ends of both supply and demand curves may not always tell us something that is economically meaningful. In this case, for example, it is unlikely that suppliers would give away 40 cases of Spam per week if the price were zero.

Case 2:

Step 1: Find the equilibrium price at the top of Everest by remembering that equilibrium requires that the price adjust to the point where quantity supplied, Q_s, equals quantity demanded, Q_d. Algebraically:

$$100 - 2p = -80 + p \quad \text{or}$$
$$180 = 3p \quad\quad\quad \text{or}$$
$$60 = p$$

Step 2: Find the equilibrium quantity by plugging the equilibrium price into the equations for supply and demand.

$$Q_d = 100 - (2 \cdot 60) = -20$$
$$Q_s = -80 + 60 = -20$$

Something looks odd here! It is tough to buy or sell a negative amount of a good.

Step 3: Graph the equations.

The demand equation is unchanged from part a, but the supply equation's intercept is now –80. The intersection, found in steps one and two, is at a price of $60 and a quantity of –20. This is point E in Figure 2.4. Now find the price at which the quantity supplied equals zero.

$$Q_s = 0 = -80 + p, \quad \text{so}$$

$p = 80$ where the supply curve hits the vertical axis. This is point C in Figure 2.4.

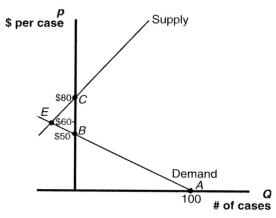

Figure 2.4

The graph shows that supply and demand do not intersect in the positive quadrant of the graph. At every price, the supply curve is above the demand curve. Firms will not supply any Spam unless the price is $80 or more. Consumers will not buy any Spam unless the price is $50 or less. It is not necessary to graph the part of the supply curve corresponding with negative quantities, because this section is economically meaningless.

There are many markets like this—where a product is not bought and sold because no one is willing to pay enough to convince firms to supply the product. Other examples might include air conditioners in Nome, Alaska and leather-bound, gilt-edged copies of Jeffrey Perloff's textbooks. In this case, the reason that the Spam supply curve has shifted leftward and/or upward probably has a lot to do with the additional costs of transporting Spam to the top of the world's highest mountain.

2. The European Union has a policy of subsidizing farmers and then exporting the excess supply to poorer countries. One report examined how these policies have affected the beef market in West Africa. In 1975, cattle from the Sahel (the part of Africa just south of the Sahara) accounted for two-thirds of the beef consumed in the Ivory Coast. By 1991, beef from the Sahel accounted for only one-quarter of the beef in the Ivory Coast market. In 1991, the EC dumped tens of millions of tons of beef in West Africa. Assuming that nothing else changed between 1975 and 1991, draw a graph showing how the EC's beef exports influenced the market in the Ivory Coast. (*Source:* "Overstuffing Africa," *The Economist,* May 8, 1993.)

Step 1: Graph the initial market outcome.

We don't have an equation for demand. We don't know the initial price. We don't know the initial quantity. However, we can reason that the demand curve, D, slopes downward. Likewise, we don't know much about supply, but we can reasonably assume that the supply curve slopes upward. Since there is no information to the contrary, we will assume that competition drives the market to an equilibrium where the supply and demand curves cross, at p_1, Q_1. The supply curve, S_1, is the sum of supply from the Sahel, S_s, and the supply from other places, S_0.

The problem states that beef from the Sahel initially accounted for two-thirds of the quantity. This leaves one-third for the supply from other places. Therefore the S_0 curve must equal $1/3Q_1$ at p_1, as is shown in Figure 2.5.

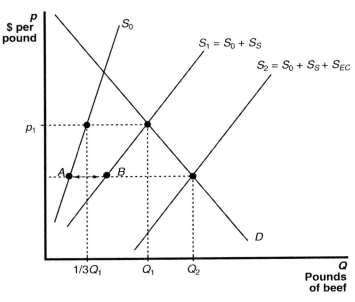

Figure 2.5

Step 2: Graph the final market outcome.

The problem assumes that the only change is the addition of European beef to the market. This will shift out the supply curve to S_2, causing it to move along the demand curve. How far out will the supply curve shift? The new equilibrium must be consistent with suppliers from the Sahel producing one-fourth of the new level of output, Q_2, so the horizontal distance from A to B is $1/4Q_2$.

3. In the following two cases, find and graph the market demand curve.

   Case 1: There are 5 identical consumers with the following demand curve:

   $$Q_{di} = 100 - 2p$$

   Case 2: There are two consumers. Demand for the first consumer is:

   $$Q_{d1} = 100 - 2p$$

   Demand for the second consumer is:

   $$Q_{d2} = 200 - p$$

Case 1:

Step 1: To find a market demand curve, recall that you must add the quantity of each consumer at each price.

To do this, always be sure that the demand equation is arranged so that quantity is on the left-hand side.

$$Q_{di} = 100 - 2p$$

Step 2: Total market demand, Q, is equal to the sum of the individual demand curves. Since price must be equal for all consumers, we can simply add the p variables together.

$$Q = \sum_{i=1}^{5} Q_{di} = \sum_{i=1}^{5}(100 - 2p) = \sum_{i=1}^{5}100 - \sum_{i=1}^{5}2p = 500 - 10p$$

$$Q = 500 - 10p$$

Step 3: Graph the demand curve (see Solved Problem 1 to review how to graph demand).

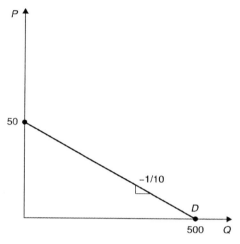

Figure 2.6

Case 2:

Step 1: Again, to find a market demand curve, recall that you must add the quantity of each consumer at each price.

To do this, always be sure that the demand equation is arranged so that quantity is on the left-hand side.

$$Q_{d1} = 100 - 2p:$$
$$Q_{d2} = 200 - p$$

Step 2: Total market demand, Q, is equal to the sum of the individual demand curves.

$$Q = \sum_{i=1}^{5} Q_{di} = (100 - 2p) + (200 - p) = 300 - p$$

$$Q = 300 - 3p$$

However, note that in this case, since the demand curves are not identical, the equation found above is only valid when price is low enough for both consumers to enter the market. To see what range this is, we go to the next step and graph the demand curves.

Step 3: First, graph the individual demand curves.

We can see that the vertical intercept for Demand 1 is $50. The vertical intercept for Demand 2 is $200. Thus the first consumer will only enter the market after the price falls to $50 or less, and the market demand curve is kinked. At prices of $50 and higher, the market demand curve is equal to the demand curve for Consumer 1. After the price falls to $50, the equation is as found in Step 2. To find the quantity coordinate for the point at the kink, note that if $P = \$50$, $Q_{d2} = 200 - (50) = 150$.

Thus, the equation of the market demand curve is:

$$Q = 200 - p, \, p \geq 50$$
$$Q = 300 - 3p, \, p > 50$$

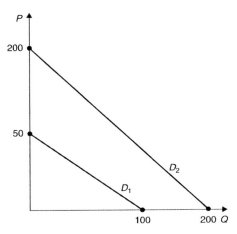

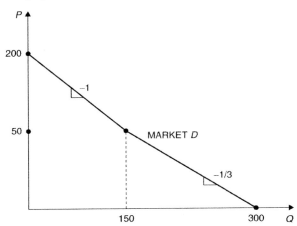

Figure 2.7

4. The market demand curve is: $Q = 600 - 2p$.

    Find   a.   the price and quantity at which $\varepsilon = -2$
          b.   the price and quantity at which $\varepsilon = -\frac{1}{2}$
          c.   the price elasticity of demand when $p = \$125$.

Step 1: Recall the formula for price elasticity of demand,

$$\varepsilon = \frac{dQ}{dp} \frac{p}{Q}$$

First, note that demand is linear in this case, so the derivative of quantity with respect to price will be constant. $dQ/dp = -2$, and this can be used for all parts of the question. (This is the inverse of the slope of the line; $dp/dQ = -\frac{1}{2}$.)

Step 2: To find the point at which elasticity is equal to a specific number, first set up the elasticity equation, substituting in the specific elasticity that you with to find and the value of the derivative found in Step one. For part (a):

$$-2 = -2\frac{p}{Q}$$

Rearrange the equation to find a relationship between price and quantity. In this case,

$$p = Q$$

Substitute the relationship into the demand curve, and solve for price and quantity.

$$Q = 600 - 2p$$
$$Q = 600 - 2(Q)$$
$$Q = 200$$
$$p = \$200$$

You can solve part (b) in exactly the same way.

$$-\frac{1}{2} = -2\frac{p}{Q}$$

Rearrange the equation to find a relationship between price and quantity. In this case,

$$Q = 4p$$

Substitute the relationship into the demand curve, and solve for price and quantity.

$$Q = 600 - 2p$$
$$4p = 600 - 2p$$
$$p = \$100$$
$$Q = 400$$

Step 3: For a problem like part (c), again, we use the elasticity relationship.

$$\varepsilon = \frac{dQ}{dp}\frac{p}{Q}$$

$$\varepsilon = -2\frac{p}{Q}$$

Using the demand curve relationship, when $p = \$150$, $Q = 600 - 2(150) = 300$. Plug these numbers into the relationship above.

$$\varepsilon = -2\frac{150}{300} = -1$$

At this point, elasticity is unitary.

If you consider your answers to (a), (b), and (c), the three points you found represent different elasticity points along a linear demand curve. In part (a), the point is on the upper part of the demand curve, where demand is elastic. In part (c), you have found the midpoint of the demand curve, where elasticity is unitary. In part (b), the point is on the lower part of the demand curve, where demand is inelastic.

5. Suppose that the market for grape jelly has the following pretax supply and demand curves:

$$Q_d = 100{,}000 - 2{,}000p$$
$$Q_s = -20{,}000 + 4000p,$$

where Q = crates per month and p = dollars per crate.

The pretax equilibrium is $p = \$20$, $Q = 60{,}000$.

Show that a tax of $5 per crate levied on sellers has the same impact as a tax that is levied on buyers. Explain the incidence of the tax.

Step 1: Show the impact of a tax levied on sellers.

A tax on sellers raises the cost of supplying the market and shifts up the supply curve by the amount of the tax. Graphing the initial supply curve shows that it intersects the vertical axis at $5. The after-tax supply curve's intercept must be $10, and it has the same slope as the pretax supply curve. If you rearrange the original supply curve so that price is on the left-hand side,

$$p = 5 + 0.00025Q$$

Add the $5 tax to the price.

$$p_1 = p + 5 = (5 + 0.00025Q) + 5$$
$$p_1 = 10 + 0.00025Q$$

As expected, the new supply curve has the same slope, but the vertical intercept is $10. To solve the problem, set supply equal to demand and solve for the equilibrium price and quantity.

The after-tax equation is $Q_s = -40,000 + 4000p$. Thus, the after-tax equilibrium is $100,000 - 2000p = Q_d = Q_s = -40,000 + 4000p$, so $p = \$23.33$, and $Q = 53,333$. (Figure 2.8(a) shows this.)

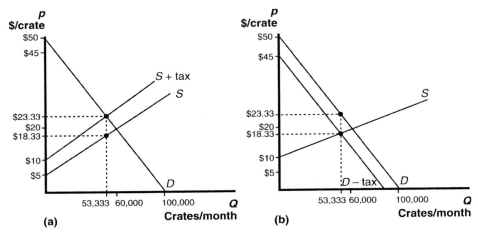

Figure 2.8

Step 2: Show the impact of the same tax levied on buyers.

A tax on buyers reduces the amount that they wish to purchase. If, for example, consumers were willing to buy 60,000 crates at a price of $20 per crate, after paying a $5 per crate tax, they will be willing to buy 60,000 crates only if the price is $15 per crate. Thus, the demand curve shifts down by the amount of the tax. Graphing the initial demand curve shows that it intersects the vertical axis at $50. The after-tax demand curve's intercept must be $45 and it has the same slope at the pretax demand curve. If you rearrange the original demand curve so that price is on the left-hand side,

$$p = 50 - 0.02Q$$

Subtract the $5 tax to the price.

$$p_1 = p - 5 = (50 - 0.02Q) - 5$$
$$p_1 = 45 + 0.02Q$$

As expected, the new demand curve has the same slope, but the vertical intercept is $45. To solve the problem, set supply equal to demand and solve for the equilibrium price and quantity. The after-tax equation is $Q_d = 90,000 - 2000p$. The after-tax equilibrium is $90,000 - 2000p = Q_d = Q_s = -20,000 + 4,000p$, so $p = \$18.33$, $Q = 53,333$. (Figure 2.8(b) shows this.)

Step 3: Compare the two.

The quantity is the same. In Figure 2.8(a) the price is $23.33. This is the price including the tax. In Figure 2.8(b) the price is $18.33. This is the price excluding the $5 tax. Thus, the two approaches yield the same result. The buyer pays $23.33. The seller receives $18.33. The government receives $5.

Step 4: Find the incidence of the tax.

$$\varepsilon = \frac{dQ}{dp}\frac{p}{Q} = -2000\frac{20}{60,000} = -\frac{2}{3}$$

$$\eta = \frac{dQ}{dp}\frac{p}{Q} = 4000\frac{20}{60,000} = 1\frac{1}{3}$$

To find the incidence of the tax, always start from the initial equilibrium point. The incidence of the tax on consumers, $dp/d\tau = \eta/(\eta - \varepsilon)$. Thus we must find the price elasticity of supply and the price elasticity of demand at the original equilibrium point. (See Solved Problem 4 to review finding the derivative terms in the elasticity formulas.)

$$\text{Incidence of the tax on consumers} = \frac{\eta}{\eta - \varepsilon} = \frac{1\frac{1}{3}}{1\frac{1}{3} - \left(-\frac{2}{3}\right)} = .60$$

60 percent of the tax is paid by consumers (the more inelastic group), and thus 40 percent of the tax is paid by producers. (Note that this is confirmed by your results in Step one; the price rose by $3.33, or 60 percent of the $5 tax. Firms take home $23.33 – $5, or $18.33, after paying the tax, which is 40 percent less than the original price.)

6. Draw a demand curve whose elasticity of demand is always –2.

    Step 1: Begin by picking a point on your demand curve – at p_1 the quantity demanded is Q_1.

    Step 2: Raise the price by a certain percent and calculate how much the quantity demanded must fall.

    Because the elasticity of demand is –2, the percentage change in quantity is twice the percentage change in price. Suppose that you began with $p = \$10$ and $Q = 100$ (you could pick any arbitrary two points). If you raise the price by 10 percent to $11, the quantity demanded must fall by 20 percent to 80.

    Step 3: *Reduce* the price by a certain percent and calculate how much the quantity demanded must fall.

    Again, because the elasticity of demand is always –2, the percentage change in quantity is twice the percentage change in price. Suppose again that you began with $p = \$10$ and $Q = 100$. If you reduce the price by 10 percent to $9, the quantity demanded must rise by 20 percent to 120. This is shown in Figure 2.9.

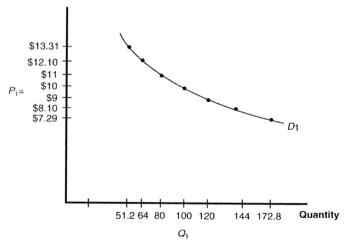

Figure 2.9

Step 4: Repeat this process by raising and reducing the price again and finding the new quantity demanded.

For example, raising the price by another 10 percent from $11 to $12.10 will reduce the quantity demanded by another 20 percent from 80 to 64. Reducing the price by another 10 percent from $9 to $8.10 will increase the quantity demanded by another 20 percent from 120 to 144.

Step 5: Draw a curve connecting all the points that you've plotted.

As the textbook explains, the elasticity of demand varies along a *linear* demand curve, but this demand curve actually *curves* since its elasticity is constant. (The method we've just used will give a constant elasticity demand curve only if the price changes are sufficiently small.)

■ Practice Problems

Problems with (*) refer to the Appendix

Multiple-Choice

1. A shift in the demand curve for shoes could be caused by all of the following except a rise in
    a. the price of boots.
    b. the price of shoelaces.
    c. the price of shoes.
    d. incomes.

2. Consumers learn that drinking wine helps prevent heart attacks. This will cause the
    a. demand curve for wine to shift outward and the price of wine to rise.
    b. supply curve for wine to shift outward and the price of wine to fall.
    c. supply curve for wine to shift inward and the price of wine to rise.
    d. demand curve for wine to shift outward, the supply curve of wine to shift outward, and the price of wine to rise, fall, or remain unchanged.

3. The wages of workers in the tire-making industry rise. At the same time, the price of gasoline climbs. Gasoline and tires are complementary goods. The resulting shifts in the supply and demand for tires imply that the equilibrium quantity of tires
    a. could rise or fall.
    b. will fall, while the price rises.
    c. will fall, while the price falls.
    d. will fall, while the price could fall, rise, or stay the same.

4. If costs of production rise, the supply curve will shift _____ and the price will _____.
    a. leftward; rise.
    b. leftward; fall.
    c. rightward; rise.
    d. rightward; fall.

5. When the automatic milking machine was invented, replacing the traditional method of milking by hand,
    a. the price of milk fell because the invention made the demand for milk fall.
    b. the price of milk fell because the invention made the supply of milk rise.
    c   the price of milk fell because the invention made the supply of milk fall.
    d. the price of milk rose because the invention made the demand for milk rise.

6. If the demand for frisbees is $Q_d = 150 - 50p$, then at a price of $1 the elasticity of demand
    a. is −0.5.
    b. is −1.0.
    c. is −2.0.
    d. cannot be determined.

7. The demand curve for zucchini is horizontal. The supply elasticity at the current price is 2. If the government levies a tax on zucchini, the percent of the tax borne by the buyers
    a. will be 0 percent.
    b. will be 50 percent.
    c. will be 100 percent.
    d. cannot be calculated without more information.

8. The elasticity of demand for Slinkies is −4.0. The elasticity of supply for Slinkies is 6.0. If a tax of 10 cents per Slinky is sprung on to the market, the price paid by buyers will increase by
    a. 3 cents.
    b. 4 cents.
    c. 6 cents.
    d. 7 cents.

Fill-in

9. A _____ is a good that you view as similar to the one you are considering purchasing, while a _____ is a good that you like to consume at the same time as the product you are considering.

10. A high minimum wage creates _____, which is an excess _____ of labor.

11. _____ are the expenses of finding a trading partner and setting up a trade for a good or service.

12. If the demand for jelly beans is unitary elastic and the price of jelly beans rises, then total revenue from sales of jelly beans will _____.

13. With an _____ tax, for every dollar the consumer spends, the government keeps a fraction, which is the tax rate.

14. When the supply of apricots falls and the price of apricots rises, this causes the price of peaches to rise. This implies that peaches are a _____ for apricots.

True-False-Ambiguous and Explain Why

15. When Hurricane Katrina ripped through Mississippi in 2005, the wages of carpenters doubled. This price rise indicates a shortage of carpenters.

16. If the demand for a product rises, then a shortage will occur.

17. In Catmandoo, the city government pays dog catchers $50 per hour; therefore, the equilibrium wage for dog catchers must be $50 per hour.

18. The equilibrium price of elbow grease is $5 per kilogram, but the government has in place a price ceiling at $3 per kilogram. Therefore, if technological improvements are made in the elbow grease-making process, the price of elbow grease will fall.

19. The equilibrium price of elbow grease is $5 per kilogram, but the government has in place a price ceiling at $3 per kilogram. Midnight oil is a complement of elbow grease. If the price of midnight oil falls, then the shortage of elbow grease will grow larger.

20. Equilibrium in the printer paper market is 2 million reams per week and $2 per ream. The government puts in place a price ceiling of $1.75 per ream and the quantity purchased falls to 1.8 million reams. Therefore, the demand curve for printer paper slopes upward, since quantity demanded falls as the price falls.

21. Equilibrium in the printer paper market is 2 million reams per week and $2 per ream. The government puts in place a price ceiling of $1.75 per ream and the quantity purchased stays at 2 million reams. Therefore, the supply curve is vertical.

22. On February 13 the price of a rose was $1 and 80 roses were purchased. On Valentine's Day (February 14), the price of a rose jumped to $2 and 200 roses were purchased. Therefore, the elasticity of demand is approximately 1.28.

23. The government places a tax of $5 per unit on beeswax and we find that the price buyers pay increases by $2.50. If the tax is increased to $15, then the price buyers pay will increase by $7.50.

24. If the government increases the tax on alcohol, use of marijuana will increase.

Short-Answer

25. In each case below use a single supply-and-demand graph to show the events in the indicated market. Label the initial and final price and quantity on the graph. Provide a brief explanation.
    a. Cotton textiles. The initial equilibrium price for a piece of cloth in Britain in 1807 was 2 shillings. Then the U.S. imposed an embargo on exports of raw cotton to Britain.
    b. Lumber. The price of lumber is initially $5 per board-foot. Then the chainsaw is invented and replaces hand-powered saws.
    c. Cotton. Farmers can grow either cotton or melons on their land, and the initial equilibrium price of cotton is 40 cents per pound. Then the demand for melons rises.
    d. Wine. The initial equilibrium price of bottle of wine is $20. Then there is a drought in the wine growing region *and* the drought makes the wine taste worse than before.
    e. The tomato market. The initial equilibrium price of tomatoes is $2 per pound. Then the price of tomato fertilizer falls.

26. The price of a hotel room in Stowe, Vermont rises by $20 per night during the winter season. The price of a hotel room in Ocean City, Maryland falls by $50 per night during the winter season. Explain these results using supply and demand.

27. A traveler wandering on an island inhabited by cannibals comes to a butcher shop. The shop specializes in human brains. The sign in the shop reads:

Artists' Brains	$10 per pound
Doctors' Brains	$10 per pound
Economists' Brains	$10 per pound
Lawyers' Brains	$40 per pound

After reading the sign, the traveler remarks, "Gosh, those lawyers' brains must be popular!" What does the butcher (who knows a bit of economics) reply?

*28. Explain how to use a regression to estimate the relationship between the hourly wage and the age of individual workers shown in Figure 2.10. (See Appendix 2A.)

Figure 2.10

29. Most desirable things, such as ice cream cones, cost money to buy. Why are some things, such as the air we breathe, free?

30. When the demand for a product rises, the price will rise and many producers will earn higher profits. Is this price rise fair for customers? Explain.

31. In early 1994, city governments had to pay the owners of processing centers about $10 per ton to take old newspapers off their hands. By fall 1994, the processing centers paid the cities nearly $25 per ton for old newspapers. The cause of this change was a rising demand for old newspapers ("Cities Couldn't Give Away Their Trash: Now They Get Top Dollar From Recyclers," *The Wall Street Journal,* September 19, 1994, B1). Demonstrate this change using supply-and-demand analysis.

32. The domestic supply (S_D), foreign (import) supply (S_I), and domestic demand (D) for widgets are given in Figure 2.11 below. What is the equilibrium price and quantity if there are no import barriers and no shipping costs for imports? What are the equilibrium price and quantity if there are no import barriers and shipping costs are $2 per pound for the foreign output? Use a graph to show your answer.

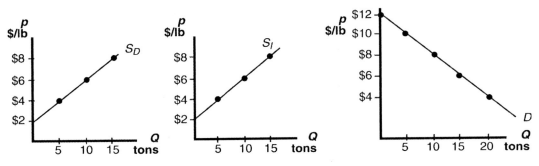

Figure 2.11

33. In the market for mudwrestling, the quantity demanded is

$$Q_d = 100 - 3p,$$

where Q is the number of matches per month, and p is the price in dollars per match. The quantity supplied is

$$Q_s = 20 + 2p.$$

The government puts in place a price ceiling of $10 per match. How will this affect the market? How would a price ceiling of $20 per match affect the market?

34. Initially, the demand and supply for Wapanzo beans are

$$Q_d = 100,000 - 5000p$$
$$Q_s = -50,000 + 10,000p,$$

where p = price in cents per pound and Q = pounds per day. Then the government decides that Wapanzo beans are bad for people and a law is passed requiring that half of all Wapanzo beans produced must be destroyed. How will this affect the supply and demand curves and the market price and quantity of Wapanzo beans?

35. Initially, the demand and supply for Wapanzo beans are

$$Q_d = 100,000 - 5000p$$
$$Q_s = -50,000 + 10,000p,$$

where p = price in cents per pound and Q = pounds per day. The government has a stockpile of Wapanzo beans (which is not included in the initial supply equation). It wants to cut the price of Wapanzo beans to 8 cents per pound. How much should it sell from its stockpile?

36. Initially, the demand and supply for grain are

$$Q_d = 100,000 - 5000p$$
$$Q_s = 10,000 + 10,000p,$$

where p = price in shekels per measure and Q = measures per year. Fearing that a drought was coming, the government has stockpiled a huge amount of grain. Joseph is in charge of the granary and wants to increase the consumption of grain to 80,000 measures this year so that people don't starve. How many measures of grain must the government sell to push the consumption up to 80,000 measures?

37. Ernest's demand for haircuts is $Q_d = 10 - 2p$. What is the market demand equation for haircuts if there are a total of five people identical to Ernest in the market?

*38. You run a regression in which the quantity of gasoline demanded per capita per day in each state is the dependent variable. The computer printout reports these estimates:

$$q = -0.791 + 0.0000631I,$$
$$(2.12)\ \ (0.0000272)$$

where q = quantity of gasoline demanded per capita per day in the state and I is the average income in the state in dollars per capita.

   a.   What is the estimated demand for gasoline if per capita income is $40,000?
   b.   Can we reject the hypothesis that income has no effect on quantity demanded?

39. Corn growers secretly cheered when Hurricane Andrew flattened part of the U.S. sugar crop. Explain their reaction using supply-and-demand analysis.

40. Initially, the demand and supply for unskilled teenage workers are

$$L_d = 350 - 50w$$
$$L_s = -400 + 100w,$$

where w = wage in dollars per hour and L = number of workers hired per day.

   a.   The government then imposes a minimum wage at $6 per hour. How will this affect employment and unemployment in this market?
   b.   At the end of the summer a lot of these teenagers drop out of the labor market and go to school full time. Which of these is more likely to be the subsequent labor supply curve? Explain.

$$L_{s1} = -200 - 50w \ \ \text{or} \ \ L_{s2} = -600 + 150w$$

   c.   Based on your answer to part b, how will the withdrawal of these workers from the labor supply affect wages, employment, and unemployment?

41. In the market for fast food workers, the quantity demanded is

$$L_d = 5000 - 400w,$$

where L is the number of hours of labor per day and w is the hourly wage in dollars. The quantity supplied is

$$L_s = -1000 + 800w.$$

How many workers will lose their jobs if the minimum wage is increased from $6 to $7 per hour? Does this increase in the minimum wage decrease total wage payments?

42. In the market for apartments, the quantity demanded is

$$Q_d = 1900 - 2p,$$

where Q is the number of apartments and p is the rent in dollars per month. The quantity supplied is

$$Q_s = -500 + p.$$

What will be the impact of a price ceiling of $900 per month?

43. In which of these markets—gasoline, bread, or babysitting services—would the supply-and-demand model be the most appropriate? In which is it least appropriate?

44. Pizza makers in College City face the following demand curve: $Q_d = 20,000 - 1000p$, where $Q_d =$ pizzas per week and $p =$ price in dollars per pizza. Will these pizza makers increase their collective revenue if they increase the price per pizza? What explains this result?

45. The Dog Catchers' Union calculates that it faces a demand elasticity of −3.0. The Brain Surgeons' Guild calculates that it faces a demand elasticity of −0.5. Does it make sense that the Dog Catchers would face a more elastic demand curve? Why might the dog catchers vote against recognition of a union that promised to increase wages by 20 percent?

46. Frank's Fitness Center decided to cut fees by 20 percent in an attempt to increase revenue. The Metropolitan Transit Authority decided to raise fares by 20 percent in an attempt to increase revenue. Was one of these two opposite approaches to raising revenues necessarily wrong? Explain.

47. Senator Blob strides up to the microphone and says, "It's time to increase the cigarette tax. Not only will increasing the cigarette tax bring in a lot of extra tax revenue, but it will increase the amount of income that families of those who are addicted to the noxious weed will be able to spend on other goods and services, such as food and health care." Is the Senator's reasoning sound?

48. The price of Marcel Duchamp's *Nude Descending a Staircase (No. 2)* (wits called it "Explosion in a Shingle Factory") has risen from about $300 when it was first exhibited in 1913 to roughly $10 million today. Assuming that these prices are real (i.e., adjusted for inflation), explain this using the supply-and-demand model.

49. The demand curve for wheat is

$$Q_d = 50,000,000 - 600,000p,$$

where Q_d is number of tons per year, and p is price per ton.

The industry supply curve is

$$Q_s = -10,000,000 + 400,000p.$$

Find the elasticity of supply and the elasticity of demand at equilibrium.

Old MacDonald asks, "If the demand curve really slopes downward, then why can I sell as much wheat as I can grow without any noticeable effect on the price?"

50. "Wheat farmers would all be better off if they suffered from bad weather or didn't work so hard, yet they all pray for good weather and work very hard." Explain this paradox. In one graph, show the workings of supply and demand in the entire wheat industry. In another graph, show the situation facing a single farmer.

51. The supply is Nerf balls $Q_s = -100{,}000 + 8{,}000p$ and the demand is $Q_d = 140{,}000 + 2Y - 7000p$, where Q = Nerf balls per month, p is the price (in cents) of one Nerf ball, and Y is income in dollars. Initially, Y is \$30,000. The government imposes a tax of 10 cents per Nerf ball. What percent of the tax is borne by buyers? If income rises to \$40,000, how much will tax revenue rise?

52. The supply of cotton in Enterprise, Alabama (home of the boll weevil monument) is $Q_s = -1000 + 50p - 700p_{soy}$, where quantity is in bales per year, p = the price per bale in dollars, and p_{soy} is the price of soybeans in dollars per bushel. Initially, the price of a bale of cotton is \$500 and the price of a bushel of soybeans is \$8. What is the cross-price elasticity of the quantity supplied of cotton with respect to the price of soybeans?

53. After the United States Postal Service issued Elvis stamps, their price almost immediately climbed above the amount shown on the front of the stamp. This is different from those generic looking stamps featuring a United States flag which always trade for a price that is equal to the value printed on the front. How can this be explained?

54. The equilibrium wage in the fast-food market is \$5 per hour and the equilibrium employment level is 400 hours per day. The elasticity of demand for labor is −0.3 and the elasticity of labor supply is 0.8. What will be the impact of a minimum wage that is 20 percent above the equilibrium?

55. The price per bag of marijuana is currently \$50 and 1000 bags are purchased each month. The elasticity of demand is −0.6. How much will the price rise if a police crackdown succeeds in reducing the supply so that only 800 bags per month are purchased?

56. In Figure 2.12, the demand curve for CD players has shifted outward because the price of CDs has fallen from \$15 to \$12. Using the information in the figure, calculate the cross-price elasticity of demand.

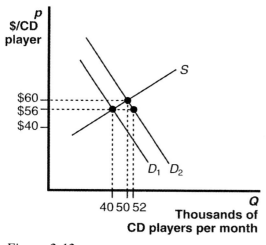

Figure 2.12

57. In the market for milk, the quantity demanded is $Q_d = 300 - 3p$, where Q is pints per day, and p is the price in cents per pint. At what point on the demand curve is the elasticity of demand = −0.5? = −1.0? = −1.5?

58. Will the share of gasoline tax paid by consumers be greater shortly after the tax has been enacted or several years after the tax has been enacted?

■ Answers to Practice Problems

1. c.   A rise in the price of shoes will cause a movement along the demand curve for shoes. It will not shift the demand curve for shoes.

2. a.   This is a change in tastes and preferences, and thus demand will increase.

3. d.   The supply curve shifts leftward due to the rise in the input price. The demand curve shifts leftward due to the rise in the price of a complementary good. The shift in supply drives the price of tires up. The shift in demand drives the price of tires down. Without more information we cannot tell which effect is greater, so we cannot predict the change in the price of tires.

4. a.   An increase in the cost of production causes a decrease in supply, which is a shift leftward. With a decrease in supply, the price will rise.

5. b.   A reduction in the cost of production causes an increase/rightward shift in supply. With an increase in supply, the price will fall.

6. a. $\varepsilon = (dQ/dp)(p/Q) = (-50)(1/100) = -0.5$.

7. a.   The share of the tax borne by consumers $= \eta/(\eta - \varepsilon) = 2/(2 - [-infinity]) = 0$.

8. c.   The portion of a specific tax that falls on consumers equals $\eta/(\eta - \varepsilon)$, where η is the elasticity of supply and ε is the elasticity of demand. Here this is $6/(6 - -4) = 0.6$, so consumers bear 60 percent of the tax, or 6 cents. These elasticities are pretty high, but Slinkies are pretty elastic. ;–)

9. substitute; complement

10. unemployment; supply

11. Transactions costs

12. stay the same. If demand is unitary elastic, then the quantity will fall by the same percentage that price rises.

13. ad valorem

14. substitute

15. False. The hurricane increased the demand for carpenters. If the price had been fixed at the initial level, then a shortage would have developed. However, the price rose, which eliminated the shortage. (A rise in price due to an increase in demand or a decrease in supply reflects increased *scarcity*, but the market is still in equilibrium.)

16. Ambiguous (but generally false). Market forces will generally cause the price to rise, which will eliminate the shortage. If there is some force, such as a government regulation, that blocks the movement to equilibrium, then a shortage will occur.

17. False. This may be the equilibrium wage, but there is no guarantee of this. An employer will have an excess demand for labor (a shortage with vacancies) if it pays less than the equilibrium wage, and it can throw money away by paying more than the equilibrium wage. If someone is paying more than the equilibrium wage, we would expect to see a long line of applicants for these positions. Profit maximizing firms will not generally do this, but city governments sometimes "overpay" their workers.

18. Ambiguous. If the technological improvements cause the supply curve to shift out enough to drive the equilibrium price below \$3, then the price will fall. This is shown by supply curve S_1 in Figure 2.13. If the supply curve shifts out by less than this, then the price will stay at \$3. This is shown by supply curve S_2 in Figure 2.13.

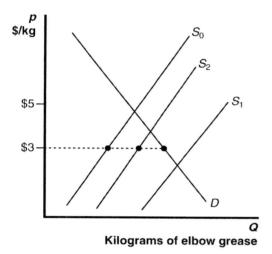

Figure 2.13

19. True. If the price of midnight oil falls, people will buy more of it. They will also increase their demand for its complement—elbow grease. As the demand curve for elbow grease shifts outward, from D_0 to D_1 in Figure 2.14, this will increase the shortage, which grows from $(Q_1 - Q_0)$ to $(Q_2 - Q_0)$.

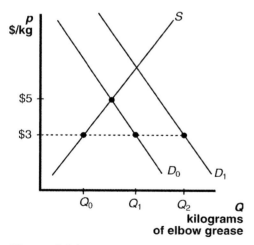

Figure 2.14

20. False. We cannot infer anything about the quantity *demanded*. The price ceiling causes a movement along the supply curve and it is the supply response that causes purchases to fall, not the demand response.

21. Ambiguous though generally true. The answer is true if nothing has been done to evade the law. In this case a price reduction has resulted in the same quantity supplied, so the supply curve is vertical. However, sales could have remained the same because the law was ignored and the price has actually stayed at $2 per ream. Likewise, the suppliers may have responded by changing the product—for example, reducing the cost by making each sheet of paper thinner.

22. False. Remembering that

$$\varepsilon = \frac{percentage\ change\ in\ quantity\ demanded}{percentage\ change\ in\ price} = \frac{\Delta Q/Q}{\Delta p/p} = \frac{dQ}{dp}\frac{p}{Q}$$

it is easy to automatically take numbers and plug them into the formula. In this case, $\Delta Q = 120$ and $\Delta p = \$1$, so putting these numbers into the demand elasticity formula yields a positive number. This is a problem. As the price has risen, the quantity has also risen. This doesn't sound like a movement along a demand curve. Figure 2.15 illustrates what may be happening. As we move from an ordinary day to Valentine's Day, the demand for flowers rises from D to D_v, causing a movement along the supply curve. There is no reason to think that the supply curve has shifted. Thus, by automatically plugging the numbers into the formula, we would have estimated the elasticity of supply, not the elasticity of demand.

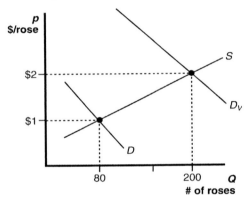

Figure 2.15

23. Ambiguous. If both the demand and supply curves are linear, then the statement would be true. However, the curves may take other shapes. Figure 2.16(a) shows a case in which the pretax price was $22.50 and in which the tax continues to be split evenly by buyers and sellers. Figure 2.16(b) shows a case in which the tax is no longer split evenly by buyers and sellers after it is raised to $15.

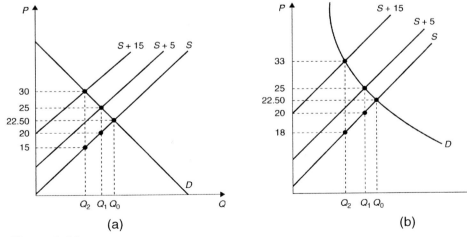

Figure 2.16

24. Ambiguous. This depends on whether alcohol and marijuana are substitutes. If they are substitutes, the rising price for booze will induce consumers to switch away from it to marijuana. If they are complements, i.e., used together, consumers will purchase less alcohol and less marijuana. (Some research has suggested that these goods may be complements; others have suggested that they may be substitutes.)

25. a. As Figure 2.17(a) shows, the U.S. embargo—which stopped the export of raw cotton from the U.S. to Britain—shifted the British supply of cloth inward from S_0 to S_1, driving up the price of cloth to P_1, as the quantity fell from Q_0 to Q_1.

b. As Figure 2.17(b) shows, the invention shifts the supply curve outward from S_0 to S_1, driving down the price of lumber to P_1, as the quantity rises from Q_0 to Q_1.

c. As Figure 2.17(c) shows, the farmers will reduce their supply of cotton in order to plant more melons. This will shift the cotton supply curve inward from S_0 to S_1, driving up the price of cotton to P_1, as the quantity falls from Q_0 to Q_1.

d. As Figure 2.17(d) shows, the drought shifts the supply curve inward from S_0 to S_1. Simultaneously, the demand curve shifts inward from D_0 to D_1, because people don't like the taste of the wine as much. We cannot tell if the price will rise, fall or remain unchanged—it depends on the relative size of the supply and demand shifts—but the quantity falls from Q_0 to Q_1.

e. As Figure 2.17(e) shows, the supply curve shifts outward from S_0 to S_1, driving down the price of tomatoes to P_1, as the quantity rises from Q_0 to Q_1.

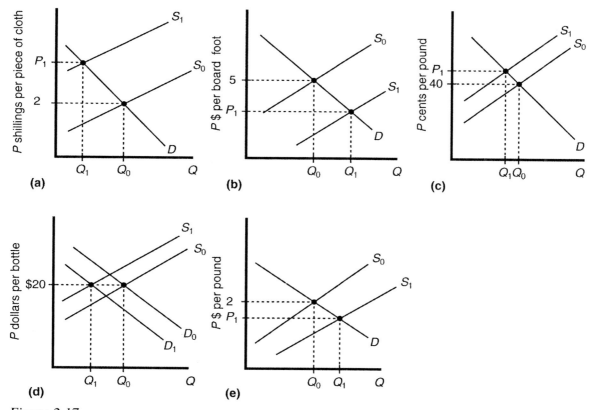

Figure 2.17

26. The demand for hotel rooms in Stowe, Vermont (a ski resort) rises during the winter. The demand for hotel rooms in Ocean City, Maryland (a beach resort) falls during the winter.

27. The punch line to the joke is: "Are you kidding? You must be confusing demand with supply. Do you have any idea how many lawyers are needed to get a pound of brains?" The point is that you cannot deduce the reason for a high (or low) price solely from one factor—such as demand. The price is set by the *interaction* of supply and demand. Figure 2.18 compares the traveler's explanation of the high price with the butcher's version. If we know only the price, either story is possible—as are a lot of others.

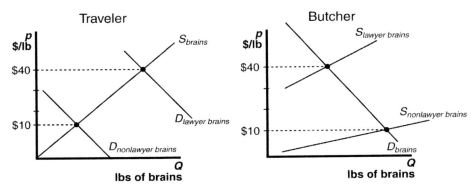

Figure 2.18

28. As Appendix 2A explains, a regression is a method of fitting a line through a scatter plot of points. Each point in this graph represents one individual's age and hourly wage. Before we can run a regression, we must begin with a theory explaining how each point is determined. Just by eyeballing Figure 2.6 we can see that there is a positive relationship between age and wage. Does a higher wage cause a higher age? This theory seems pretty weak. Earning more won't make your older. Does a higher age cause a higher wage? This sounds more plausible. Economic theory says that all prices, including wages, are determined by the supply and demand. The demand for labor depends on how productive the worker is and productivity is known to be related to maturity, plus mental and physical abilities, which generally rise as a person ages from 15 to 25. Thus our theory says that a person's wage is caused, at least in part, by his or her age. A linear representation of this theory is

$$\text{wage} = a + (b \times \text{age}) + e,$$

where a and b are the coefficients we want to determine (the intercept and slope of the line) and e is an error term that captures random effects that are not otherwise reflected in our equation; that is, there are a lot other things, such as effort and aptitude, that influence wages and are independent of age. The most widely used method to fit the line through this plot is called ordinary least squares (*OLS*). It selects the line that minimizes the sum of the squared residuals, where a residual is the vertical distance between the estimated line and each point. There is no point in calculating the line by hand, because a computer can do it in less than a second, providing a regression line and statistics telling how confident we are that the slope is actually different from zero. If we are confident that the slope is different from zero, we are confident that a relation does exist between age and wage.

29. To explain why an ice cream cone costs 75 cents, we would draw a demand curve and a supply curve and show that they intersect at 75 cents per cone. Supply and demand can also be used to explain why some things are free. Although the idea may seem strange, there is a downward-sloping demand curve for air. If the price of air were really high, say $1,000 per breath, not many people would buy it, since they wouldn't have enough money to pay for it. At a lower price, more people could afford to pay for air. Luckily for us here on Earth, at every price the natural supply of air is greater than the quantity that is demanded. Figure 2.19 shows this situation. The supply of air on Earth, S_{Earth}, is greater than the demand, D, at any positive price and at the price of zero. Thus, there is an excess supply of air at the price of zero. Air need not be free. If the supply of air were smaller, the price would become positive. For example, people scaling Mount Everest often pay for breathable air, which they must carry up in oxygen tanks. This is because the natural supply of oxygen is much less at such high elevations. Other examples are astronauts and scuba divers. In *Total Recall*, a futuristic thriller starring Arnold Schwartzenegger, residents of Mars were required to pay for oxygen, because

it was so scarce. Figure 2.19 shows that this supply curve, S_{Mars}, intersects the demand curve at a positive price. At the end of the movie, Schwartzenegger's character activates a gigantic machine that produces oxygen for the Martian atmosphere. In essence, he (almost single-handedly!) has shifted the supply curve to the right so far that it no longer intersects the demand curve and the price of oxygen falls to zero. (I hope this doesn't spoil the end of the movie for you.)

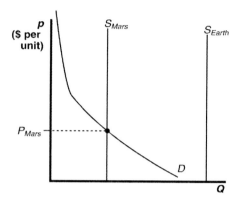

Figure 2.19

30.   Because fairness is a normative issue, different people will answer this question differently. However, economic analysis allows us to make well-informed judgments. Suppose that a law was passed making it illegal to raise prices as demand increases. Mandating that price be kept at p_1, in Figure 2.20, would cause a shortage, $(Q_2 - Q_0)$. In reaching a judgment, we must weigh the claims of those who prefer the price to stay at the initial level—those who can buy it at the initial price, against the claims of those who want the price to rise—the sellers, plus those who are willing to pay more than p_1 but who cannot get the product because output won't rise if there is a price ceiling. Without economic analysis it is easy to overlook the fact that many consumers are hurt by price ceilings. While fairness includes many dimensions that are not included in Figure 2.20 (for example, we don't know anything about the producers' profit rates), economic analysis can help us better weigh the pros and cons of many policies. In a recent study, students were asked a number of questions about fairness. One question was "On a holiday, when there is a great demand for flowers, their prices usually go up. Is it fair for flower sellers to raise their prices like this?" Among students who had not taken any economics courses, 18 percent felt that the price rise was not fair. Among students who had nearly completed a semester of economics, only 10 percent felt that the price rise was not fair. Thus, the proportion who felt the price rise was not fair fell almost in half. (See Robert Whaples, "Changes in Attitudes among College Economics Students about the Fairness of the Market," *Journal of Economic Education*, Fall 1995, for additional findings.)

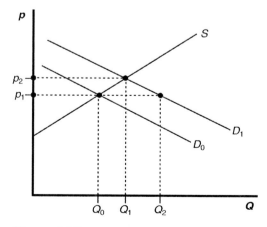

Figure 2.20

31. The supply of old newspapers was so high and the demand for old newspapers was initially so low that the cities had to pay recyclers to take them off their hands. This is shown in Figure 2.21, as D_0 and S initially intersect at a price of –$10. As new uses for old newspapers were found, the demand rose to D_1 and the intersection rose above the price of zero. Disposal of unwanted goods is not always free.

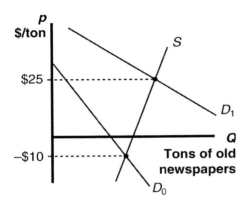

Figure 2.21

32. Figure 2.22 replicates the demand curve in Figure 2.7. Supply curve S_{D+I} is the horizontal sum of supply curves S_D and S_I from Figure 2.7. This represents the supply curve when there are no barriers to trade and no transportation costs. It intersects the demand curve where price = $5.33 per pound and quantity = 16.67 tons. If transportation costs are $2 per pound, then S_I will shift upward by $2 per pound. When this higher import supply curve is added horizontally to S_D it gives us S_{D+IT}, which is the same as S_D below $4 per pound and has the same slope as S_{D+I} above $4 per pound. It intersects the demand curve where price = $6 per pound and quantity = 15 tons.

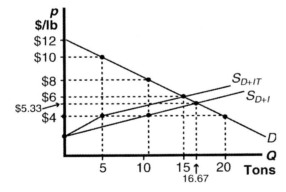

Figure 2.22

33. At equilibrium, $100 - 3p = 20 + 2p$ or $80 = 5p$, so $p = \$16$. The equilibrium quantity of matches is 52 per month ($100 - (3 \times 16) = 52$). At $10 per match, the quantity demanded is 70 matches per month ($100 - (3 \times 10) = 70$), but the quantity supplied is only 40 per month ($20 + (2 \times 10) = 40$). Thus only 40 matches are staged per month, and there is a shortage of 30 matches per month. This may give rise to illegal trading. Notice that the supplier of the fortieth match is willing to stage the match for only $10, but customers are willing to pay $20. (We can find this by plugging $Q = 40$ into the demand equation and solving for price. $40 = 100 - 3p$, so $p = \$20$.) See Figure 2.23.

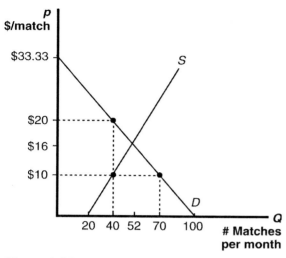

Figure 2.23

A price ceiling of $20 per match would have *no* impact on the market at all. The equilibrium price is $16 per match and this is below the ceiling, and therefore quite legal. There are no forces that will drive the price up to the ceiling. Remember: You only bump your head when the ceiling is too low.

34. The initial equilibrium is at price = 10 cents and quantity = 50,000 pounds. (Set $Q_d = Q_s$ and solve for p. $100,000 - 5000p = -50,000 + 10,000p$, so $150,000 = 15,000p$, and $p = 10$. Plug $p = 10$ into the demand and supply equations and verify that $Q = 50,000$.)

Next construct a supply curve that reduces output to half of its previous level at each price. The initial supply curve, S, and the demand curve, D_1, are plotted in Figure 2.24. The new supply curve, S_2, hits the vertical axis at the same level as S_1 but at each price the quantity is half that of S_1, (for example, at 10 cents per pound, S_2 is 25,000 pounds and S_1 is 50,000 pounds)—therefore, S_2 has a slope that is twice as steep. The equation for S_2 is $Q_{S2} = -25,000 + 5000p$. Notice that this hits the vertical axis at $p = 5$ and that output rises only 5000 pounds for each one cent increase in price, not 10,000 pounds as in the case of the original supply curve.

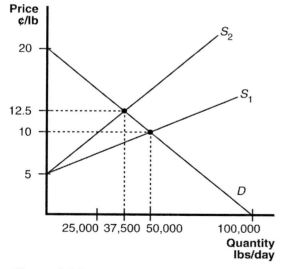

Figure 2.24

Find the new equilibrium by setting $Q_d = Q_{s2}$ and solving to find that $p = 12.50$ cents and $Q = 37,500$. ($100,000 - 5000p = -25,000 + 5000p$, so $125,000 = 10,000p$, and $p = 12.50$. Plugging $p = 12.50$ into the demand and supply equations shows that $Q = 100,000 - (5000 \times 12.5) = 100,000 - 62,500 = 37,500$.) Notice that the policy of destroying half the Wapanzo bean crop has reduced production and consumption by only one-fourth, because this action has driven up the price and induced the producers to move up along the new supply curve.

35. As in the last question, the initial equilibrium is at price = 10 cents and quantity = 50,000 pounds. To find out how much the government must sell to push the price down by 2 cents per pound, we need to see how much consumers will buy at 8 cents per pound and how much producers will sell. Plugging 8 cents into the demand and supply equations yields:

$$Q_d = 100,000 - (5000 \times 8) = 100,000 - 40,000 = 60,000 \text{ pounds per day.}$$
$$Q_s = -50,000 + (10,000 \times 8) = -50,000 + 80,000 = 30,000 \text{ pounds per day.}$$

Thus the quantity demanded is 30,000 pounds per day greater than the quantity supplied at 8 cents per pound. The government must supply 30,000 pounds per day to make the quantity demanded equal the quantity supplied (by producers and the government) at 8 cents per pound.

36. First solve to find the equilibrium when the government does not intervene into the market. (Set $Q_d = Q_s$ and solve for p. $100,000 - 5000p = 10,000 + 10,000p$, so $90,000 = 15,000p$, and $p = 6$ shekels. Plug $p = 6$ into the demand and/or supply equations. $Q_d = 100,000 - (5000 \times 6) = 100,000 - 30,000 = 70,000$ measures.) Thus consumption is too low by 10,000 measures. However, Joseph cannot simply solve the problem by supplying 10,000 measures from the government granary. If he does, he will drive the price down and other suppliers will reduce their production somewhat, so the quantity supplied won't rise by the whole 10,000 measures.

Joseph must find the price that will push consumers far enough down their demand curve so that they will demand 80,000 measures of grain, then he must calculate the supply that producers will sell at this price. The government must sell enough to close this gap.

Set Q_d equal to 80,000 and solve for p. $80,000 = 100,000 - 5000p$ or $20,000 = 5000p$, so $p = 4$ shekels if consumers are to buy 80,000 measures of grain.

Plug $p = 4$ into the supply equation. $Q_s = 10,000 + 10,000 \times 4 = 50,000$. Thus, the government needs to sell 30,000 measures of grain to boost consumption to 80,000 measures. Two-thirds of this is to make up for the reduction in supply by producers (who slide down their supply curve in the face of lower prices).

37. It is probably easiest to answer this question by using a graph. Figure 2.25(a) plots out $Q_d = 10 - 2p$. (As usual, the horizontal intercept can be found by solving for Q_d when $p = 0$ and the vertical intercept can be found by setting $Q_d = 0$ and solving for p.) To find the market demand curve we sum *horizontally* across individuals. Since these five people are identical, the market demand curve will simply be five times higher than Ernest's demand curve at each price. Thus, at $p = 0$, the quantity demanded is 50 rather than 10, and at $p = 2.5$, the quantity demanded is 25 rather than 5. The equation that goes with this market demand curve—seen in Figure 2.25(b)—has an intercept that is five times farther out and a slope that indicates that the quantity demanded falls by five units, not one unit, each time price climbs by one. The appropriate equation, therefore, is $Q_d = 50 - 10p$. Notice that we could have found this by simply multiplying the initial demand equation by five or adding it to itself five times.

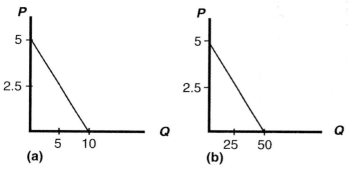

Figure 2.25

Warning! This simple addition (or multiplication) only works when we have identical customers. If, for example, we had two customers whose demand equations were $Q_{d1} = 10 - 2p$ and $Q_{d2} = 20 - 2p$, we couldn't simply add these equations to get a market demand of $Q_{d3} = 30 - 4p$. This equation is plotted as a dashed line in Figure 2.26, along with the kinked demand curve that comes from correctly aggregating demand by adding the individual demand curves together horizontally. (They lie on top of each other below a price of 5.) A linear demand equation cannot describe the resulting market demand curve. The correct demand curve's formula must be given in two steps: If $p > 5$ then $Q_d = 20 - 2p$. If $p \leq 5$ then $Q_d = 30 - 4p$. (See Solved Problem 3 for another example of this type of demand curve problem.)

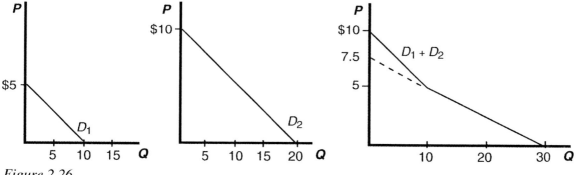

Figure 2.26

38.   a.   To find the estimated quantity demanded, plug $I = 40,000$ into the regression equation:
      $q = -0.791 + (0.0000631 \times 40,000) = -0.791 + 2.524 = 1.733$ gallons per capita per day.

      b.   If zero were to lie in the confidence interval around our coefficient estimate (0.0000631), we would not be able to reject the hypothesis that income has no effect on the quantity of gasoline demanded. To build the 95 percent confidence interval, take the coefficient estimate plus and minus two times the estimated standard error of the coefficient, which is given in parentheses below the estimated coefficient. The 95 percent confidence interval, therefore, runs from $(0.0000631 - (2 \times 0.0000272))$ to $(0.0000631 + (2 \times 0.0000272))$, i.e., from 0.0000087 to 0.000118. Because zero is not in this confidence interval, we are 95 percent confident that income *does* have an effect on per capita gasoline consumption.

39.   The effect of the hurricane on the sugar market is straightforward (see Figure 2.27(a)). The storm has shifted the supply curve to the left, moving it along the demand curve and yielding a higher price for sugar. It stands to reason that corn growers will only cheer such an event if they have gained from the disaster. Corn growers must think that the price of corn will rise. Since their own supply curve hasn't been affected by the hurricane, this must mean that the demand for corn has risen and driven up the price of corn (see Figure 2.27(b)). If sugar and corn (the source of corn syrup) are substitutes, then the rising price of sugar will shift the demand for corn outward. Notice that we have been able to use

economic reasoning to deduce that corn and sugar *must* be substitutes if an inward shift of the sugar supply curve were to make corn producers better off (unless there is some other link between these markets that we don't know about.)

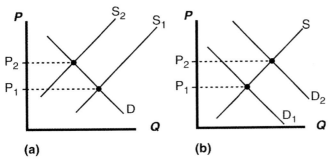

(a)   (b)

Figure 2.27

40. a. The market equilibrium wage equates L_d and L_s ($350 - 50w = -400 + 100w$, or $750 = 150w$), so $w = \$5$ per hour. At this wage rate the quantity supplied and demanded is 100 workers. (See Figure 2.28.) To find the effect of the minimum wage, plug $6 per hour into the demand-and-supply equations. $L_d = 350 - (50 \times 6) = 50$. $L_s = -400 + (100 \times 6) = 200$. Employers will only hire 50 workers, but 200 workers want jobs. Therefore, employment falls by 50 (from 100 to 50). Unemployment (excess supply) grows from 0 to 150 workers.

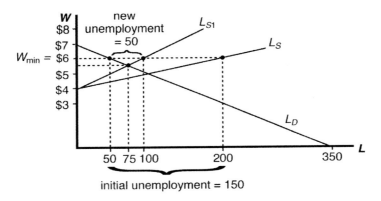

Figure 2.28

b. The withdrawal of workers from the market shifts the labor supply curve inward. Both of the proposed labor supply curves hit the vertical axis at $4 per hour (the same as the initial labor supply curve) but the first of these, $L_{s1} = -200 + 50w$, is steeper than the original (each one-dollar increase in the wage pulls 50 workers into the labor market), while the second equation, $L_{s2} = -600 + 150w$, is flatter. Therefore, the first equation better shows a decline in the supply of labor.

c. After students return to school, the equilibrium wage rises to $5.50 (where $L_d = 350 - 50w = -200 + 50w = L_{s1}$) and equilibrium quantity rises to 75 workers. This is still below the minimum wage, so employment is not changed. Only 50 workers are hired. However, the excess supply has diminished. At $6 per hour, there are now only 100 teenagers willing to work ($-200 + (50 \times 6) = -200 + 300 = 100$), so unemployment (excess supply) has fallen to 50 workers.

41. The original minimum wage is set above equilibrium. (The equilibrium wage, where $L_d = L_s$, is $5 per hour. Check this by verifying that both L_d and L_s equal 3000 at $5.) To find the outcome when the minimum wage is $6 per hour, plug $6 into the demand equation. Do the same for $7 per hour. As Figure 2.29 shows, the quantity demanded falls from $L_d = 5000 - (400 \times 6)$ to $L_d = 5000 - (400 \times 7)$, i.e., from 2600 to 2200. Thus, employment of fast food workers falls by 400. The total wage payments to fast food workers, on the other hand, barely falls. Total payments $= wL$. This has fallen from ($6 \times 2600) = \$15,600$ to ($7 \times 2200) = \$15,400$.

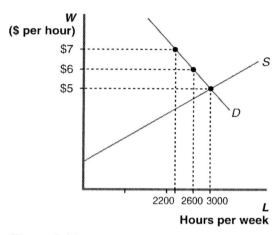

Figure 2.29

42. $Q_d = 1900 - 2p = -500 + p = Q_s$, so $2400 = 3p$, and p, the equilibrium price, is 2400/3 = $800. At this price the quantity demanded and supplied is 300. Because the rent ceiling is above the equilibrium price of $800, it will have no impact on the market.

43. The supply-and-demand model is most applicable when everyone is a price taker, firms sell identical products, everyone has full information about the price and quality of goods, and costs of trading are low. By these criteria, the model is *least* appropriate in the babysitting market. In this market it can be time consuming, difficult, and expensive for a buyer to find a seller (and vice versa)—lots of phone calls might need to be made to find a sitter. In addition, few people know the going price for sitter services in the market, and the product quality differs dramatically from one seller to another. The *most* applicable market is probably gasoline. Brands of gasoline are likely to be more similar than brands of bread, and consumers are much more informed about prices. They learn the latest gasoline prices as they drive around town (on the way to work, for example) because almost all sellers post their prices on large signs that can be seen from the road. To find out the price of bread one must usually go into the store and look, so information is much less complete.

44. To answer this question, pick an initial price of pizza and a higher final price and compare the revenue in the two cases.

    Case 1: Increase the price from $5 to $10. Sales fall from 15,000 to 10,000. Revenue equals pQ, so revenues have risen from $75,000 per week to $100,000 per week.

    Case 2: Increase the price from $10 to $15. Sales fall from 10,000 to 5000, so revenues have fallen from $100,000 per week to $75,000 per week.

    Thus revenue could rise or could fall. Notice that changes in revenue depend on the elasticity of demand, which changes as we move along the demand curve. In Case 1 we are in an inelastic section of the demand curve; thus the percentage rise in price is greater than the percent fall in quantity, so pQ rises. In Case 2, we are in an elastic section of the demand curve; thus the percentage rise in price is smaller than the percentage fall in quantity, so pQ falls.

45.   The elasticity of demand is a measure of responsiveness of the quantity demanded (of labor) to the wage, and is tied closely to the availability of substitutes. The elasticity of demand for members of the Dog Catchers' Union is likely to be high because it will be easy to replace them with nonmembers or do without their services. On the other hand, the elasticity of demand for members of the Brain Surgeons' Guild is likely to be low, since brain surgeons are much harder to replace (it takes a lot of training, degrees, and licenses).

The dog catchers would probably vote against recognition of a union that promised to increase wages by 20 percent because they know that the elasticity of demand for their services is high. Since

$$-3.0 = \frac{percentage\ change\ in\ quantity\ demanded}{percentage\ change\ in\ wage} = \frac{\Delta Q/Q}{20\%}$$

this implies that a 20 percent increase in wages will cause a 60 percent decrease in the quantity demanded. Many members of the union will lose their jobs.

46.   Neither of these opposite strategies is necessarily wrong. If Frank's Fitness Center faces an elastic demand curve, then cutting fees by 20 percent will increase the quantity demanded by a greater percentage and revenues will increase. Frank probably faces an elastic demand curve, since there are lots of other firms in the industry—lots of substitutes for his product. If the Metropolitan Transit Authority faces an inelastic demand curve, then raising fares by 20 percent will decrease the quantity demanded by less than 20 percent, and revenues will increase. The MTA probably faces an inelastic demand curve since there are few good substitutes for public transportation in many large cities.

47.   Senator Blob's reasoning is squishy. He assumes (correctly, according to the figures in the text) that the demand for cigarettes is inelastic. Thus a tax hike will probably increase tax revenues because the quantity demanded won't fall much (provided that the tax it is not so high that widespread bootlegging arises). However, if demand is inelastic, the price will rise by a greater percentage than the quantity demanded, so total expenditures on cigarettes will rise and "those who are addicted to the noxious weed" will have less to spend on other goods and services.

48.   There is only one original of *Nude Descending a Staircase (No. 2)*, so the supply curve is vertical (perfectly inelastic) at a quantity of one. In cases of such a product, demand alone determines the price of the good. As the demand has risen, from D_{1913} to D_{2004}, the price has skyrocketed. See Figure 2.30.

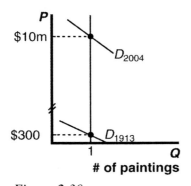

Figure 2.30

49. $50{,}000{,}000 - 600{,}000p = -10{,}000{,}000 + 400{,}000p$ or $60{,}000{,}000 = 1{,}000{,}000p$, so the equilibrium price is \$60 per ton and the equilibrium quantity is 14 million tons ($50{,}000{,}000 - 600{,}000 \times 60 = 14{,}000{,}000$).

The elasticity of demand is

$$\varepsilon = \frac{dQ}{dp}\frac{p}{Q} = -600{,}000\frac{\$60}{14{,}000{,}000} = -2.57$$

The elasticity of supply is

$$\eta = \frac{dQ}{dp}\frac{p}{Q} = 400{,}000\frac{\$60}{14{,}000{,}000} = 1.71$$

The reason that Old MacDonald's decisions have no noticeable effect on the price is that his output is such a miniscule part of the entire supply. Suppose that he doubled his output from 10 tons to 20 tons. This would shift the supply curve outward imperceptibly, since the total quantity supplied is 14 million tons. To accommodate this outward shift in supply, the price would fall by a tiny amount as we move along the demand curve. For example, if Old MacDonald's output rises by 10 tons, the output would rise by .00000071 percent and the price would fall by .00000047 percent.

50.   Figure 2.31(a) shows the entire wheat industry. Bad weather would shift the supply curve inward, but could make all farmers better off if demand is inelastic, so that the price would rise by a greater percentage than the drop in the quantity demanded. Revenue will rise because $p_2 Q_2 > p_1 Q_1$.

Figure 2.31(b) shows the situation facing a single farmer. Each farmer faces a perfectly elastic demand curve for wheat, because other farmers' wheat will substitute for their own. If an individual farmer supplies less, quantity will fall, but price will stay the same, so revenue will fall from $p_1 q_1$ to $p_1 q_2$.

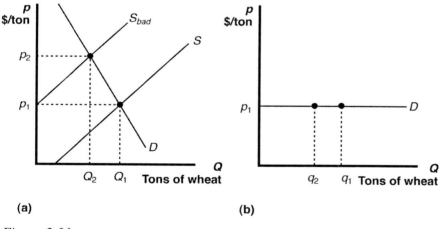

(a)   (b)

Figure 2.31

51. What percentage of the tax is borne by the buyers?

Remember that the share of the tax paid by the consumer equals $\eta/(\eta - \varepsilon)$.

The pretax equilibrium is

$$Q_d = 140,000 + 2 \times 30,000 - 7000p = -100,000 + 8000p \text{ or}$$
$$200,000 - 7000p = -100,000 + 8000p \text{ or}$$
$$300,000 = 15,000p, \text{ so}$$

$$p = 20 \text{ cents per Nerf ball and } Q = 60,000 \text{ Nerf balls per month.}$$

Therefore, the demand elasticity $= -7000(20/60,000) = -2.33$ and the supply elasticity $= 8000$ $(20/60,000) = 2.67$.

The share of the tax borne by the consumers is $\eta/(\eta - \varepsilon) = 2.66/(2.66 - -2.33) = .5333$, so the consumers bear 53.33 percent of the tax.

The 10-cent tax will raise the price paid by the buyers to 25.33 cents, but cut the price received by the sellers to 15.33 cents. At these prices $Q_d = Q_s = 22,667$.

This generates tax revenues of $tQ = \$.10 \times 22,667 = \$2267$.

The increase in income shifts out the demand curve to

$$Q_d = 140,000 + 2 \times 40,000 - 7000p, \text{ so the new pretax equilibrium is}$$
$$Q_d = 220,000 - 7000p = -100,000 + 8000p$$
$$320,000 = 15,000p$$

$$p = 21.33 \text{ cents per Nerf ball and } Q = 70,667 \text{ Nerf balls per month.}$$

The demand elasticity at the new equilibrium $= -7000(21.33/70,667) = -2.113$ and the supply elasticity $= 8000(21.33/70,667) = 2.415$, so the incidence of the tax is the same as before, $2.415/(2.415 - -2.113) = .5333$.

After the tax, the price paid by the buyer is $21.33 + 5.33 = 26.66$ and the price received by the seller is 16.66. $Q_d = Q_s = 33,333$.

The new tax revenue is $\$.10 \times 33,333 = \$3333$, so the increase in income drives up tax revenues by $\$3333 - \$2266 = \$1067$.

52. $Q_s = -1000 + 50p - 700p_{soy}$, $p = \$500$ and $p_{soy} = \$8$.

The formula for cross-price elasticity of supply is

$$\frac{percentage\ change\ in\ quantity\ supplied\ of\ cotton}{percentage\ change\ in\ price\ of\ soybeans} = \frac{Q_{cot}}{P_{soy}} \frac{P_{soy}}{Q_{cot}}$$

The quantity supplied is $-1000 + (50 \times 500) - (700 \times 8) = 18,400$, so the cross-price elasticity is $-700(8/18,400) = -0.304$. Thus, soybeans and cotton are substitutes on the supply side. As the price of soybeans rises, farmers decrease their supply of cotton, switching away from cotton production and into soy production.

53. For stamps featuring a U.S. flag, the USPS will issue an unlimited amount at the face value on the stamp. Thus, the supply curve for 39-cent flag stamps is a horizontal line at 39 cents, $S_{Flag.}$ As Figure 2.32(a) shows, the demand for these stamps could be high, D_H, or low, D_L, but the price will stay at 39 cents. People knew that there were a limited number of Elvis stamps to be produced. The USPS would sell these stamps for, say, 39 cents each, but would only sell a limited quantity, Q_{max}, in Figure 2.32(b). Thus, the supply curve looked like $S_{Elvis.}$ Demand for these stamps was high enough that D_{Elvis} intersected S_{Elvis} at a price higher than 39 cents.

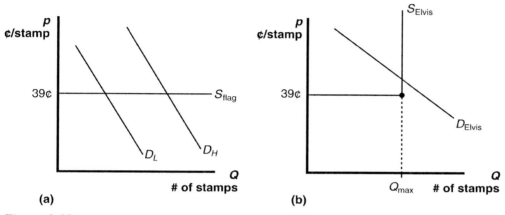

Figure 2.32

54. The employers will move back along the demand for labor curve. By definition ε, the elasticity of demand for labor, equals (percentage change in quantity demanded)/(percentage change in wage). Here $\varepsilon = -0.3$ and percentage change in wage = 20 percent, so percentage change in quantity demanded = −6 percent. Thus, the quantity of labor demanded will fall by 6 percent, from 400 to 376 hours per day.

The workers will attempt to move up along their labor supply curve. By definition η, the elasticity of supply of labor, equals (percentage change in quantity supplied)/(percentage change in wage). Here $\eta = 0.8$ and percentage change in wage = 20 percent, so percentage change in quantity supplied = 16 percent. Thus, the quantity of labor supplied will rise by 16 percent, from 400 to 464 hours per day. All in all, employment drops by 24 hours per day and unemployment (the gap between the quantity of labor supplied and the quantity demanded) rises from zero to 88 (464 − 376).

55. The police crackdown will cause the supply curve to shift inward, moving people up along the demand curve. The elasticity of demand, ε, equals (percentage change in quantity demanded)/(percentage change in price). Here $\varepsilon = -0.6$ and percentage change in quantity demanded is −20 percent (a drop from 1000 to 800). Therefore, the percentage change in price must be 33.3 percent (−0.6 = 20 percent/ (−33.3 percent)), so price rises from $50 per bag to $66.67 per bag.

56. We need to measure the impact of the change in the price of CDs on the quantity demanded of CD players—holding everything else constant including the price of CD players. This cross-price elasticity = $(\Delta Q_{Dplayers}/Q_{Dplayers})/(\Delta p_{CDs}/p_{CDs})$. Holding the price of CD players constant at $56 we see that the drop in the price of CDs from $15 to $12 causes the quantity demanded of CD players to rise from 40,000 to 52,000 per month; thus a $3 price drop has caused a 12,000-unit increase in the quantity demanded. Plugging in these numbers, the cross-price elasticity equals (12,000/40,000)/ (−$3/$15) = −0.3/0.2 = −1.5. (If you used the arc elasticity method, the answer is −1.17.)

57.   Recall that $\varepsilon = (dQ/dp)(p/Q)$ and that (dQ/dp) is the derivative of the demand equation. Thus we need to find where $-3(p/Q)$ equals each of these totals. Substituting in $(300 - 3p)$ for Q, we get $-3(p/(300 - 3p))$. Set this equal to each of the numbers and solve. For example, $-3(p/(300 - 3p)) = -0.5$, implies that $6p = 300 - 3p$, or $9p = 300$, so $p = 33.33$ when the elasticity of demand is -0.5. Let's check this. At $p = 33.33$, the quantity demanded is 200. Plugging these numbers into the elasticity formula yields $\varepsilon = (dQ/dp)(p/Q) = -3 \times (33.33/200) = -0.5$. The elasticity equals -1.0 at a price of 50, and -1.5 at a price of 60.

58.   The incidence of the tax depends on the size of the demand elasticity relative to the supply elasticity. The portion of the tax that falls on consumers equals $\eta/(\eta - \varepsilon)$, where η = the supply elasticity and ε = the demand elasticity. Each of these elasticities tends to change over time. In most cases demand elasticities get larger in magnitude over time, as consumers can make more adjustments. For example, the elasticity of demand for gasoline in Canada rises in magnitude from -0.35 in the short run to -0.7 in the long run (five years). On the other hand, supply elasticities also generally get larger as suppliers have more time to adjust. In such cases, the portion of the tax falling on the consumer depends on which elasticity changes faster. For example, suppose that the supply elasticity of gasoline in Canada is 2.0 in the short run and rises to 3.0 in the long run. In this case, the portion of the tax falling on consumers in the short run is $\eta/(\eta - \varepsilon) = 2/(2 - -0.35) = 85$ percent. In the long run the portion is $\eta/(\eta - \varepsilon) = 3/(3 - -0.7) = 81$ percent.

Finally, note that the elasticity of demand falls over time for some goods, especially those that are durable or easily stored. For such products, it is likely that the proportion of the tax falling on the consumer will rise over time, even if the supply elasticity is unchanged with time.

■ Exercises

True-False-Ambiguous and Explain Why

1.   The equilibrium price of elbow grease is $5 per kilogram, but the government has in place a price ceiling at $3 per kilogram. If the government removes the price ceiling, this will cause the price to rise and people will buy more.

2.   The equilibrium price of elbow grease is $5 per kilogram, but the government has in place a price ceiling at $3 per kilogram. Shoulder grease is a substitute for elbow grease. If the price of shoulder grease falls, then the shortage of elbow grease will grow larger.

3.   The tax on gasoline in the District of Columbia is 20 cents per gallon. If the government raises the rate, then total tax revenue will increase.

4.   The demand for used lawn mowers is $Q_d = 5000 - 50p$, where Q_d = number of lawn mowers per week, and p = price in dollars. Therefore, the elasticity of demand is -1.

Short-Answer

5.   The former Drug Czar said, "We think that we are winning the war on drugs. Recently the price of cocaine has climbed and this indicates that we are cutting off the supply of cocaine smuggled into the United States. Unfortunately, we have no statistics on the amount of cocaine being sold." Was his reasoning sound? Explain.

6. Producers of Wapanzo beans convince the government to support the price of their product. If the price is lower than 15 cents per pound, the government will buy up enough Wapanzo beans to boost the price up to 15 cents per pound. The demand and supply for Wapanzo beans are

$$Q_d = 100,000 - 5000p$$
$$Q_s = -50,000 + 10,000p,$$

where p = price in cents per pound and Q = pounds per year. How much will this price-support program cost per year?

7. Figure 2.33 shows the quantity of blueberries bought and sold in various months. Can we use a regression line to estimate the supply of blueberries based on this data? Explain.

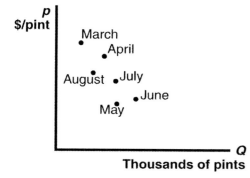

Figure 2.33

8. The monthly demand curve for pizza for a typical college student, and the monthly supply curve for a typical pizzeria in a college town are given below.

$$q_d = 50 - 5p$$
$$q_s = -15,000 + 5,000p$$

Assume that the demand and supply curves are linear and that there are 10,000 identical consumers and 10 identical pizza makers. Find the equilibrium price and quantity in this market.

9. The demand and supply equations for peaches are

$$Q_d = 2,000,000 - 20,000p + 10Y + 5000p_A,$$

where quantity is in crates per week, p is the price of peaches in cents per pound, Y is average yearly household income in dollars, and p_A is the price of apricots in cents per pound, and

$$Q_s = -1,700,000 + 10,000p + 50,000R,$$

– where quantity is in crates per week, p is the price of peaches in cents per pound, and R is the number of inches of rain per year in the peach growing district. Assume that incomes average \$30,000, the price of apricots is 80 cents per pound, and the annual rainfall was 40 inches.

a. What is the equilibrium price of peaches?

b. How does the equilibrium price of peaches vary with the number of inches of rain per year in the peach-growing district?

c. Based on the equation, are peaches and apricots substitutes or complements?

10. In the market for apartments, the quantity demanded is

$$Q_d = 1800 - 3p,$$

where Q is the number of apartments and p is the rent in dollars per month. The quantity supplied is

$$Q_s = -200 + p.$$

Suppose the city council sets a price ceiling $100 below equilibrium. How will the market respond? If you are the only landlord in town who breaks the law, for how much can you rent your apartment?

11. In the market for tutoring in microeconomics, the quantity demanded is

$$Q_d = 500 - 10p,$$

where Q is the number of hours and p is the price per hour. The quantity supplied is

$$Q_s = 100 + 6p.$$

Because of their wild behavior, Alex and Mac's frat has been kicked out of school. This has caused the equilibrium quantity of tutoring to fall by 90 hours. Assuming that the demand curve's shift has been parallel, how much tutoring did their frat originally purchase?

12. In the market for portable gasoline generators, the quantity demanded is

$$Q_d = 4000 - 5p,$$

where Q is the number per week and p is the price per unit. The quantity supplied is

$$Q_s = -500 + 4p.$$

An ice storm hits and demand for generators "doubles"—i.e. at every price, people desire to buy exactly twice as much. How does this affect the equilibrium price and quantity? Draw a graph and explain.

13. In the market for portable gasoline generators, the quantity demanded is

$$Q_d = 4000 - 5p,$$

where Q is the number per week and p is the price per unit. The quantity supplied is

$$Q_s = -500 + 4p.$$

An ice storm hits and demand for generators "doubles"—but this time people are willing to pay twice as much for each quantity. How does this affect the equilibrium price and quantity? Draw a graph and explain.

14. The Cineplex is showing *Lord of the Rings: The Return of the King*. The current price for a ticket is $6 and there are 1000 tickets sold daily. The estimated price elasticity of demand is −1.5 and the theater is currently filled to 80 percent of capacity. The manager proposes a 10 percent increase in the price of a ticket. Is this a sensible policy? What ticket price will maximize revenue?

15. The residents of Eastford, Connecticut have downward-sloping, linear demand curves for ice cream. An art aficionado notices an original landscape by Frederick Church hanging in the town hall. After it is sold, each resident in town is mailed a check for $10,000. Because of this, their demand curves shift so that at any price they are willing to buy two more ice cream cones per month than before. The supply curve of ice cream cones they face is flat at 75 cents per cone.

Draw a graph showing the demand curve for a representative individual before and after the increase in income and the supply curve faced by the representative individual.

How will the increase in income influence the price elasticity of demand for ice cream cones?

16. Before the government started regulating the market for rental apartments, landlords charged a monthly rent of $500, and 1000 apartments were rented. The short-run elasticity of supply at this equilibrium is 0.2 and the short-run elasticity of demand is −0.4. What will happen if the government sets a rent ceiling at $450 per month?

17. The supply of apartments is $Q_s = -20 + 0.2p$ and the demand is $Q_d = 230 - 0.3p$, where quantity is the number of units and price is in dollars per month. The government imposes a price ceiling of $450. Later it slaps on a tax of $50 per month. How does this tax affect the market?

18. The supply of clam chowder is $Q_s = 1000 + 20p$. The demand for clam chowder is $Q_d = 14,000 - 40p_A - 100p$, where Q is the number of crates per day, p is the price per crate in dollars, and p_A is the price of crackers in dollars per case. The supply of crackers is $Q_s = 500 + 20p_A$. The demand for crackers is $Q_d = 2000 - 40p_A$, where Q = cases per day and p_A is the price of crackers per case in dollars. What is the cross-price elasticity of the demand for clam chowder with respect to the price of crackers?

19. The table below gives the quantity of gasoline demanded, $Qd_{Gasoline}$ (in millions of gallons per day), and the quantity of tires demanded, Qd_{Tires} (in millions per year), in periods 1 and 2.

Period			$Qd_{Gasoline}$	Qd_{Tires}	$P_{Gasoline}$	P_{Tires}
1	90	70	$1.20	$ 80		
2	85	60	$1.50	$100		

Why can no elasticities be calculated based on the changes that occur between periods 1 and 2?

20. Figure 2.34 shows the demand for tickets to the Pat Boone Fourth of July concert. If the concert promoters charge $10 per ticket, what will be the elasticity of demand?

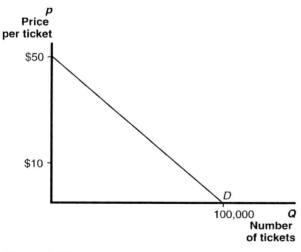

Figure 2.34

21. The market for a product has the following pretax supply and demand curves: $Q_d = 100,000 - 2000p$ and $Q_s = -20,000 + 4000p$, where Q = units per month and p = dollars per unit. The government has just levied a tax, which has caused the price paid by buyers to rise by $2 per unit. How big was the tax?

22. Suppose that consumers currently use ATM machines 10 billion times per year. If the government adds a tax of 10 cents per ATM use (and nothing else happens that shifts the supply and demand curves), will it raise $1 billion in tax revenue per year? Draw a graph and explain.

23. The demand for beef is

$$Q_d = 1,000,000 - 300,000p + 15Y$$

where Q is the pounds per week, p is the price per pound and Y is income per capita.

The quantity supplied is

$$Q_s = -400,000 + 200,000p.$$

If income per capita equals $40,000, what is the income elasticity for beef?

Chapter 3
A Consumer's Constrained Choice

■ Chapter Summary

Economists almost always assume that consumers are rational maximizers. This chapter spells out the characteristics of rational maximizing consumers and develops a set of tools to analyze their decision-making process.

People are complex and their preferences differ dramatically, but economists make three simplifying assumptions that seem consistent with consumer behavior. We assume that preferences are **complete** and **transitive**, and that **more is better**. The first two assumptions reflect a broader belief that consumers are rational—that they make logically consistent decisions. **Completeness** means that when faced with a choice between any two bundles of goods, a consumer *can* rank them so that the consumer prefers the first bundle to the second, prefers the second to the first, or is indifferent between them. (Being indifferent means that the two are valued equally.) **Transitivity** means that if a consumer prefers Bundle A to Bundle B and prefers Bundle B to Bundle C, then the consumer prefers Bundle A to Bundle C. These three assumptions are not always correct, but they adequately describe most people and most ordinary choices. **More is better** (or *nonsatiation*) means that for economic **goods**, consumers always receive some happiness from more, or at least can freely dispose of any excess (if more is not preferred to less, the good is an economic **bad**). Two more mathematical properties of preferences are **continuity** and **strict convexity**. Continuity is similar to transitivity and ensures that consumers don't change preferences in response to very small changes in bundles. Strict convexity means that consumers prefer averages to extremes, and again is a technical condition that simplifies the mathematics of consumer optimization.

A **utility function** converts a consumption bundle into a number that can be used for the purpose of ranking. A person receives a higher level of satisfaction (or utility) when consumption of almost any good rises. Utility functions are *ordinal* rather than *cardinal;* that is, they represent relative rankings of bundles but do not allow absolute comparisons of how much better one bundle is than another. Since only ranking and not absolute number is important, utility functions are also not unique. (Economists say that utility functions are *unique only up to a positive monotonic transformation;* or in other words, if you transform a function in a way that preserves relative order, the ranking of bundles will be the same.)

An **indifference curve** is a map showing the set of all bundles of goods that a consumer views as equally desirable. On any two-good graph, a consumer has an infinite number of indifference curves—one for each level of satisfaction. An indifference curve's slope is the consumer's **marginal rate of substitution** (MRS)—the maximum amount of one good the consumer will sacrifice to obtain one more unit of another good. **Marginal utility** measures the extra satisfaction from consuming one extra unit of the good, and is equal to the partial derivative of the utility function with respect to the particular good. The slope of an indifference curve (its MRS) equals the negative of the ratio of the marginal utility from the good on the horizontal axis to the marginal utility from the good on the vertical axis,

$$MRS = -\frac{\delta U/\partial q_1}{\partial U/\partial q_2}$$

Indifference curves can take a wide range of shapes, because rational consumers can have a wide array of tastes. However, if our assumptions about preferences are correct, then all indifference curve maps must have these properties: (1) Bundles on indifference curves farther from the origin are preferred to those on indifference curves closer to the origin. (Likewise, any point to the "northeast" direction of another point must be preferred to one to the "southwest" of it.) (2) Every point in the graph has an indifference curve running through it. (3) Indifference curves cannot cross. (4) Indifference curves slope down. (5) Indifference curves cannot be thick. The slope of an indifference curve usually (but not always) changes as you move along the indifference curve because the consumer's willingness to trade off the two goods depends on how much of each good the consumer has; marginal utility decreases as a consumer acquires more and more of any one good. Most indifference curves are convex to the origin—that is, the slope gets flatter as you move down and to the right along the curve, because there is a *diminishing marginal rate of substitution (MRS)*. Two important exceptions to convexity are **perfect substitutes** (linear indifference curves) and **perfect complements** (L-shaped indifference curves).

A **budget constraint** is an equation or line on a graph showing all the possible combinations of goods that a consumer can purchase if the entire budget is spent on those goods. The budget constraint plus the area inside it are called the **opportunity set**. The slope of the budget constraint reflects the relative prices of the two goods, the **marginal rate of transformation (MRT)**. The budget constraint depends only on the consumer's income and the prices of the goods. When the price of one good changes, the budget constraint will rotate. When the price rises, it rotates inward, giving the consumer a smaller opportunity set. When the price falls, the consumer can get more, so the budget constraint rotates out, creating a larger opportunity set. Thus an income rise yields a parallel outward shift in the budget constraint: The slope does not change, but the opportunity set grows.

The consumer's budget constraint is determined by the market, since this is where prices and incomes are determined. Economists are usually silent about where preferences come from. (Maybe they are innate? Maybe Mom and Dad had something to do with it? Maybe it's culture? Maybe it's too complicated and outside our area of expertise, so we'll just say nothing.) We generally assume that a person has a preexisting set of preferences that are independent of the position of the budget constraint. However, by bringing together preferences and the budget constraint, we can determine the **constrained choices** a rational maximizing consumer will make. The maximizing consumer will choose the point along the budget constraint that yields the highest level of utility. This will occur at a point of tangency between the budget constraint and the highest attainable indifference curve (an **interior solution**) or at one of the ends of the budget constraint (a **corner solution**—when all the income is spent on one good and none on the other). In the cases where both goods are purchased, the tangency of the budget constraint and the indifference curve means that the MRS = MRT, or rearranging this condition, utility is maximized if the last dollar spent on the first good yields as much extra utility as the last dollar spent on the second good.

To maximize utility subject to a constraint, you can use either the substitution method or the **Lagrangian** method (see Solved Problem 1). The *dual* of this problem is minimizing expenditure subject to a utility constraint; from this problem, we can also find the **expenditure function**, the relationship showing the minimal expenditures required to achieve a specific level of utility, given prices.

■ Key Concepts and Formulas

- Indifference curve: combinations of goods that give the same level of satisfaction.
- Budget constraint: all the possible combinations of goods that can be purchased.
- Consumer's constrained choice: picking the affordable bundle that maximizes utility.
- If V = good on the vertical axis and H = good on the horizontal axis, then:
  Indifference curve's slope = marginal rate of substitution (MRS) = $(\Delta V/\Delta H) = -MU_H/MU_V$
  Slope of budget constraint = marginal rate of transformation (MRT) = $-p_H/p_V$
  Interior solution: MRS = MRT or $-MU_H/MU_V = -p_H/p_V$ or $MU_H/p_H = MU_V/p_V$

- Substitution method: method of solving constrained choice problems by substituting the constraint into the objective function.
- Lagrangian method: method of solving constrained choice problems by optimizing a Lagrangian function.
- Expenditure function: the relationship showing the minimal expenditures necessary to achieve a specific utility level for a given set of prices.

■ Application: Does Money Buy Happiness?

The economic theory developed in this chapter relies on the assumption that "more is better." If this assumption is correct, people with higher incomes—who can reach higher indifference curves—will be better off.

Question: Does having a higher income—a budget constraint that is further out—*really* make people better off?

Answer: Economists conceptualize consumer behavior using the concepts of utility and the utility function, but admit (as the textbook puts it) that "utility functions do not exist in any fundamental sense." If you ask someone if they have a little or a lot of utility, they probably cannot give a meaningful answer. On the other hand, if you ask people if they would rather have more goods and services or less, almost all with say that more *is* better. (If they speak "econ," they may even say that more goods and services give them more "utility.") Unfortunately, these responses don't necessarily answer the question about whether or not they are really better off when they get more goods and services. An alternative to asking about someone's utility is to simply ask people how happy they are. Happiness and utility are not exactly the same thing, but most people would say that they are closely related and that happiness is essential to being "well off." If the assumptions used in this chapter are correct, we might expect that people who have a higher income—and can therefore reach a higher indifference curve with more utility—would report being better off and happier.

A wide range of surveys have asked questions related to both happiness and income, so it is easy to examine the correlation between these two important factors. The general finding from these surveys is that in some ways money does buy happiness, but in other ways it does not. On average, people in rich countries are happier than are those in poor countries. The positive relationship is especially strong among countries with average incomes below about $13,000 per year. However, for rich countries it does not seem that rising per capita income has any discernible effect on reported happiness. In rich countries like the United States or Japan, average real incomes have risen considerably since 1960, but average reported happiness has not risen.

On the other hand, within rich countries people from households with higher incomes report being happier than those from households with lower incomes. According to the General Social Survey, in 2005 34 percent of Americans reported being "very happy," 50 percent reported being "pretty happy," and 15 percent were "not too happy." However, among those in families earning under $30,000 per year only 24 percent reported being very happy, with the share climbing steadily so that 49 percent in *families* earning $100,000 or more reported being very happy. Within rich countries, like the United States, it may be that relative income rather than absolute income is more important for overall happiness. Economists David Blanchflower and Andrew Oswald have developed a simple model in which reported happiness is a function of utility and estimate some of the trade-offs within this function, using survey data from 1972 to 1998. They find that more income makes people somewhat happier but so do other things like marriage, a job, and regularly attending a religious institution. Blanchflower and Oswald's estimates show that among Americans extra income buys some—but not a lot—more happiness. They find that "to 'compensate' men for unemployment would take a rise in income . . . of approximately \$60,000 per annum" (which is well above the average income in the U.S.) and that "a lasting marriage is worth \$100,000 per annum when compared to being widowed or separated."

Critics worry that an individual's self-reported level of happiness is too subjective and tells us very little, but these measures are strongly correlated with friends' and family members' assessments and even biological indicators of well-being—such as smile duration and electroencephalogram measures of prefrontal brain activity. Still, measuring absolute well-being this way is imperfect. Happiness might be like tallness. The proportion of people reporting that they are "tall" wouldn't rise as average heights rise, and the proportion saying they are "happy" might not rise much as average well being rises, for the same reason—people's comparisons may be relative rather than absolute. No method of assessing utility, well-being, or happiness is perfect, so economists have begun to use a wide array of measurements and continue to ponder the relationship between these measures and their basic assumptions about human behavior—such as "more is better."

Sources: Bruno S. Frey and Alois Stutzer, *Happiness and Economics: How the Economy and Institutions Affect Human Well-Being*. Princeton: Princeton University Press, 2002. David G. Blanchflower and Andrew J. Oswald, "Well-Being over Time in Britain and the USA," NBER Working Paper 7487 (January 2000). Daniel Nettle, *Happiness: The Science Behind Your Smile*, New York: Oxford University Press, 2005. Pew Research Center, "Are We Happy Yet?" (February 2006) http://pewresearch.org/social/pack.php?PackID=1.

■ Solved Problems

1. Michael spends all of his food budget on pizza and milk. Michael's utility function is:

$$U(q_1, q_2) = q_1 q_2,$$

where q_1 is the quantity of pizza and q_2 is the quantity of milk. His monthly food budget is \$120, the price of pizza (p_1) is \$3, and the price of milk (p_2) is \$2. Find Michael's utility-maximizing choice of pizza and milk, using both the Lagrangian method and the substitution method, and then carefully graph your results.

Step 1: First, find Michael's utility-maximizing combination of pizza and milk using the Lagrangian method.

In any constrained maximization problem, you will have an objective function to be maximized or minimized and a constraint. In this case, we want to maximize Michael's utility subject to his budget constraint.

$$\textbf{Max } U(q_1, q_2) = q_1 q_2$$
$$\textbf{subject to: } 120 = 3q_1 + 2q_2$$

1:   Write the Lagrangian function.

The Lagrangian function consists of two parts: what you are trying to optimize and a constraint. In this case, the constraint, or what is keeping Michael from reaching infinite utility, is the budget constraint.

$$\mathbf{L} + = (\text{function to be maximized}) + (\mathbf{L})$$
$$= q_1 q_2 + \lambda(120 - 3q_1 - 2q_2)$$

What you are really doing here is adding zero. The term in the parentheses is the budget constraint, rearranged so that its value is zero (that is, it's what you would get if you move the right-hand side terms to the left-hand side; the right-hand side would then be zero.). Regardless of the value of λ, the Lagrangian multiplier, the whole term equals zero.

2:   Take partial derivatives with respect to q_1, q_2, and λ, and set the partial derivatives equal to zero.

$$\frac{\partial \mathbf{L}+}{\partial q_1} = q_2 - 3\lambda = 0$$

$$\frac{\partial \mathbf{L}+}{\partial q_2} = q_1 - 2\lambda = 0$$

$$\frac{\partial \mathbf{L}+}{\partial \lambda} = 120 - 3q_1 - 2q_2 = 0$$

These are known as the **first order conditions**; these things must be true if you are at a maximum or minimum (but you may not know which it is).

3:   Use the first two equations to find a relationship between the two goods.

$$\frac{q_2}{q_1} = \frac{3}{2}$$

(Note that this is the same expression that you would get if you set up the appropriate tangency condition, in this case $MU_1/MU_2 = P_1/P_2$, as you do with the substitution method.)

4:   Substitute into the original constraint

Rearrange the above to read $q_2 = 3/2\ q_1$. Then substitute into the original budget constraint and solve for q_1.

$$120 = 3q_1 + 2q_2$$

$$120 = 3q_1 + 2\left(\frac{3}{2}q_1\right)$$

$$120 = 6q_1$$

$$q_1 = 20$$

$$q_2 = \frac{3}{2}(20) = 30$$

We thus know that at the utility-maximizing point, $q_1 = 20$, $q_2 = 30$, and $U = (20)(30) = 600$. Michael reaches his highest level of utility, 600, when he consumes 20 slices of pizza and 30 quarts of milk. (Note that technically we do not know if this is a maximum or a minimum. We would then need to check the **second-order conditions**, which have to do with what is happening to the second derivatives. In this case, the second derivatives [f_{xx} and f_{yy}] should be negative, which would tell us that moving away from the optimal point in any direction would result in a reduction in the objective function.)

5:   Check your work.

It's a good idea to now check your answer. Plug the optimal values into the budget constraint, and see if it balances. Check for sense. For example, in the above example, pizza is more expensive than milk is. Thus, if both goods enter the budget constraint symmetrically (for example, have the same exponent in the utility function), you should buy less pizza than milk. Did you get a zero value or a negative value for either good? Such an answer must be incorrect with convex indifference curves.

Step 2: Find Michael's utility-maximizing combination of pizza and milk using the substitution method.

Note that you will (presumably!) get the same answer this way; it's just another method of reaching the same result. Why learn both methods? Your professor may prefer that you do this with one method or the other. Additionally, the Lagrange method can be used in more complex problems with more constraints, when the substitution method will not work.

To use the substitution method, first rewrite the budget constraint as

$$q_1 = \frac{(120 - 2q_2)}{3}$$

You are trying to maximize the utility function $U = q_1 q_2$. Substitute the expression you found above for q_1 in the utility equation.

$$U = \frac{(120 - 2q_2)}{3} q_2 = 40q_2 - \frac{2}{3}q_2^2$$

This is now an *unconstrained* maximization problem (with respect to q_2). To find the maximum of the function, take the derivative with respect to q_2, and set the derivative equal to zero.

$$\frac{dU}{dq_2} = 40 - \frac{4}{3}q_2 = 0$$

Solving for q_2 gives $q_2 = 30$. Substitute into the budget constraint to get $q_1 = 20$ (and $U = 600$), and note that this is the same answer that you found using the Lagrangian method. (And, as with the Lagrangian method, to be sure that this point is a maximum, you would again need to check the second-order conditions.)

Step 3: Carefully graph your results.

The budget constraint is a straight line, so you can find the endpoints by setting the quantity of each good equal to zero and solving for the other. For example, if the quantity of milk (the good on the vertical axis) is zero, the quantity of pizza is $120/3 = 40$. In other words, the most pizza that Michael can buy, if he spends all his money on pizza, is 40 pizzas. Likewise, the most milk that he can buy is $120/2 = 60$ quarts of milk. The slope of the budget line is equal to $-p_1/p_2 = -3/2$.

Michael's indifference curves are smooth and convex; one way to find the shape of these curves is set utility equal to any arbitrary value and find combinations of the two goods that give this level of utility.

Be sure that your completed graph shows indifference curves, the budget constraint, the slope and intercepts of the budget constraint, and the coordinates of the utility-maximizing point that you found!

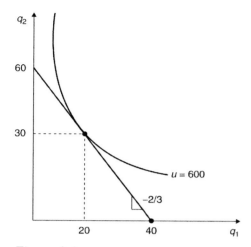

Figure 3.1

2. Michael now wants to find the minimum amount of money that he needs to spend to reach a utility level of 3750. Prices and the utility function are the same as in Solved Problem 1. Find the necessary expenditure to reach a utility level of 3750, and find Michael's expenditure function.

    Step 1: This problem is the *dual* of Solved Problem 1.

    In the previous problem, you maximized utility subject to a budget constraint. In this problem, you want to <u>minimize</u> spending subject to a utility constraint.

    $$\text{Min } E = 3q_1 + 2q_2$$
    $$\textbf{subject to: } 3750 = q_1 q_2$$

    1: Write the Lagrangian function.

    Again, the Lagrangian function consists of two parts: what you are trying to optimize and a constraint. In this case, the constraint is the utility level that Michael wishes to reach, which is what is keeping Michael from minimizing his expenditures (spending nothing!).

    $$\textbf{L} + = (\text{function to be minimized}) + (\textbf{L})$$
    $$= 3q_1 + 2q_2 + \lambda(900 - q_1 q_2)$$

    2: Take partial derivatives with respect to q_1, q_2, and λ, and set the partial derivatives equal to zero.

    $$\frac{\partial \textbf{L} +}{\partial q_1} = 3 - q_2 \lambda = 0$$

    $$\frac{\partial \textbf{L} +}{\partial q_2} = 2 - q_1 \lambda = 0$$

    $$\frac{\partial \textbf{L} +}{\partial \lambda} = 3750 - q_1 q_2 = 0$$

    3: Use the first two equations to find a relationship between the two goods.

    $$\frac{q_2}{q_1} = \frac{3}{2}$$

4: Substitute into the original constraint.

Rearrange the above to read $q_2 = 3/2\ q_1$. Then substitute into the original utility constraint and solve for q_1.

$$3750 = q_1 q_2$$

$$3750 = q_1 \left(\frac{3}{2} q_1 \right)$$

$$3750 = \frac{3}{2} q_1^2$$

$$q_1 = 50$$

$$q_2 = \frac{3}{2}(50) = 75$$

$$E = 3(50) + 2(75) = \$300$$

In order to achieve a utility level of 3750 at the *least cost*, Michael must spend $300 and purchase 50 pizzas and 75 quarts of milk. There are other ways that Michael could achieve this utility level, but they would cost more.

5: Find the expenditure function.

The expenditure function is a function of prices and a fixed level of utility. As before, we set up the Lagrange function and differentiate with respect to q_1, q_2, and λ. This time, though, instead of using the actual prices and level of utility given in the problem, we will use algebraic equivalents.

$$\mathbf{L} + = (\text{function to be minimized}) + (\mathbf{L})$$

$$= p_1 q_1 + p_2 q_2 + (\overline{U} - q_1 q_2)$$

$$\frac{\partial \mathbf{L}+}{\partial q_1} = p_1 - q_2 \lambda = 0$$

$$\frac{\partial \mathbf{L}+}{\partial q_2} = p_2 - q_1 \lambda = 0$$

$$\frac{\partial \mathbf{L}+}{\partial \lambda} = \overline{U} - q_1 q_2 = 0$$

As you did before, use the first two equations to solve for a relationship between the two goods.

$$\frac{q_2}{q_1} = \frac{p_1}{p_2}, \quad \text{or} \quad q_1 = \frac{p_2}{p_1} q_2, \quad \text{or} \quad q_2 = \frac{p_1}{p_2} q_1$$

Now use the equation for the expenditure function to solve for q_1 and q_2 in terms of the prices and expenditure.

$$E = p_1 q_1 + p_2 q_2$$

$$E = p_1 \left(\frac{p_2}{p_1} q_2 \right) + p_2 q_2$$

$$q_2 = 2 \frac{E}{p_2}$$

$$\text{Similarly, } q_1 = 2 \frac{E}{p_1}$$

Then use the expressions that you found above to substitute into the utility function. Finally, solve for E, the expenditures function.

$$\bar{U} = q_1 q_2$$

$$\bar{U} = \left(2\frac{E}{p_1}\right)\left(2\frac{E}{p_2}\right) = 4\frac{E^2}{p_1 p_2}$$

$$E = \frac{1}{2}\sqrt{\bar{U} p_1 p_2}$$

The expenditure function tells us how much Michael would have to spend to attain any specific level of utility, given prices. For example, if the price of pizza is $1, the price of milk is $5, and Michael wishes to reach utility of 2,000, he would have to spend $200. (You can check whether your expenditure function is correct by plugging in the numbers that you found in the first part of the problem.)

3.   Draw a representative indifference curve for Faye in each of the following cases:

Case 1: Draw a representative indifference curve for Faye for right shoes and left shoes (assuming that Faye has two feet).

Step 1: Make a graph with quantities of the two goods on the axes, then pick a point, any point, and think about how much utility this consumption bundle yields.

For example, begin at point a, in Figure 3.2(a), where Faye has one right and one left shoe.

Step 2: Think of other points in the graph that will give the same amount of satisfaction.

What will give the same satisfaction as point a? Will point b, two right shoes and two left shoes? No. Point b gives more of both, so it cannot be on the same indifference curve as point a. It must be on a higher indifference curve. A consumption bundle like the one at point c (one right shoe and two left shoes) will give the same amount of satisfaction as the initial consumption bundle (one right shoe and one left shoe). The second, unmatched left shoe does not make Faye any better off, nor does it make her worse off (she can throw it away). Because she is no better off and no worse off, she must be on the same indifference curve, I_0, as she was initially.

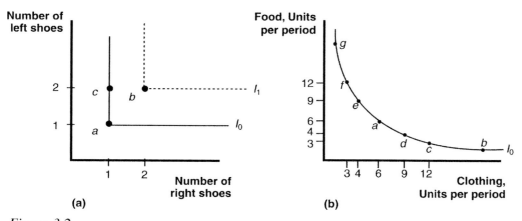

Figure 3.2

Step 3: Connect the dots.
Hook up all the bundles that give the same amount of utility. See I_0 in Figure 3.2(a).

You can repeat the process for additional indifference curves representing different levels of utility. See I_1 in Figure 3.2(a).

Case 2: Draw a representative indifference curve for Faye's consumption of food, F, and clothing, C, assuming that Faye's utility function is $U = 2FC$.

Step 1: Make a graph with the two goods as the axes, then pick a point and think about how much utility this consumption bundle yields.

Suppose we pick point a—6 units of food and 6 units of clothing. Plugging these numbers into the utility function yields 72 units of utility ($U = 2CF = 2 \times 6 \times 6 = 72$).

Step 2: Think of other points in the graph that will give the same amount of satisfaction.
What other combinations of food and clothing yield 72 units of utility? Any combination of food and clothing whose product is 36—e.g., 2 food and 18 clothing (point b), 3 food and 12 clothing (point c), 4 food and 9 clothing (point d), 9 food and 4 clothing (point e), 12 food and 3 clothing (point f), 18 food and 2 clothing (point g), and so on.

Step 3: Connect the dots.
Hook up all the bundles that give the same amount of utility. See I_0 in Figure 3.2(b).

■ Practice Problems

Multiple-Choice

1. Picture a graph with chicken on the vertical axis and pork on the horizontal axis. Larry's indifference curves are vertical. This implies that he
   a. receives no satisfaction from pork.
   b. receives no satisfaction from chicken.
   c. dislikes pork.
   d. dislikes chicken.

2. Wrestling tickets sell for $10 and stock car race tickets sell for $20. Suppose that Billy Bob, whose preferences satisfy all the usual assumptions, buys five wrestling tickets and two stock car race tickets each month. With this consumption bundle, his marginal rate of substitution of wrestling matches for stock car races is 3. Which of the following is correct?
   a. Billy Bob could increase his utility by buying more wrestling tickets and fewer stock car race tickets.
   b. Billy Bob could increase his utility by buying more stock car race tickets and fewer wrestling tickets.
   c. Billy Bob is at an interior solution and is maximizing his utility.
   d. Billy Bob is at a corner solution and is maximizing his utility.

3. Ginny must spend her entire income on sunscreen and Silly Putty and chooses to spend it all on sunscreen, buying ten bottles. Which of the following statements *must* be true?
    a. she considers Silly Putty to be a bad.
    b. the first unit of Silly Putty must have zero marginal utility.
    c. the first unit of Silly Putty must generate less utility than the tenth bottle of sunscreen.
    d. the first unit of Silly Putty must generate less utility per dollar than the tenth bottle of sunscreen.

Fill-in

4. If Gaston's marginal rate of substitution for two goods is the same, no matter how much of each good he buys, then the two goods must be ___substitutes___.

5. Indifference curves are convex to the origin because of ___diminishing___ marginal rates of substitution.

True-False-Ambiguous and Explain Why

6. People's indifference curves for oatmeal and caviar are parallel to one another. *Yes?*

7. If you know the slope of the budget constraint for two goods, then you know the prices of the two goods.

8. Derek likes one scoop of chocolate ice cream better than one scoop of vanilla ice cream and one scoop of vanilla ice cream better than one scoop of strawberry ice cream. Therefore, he will like one scoop of chocolate ice cream better than one scoop of strawberry ice cream.

9. Both Tums and Rolaids will cure David's heartburn, and he regards them as perfect substitutes. Therefore, his indifference curves will be linear with a slope of -1.

Short-Answer

10. Rose loves to eat eggs, but they make her break out in a rash. Luckily, two capsules of Rash-B-Gone per egg are a perfect antidote. Rose has budgeted $5 for eggs and Rash-B-Gone this month. The cost of an egg is 10 cents and the cost per Rash-B-Gone tablet is 20 cents. Rose will therefore buy how many eggs and how many capsules of Rash-B-Gone?

11. Jonathan likes PlayStation games (P) and Hot Pockets (H). PlayStation games cost $40. Hot Pockets cost $2. Jonathan's monthly budget for these items is $100, and his utility function is, $U(P, H) = P^2H^{1/2}$. Find Jonathan's utility-maximizing bundle and his level of utility.

12. Caitlin likes to go to the mall to buy sandals (S) and handbags (H). Her utility function is $U(S, H) = S^{1/2}H^{1/2}$. The price of sandals is $10, and the price of handbags is $40. How much money should Caitlin bring with her if she wishes to receive a utility level of 16 from her trip to the mall?

13. Katrina (who owns a cat) has the following utility function. $U = F + N$, where $F =$ cans of Friskies cat food and $N =$ cans of Nine Lives cat food. The price of Friskies is $1 per can. The price of Nine Lives is $2 per can. How much of each will Katrina buy if she has $20 to spend on cat food?

14. Boris has an income of $100 per month. Initially the price of food is $1 per bag, the price of prune juice is $2 per bottle, and Boris buys no prune juice. Then the California prune growers launch a slick advertising campaign convincing Boris that prune juice is very hip, so he starts buying 10 bottles per month. Boris's income, the price of food, and the price of prune juice have all remained the same. Show graphically why and how Boris has changed his consumption bundle.

15. Bulk Phone, Inc. offers a discount for bulk purchases. Calls cost 10 cents per minute, but if you call for 100 minutes or more, you get a 10 percent discount on your entire phone bill. Draw the budget constraint facing the firm's customers.

16. Bonus Phone, Inc. offers a bonus to frequent callers. Calls cost 10 cents per minute, but for every 100 minutes that you call during that month, you receive 100 free "bonus" minutes. Draw the budget constraint facing the firm's customers. How many minutes would *you* select if faced with this budget constraint?

17. A newspaper article says, "Sales of SUVs have plunged in recent months as the price of gasoline has soared. Manufacturers have noticed this change in tastes for SUVs and have begun pouring their resources into producing more fuel-efficient vehicles." Do you agree with the article that consumers' "tastes" for SUVs have changed? Explain.

18. LaTonya's utility function is $U = 5A^{.6}B^{.2}$. The price of A is $p_a = \$10$, the price of B is $p_b = \$5$, and her income, Y, is $200. What is her optimal consumption bundle? How much utility does she receive from this bundle? If her utility function was $U = 10A^{.6}B^{.2}$, how would her consumption decision change?

19. Use an indifference mapping to show Blanchflower and Oswald's finding about happiness (from the Application at the beginning of this chapter) that "to 'compensate' men for unemployment would take a rise in income . . . of approximately $60,000 per annum."

20. a. Lauren is at the grocery store, where there is a sale on cereal. Cereal is only $1 per box, but next week it will be $2 per box. Lauren has $20 to spend on cereal in this two-week period. Show her cereal budget constraint and predict the point on the budget constraint that she'll select.

    b. Lauren is at the grocery store, where there is a sale on bananas. Bananas are only 25 cents per pound, but next week they will be 50 cents per pound. Lauren has $1 to spend on bananas in this two-week period. Show her banana budget constraint and predict the point on the budget constraint that she'll select. Explain why this is likely to differ from the point that she selected on her cereal budget constraint.

21. Addie can buy vitamins at the corner store for $5 per bottle or over the Internet at $4 per bottle. (The vitamins are identical.) The $4 per bottle includes the shipping cost, but there is a $5 fee for handling each order on the Internet. Draw a budget constraint showing the trade-offs she faces, then explain, using indifference curves, where she'll buy the vitamins.

22. Suppose that Zach's monthly income is $1000, the price of food is $10 per unit, and the price of housing is $50 per unit. He initially consumes 50 units of food each month and 10 units of housing. Then Zach's income climbs to $1200 per month, the price of food climbs to $13.33 per unit, and the price of housing falls to $40 per unit. Show how these changes shift Zach's budget constraint. Is he better off before or after the shift in the budget constraint?

23. The Hormsbury family's income is $3000 per month. They purchase two things: doctor visits (*DV*), and other stuff (*OS*). Doctor visits cost $100 each and other stuff costs $1 per unit. Originally no medical insurance is available, but then a plan is offered that costs $300 per month and pays 80 percent of the cost of doctor visits, up to 10 visits per month. Show how the availability of this medical insurance will affect the Hormsbury's budget constraint.

24. In Figure 3.3, the price of A is $5. What is Nicole's income and what is the price of B?

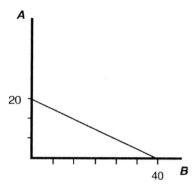

Figure 3.3

25. Khalid buys soccer tickets and opera tickets. The marginal utility he receives from an opera is 30 and the marginal utility he receives from a soccer match is 10. Does this mean that he likes attending the opera more than going to a soccer match? If the price of a soccer ticket is $20, how much does an opera ticket cost?

■ Answers to Practice Problems

1. b.

2. b.   Maximization requires that $MU_{races}/MU_{wrestling} = p_{races}/p_{wrestling}$. We know that $p_{races}/p_{wrestling} = 2$, so $MU_{races}/MU_{wrestling}$ should equal 2 also. Billy needs to reduce this ratio from 3 to 2 and can do so by going to more races (the marginal utility per race falls as he sees more) and fewer wrestling matches (the marginal utility per match rises as he sees fewer).

3. d.

4. perfect substitutes

5. diminishing

6. Ambiguous. While textbooks, professors, and students often automatically draw a set of indifference curves so that each is always the same distance away from the others, this need not be the case. This type of indifference curves (which are usually called *homothetic*) imply that as income rises the tangency between the budget constraints and the indifference curves will always fall along a ray from the origin. This implies that the person always buys the same ratio of the two goods at all incomes. This is quite unlikely in the case of oatmeal and caviar (and for many other goods!). Oatmeal is probably an inferior good, while caviar is not.

7. False. If you know the slope of the budget constraint, you know the relative prices. The slope of the budget constraint—a.k.a. marginal rate of transformation (*MRT*)—is equal to $-p_a/p_b$, so you only know the price of one in relation to the price of the other.

8. Ambiguous, but probably true. Derek may be one of those odd (irrational?) people whose preferences are not transitive. Economists generally assume transitivity, and test results (see Arnold Weinstein, "Transitivity of Preferences: A Comparison among Age Groups," *Journal of Political Economy*, March/April 1968) verify that almost all adults (93.5 percent in this study) have transitive preferences. Derek might be a child, and many children have intransitive preferences.

9. False. Perfect substitutes are represented by linear indifference curves. However, not all perfect substitutes are traded one-for-one. If, for example, David needs two Tums tablets but only one Rolaids tablet to cure his heartburn, then the slope of his indifference curves is $-1/2$ or -2 (depending on which good goes on which axis).

10. 10 eggs and 20 capsules. Because they are perfect complements (L-shaped indifference curves), she always buys one egg with two capsules. One egg and two capsules cost 50 cents, so she can afford 10 eggs and 20 capsules.

11. This problem can be solved using either the Lagrangian method or the substitution method. The solution below uses the Lagrangian method.

$$\textbf{Max } U(P, H) = P^2 H^{1/2}$$
$$\textbf{subject to: } 100 = 40P + 2H$$
$$\textbf{L} + = P^2 H^{1/2} + \lambda(100 - 40P + 2H)$$

Take partial derivatives with respect to *P*, *H*, and λ, and set the partial derivatives equal to zero.

$$\frac{\partial \textbf{L}+}{\partial P} = 2PH^{\frac{1}{2}} - 40\lambda = 0$$

$$\frac{\partial \textbf{L}+}{\partial H} = \frac{1}{2}P^2 H^{-\frac{1}{2}} - 2\lambda = 0$$

$$\frac{\partial \textbf{L}+}{\partial \lambda} = 100 - 40P - 2H = 0$$

Use the first two equations to find a relationship between the two goods.

$$H = 5P$$

Substitute into the original constraint

$$100 = 40P + 2H$$
$$P = 2$$
$$H = 10$$

$$U(P,H) = (2)^2 (10)^{\frac{1}{2}} = 12.6$$

12. This is an expenditure function problem, and you can solve it either by using the Lagrangian method or the substitution method. The answer below shows the Lagrangian method.

$$\textbf{Min } E = 20S + 40H$$
$$\textbf{subject to: } 16 = S^{1/2} H^{1/2}$$
$$\textbf{L} + = 10S + 40H + \lambda(1200 - S^{1/2} H^{1/2})$$

Take partial derivatives with respect to q_1, q_2, and λ, and set the partial derivatives equal to zero.

$$\frac{\partial \mathbf{L}+}{\partial S} = \frac{1}{2}S^{-\frac{1}{2}}H^{\frac{1}{2}} - 10\lambda = 0$$

$$\frac{\partial \mathbf{L}+}{\partial q_2} = \frac{1}{2}S^{\frac{1}{2}}H^{-\frac{1}{2}} - 40\lambda = 0$$

$$\frac{\partial \mathbf{L}+}{\partial \lambda} = 16 - S^{\frac{1}{2}}H^{\frac{1}{2}} = 0$$

Use the first two equations to find a relationship between the two goods.

$$S = 4H$$

Substitute into the original constraint

$$12 = S^{\frac{1}{2}}H^{\frac{1}{2}}$$

$$16 = S^{\frac{1}{2}}(4S)^{\frac{1}{2}}$$

$$S = 8$$

$$H = 2$$

$$E = 10(8) + 40(2) = \$160$$

Caitlin will need to take $160 to the mall with her.

13. First draw Katrina's budget constraint, then draw her indifference curves. See Figure 3.4. The budget constraint is a solid line; the indifference curves are dashed. The subscript on each indifference curve gives the level of utility. Notice that the indifference curves do not have the usual convex shape. Any time that N falls by 1, a rise of F by 1 will give her the same amount of utility. Therefore, her indifference curve is linear with a slope of –1. In other words, Friskies and Nine Lives are perfect substitutes. The highest level of utility that she can reach is when she buys nothing but Friskies—at point a. This is a corner solution. Because the two goods are perfect one-for-one substitutes, she will buy whichever is cheaper.

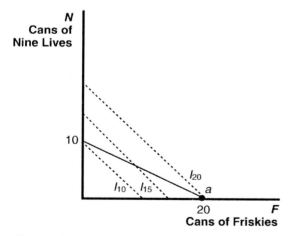

Figure 3.4

14. See Figure 3.5. Initially Boris has a corner solution at point *a*, because he did not value the first bottle of prune juice enough to give up 2 bags of food for it. Later Boris has an interior solution at point *b*. His budget constraint has not changed; his tastes have changed. Figure 3.8 shows the new indifference curve, I_2, crossing the initial indifference curve, I_1. They cross because advertising has changed his willingness to trade off food and prune juice. (Although his indifference curves have shifted, we can still assume that the indifference curves *within* his initial set do not cross one another, nor do the curves within his new set of indifference curves cross one another.)

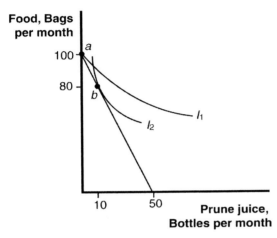

Figure 3.5

15. See Figure 3.6. For the first 100 minutes, the slope of the budget constraint is −10 cents per minute. 100 minutes would normally cost $10, but this is where the 10 percent discount kicks in, so 100 minutes cost only $9. Past 100 minutes, the slope of the budget constraint is −9 cents per minute.

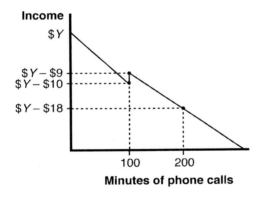

Figure 3.6

16. See Figure 3.7. For the first 100 minutes, the slope of the budget constraint is −10 cents per minute; then there is a "flat" section that is 100 minutes long. The pattern repeats itself every 200 minutes. What point on the budget constraint would you pick? It all depends on your tastes, so it is hard to predict. However, we can predict that you will be unlikely to select somewhere between 100 and 200 minutes and waste your bonus minutes. Doing so will put you on a lower indifference curve than you could otherwise reach. Many people will end up at the kink in the budget constraint.

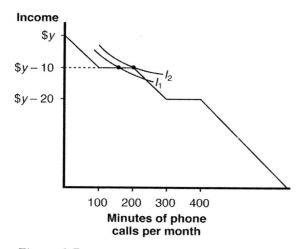

Figure 3.7

17. The newspaper article is using the term "tastes" differently than economists do, so you'll probably disagree. The reason that people are buying fewer SUVs isn't that individual tastes or preferences—which "determine the amount of pleasure people derive from the goods and services they consume"—have changed. The reason that people are buying fewer SUVs is that the budget constraint facing them has changed—i.e., driving an SUV has become more expensive.

18. Using either the Lagrangian method or the substitution method, LaTonya's optimal consumption bundle is $A = 15$, $B = 10$. To find utility, plug $A = 15$ and $B = 10$ into the utility function:

$$U = 5A^6B^2 = 5(15^6)(10^2) = 40.24.$$

Her consumption bundle will not change at all if she has the alternative utility function, $U = 10A^6B^2$, because this merely doubles all the values in the initial utility function. Thus the utility that she receives increases, but her optimal consumption bundle does not change.

19. Figure 3.8 puts annual income on the vertical axis and employment status on the horizontal axis. Point A—income of $100,000 per year and being unemployed—yields the same amount of happiness (or utility) as point B—annual income of $40,000 per year (i.e. $60,000 lower than point A) and being employed. Unlike conventional indifference mappings, however, we can't simply hook up points A and B and draw an indifference curve, because the quantity on the horizontal axis isn't a continuous variable. The figure shows a dashed indifference curve linking them, but the points in between them have no meaning, since one can't be half employed and half unemployed. Points C and D, which are $10,000 lower than points A and B, yield less happiness and are along a lower indifference "curve." At first glance, these results seem to contradict economists' assumption that leisure is a good. Shouldn't an unemployed person be happier than an employed person with the same income, since he has more leisure time? Perhaps not. It may be that the status of looking for work but not having it subtracts so much utility that it offsets the gain from more leisure time. Note also that Blanchflower and Oswald find that other non-work situations, such as retirement and being a full-time student, don't reduce happiness.

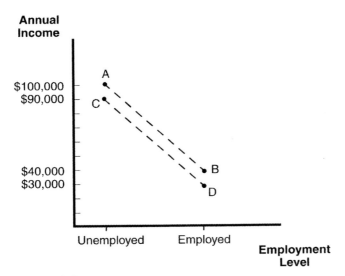

Figure 3.8

20. a.   Figure 3.9(a) shows the cereal budget constraint, B_1. If Lauren buys all the cereal this week, she can get 20 boxes. If she buys it all next week, she can get only 10 boxes. Her indifference curves may be linear with a slope of −1, since cereal purchased this week may be a perfect substitute for cereal purchased next week, due to its storability. (In this case her indifference curves look like I_1, which is shown as a dashed line.) If this is the case, Lauren will select the corner solution, at point *a*, where she spends all $20 this week, while cereal is on sale.

   b.   Figure 3.9(b) shows the banana budget constraint. It is just like the cereal budget constraint in that Lauren can buy twice as many bananas this week than she can next week. In this case, however, her indifference curves are very unlikely to be linear, since bananas are perishable. One week from now, the squishy brown bananas she bought this week will not be a good substitute for newly purchased yellow bananas. Therefore, she'll probably have an interior solution, purchasing bananas in both periods, for example, where indifference curve I_1 is tangent to the budget constraint, B_1, at point *a*.

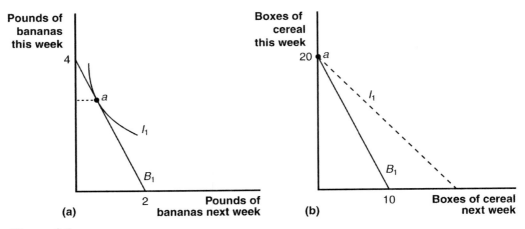

Figure 3.9

21. Figure 3.10(a) shows one way to graph Addie's budget constraint. Her income is $Y and purchases at the corner store are shown by B_{cs}, whose slope is –$5 per bottle. Internet purchases are shown by B_I, which begins at $(Y - \$5)$ because of the handling fee—this must be paid regardless of the number of bottles shipped. Its slope is –$4 per bottle. The two lines cross at 5 bottles—since $25 will be spent for 5 bottles at either source. Whether Addie purchases from the corner store or over the Internet depends on the shape of her indifference curves. If they are like I_1, she'll buy at the corner store. If they are like I_2, she'll buy over the Internet

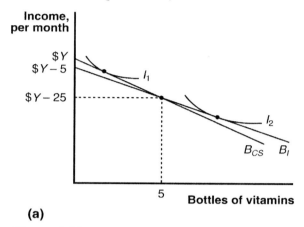

(a)

Figure 3.10

Another way to draw the budget constraint is to put store-bought bottles on one axis and Internet-bought bottles on the other axis, as in Figure 3.10(b). (This is similar to the way the text analyzes purchases of books over the Internet.) In this case, vitamins purchased at the corner store and vitamins purchased over the Internet are perfect substitutes, so her indifference curves are linear, with a slope of −1, as is shown by I_1 and I_2 (which are dashed lines). Figure 3.10(b) includes two budget constraints—one for a case in which Addie doesn't have much money allocated to vitamins (only $15) and another where she has more money to spend on vitamins ($45). The maximum quantities of vitamins that can be purchased from each source are $\$Y/P_{store}$ and $\$(Y - 5)/P_{Internet}$. The slopes of the budget constraints are $P_{Internet}/P_{store}$ or −4/5. The budget constraints have a vertical drop along the vertical axis because one bottle of store-bought vitamins ($5 worth) must be given up in order to get any Internet-bought vitamins (to cover the $5 handling fee). With the lower budget constraint, she'll purchase all her vitamins at the corner store—point *a*. With the higher budget constraint, she'll buy over the Internet—point *b*.

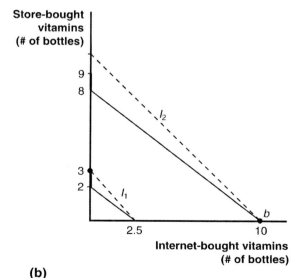

(b)

Figure 3.10

22. Figure 3.11 shows the initial and new budget lines, B_1 and B_2. The endpoint of B_1 on the food axis is $Y/P_F = \$1000/\$10 = 100$ units. The endpoint of B_1 on the housing axis is $Y/P_H = \$1000/\$50 = 20$ units. Point a marks Zach's original consumption point. The endpoint of B_2 on the food axis is $Y/P_F = \$1200/\$13.33 = 90$ units. The endpoint of B_2 on the housing axis is $Y/P_H = \$1200/\$40 = 30$ units. B_2 allows Zach to consume beyond point a, so the shift makes him better off.

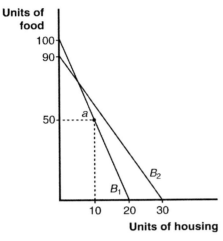

Figure 3.11

23. See Figure 3.12. BC_0 is the original budget constraint—the maximum the family can buy is 3000 units of other stuff each month or 30 doctor visits. Under the insurance plan, the family gives up $300, dropping down to 2700 units of other stuff on the vertical axis. From this point the slope of the budget constraint is much gentler than before. The slope shows that the family gives up only 20 units of other stuff for each doctor visit—previously they gave up 100 units of other stuff to get a doctor visit. Ten doctor visits, therefore, cost 500 units of other stuff (300 for the insurance + 20 for each of the 10 visits). Beyond 10, however, doctor visits are no cheaper than before, so the new budget constraint parallels the original budget constraint.

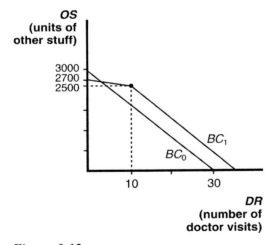

Figure 3.12

24. If Nicole spends all her money on A, she can buy 20 of them. Since they cost $5 each, she must have $100 to spend. Because the maximum amount of B that she can buy is 40, the price of B must be $2.50 = \$100/40$.

25. We can't really tell how much Khalid likes soccer versus opera. All we know is the marginal utility— the utility from the last unit consumed. His total utility from watching soccer may be much greater because he may value the non-marginal games a lot more and he may go to a lot more matches than operas—so many matches that the last one he attends doesn't provide much additional entertainment. However, because he consumes some of both, we know that he's at a point of tangency, where $MU_s/p_s = MU_o/p_o$ (with S = soccer and O = opera). Substituting in the numbers from the problem, $10/20 = 30/p_o$. Thus the price of an opera ticket must be $60.

■ Exercises

True-False-Ambiguous and Explain Why

1. Nikeya and Vicky both purchase milk and cookies at the same Quik Mart. They have different tastes for milk and cookies and different incomes. They both end up purchasing some milk and some cookies, but they buy considerably different amounts of the two goods. Therefore, we can conclude that they have the same marginal rate of substitution of milk and cookies at their optimal consumption bundles.

2. Economists assume that people are out to maximize their own well-being, therefore ruling out the possibility of altruism.

3. Every point on an indifference curve represents the same amount of money.

Short-Answers

4. Almost anyone would say that the standard of living of people in developed countries, such as the United States, Europe, and Japan, is currently much higher than it was in the preindustrial era. Think about the things we now have that people did not have then such as full stomachs, big sturdy houses, cars, and TVs. In fact, we have more of almost everything and our life expectancy is much higher as well. There are few people, other than the Unabomber, who think the "good old days" were really better than today. Can we prove that people are better off today than they were in the preindustrial period?

5. Consider three consumers. All three buy bread (B) and cheese (C), and no other goods. The price of bread (B) is $1 per loaf, and the price of cheese (C) is $2 per pound. Each consumer has a weekly budget of $60. Given the information below, find the utility-maximizing combination of bread and cheese for each consumer and each consumer's level of utility.
   a. Stephanie's utility function is $U(B, C) = B^{1/2}C^{1/2}$.
   b. Evan's utility function is $U(B, C) = \min(B, C)$. In other words, he likes 1 loaf of bread with 1 pound of cheese, and likes no other combination.
   c. Ian doesn't care whether he has bread or cheese as long as he has some food. These goods are perfect substitutes for him, and his utility function is $U(B, C) = B + C$.

6. For the three consumers in Question 4 (above), draw graphs showing at least two indifference curves, the budget constraint, and the utility-maximizing point. Be sure to label everything carefully!

7. In Fairfax, Virginia, a price war recently broke out between competing grocery stores.
   a. The price of bananas was originally 50 cents per pound.
   b. Super Big then cut the price to 25 cents per pound.
   c. Market Max responded by giving away the first pound for free and charging 50 cents per additional pound.

d. Groceries Galore then began to tape quarters (25 cents) to each 1-pound bunch of bananas, giving away the first pound for free, while charging 50 cents per additional pound.

   i. Graphically show the price war by drawing a typical consumer's budget line in each situation, and labeling each budget line with its Roman numeral.

   ii. Which of the first three pricing schemes was the favorite of customers in Fairfax? Explain.

8. Cassandra buys tomatoes (*T*) and cauliflower (*C*), and her utility function is $U(T, C) = TC$. The price of tomatoes is \$2 per pint, and the price of cauliflower is \$1 per head. If Cassandra wants to buy enough vegetables to reach a utility level of 30, how much money will she need to spend, and what will she buy?

9. A consumer's utility function is $U(B, Z) = B + AB^a Z^b + Z$, where *A*, *a*, and *b* are constants, *B* is burritos, and *Z* is pizzas. What is the slope of the consumer's indifference curve?

10. Justin's consumption bundle is shown in Figure 3.13. Would he prefer that the price of cherries fall in half or that the price of raspberries fall by two-thirds? Show the comparison graphically and explain.

11. Draw a set of indifference curves for $U = B + Z + BZ$, where B = burritos and Z = pizzas.

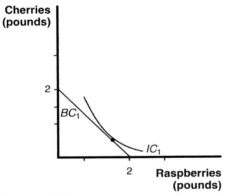

Figure 3.13

12. Figure 3.14 shows that given Mandi's budget constraint and her tastes for grapefruit juice and orange juice (*OJ*), she buys one case of grapefruit juice and four cases of (*OJ*) each month at point *A*. Show how the situation would change if grapefruit juice makers improve their product's flavor and her budget constraint remains the same. Will Mandi be better off?

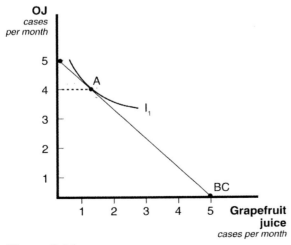

Figure 3.14

Chapter 4
Demand

■ Chapter Summary

In Chapters 2 and 3, we examined the properties of the supply-and-demand model. In this chapter and those that follow it, we use our most fundamental principle—rational maximization—to show why supply and demand curves have their characteristic shapes.

As the price of one good falls, while the price of the other good stays the same, the budget line rotates outward. The points of tangency between this rotating budget line and the individual's indifference curves trace out the **price-consumption curve**. The information in the price-consumption curve, when plotted onto a price-quantity graph, yields the demand curve.

As income rises, the budget line makes a parallel outward shift. The points of tangency between this shifting budget line and the individual's indifference curves trace out the **income-consumption curve**. When plotted onto an income-quantity graph, this yields an **Engel curve**: the relationship between the quantity demanded of a good and income, holding prices constant. The income elasticity, ξ, equals (percentage change in quantity demanded)/(percentage change in income), or

$$\frac{\%\Delta Q}{\%\Delta Y} = \frac{\partial Q}{\partial Y}\frac{Y}{Q}$$

A good is **normal** if it has a positive income elasticity, and **inferior** if it has a negative income elasticity. If a good is normal and income increases, then the demand curve for that good will shift outward. For an inferior good, an increase in income causes its demand curve to shift inward. Income elasticities greater than 1 imply that spending on the good rises more than in proportion to income; this is called a **luxury** good. Goods with income elasticities greater than or equal to zero and less than or equal to 1 are called **necessities**; spending on these goods rises less than proportionately to income. Since as income rises, a consumer must spend more on some goods, not all goods can be inferior. The same good may be normal at a lower income level but inferior if income is sufficiently high. The weighted sum of a consumer's income elasticities (the sum of income elasticity times budget share) must always add up to 1.

When a price changes, the total change in the quantity demanded is the sum of two effects—the substitution effect and the income effect. The **substitution effect** is the change in the quantity demanded because of the change in the good's price, *holding other prices and the consumer's utility constant* (a *compensated change in price*). The income effect recognizes that changing prices effectively change a consumer's real income. The **income effect** is the change in the quantity demanded by the consumer because of the change in income, *holding prices constant*. Because indifference curves are convex to the origin, the substitution effect must be negative, in the sense that a rise in price of a good will cause a substitution away from the product (a fall in quantity), holding utility constant. The direction of the income effect depends on the income elasticity.

For normal goods the demand curve *must* slope downward, as both the substitution and the income effects cause quantity demanded to rise when price falls. If a good is inferior, the income effect goes in the opposite direction of the substitution effect. For most inferior goods, the income effect is smaller than the substitution effect, so the total effect moves in the same direction as the substitution effect, and the demand curve still slopes downward. If an inferior good's income effect is larger than its substitution effect, a decrease in price causes the quantity demanded to *fall,* and thus the demand curve would slope upward. A good with an upward-sloping demand curve is called a **Giffen good**. Although it is theoretically possible for a demand curve to slope upward, economists have found few, if any, real-world examples of Giffen goods.

An ordinary demand curve, also called a *Marshallian* demand curve, reflects the combined influence of income and substitution effects. We could also derive a **compensated demand curve**, showing how quantity demanded varies with price, holding utility constant. The compensated demand curve, also called the *Hicksian* demand curve, reflects only substitution effects and must always be downward sloping.

The Slutsky equation shows the relationship between the price elasticity of demand (ε), the substitution elasticity of demand (ε^*), and the income elasticity of demand ($\bullet$).

Total effect = substitution effect + income effect

$$\varepsilon = \varepsilon^* + (-\theta\xi),$$

where θ = the budget share of the good. The Slutsky equation can be used to decompose the total effect of a price change into its separate components, and also to show why Giffen goods are so unlikely to occur. To be a Giffen good, the total effect of a price increase must be positive, or in other words, price elasticity of demand must be positive. For ε to be positive, it must be true that $\bullet$ is negative (the good is inferior), and that it accounts for a large share of the budget. However, most goods that account for a large share of consumer budgets, such as food and housing, are normal goods, not inferior goods.

Adjusting nominal prices for the effects of inflation yields **real prices**. The most widely used measure of inflation in the United States is the **Consumer Price Index** (CPI). The CPI reports how much it costs now to buy the bundle of goods that an average consumer purchased in a base year. To find the rate of inflation, we calculate the percentage increase in income needed to buy the first year's bundle in later years. However, if income rises by the amount of the CPI, a consumer will be overcompensated for the effects of rising prices because his utility will increase. If his income rose at the same rate as the cost of the initial consumption bundle, the consumer would substitute away from the goods whose prices have risen relatively, and purchase a new bundle that yields more utility. The CPI has an upward bias in the sense that an individual's utility rises if we increase that person's income by the same percentage as the CPI rises.

This overcompensation is called **substitution bias**. Several studies estimate that due to the substitution bias, the CPI inflation rate is about half a percentage point too high per year. (In addition, the CPI is biased upward due to other problems, especially its inability to reflect the value of quality improvements and new goods.) The CPI is a **Laspeyres** index, using quantities from an earlier base period. An alternative is to use a **Paasche** index, which weights prices using the *current* quantities of goods purchased. However, a Paasche index generally overstates the degree of substitution and thus understates the change in the cost of living. The **Fisher** index tries to balance the overstatement and understatement of the other two by multiplying the Laspeyres and Paasche indexes and taking the square root.

The **theory of revealed preferences** is a way of inferring the shapes of consumer indifference curves from observed behavior. The theory assumes that consumers maximize utility subject to a budget constraint, and that indifference curves are smooth and convex, so that there is a unique utility-maximizing bundle. If a consumer prefers Bundle *a* to Bundle *b*, and Bundle *b* to Bundle *c*, then a rational consumer must prefer Bundle *a* to Bundle *c*. We say that Bundle *a* is *revealed to be preferred* to Bundle *c*. If a large number of consumer choices can be observed, then we can determine the shape of a consumer's indifference curves. The theory of revealed preferences can be used to derive the (negative) substitution effect, even without making any assumptions about the shape of indifference curves or having knowledge of the utility function.

■ Key Concepts and Formulas

- Price-consumption curve: line through equilibrium bundles consumed at each price of a given good.
- Income-consumption curve: line through equilibrium bundles consumed at each income level.
- Engel curve: the relationship between the quantity demanded and income.
- Normal good: income elasticity (•) > 0.
  Necessity: $0 \leq • \leq 1$.
  Luxury: $• \geq 1$.
- Inferior good: $• < 0$.
- The weighted share of a consumer's income elasticities must add up to 1.
- Substitution effect: the change in the quantity of a good that a consumer demands due to the change in the good's price, holding other prices and utility constant.
- Income effect: the change in the quantity of the good a consumer demands due to a change in income, holding prices constant.
- Giffen good: strongly inferior good with an upward-sloping demand curve.
- The Slutsky equation: total effect of a price change on quantity demanded, ε, equals the substitution effect, ε^*, plus the income effect, $-\theta\xi$ (where θ = the budget share of the good, and ξ = the income elasticity of the good).
- Laspeyres price indices, such as the CPI, overstate the effects of inflation on the cost of living, because they do not account for substitution.
- The theory of revealed preferences shows how the shape of indifferences can be inferred from a consumer's observed choices, and can be used to confirm the existence of a negative substitution effect.

■ Application: More Problems with the CPI

As discussed in the text, the Consumer Price Index (CPI) is a Laspeyres price index that measures price changes in a fixed market basket of goods over periods of time, but is not a true cost-of-living index. Let's consider more of the issues relating to measuring the cost of living with the CPI.

Question: How accurately can changes in the CPI be related to changes in consumer well-being?

Answer: There are a number of problems in using the CPI to measure true changes in the cost of living, as discussed previously. The most clear is the substitution bias. Since the CPI uses a fixed market basket of goods, it overstates inflation and cost-of-living changes to the extent that consumers are able substitute away from more expensive goods. Recent adjustments in CPI calculation, such as use of geometric means in calculating average prices for broad categories of goods, have minimized some of the within-category bias but have no impact on the between-category bias. Additionally, these adjustments cannot accurately measure changes in utility. For example, you might substitute chicken for fish when fish prices rise, but if you greatly prefer your original choice, your level of utility has changed much more than your cost of living.

Substitution bias is only one problem with the CPI. Another is the issue of new products and the quality of products. For example, a very good personal computer purchased in the mid-1980s might have a 40 megabyte hard drive and run at 16 megahertz, and that machine would cost more than twice what a computer with many gigabytes of storage space and running more than 30 times faster would cost. In the 1970s, such a product would not have been available. Thus if you consider the effect on a consumer's utility, the existence of the computer in the 1980s increases utility (relative to the 1970s, assuming that the consumer values a computer), but also increases the cost of living. The subsequent changes in technology increase utility, both by causing prices to fall and by improving the quality of the product. Only the fall in prices is measured by the CPI. This makes comparison of the cost of living in different times particularly difficult, as typical consumption bundles are likely to change dramatically.

Like all aggregate measures, the CPI only measures changes in your cost of living accurately if you are very like the average. If you live in an urban area, are a member of a family of four living on the median income in the United States, and you consume a typical market basket of goods, the CPI probably comes close to measuring your cost of living change from year to year. If you are a single vegetarian living in a rural area, you may consume very different items! Likewise, if you are elderly or disabled, your cost of living may be rising more rapidly than the average, as the cost of health care and prescription medicines has exceeded the average rate of inflation for some time.

A quick Internet search will show you the extent of controversy on these and related points, and you will find that some people argue that the CPI is understated, while others argue the reverse. Some of these issues come from a very fundamental problem with measuring both the cost of living and GDP, issues relating to goods that either do not go through markets in any direct way (such as the value of work that you do for yourself) and the value of things that are measured only indirectly by market prices. An important example of the latter is called Owner's Equivalent Rent (OER). If you own a house, you don't pay rent, but living in your house has an implicit cost, the cost of renting some equivalent property. A full explanation of how OER is measured would take a great deal of space, but it is easy to see how OER fluctuates with changes in the housing market. If housing prices rise, then the demand for rental properties will also increase, since some people will not be able to afford to buy houses. This causes rental prices to increase and thus, since it is more expensive to rent equivalent properties, the OER component of the CPI increases. It appears that inflation has risen. But if you already live in a house that you own, has your cost of living changed at all? The answer is, yes and no. Your direct cost of living has not changed at all. However, if you said that your opportunity cost has risen, you would also be correct! Has your level of utility changed? The answer to that is ambiguous as well.

Sources: Bureau of Labor Statistics, (http://www.bls.gov, various pages). See also http://www.aw-bc.com/perloff/ for further sources on quality and new product issues. Numerous magazine and newspaper sources discuss the issue of OER in inflation changes in recent years.

■ Solved Problems

1. Michael (from Chapter 3, Solved Problem 1) spends all of his food budget on pizza and milk. Michael's utility function is:

$$U(q_1, q_2) = q_1 q_2,$$

where q_1 is the quantity of pizza (slices) and q_2 is the quantity of milk (quarts). His monthly food budget is $120, the price of pizza (p_1) is $3, and the price of milk (p_2) is $2. Previously, we found that with this level of income and prices, Michael's utility-maximizing bundle is $q_1 = 20$, $q_2 = 30$, and with this combination, his level of utility is 600.

Now suppose that the price of pizza falls to $2. Find Michael's new utility-maximizing bundle, his new level of utility, and then find the substitution and income effects of the price change. Carefully graph your results.

Step 1: Find the new utility-maximizing bundle.

First, find Michael's new utility-maximizing bundle. Since this is just a repeat of the Lagrangian problem in the last chapter (and you're an expert on this by now!), we're going to skip that part and just note that the new utility-maximizing bundle is $q_1 = 30$, $q_2 = 30$, and with this combination, his level of utility is 900. As expected, a fall in the price of one of the goods that Michael buys increases his utility.

Step 2: Find the compensated bundle at the new price ratio.

What you found in Step 1 is the *total* effect of the fall in the price of pizza. Now, we want to separate the total effect into income and substitution effect points. In order to do this, we must find the consumption bundle that would correspond with a *compensated* fall in the price of pizza. In other words, if the price of pizza fell, but enough money were *taken away* from Michael so that he could not increase his utility, what bundle would he buy?

To find this bundle, consider what we know about this point. First, it must be on the original indifference curve, $600 = q_1 q_2$. Secondly, it must be true that at this new point, the MRS (slope of the indifference curve) is equal to the new price ratio. Since we can write the MRS as the ratio of the marginal utilities,

$$\frac{MU_1}{MU_2} = \frac{\partial U / \partial q_1}{\partial U / \partial q_2} = \frac{p_1}{p_2}$$

$$\frac{q_2}{q_1} = \frac{1}{1}$$

$$q_1 = q_2$$

We can use this relationship between the quantities of the goods to substitute back into the indifference curve equation.

$$600 = q_1 q_2$$

$$600 = (q_1)^2$$

$$q_1 = q_2 = 24.5 \text{ (rounded to one decimal place)}$$

In other words, if the price of pizza fell to $1, but we take away some income from Michael so that he cannot increase his utility above 600, he would now choose to buy 24.5 slices of pizza and 24.5 quarts of milk (we might want to round this to a whole number since you usually can't buy half a slice of pizza). Note that as compared to his original bundle (20, 30), Michael buys relatively more pizza and relatively less milk. Since pizza has become relatively less expensive, he substitutes away from milk and buys more pizza.

Step 3: Find the income and substitution effect quantities.

Michael originally consumed 20 slices of pizza and 30 quarts of milk. If the price of pizza falls, but Michael is compensated (which in this case means that he loses income) so that he must remain at the original level of utility, he will consume 24 slices of pizza and 24 quarts of milk (quantities rounded to whole numbers). Thus the *substitution effect* of the fall in the price of pizza is (+4, −6). Michael consumes 4 more slices of pizza and 6 fewer quarts of milk. If Michael is not compensated, he will now consume 30 slices of pizza and 30 quarts of milk (this is the bundle you found in Step 1). Thus the *income effect* is (+6, +6). The increase in real income resulting from the fall in the price of pizza causes Michael to consume 6 more slices of pizza and 6 more quarts of milk. Since Michael's real income *rose* and he consumed more of both goods, both goods are normal. The total effect of the price change is equal to the substitution effect plus the income effect.

Total effect = substitution + income

Total effect (on pizza consumption) = 4 + 6 = 10

Step 4: Carefully graph your results.

As you did before, graph the original budget constraint (L^1) and the new budget constraint (L^2), being careful to label your endpoints. Michael's indifference curves are smooth and convex, and you should draw at least two, representing the original level of utility and the new level of utility. To show the substitution effect, draw a line that is parallel to the *new* budget constraint and *tangent* to the old indifference curve (L^*). Note that you don't know the intercepts of this line (although we will find them in the next chapter). Label the consumption bundles and their coordinates. Finally, label the income, substitution, and total effects on the axis corresponding with the good whose price has changed.

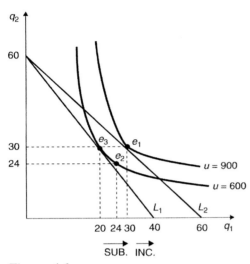

Figure 4.1

2. Find Michael's compensated and uncompensated demand curves for pizza, and graph your results.

Step 1: Find the ordinary (Marshallian or uncompensated) demand curve for pizza.

Demand curves are a function of prices and income. The easiest way to find ordinary demand functions is to return to the original Lagrangian problem, but this time we want to write the budget constraint in terms of variables rather than specific prices.

$$\textbf{Max } U(q_1, q_2) = q_1 q_2$$
$$\textbf{subject to: } I = p_1 q_1 + p_1 q_2$$

Now follow exactly the same steps that you did before. Write the Lagrangian function, take partial derivatives with respect to q_1, q_2, and λ, and set the partial derivatives equal to zero. Your first-order condition will now be

$$\frac{q_2}{q_1} = \frac{p_1}{p_2}$$

$$q_2 = \frac{p_1}{p_2} q_1$$

Now substitute into the original budget constraint, and solve for q_1 (since you are trying to find the demand for pizza).

$$I = p_1 q_1 + p_2 q_2$$

$$I = p_1 q_1 + p_2 \left(\frac{p_1}{p_2} q_1 \right)$$

$$q_1 = \frac{I}{2p_1}$$

This is the general form of Michael's ordinary demand function. Since we know that his income is $120, we can substitute this value into the equation.

$$q_1 = \frac{60}{p_1}$$

Step 2: Find the compensated (Hicksian) demand curve for pizza.

The compensated demand curve is a function of prices and utility. To find the compensated demand curve, you first need to find the expenditures function, since that tells you what amount of money Michael must spend to achieve a given level of utility. In Chapter 3, Solved Problem 2, you found this for a given level of utility. To find the expenditures function in general, start in the same way, by minimizing spending subject to a utility constraint. To get the general form of the expenditures function, we write the problem with variables for prices and utility.

$$\textbf{Min } E = p_1 q_1 + p_2 q_2$$
$$\textbf{subject to: } U^* = q_1 q_2$$

Remember that U^* refers to a fixed level of utility. As you did before, take partial derivatives with respect to with respect to q_1, q_2, and λ, and set the partial derivatives equal to zero. Your first-order condition will now be exactly the same as what you found in Step 1 (since this is the dual of that problem).

$$\frac{q_2}{q_1} = \frac{p_1}{p_2}$$

$$q_2 = \frac{p_1}{p_2} q_1$$

Now substitute into the constraint, and solve for q_1.

$$U^* = q_1 q_2$$

$$U^* = q_1 \left(\frac{p_1}{p_2} q_1 \right)$$

$$q_1 = \sqrt{\frac{U^* p_2}{p_1}}$$

This is the general form of the compensated demand curve. In this problem, Michael's original level of utility is 600. Thus

$$q_1 = \sqrt{\frac{600(2)}{p_1}} = \sqrt{\frac{1200}{p_1}}$$

This is the compensated demand curve for this problem.

Step 3: Graph the compensated and ordinary demand curves.

See the graph below. It must always be true that the compensated and ordinary demand curves intersect at the original utility-maximizing point, so this is one way to double-check your math.

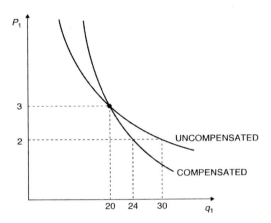

Figure 4.2

3. In Figure 4.3, BC_1 represents the consumer's budget line when she has $100. Calculate her income elasticity of demand for both Good A and Good B.

Income elasticity of demand, ξ, equals the percentage change in quantity demanded divided by the percentage change in income. We need to deduce both of these changes from the graph, then put them together into the income elasticity formula.

Step 1: Find the percentage change in quantity demanded of A and B.

Consumption of A falls from 10 to 9, so the percentage change is $-1/10 = -10$ percent.

Consumption of B rises from 5 to 8, so the percentage change is $= 3/5 = 60$ percent.

Step 2: Find the percentage change in income.

Initially, the maximum amount of A that she can purchase is 20 and the maximum amount of B is 10. After the increase in income, these rise to be 1.25 times higher than initially, an increase of 25 percent.

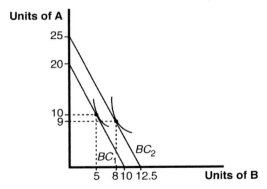

Figure 4.3

Step 3: Calculate the income elasticities.

Income elasticity of demand for $A = -10$ percent/25 percent $= -0.4$, which is inferior.

Income elasticity of demand for $B = 60$ percent/25 percent $= 2.4$, which is normal.

■ Practice Problems

Multiple-Choice

1. If the demand curve for skiing slopes downward, which of the following is true?
    a.   The substitution and income effects work in the same direction.
    b.   The substitution and income effects work in opposite directions, with the income effect being larger in magnitude.
    c.   The substitution and income effects work in opposite directions, with the income effect being smaller in magnitude.
    d.   Either a or b.
    e.   Either a or c.

2. An Engel Curve for a good has a positive slope if
    a.   the good is an inferior good.
    b.   the good is a Giffen good.
    c.   the good is a normal good.
    d.   the demand curve also slopes downward.

3. When Marcia's income rises, she buys more peanut butter, but the share of her budget spent on peanut butter falls. For Marcia, peanut butter can best be described as
    a.   a necessity.
    b.   a luxury.
    c.   a Giffen good.
    d.   an inferior good.
    e.   There is not enough information to determine what kind of good this is.

Fill-in

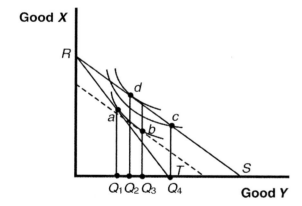

Figure 4.4

4. In Figure 4.4, the budget line rotates from *RT* to *RS*. The substitution effect causes consumption of good *Y* to change from _____ to _____. The income effect causes consumption of good *Y* to change from _____ to _____. The total effect causes consumption of good *Y* to change from _____ to _____.

5. A true cost-of-living index is an inflation index that holds _____ constant over time.

True-False-Ambiguous and Explain Why

6. If there are only two goods, both goods cannot be luxuries.

7. The demand curve for a normal good *must* slope downward.

8. The income elasticity of demand for a good can be negative at all income levels.

Short-Answer

9. Show the total, substitution, and income effects if the price of tires rises for an individual who views tires and gasoline as perfect complements.

10. In each case below use a single supply-and-demand graph to show the events in the indicated market. Label the initial and final prices and quantity on the graph. Provide a brief explanation.
    a. Possum. The initial equilibrium price for a pound of possum meat is $2. Then incomes rise. (Possum meat is an inferior good.)
    b. Caviar. The initial equilibrium price for caviar is $100 per ounce. Then stocks of sturgeon (the fish that is the source of caviar) plummet and incomes rise among caviar consumers. (Caviar is a normal good.)

11. Official statistics estimate that the median family income of Americans was constant between 1979 and 1995. These statistics adjust for inflation using the Consumer Price Index. How should we interpret the official statistics?

12. *Reader's Digest* reported the results of a survey of American buyers. The typical buyer reported that if his or her income were to rise by $1000, he or she would spend an additional $400 on clothing. Does this sound plausible? Explain.

13. Suppose that Tonya's quantity demanded of jelly beans is $Q_d = 10,000 - 500,000p + 5000Y + 25Y^2$, where quantity is in jelly beans per year, the price, p, is $0.10 per jelly bean, and Y = income in thousands of dollars. The other good that she purchases is gummy bears, which sell for $0.10 each. Draw Tonya's Income-Consumption Curve and her Engel Curve for jelly beans as her income rises from $20,000 to $30,000 to $40,000.

14. Laura earns $50 per week, which she spends exclusively on Dove Bars and Spam. Initially the price of a Dove Bar is $2 and the price of a can of Spam is $1. At first, she consumes 40 cans of Spam (she's desperate). Laura receives a raise and now earns $100 per week. Spam is an inferior good. Show how Laura is likely to adjust her consumption bundle as her income rises.

15. Using budget lines and indifference curves show the income and substitution effects for a good whose demand is perfectly inelastic.

16. Rachna's consumption of apples and oranges in the base period and the current period are given below, along with the prices. Using this information, calculate the Consumer Price Index for fruit for Rachna. Compare this result, which uses the Laspeyres index, with a Paasche index and a Fisher index.

	Base Period		Current Period	
	Quantity	Price	Quantity	Price
Apples	20	$0.50	15	$1
Oranges	10	$0.50	15	$0.50

17. Andy has $90 per month to spend on bicycle magazines and computer magazines. The price of bicycle magazines is $3 and the price of computer magazines is $2. Initially, he buys 20 bike magazines. His income elasticity for bike magazines is zero. If his income climbs to $110 per month, what must his income elasticity for computer magazines be?

18. The demand equation for CD players is $Q_D = 300,000 - 2000p + 3I$ where Q_D = number of CD players per year, p = price in dollars, and I = average annual income. What is the income elasticity of demand for CD players when $p = \$100$ and $I = \$40,000$?

19. Suppose that a good's income elasticity is -2 and its budget share is 10 percent. If the good is a Giffen good, what must its substitution elasticity of demand, ϵ^*, be?

20. Suppose that a person's indifference curves for combinations of A and B are convex. Using budget constraints and indifference curves, show that if the cross-price elasticity of demand between A and B is zero, as the price of A falls, then B must be a normal good.

21. In Figure 4.5, Ike's demand curve for DVD rentals has shifted because his income has risen by 40 percent. Show this shift using a budget constraint and indifference curve graph and assuming that his income is initially $1000 per month.

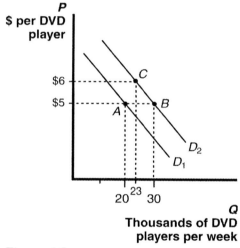

Figure 4.5

22. In Figure 4.5, Ike's demand curve for DVD rentals has shifted because his income has risen by 40 percent. Simultaneously (because overall demand has risen) the price of a DVD rental has increased from $5 to $6. Show the movement from point A to point C using a budget constraint and indifference curve graph and assuming that Ike's income is initially $1000 per month.

23. Using the information in Figure 4.5, calculate Ike's income elasticity of demand for DVD rentals.

24. In Figure 4.6, the demand curve has shifted because incomes have risen by 50 percent. Using the information in the figure, calculate each of these elasticities over the appropriate ranges:
    a. elasticity of demand
    b. elasticity of supply
    c. income elasticity

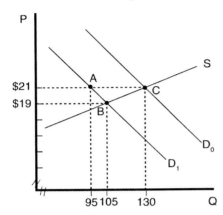

Figure 4.6

25. During the initial period of industrialization, a debate raged about whether industrialization was bringing a higher standard of living. In the United States, for example, the average height of adult males fell from 5 feet 8.3 inches for those born in 1830 to 5 feet 7.1 inches for those born in 1860. Some historians contend that this drop in heights occurred because the price of food (especially meat) was rising, causing people to eat less and thus grow less. Suppose that the declining heights were caused by increased meat prices. Does this decline in meat consumption mean that the overall standard of living was declining? In your answer, use budget constraints and indifference curves with meat on one axis and "other goods" on the other axis. Consider the case where the price of other goods remains the same and the case where the price of other goods falls.

26. Stefan consumes bread (B) and cheese (C). His utility function is $U = BC$, the price of bread is $5/loaf, and the price of cheese is $5/lb. He currently spends his $100 weekly budget buying 10 loaves of bread and 10 pounds of cheese.
    a. If the price of cheese rises to $10, what will Stefan consume now?
    b. Find the income and substitution effects of the rise in the price of cheese, and carefully graph your results.

27. Using the information from Problem 26, find Stefan's ordinary and compensated demand curves, and graph them.

28. Consider three consumers, Mollie, and Maggie, and May. Mollie likes to eat sandwiches with one slice of ham and one slice of cheese, and will not eat any other combination. Maggie doesn't care what she puts on her sandwich; she just wants two slices of either product on her sandwich. May has ordinary, convex indifference curves and a utility function of $U = HC$. Each has $24 to spend on sandwiches, and there is an unlimited supply of free bread.
    a. Initially the price of ham is $3, and the price of cheese is $1. Find each consumer's utility-maximizing combination of ham and cheese.

b.   Now suppose that the price of ham rises to $5. Find the new utility-maximizing combination for each consumer, and find the income and substation effects of the price change.

c.   Carefully graph your results.

29.   Using Problem 28, explain how Mollie, Maggie, and May's actions could be expressed in terms of the Slutsky equation.

30.   Two economists are walking down the street. The first economist sees a beautiful British racing green Jaguar being driven down the street and says, "I want one of those." The second economist says, "Obviously not." Explain why this economist joke is (supposed to be) funny, using the concept of revealed preference.

■ Answers to Practice Problems

1.   e.   If the income effect worked in the opposite direction and was larger in magnitude, this would be a Giffen good, and the demand curve would slope upward.

2.   c.

3.   a.   Since Marcia buys more as her income rises, the peanut butter is a normal good. But since the share of her budget is falling, the percentage increase in quantity must be less than the percentage increase in income. Thus income elasticity is less than 1 (but greater than zero), and peanut butter is best described as a necessity.

4.   substitution effect $= Q_1$ to Q_3

income effect $= Q_3$ to Q_2

total effect $= Q_1$ to Q_2

5.   utility

6.   True. A luxury is a good that has an income elasticity greater than 1. In other words, as income rises, spending increases more than proportionately. If there are only two goods, you can spend *absolutely* more on each good, but you cannot spend *relatively* more on both goods. If you increase the proportion spent on one good, then you must decrease the proportion spent on the other good, and thus it must be a necessity or an inferior good.

7.   True. For a normal good both income and substitution effects lead the consumer to purchase more as the price falls.

8.   False. The income elasticity of demand for a good cannot be negative at all income levels. A negative income elasticity implies that a rise in income will cause the person to buy *less*. To buy less, the person must have bought some of the product at some income level. A person whose income is zero cannot buy anything, so if the person is ever to buy any of the product, it must be normal in the range between zero income and the income at which the good is first purchased.

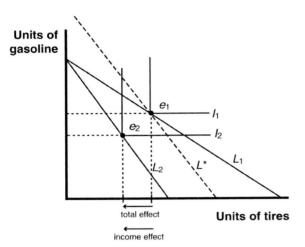

Figure 4.7

9. Figure 4.7 shows that the inward rotation of the budget line induces the consumer to move from e_1 to e_2. The line L^* has the same slope as L_2. Notice that because the goods are perfect complements, the slope of the indifference curves changes so abruptly that L_1 and L^* touch I_1 at exactly the same point. Therefore, the change in relative prices causes no substitution between gasoline and tires (after all, they are *perfect* complements). Because there is no substitution effect, all of the decrease in consumption is due to the income effect.

10. a. As Figure 4.8 (a) shows, a rise in income will cause the demand curve to shift inward from D_0 to D_1, because the possum meat is an inferior good. This will cause the price to fall to P_1, as the quantity falls from Q_0 to Q_1.

    b. As Figure 4.8 (b) shows, a rise in income will cause the demand curve to shift outward from D_0 to D_1, because the caviar is a normal good. Simultaneously, the supply curve shifts inward from S_0 to S_1. This will cause the price to rise to P_1. Q_1 could be higher, lower, or the same as Q_0, depending on the relative size of the supply and demand shifts.

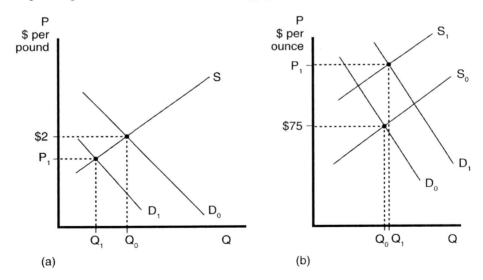

Figure 4.8

11. Because the Consumer Price Index assumes that consumers do not substitute toward goods whose relative prices have fallen (and because it ignores many quality improvements and the introduction of new goods), it overstates inflation. Most economists accept the Boskin Commission's estimate that the overstatement was about 1.1 percentage points per year. Therefore, real incomes did not remain constant, but rose by about 1.1 percent per year between 1979 and 1995.

12. These responses do not seem very reasonable. The median household income in the United States is about $44,400 per year (2004). Thus, the $1,000 increase is an increase of about 2.25 percent. Household surveys show that about 5.5 percent of consumer expenditures go to clothing; that is, about $2,442 per household. If spending rose by $400 (as the survey claims), this would be a 16.38 percent increase in clothing expenditure. This implies an income elasticity of demand for clothing that is awesomely large, (percentage change in quantity demanded)/(percentage change in income) = 16.38%/2.25% = 7.28, which is much larger than any known income elasticity estimates for clothing. (Even if we do not know the exact percentage changes in income and quantity of clothing demanded, we could use rough estimates and reach the same conclusion that the elasticity implicitly in the *Reader's Digest* numbers is extremely high.)

13. The quantity of jelly beans demanded and expenditure on jelly beans can be found by plugging the price and various income levels into the equation. Subtract the jelly bean expenditure from income to find gummy bear expenditure and divide this by $0.10 to find the quantity of gummy bears demanded. For example, since $Q_{d\text{Jelly Beans}} = 10,000 - 500,000p + 5000Y + 25Y^2$, plug in $p = \$0.10$, $Y = 20$, and $Y^2 = 400$ to get $Q_{d\text{Jelly Beans}} = 10,000 - (500,000 \times 0.1) + (5000 \times 20) + (25 \times 400) = 10,000 - 50,000 + 100,000 + 10,000 = 70,000$. Thus, at an income of $20,000 Tonya buys 70,000 jelly beans, spending $7000 on them (70,000 × $0.10). This leaves $13,000 for gummy bears. Since their price is $0.10 each, she can buy 130,000.

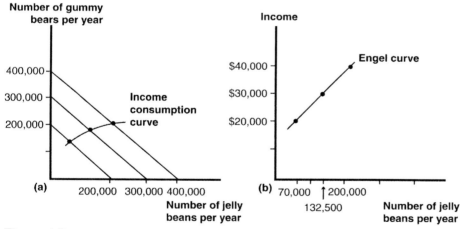

Figure 4.9

Income	Q_d Jelly Beans	Expenditure Jelly Beans	Expenditure Gummy Bears	Q_d Gummy Bears
$20,000	70,000	$ 7,000	$13,000	130,000
$30,000	132,500	$13,250	$16,750	167,500
$40,000	200,000	$20,000	$20,000	200,000

Figure 4.9(a) shows the income-consumption curve. Figure 4.9(b) shows the Engel curve for jelly beans.

14. Figure 4.10 shows Laura's initial and new budget constraints. The end points are found by dividing income by the price of each good. Because she initially spent $40 on Spam, she had $10 left over for Dove Bars and bought five of them, as shown at point *a*. Her new consumption bundle is not known exactly, but it must be a point where consumption of Spam has fallen; after all, her income has risen and Spam is an inferior good for most consumers. Because she is buying less Spam, her consumption of Dove Bars must rise. Any point from *b* to *c* is possible for Laura, depending on the shape of her indifference curves. Point *d* is one possibility.

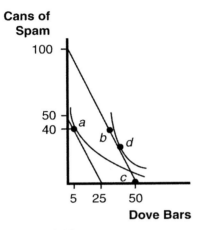

Figure 4.10

15. See Figure 4.11. The price of *B* has fallen from L_1 to L_2, but the quantity of *B* demanded has stayed the same, Q_1. Therefore, the demand for *B* is perfectly inelastic. The substitution effect (from e_1 to e^*) must be equal to the income effect (e^* to e_2), which goes in the opposite direction.

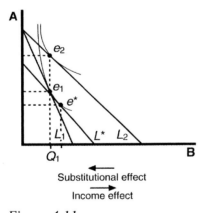

Figure 4.11

16. The CPI/Laspeyres method compares the cost of the basket of goods using the base period quantities.

Base Period Cost:
20 apples × $0.50 + 10 oranges × $0.50 = $15

Current Period Cost:
20 apples × $1.00 + 10 oranges × $0.50 = $25

Cost of Living Index = (Current Period Cost)/(Base Period Cost) = $25/$15 = $166.66

The Paasche method compares the cost of the basket of goods using the current period quantities.

Base Period Cost:

15 apples × $0.50 + 15 oranges × $0.50 = $15

Current Period Cost:

15 apples × $1.00 + 15 oranges × $0.50 = $22.50

Cost of Living Index = (Current Period Cost)/(Base Period Cost) = $22.50/$15 = $150

The Fisher method multiples the two cost of living indexes and takes the square root:

$166.66 \times 150 = 25,000$. The square root of this is 158.11. Notice that the Fisher Index estimate of the inflation rate, 58.11%, is between the Paasche estimate of 50% and the Laspeyres estimate of 66.66%

17. Initially Andy bought 15 computer magazines.

$$\text{Income} - (p_{\text{Bike Magazines}} \times Q_{\text{Bike Magazines}}) =$$
$$(p_{\text{Computer Magazines}} \times Q_{\text{Computer Magazines}}) \quad \text{or}$$
$$\$90 - (\$3 \times 20) = (\$2 \times 15).$$

Because the income elasticity for bike magazines is 0, all the extra $20 goes to computer magazines, so he buys 25. Thus as income rises from $90 to $110, the quantity of computer magazines bought rises from 15 to 25. Putting these numbers into the formula for income elasticity yields: $\xi = (\Delta Q/Q)/(\Delta Y/Y) = (10/15)/(20/90) = 3$.

18. First find the quantity demanded by plugging $p = \$100$ and $Y = \$40,000$ into the demand equation, to find $Q_D = 300,000 - (2000 \times 100) + (3 \times 40,000) = 300,000 - 200,000 + 120,000 = 220,000$. Next remember that income elasticity $= (\Delta Q_D/Q_D)/(\Delta Y/Y)$ or $(\Delta Q_D/\Delta Y)(Y/Q_D)$, where the $(\Delta Q_D/\Delta Y)$ term is the coefficient on income from the demand equation—in this case, 3. Hence income elasticity = $3(40,000/220,000) = 0.545$.

19. The Slutsky equation is: total effect = substitution effect + income effect or $\epsilon = \epsilon^* + -\theta\xi$ (where $\theta =$ the budget share of the good, and $\xi =$ the income elasticity of the good). If a good is a Giffen good, then the total effect, ϵ, is positive. Using the information in the problem, we know that $\theta = 0.1$ and $\xi = -2$. Thus we have: $\epsilon = \epsilon^* + -(0.1 \times -2)$, or $\epsilon = \epsilon^* + 0.2$. For ϵ to be positive, ϵ^* must be smaller in magnitude than 0.2. Its range is between 0 and -0.2.

20. Figure 4.12 shows the case where the cross-price elasticity between A and B is zero. A zero cross-price elasticity means that as the price of A falls (as the budget constraint rotates from L_1 to L_2), the quantity demanded of B does not change, but continues to be Q_1. This consumer's initial optimal point, e_1, and her final optimal point (after the price of A falls), e_2, both line up at Q_1. To find the substitution effect, we need to find the point on the initial indifference curve, I_1, that has the same slope as the new budget constraint, L_2. This is point e^*. (We usually find the substitution and income effects by examining the change in the consumption of the good whose price has changed, but this time we're doing it for the good whose price has stayed the same.) The income effect takes us from e^* to e_2. Obviously good B is a normal good since the movement from e^* to e_2 increases the quantity of B consumed, as the income effect cancels out the substitution away from good B.

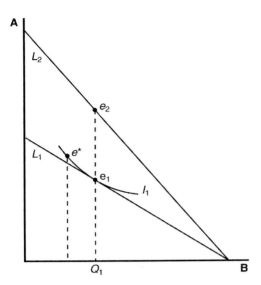

Figure 4.12

21. Figure 4.13 shows that as the budget constraint has made a parallel shift, Ike's point of tangency has moved from point A to point B. These match points A and B in Figure 5.9, with the quantity of DVD rentals rising from 20 to 30 and the amount left over for other goods rising from 900 to 1250. (The graph assumes that other goods have a price of $1 each.)

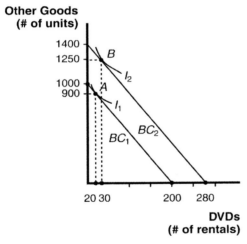

Figure 4.13

22. Figure 4.14 shows the original budget constraint, BC_1 and the new one, BC_2. BC_2's end point on the DVD axis is $1400/$6 = income/(price of a DVD rental) = $233.33. Ike's maximizing points are the quantities that he demands, with the quantity of rentals rising from 20 to 23 and the money left over for other purchases rising from 900 (= $1000 - (20 \times 5)$) to 1262 (= $1400 - (23 \times 6)$). (The graph assumes that other goods have a price of $1 each.)

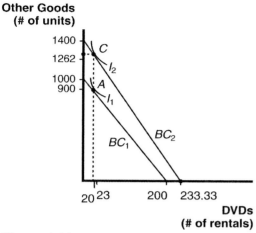

Figure 4.14

23. Income elasticity = $\%\Delta Q_d / \%\Delta Y$. In this case, as income rises by 40 percent, Ike's demand curve shifts from D_1 to D_2 and at a price of $5 per rental, his quantity demanded jumps from 20 to 30. Thus the $\%\Delta Q_d$ from point A to point B is 50%. $\%\Delta Q_d / \%\Delta Y = 50\%/40\% = 1.25$.

24   a. Find the elasticity of demand by calculating the percentage change in the quantity demanded divided by the percentage change in price between points A and B along D_1. The percentage change in quantity demanded = +10 percent; the percentage change in price = −10 percent, so the elasticity of demand = −1 in this range, along this curve. (You can estimate the demand elasticity at other points along D_1 or along D_2 if you wish, but the prices and quantities aren't marked as clearly.)

      b. Find the elasticity of supply by calculating the percentage change in the quantity supplied divided by the percentage change in price between points B and C along S. The percentage change in quantity supplied = +21.3 percent; the percentage change in price = +10 percent, so the elasticity of supply is +2.13.

      c. Find the income elasticity by calculating the percentage change in the quantity demanded divided by the percentage change in income between points C and A as the demand curve shifts inward due to the income increase. The percentage change in quantity demanded = −31.1 percent; the percentage change in income (given in the problem) = +50 percent, so the income elasticity is −0.62 and the good is inferior.

25. One of the most important things that a person can know is when a question can and cannot be answered with the evidence at hand. With only the information about meat prices and meat consumption, one may be tempted to conclude that people became worse off, but it is also possible that they became better off. The economist's concept of the standard of living is utility. If a person's utility increases, we would say that the standard of living has increased. However, with the information given above, we can draw budget constraints that are consistent with rising utility or falling utility. In Figure 4.15(a), the budget constraint rotates inward (from BC_0 to BC_1) as the price of meat rises, while the prices of other goods and income levels remain unchanged. The new consumption level of meat falls (M_1 is less than M_0). If this is what happened, then people became worse off. (Assuming that they were initially maximizing utility, they must have initially been at a point of tangency between indifference curve I_0 and BC_0 (point a). Now they cannot reach that point.) However, this is not the only possibility. If income rose or the price of other goods fell (or both), then the budget constraints could have been

something like those in Figure 4.15(b), in which both ends of the budget constraint rotate. Meat consumption falls (from M_0 to M_1), but the consumption of other goods rises (from OG_0 to OG_1). Point b is on a higher indifference curve than point a. Incomes did rise and many other prices did fall, so most economic historians believe that Figure 3.13(b) reflects what happened in the United States. In Britain, height declines were more severe, and the standard of living debate still rages.

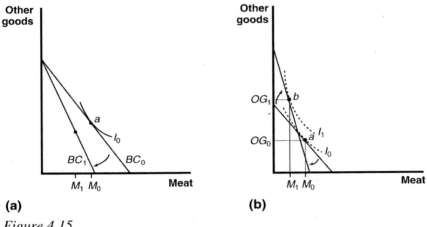

(a)   **(b)**

Figure 4.15

26. a.   Use the Lagrangian method or the substitution method to find Stefan's new bundle. Stefan will now buy 10 loaves of bread and 5 pounds of cheese.

   b.   To find Stefan's compensated bundle, note that his original level of utility is $U = (10)(10) = 100$. We need to find the bundle that Stefan would buy if his utility was still 100 but the new price ratio exists. To do this, we use the first-order condition that you found in part a, which is $C = \frac{1}{2} B$ (or $B = 2C$) You could also find this by setting the MRS equal to the price ratio. Now use the utility function for Stefan's original bundle, $100 = BC$. Substitute in the first order condition, and solve for B and C. $B = 14$; $C = 7$ (answers rounded to whole numbers). We now have three different bundles for Stefan (as we can see in Figure 4.16), and can calculate the substitution and income effects. Substitution: $7 - 10 = -3$ (when the price of cheese rises, Stefan buys 3 fewer pounds). Income: $5 - 7 = -2$ (when Stefan's real income falls, he buys 2 fewer pounds).

   In Figure 4.16, e_1 is the original utility-maximizing bundle, e_2 is the compensated bundle, and e_3 is the new utility-maximizing bundle

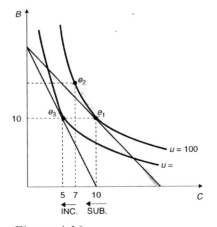

Figure 4.16

27. To find the ordinary demand curve, redo the original Lagrangian problem using algebraic expressions for prices and income (see Solved Problem 2 for exact steps). Stefan's ordinary demand curve for cheese is:

$$q_C = \frac{I}{2 p_C}$$

Thus with an income level of $100, we could rewrite this as:

$$q_C = \frac{50}{p_C}$$

To find Stefan's compensated demand curve, use the cost-minimizing version of Stefan's Lagrangian problem (see Solved Problem 2 for steps).

$$q_C = \sqrt{\frac{U^* p_B}{p_C}}$$

Since Stefan's original level of utility was 100, we can rewrite the compensated demand curve as:

$$q_C = \sqrt{\frac{U^* p_B}{p_C}} = \sqrt{\frac{100 \cdot 5}{p_C}} = \sqrt{\frac{500}{p_C}}$$

Figure 4.17 shows Stefan's ordinary and compensated demand curves.

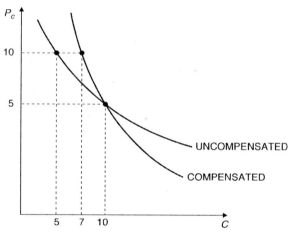

Figure 4.17

28. a. For Mollie, these goods are perfect complements. The easiest way to think about this is, what does it cost for her to get her preferred choice? She likes 1 slice of ham and 1 slice of cheese, so 1 sandwich will cost her $3 + $1 = $4. With $24, she can buy 24/4 = 6 sandwiches, so she will purchase 6 slices of ham and 6 slices of cheese.

For Maggie, these goods are perfect substitutes. She will always buy the cheapest. With her $24, she could buy 24/3 = 8 slices of ham, or she could buy 24/1 = 24 slices of cheese. Since she is indifferent between the two goods, she will choose to buy 24 slices of cheese.

May's optimal bundle can be found by setting up the Lagrangian equation or by using the substitution method. At current prices, her optimal bundle is 4 ham and 12 cheese (and her level of utility is 48).

b.   For Mollie, since these goods are perfect complements, there is no substitution effect, because she will never substitute. The only point at which she can reach her original level of utility, given the new price ratio, is her original point. However, if she is not compensated, she cannot afford that many sandwiches any more. At the new price ratio, a sandwich costs $6, and thus she will buy 4 sandwiches (4 ham and 4 cheese). This is a pure income effect.

For Maggie, since these goods are perfect substitutes, whether or not there is a substitution effect depends on whether the good she was previously purchasing has become more expensive, thus inducing her to switch. In this case, the price of ham rose, and she was not buying it before, so she will not buy it now. There is no substitution effect, and since she can still buy her original bundle, there is no income effect. (Note that for Maggie, there would be a substitution effect if the price of ham fell to less than $1, or if something happened to the price of cheese, there would possibly be substitution effects and certainly would be income effects.)

We can find income and substitution effects for May in the usual way. At the new price ratio, she will buy 2 ham (rounded to the nearest whole number) and 12 cheese. Then find May's compensated bundle, recalling that her original level of utility was 48. With the new price ratio, her compensated bundle is 3 ham and 15 cheese (rounded to whole numbers). Thus the price increase has both income and substitution effects for May.

c.   In the graphs, e_1 is the original utility-maximizing bundle, e_2 is the compensated bundle, and e_3 is the new utility-maximizing bundle.

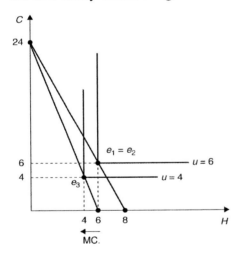

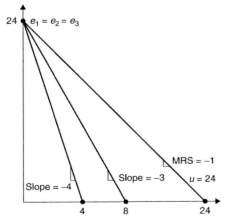

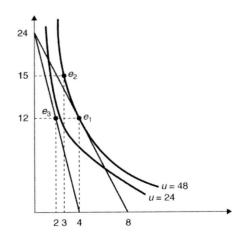

Figure 4.18

29. Recall that the Slutsky equation shows the relationship between the price elasticity of demand (ε), the substitution elasticity of demand (ε^*), and the income elasticity of demand ($\bullet$).

$$\text{total effect} = \text{substitution effect} + \text{income effect, or}$$
$$\varepsilon = \varepsilon^* + (-\theta\xi),$$

where θ = the budget share of the good.

For Mollie, since these goods are perfect complements, ε^* must be zero. Thus $\varepsilon = 0 + (-(1/2)\xi)$, or in other words, the income effect is equal to half of the income elasticity of demand, which makes sense since spending on ham accounts for half of Mollie's budget. In this case, you can see clearly the relationship between the size of the income effect and the budget share. If Mollie liked a lot more ham on her sandwich, and thus spent *relatively* more of her budget on ham, the income effect would be much larger (in absolute value).

For Maggie, ε^* is again zero, but only for ham prices above $1, the current price of cheese (it is infinite for ham prices below $1). Since ham currently accounts for zero percent of her budget, the income effect must also be zero.

Since May has more conventional preferences, there is both a substitution and an income effect of the price change. Expressed in absolute numbers, −2 (the total change in ham purchases) = −1 (the substitution effect) + (−1) (the income effect). May has some ability to substitute, and ham is not a large part of her spending (at current prices), and thus neither effect is large.

30. The joke is, if you really wanted the Jaguar, you would already have purchased it (or taken steps to). The theory of revealed preference basically states that what you want is revealed by the actions you take; in this case, the fact that the economist had taken no actions to obtain the desired object implies that other bundles were revealed to be preferred to the Jaguar. It's wise to not take the joke too literally (since, of course, there are many bundles that we might prefer that are simply unaffordable), but the sense of it does capture much of the essence of the theory: there are many things that we say we want, but our actions show that other choices are preferred.

■ Exercises

True-False-Ambiguous and Explain Why

1. When Scott was 21, the real price of general admission tickets to San Francisco Giant's games was $5 and he bought 10 tickets per season. When Scott was 35, the real price of general admission tickets to Giants games was cut to $4 and he bought only 5 tickets per season. Therefore, general admission tickets to Giants' games are a Giffen good for Scott.

2. The compensated demand curve will always be steeper than the ordinary demand curve.

3. Letitia's mother wants her to go come home for the Thanksgiving holiday. However, her mother really stresses her out, so seeing her mother reduces her utility, all other things equal. Despite that, she chooses to go home for Thanksgiving. Thus she is an irrational consumer.

Short-Answer

4. Mike regards Gatoraid and Crocaid as perfect substitutes. Assume that he has $10 per month to spend on sports drinks and that the price of a bottle of Gatoraid is $0.60, while the price of a bottle of Crocaid is initially $0.70.

    a. Draw a graph showing his budget line and how it changes as the price of Crocaid falls from $0.70 to $0.60 to $0.50 to $0.40. Mark the consumption bundles that Mike chooses.

b. Draw a second graph showing the ordinary demand curve for Crocaid.

c. Explain which part of the increase in consumption is due to the income effect and which part is due to the substitution effect.

5. The annual demand for *Study Guide to Accompany Microeconomics* consists of the demand by people attending large colleges, $Q_l = 100{,}000 - 5{,}000p + 4Y$, and the demand by people attending small colleges, $Q_d = 100{,}000 - 5{,}000p + Y$, where p = the price per study guide, and Y = parents' average income, which is initially \$40,000 for both groups. Then a new tax bill is passed and the income of parents with students at large colleges falls to \$30,000, while the income of parents with students attending small colleges rises to \$50,000. Total national income is unchanged, because the two groups are the same size. Draw a demand curve showing how the tax bill affects the demand for *Study Guide to Accompany Microeconomics*.

6. A recent study concluded that the price elasticity of demand for cigarettes is approximately −0.5, but that this elasticity decreases as income rises. Show this result using budget constraints and indifference curves. (The study is Joni Hersch, "Gender, Income Levels, and the Demand for Cigarettes," *Journal of Risk and Uncertainty,* 21 (2), November 2000.)

7. Crispin maximizes his utility by consuming tuna (T) and beef (B). His utility function is $U(T, B) = 10T^{3/4}B^{1/4}$. Crispin's income is income is \$900, the price of tuna is \$9, and the price of beef is \$3. Find Crispin's utility-maximizing bundle, and carefully graph your results.

8. Refer to Exercise 7. The price of tuna now falls to \$3. Find the income and substitution effects of the price change, and graph Crispin's indifference curve map and budget constraints, being sure to label everything carefully.

9. Refer to Exercise 7. Find Crispin's ordinary and compensated demand curves, and graph them.

10. Use budget constraints and indifference curves to show the income and substitution effects for a good whose income elasticity is zero.

11. Figure 4.19 shows Dontay's weekly demand for bottled water. Show the information in this demand curve using budget constraints and indifference curves. Assume that he has \$10 per week to spend.

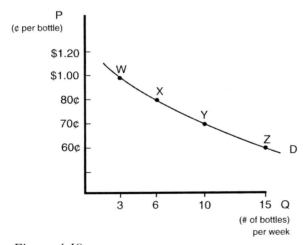

Figure 4.19

12. Use the Slutsky equation to explain why a rise in the price of gasoline is likely to have more of an effect on consumers than a rise in the price of strawberry milkshakes, even if the price of each good rises by the same percentage.

13. Suppose that an early frost destroys ALL of the Florida orange crops. California oranges are unharmed. Assuming that Florida oranges were considered to be part of a consumer's market basket prior to the frost, carefully explain why both a Laspeyres-type price index like the CPI and Paasche index will mismeasure the effect on consumer inflation.

Chapter 5
Consumer Welfare and Policy Analysis

■ Chapter Summary

In Chapter 5, we extend the tools developed in Chapters 3 and 4 to further examine the consumer's utility-maximizing problem and in particular, to measure consumer welfare and how it is changed by various government policies.

Consumer welfare is generally measured by the net benefits of consuming a good, the difference between the total benefit received and the amount paid for the good. This can be measured via to the inverse demand curve (the ordinary demand curve, $Q = f(P)$ rearranged so that $P = f(Q)$). The inverse demand curve measures a consumer's **marginal willingness to pay**, or the marginal value placed on the last unit purchased. The sum of the marginal values of each unit purchased is equal to the total value of consuming a given number of units, or the total area under the demand curve at a given price. **Consumer surplus** is the monetary difference between what a consumer is willing to pay and the actual cost of the good(s). Graphically, this is the area under the individual's inverse demand curve and above the market price, up to the quantity that the consumer actually buys. Likewise, market consumer surplus is equal to the area under the market inverse demand curve and above the market price, up to the quantity that consumers purchase. Price increases reduce consumer surplus, both by decreasing the quantity that consumers purchase and by reducing the surplus on each remaining unit.

Although economists usually use ordinary demand curves to measure consumer surplus, ideally, consumer surplus changes would be measured by the income that would be needed to offset the effect of a price change, holding utility constant. In other words, this is the amount of income that the consumer would need to compensate for a price increase, if utility does not change. Along a compensated demand curve, the change in quantity is a pure substitution effect; the income needed to reach the compensated quantity is an exact measure of consumer surplus. One method of calculating this amount of income is by finding the difference in consumer expenditure functions at different prices, holding utility constant. But which level of utility should be used? The amount of money that would be needed to compensate a consumer for the utility loss from a price increase is called **compensating variation**. The amount of money that would have to be taken from a consumer (at the original price ratio) to reduce utility *as much as the price increase does* is called **equivalent variation**. Both measures of variation are found using indifference curve analysis. The relationship between the three measures of welfare changes depends on income elasticity, as can be seen via the Slutsky equation. In practice, most goods have relatively low budget shares, and thus there is little difference between the three measures.

A change in total consumer surplus shows the total effect of price changes on all consumers in the market. In general, consumer losses from a price increase are larger when a large amount is spent on the good and when demand is inelastic. Thus policymakers can reduce consumer losses from taxation through wise choice of markets. Government policies that have an impact on market quantities and prices change consumer surplus and thus consumer welfare. In this chapter, we consider two types of policies, quota-type programs in which the government either restricts the quantity of goods in the market or provides a consumer with additional unit of a good, and tax/subsidy programs in which the government changes the price of the good.

Quotas are limits on the amount of a good that can be purchased. They reduce consumer welfare if the consumer would have purchased more than the quota amount if the quota did not exist. Likewise, government "gift" programs such as food stamps and housing vouchers increase consumer welfare, but in general, not by as much as an equivalent gift of cash. Similarly, the government subsidizes goods and services such as child care, lowering the price to the consumer. Although again, providing child-care subsidizes increases consumer welfare, a lump-sum gift of cash would increase consumer welfare by a greater amount under most circumstances.

In another application of indifference curve analysis, a consumer chooses between leisure and other goods, subject to a time constraint and a budget constraint tied to the rate at which time can be converted into money—the wage rate. As the wage rate rises, the budget constraint rotates upward. The consumer selects the quantity of income and leisure that maximizes utility. As the wage rate rises, the consumer's decisions trace out a demand for leisure curve which can be easily converted into a **labor supply curve**. A rising wage rate generates a substitution effect that induces more work—at a higher wage leisure is more expensive, so less is purchased, and more work is done. A rising wage rate also increases income and generates an income effect—if leisure is a normal good, the individual will want more leisure as rising wages bring higher income. Thus, if leisure is a normal good (and most evidence says that it is), the substitution and income effects work in opposite directions, so rising wages have an ambiguous effect on the demand for leisure and the supply of labor. If the substitution effect is stronger, the labor supply curve will slope upward. If the income effect is stronger, labor supply will decrease as wages rise—bending backward. Empirical evidence suggests that labor supply curves are nearly vertical for many people. In this case the income and substitution effects are approximately equal.

The income and substitution effects resulting from changes in the wage rate can also be used to analyze the effect of changes in marginal income tax rates. If labor supply curves are upward sloping, increases in marginal income tax rates will tend to reduce hours of work (since substitution effects exceed income effects), and thus raising income tax rates is both a bad idea in terms of economic growth and also a relatively poor way to increase government income. If the labor supply curve is vertical or backward bending, the opposite is true, since income effects exceed substitution effects, and workers will increase hours worked in response to the tax increase. Since empirical studies suggest that the labor supply is nearly vertical for many workers, small increases in tax rates must increase tax revenues, but for sufficiently high marginal tax rates, workers move to the upward-sloping part of their labor supply curves, and increases in tax rates reduce tax revenues. Thus the tax revenue curve is bell-shaped, and there is some **optimal tax rate**.

■ Key Concepts and Formulas

- **Consumer welfare:** net benefits of consuming a good; the difference between the total benefit received and the amount paid for the good.
- **Inverse demand curve:** the ordinary demand curve, $Q = f(P)$ rearranged so that $P = f(Q)$.
- **Marginal willingness to pay; marginal value:** marginal willingness to pay is the maximum amount that a consumer will pay for another unit; this is the same as the marginal value of the good, the value that the consumer receives from the last unit of the product.
- **Consumer surplus:** the area under the individual's inverse demand curve and above the market price, up to the quantity that the consumer actually buys.
- **Compensating variation:** the amount of money that would be needed to compensate a consumer for the utility loss from a price increase.
- **Equivalent variation:** the amount of money that would have to be taken from a consumer (at the original price ratio) to reduce utility as much as the price increase would.
- **Quota:** limit on the amount of a good that can be purchased.
- **Subsidy:** reduction in the price per unit of a good.

- **Labor supply curve:** the relationship between hours worked and the wage rate.
- **Marginal tax rate:** tax rate on the last dollar of income earned.
- **Optimal tax rate:** tax rate that maximized tax revenues.

■ Application: Pigeon Labor Supply Curves

Economic theory is based on the assumption that people make rational choices in the face of scarce resources. This theory has been used to examine a wide range of choices, including the decision about how much labor to supply. Animals have to make choices among scarce resources, too. Like most humans, animals have to work in order to consume.

Question: Do animals make rational choices? What is the shape of animals' labor supply curves?

Answer: Experimental evidence suggests that animals do make rational choices and that animal workers have backward-bending labor supply curves at higher wages. Researchers at Texas A&M and Washington University examined the income-leisure choices of pigeons. Male White Carneaux pigeons (with no previous experimental history) were given the job of pecking a response key for a 3-second access to a food hopper containing mixed grains. Wages could be altered by varying the number of pecks required for a payoff from 12.5 pecks to 400 pecks. Unearned income could be varied by providing free access for 3 seconds to the food hopper at regular intervals. Thus by varying both the wage rate and the unearned income, the experimenters could determine the substitution effect of a wage change and the income effect.

The researchers found that pigeons are willing to trade income for leisure if the price is right. More specifically:

- Pigeons consume more leisure as the price of work rises and they are compensated with extra unearned income. The experimenters lowered the wage (raising the number of pecks needed to get food), which decreased the price of leisure. To compensate the pigeons, they also increased the amount of food the pigeons got without working. As the price of leisure fell and they were compensated with more unearned income, the pigeons consumed more leisure.
- Leisure is always a normal good. As the pigeons' income increased—that is, as they got more food without working—the pigeons consumed more leisure by spending less time pecking.
- Pigeons' labor supply curves are backward bending. At low wages, increasing the wage yields more work, but at higher wages, increasing the wage yields less work.
- With increases in wages, both income and substitution effects get smaller, but the substitution term decreases more rapidly than the income term.

If pigeons were not rational and followed some arbitrary rule such as working a constant percent of the time, they would not respond to wage and income changes in this systematic, nonconstant manner. Rational behavior makes it much easier for this and any other species to succeed in a world of scarcity and competition.

Source: Raymond Battalio, Leonard Green, and John Kagel, "Income-Leisure Tradeoffs of Animal Workers," *American Economic Review,* September 1981.

■ Solved Problems

1. Remember Michael, from Chapter 3, Solved Problem 1, and Chapter 4, Solved Problem 2? He's back again! Michael's utility function is:

$$U(q_1, q_2) = q_1 q_2,$$

where q_1 is the quantity of pizza (slices) and q_2 is the quantity of milk (cups). His monthly food budget is $120, the price of pizza (p_1) is $3, and the price of milk (p_2) is $2. Previously, we found that with this level of income and prices, Michael's utility-maximizing bundle is $q_1 = 20$, $q_2 = 30$, and with this combination, his level of utility is 600. In Chapter 4, Michael was happy to find that the price of pizza had fallen to $2, and thus his utility increased. Now, Michael wants to know the compensating and equivalent variation from the fall in the price of pizza.

Step 1: Find compensating variation.

Since the price of pizza *fell,* compensating variation is the amount of money that we would have to *take away* from Michael to keep him at a utility level of 600, his original level of utility. Since we already found the income and substitution effects of this price change in Chapter 4, Solved Problem 1, it is easy to find compensating variation. Michael's compensated bundle was 24.5 slices of pizza and 24.5 cups of milk (we could round these quantities to whole numbers, but for exactness, let's leave them as is). The cost of this bundle at the new prices is $E = 2(24.5) + 2(24.5) = \$98$. Since Michael's income is $120, the amount that we would have to take away from him to leave his utility unchanged is $(120 - 98) = \$22$. This is compensating variation.

Note that if we had not already solved for the compensated bundle, we could have found the answer to this problem by using the expenditure function, which we also found (in Chapter 3). Plug in the new prices and the old level of utility, and solve for expenditure. Again, compensating variation will be the difference between Michael's income and the expenditure that would be required to attain the original utility level.

Step 2: Find equivalent variation.

Equivalent variation is the amount of money that it would take to make Michael *just as well off* (at the original price ratio) as he is with the price change. To find this, we need to find what Michael would have needed to spend to achieve his new level of utility, if prices had not changed. Michael's new level of utility is 900 (from Chapter 4, Solved Problem 1). From Chapter 3, Solved Problem 2, Michael's expenditure function is:

$$E = 2\sqrt{\overline{U} p_1 p_2}$$

Substituting the new utility level, 900, the old price of pizza, $3, and the price of milk, $2, gives us expenditure of $146.96. Thus, at the old level of prices, we would have to give Michael an additional $26.96 to make him just as happy as the price increase makes him.

Note that the two measures of changes in consumer welfare give very similar results. We could also find Michael's change in consumer surplus using the compensated demand curve found in Chapter 4, which would give a similar result.

2. The Hormsbury family's income is $1000 per period, the price of illegal drugs is $50 per dose, and the price of food is $10 per bag. The family initially purchases 80 bags of food and 4 doses of drugs. Both are normal goods for the Hormsburys. The government wishes to reduce the Hormsburys' drug consumption and gives them 50 bags of free food per period. There are two questions we wish to answer about the effect on the Hormsburys.

   a.   Does the policy work? That is, will the Hormsburys consumer fewer drugs?

   b.   If the government is only interested in making the Hormsburys happier and doesn't care what they consume, is this the most effective way of doing it?

Step 1: Draw the initial budget constraint and mark the initial equilibrium.

The end points are $I/p_F = \$1000/\$10 = 100$ and $I/p_D = \$1000/\$50 = 20$. Notice that 80 bags of food cost $800 and 4 doses of drugs cost $200. This total is $1000, so it does fall on the budget constraint. See budget constraint BC_0 in Figure 5.1.

Step 2: Draw the new budget constraint.

The end point on the food axis rises by 50 bags, so it is now 150 bags. The slope of the budget constraint doesn't change since the prices of food and drugs haven't changed. However, the end point of the budget constraint on the drugs axis has not changed—the family cannot buy more than 20 doses of drugs. There must be a flat section on the new budget constraint to represent the "free" food. Anytime you get something for free, you don't have to give up anything to get it; hence, this family gets the first 50 bags of food without giving up any drugs. See budget constraint BC_1 in Figure 5.1.

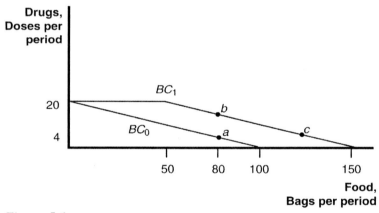

Figure 5.1

Step 3: Decide how the family reacts to the new budget constraint, and answer the questions.

Since both goods are normal and the free food shifts the budget constraint outward—just like an increase in income—then the family increases the consumption of both goods. The family's new consumption bundle is somewhere to the "northeast" of point *a*—somewhere between points *b* and *c*. The answer to the first question is, the good intentions of the government have failed: The Hormsburys have used the governmental largesse to subsidize their bad habit. Policy makers must take such a possible outcome into account. The answer to the second question is, it is likely that the Hormsburys would have been happier (and certainly would have been just as happy) with a gift of an equivalent amount of cash.

To see this, first note that the value of the government's gift is (50)(10) = $500. Draw a new graph showing the Hormsburys' budget constraint with the gift of food, and draw a new budget constraint showing the effect of a gift of cash, as in Figure 5.2. Note that every point that is attainable with the food gift is also attainable with the cash gift and that the Hormsburys originally consumed 80 bags of food, so it is unlikely that they would reduce their consumption of food if they were given more income (unless food is an inferior good). Thus they are likely to be indifferent between a cash gift and a food gift. However, for a family who would prefer to consume fewer than 50 bags of food, the cash gift would increase utility more. They would be able to buy bundles on the dashed line segment, attainable with the cash grant but not with the food gift. Thus if the government cares about increasing happiness but does not care how its gifts are used, cash grants are a more effective (and generally less costly) means of attaining a given level of utility.

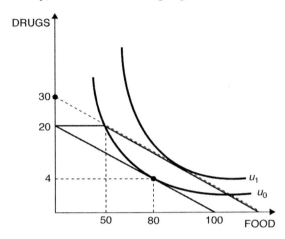

Figure 5.2

3. Andy frequents a pub called the Boar's Head, where he has been in the habit of eating 10 meals per month, at $10 per meal.

   a. The Boar's Head offers him membership in the Pig's Breath Club (ugh), which costs $50 per month to join, but lowers the price per dinner to $5 for that month. Will Andy accept the membership?

   Step 1: Carefully draw the initial and the new budget constraints.

   Problem? There is only one good, so what do I put on the other axis? Answer: Put any good, or "all other goods," or (simplest of all) income on the other axis. Income can be thought of as a good (a "composite commodity") because it measures the dollar amount of all other goods that can be purchased. Since we don't know Andy's exact income, we'll simply call it $Y. Figure 4.3 shows the initial budget constraint (BC_1) starting at $Y on the vertical axis, with a slope of –$10. It means that he can trade off $10 to get a meal. Joining the club gives him the new budget constraint (BC_2) that starts at $Y but immediately falls to $Y – 50. This shows that he must give up $50 to join the club—that is, he has spent $50 and still has no meals. BC_2's slope is flatter: only –$5 per meal. The two budget constraints intersect at $Y – 100 and 10 meals. This is exactly where Andy has been consuming (point *a*).

   Step 2: VERY carefully, draw in the indifference curve that is associated with his initial consumption bundle.

   Since we assume that he has been maximizing utility, the slope of this indifference curve (I_1) must be the same as the slope of the initial budget constraint (BC_1). If I_1 is tangent to BC_1, it cannot be tangent to BC_2. It must cut through BC_2. (You will only see this if you draw carefully.)

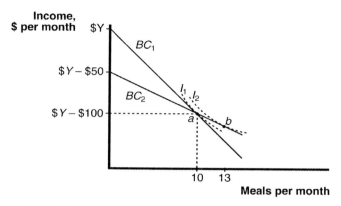

Figure 5.3

Step 3: Decide whether or not he'll go for the meal deal.

Careful examination of Figure 5.3 shows that Andy can reach a higher indifference curve, such as I_2, if he joins the club and moves to a point like *b*. The meal deal allows him to stay at his initial consumption point, *a*, but it also allows him to reach points along BC_2 past point *a*, which he couldn't reach before. In all likelihood he will join the club. The figure shows that the tenth meal is worth exactly $10 to Andy. If his indifference curves change slope slowly, this implies that the eleventh meal is worth a bit less than $10 to Andy, say, $9. But joining the club allows him to buy this meal for only $5, so he'll join the club and buy extra meals. Only if the slope of the indifference curve changes quickly, so that the eleventh meal is worth less than $5, will he decline to join the club.

b.   The Boar's Head offers Andy membership in the Pig's Breath Club, which costs $50 per month to join, but lowers the price per dinner to $6 for that month. Will Andy accept the membership offer this time?

Step 1: Carefully draw the initial and the new budget constraints.

The budget constraints are exactly the same as in the first part of this problem, except that now BC_2 is steeper, with a slope of $-\$6$ per meal. The two budget constraints intersect at 12.5 meals, where Andy has spent $125. See Figure 5.4. You can find this intersection algebraically by setting the two budget constraints equal to one another and solving for M, the number of meals

$$BC_1 = \$Y - \$10M, \quad \text{while} \quad BC_2 = \$Y - \$50 - \$6M.$$
$$\$Y - \$10M = \$Y - \$50 - \$6M.$$

Subtract $\$Y$ from both sides. Add $\$6M$ to both sides. This yields:

$$-\$4M = \$50, \quad \text{so} \quad M = 12.5.$$

Notice that Andy can no longer consume his initial consumption bundle (point *a*) if he joins the club. However, BC_2 is not entirely inside the opportunity set associated with BC_1. There are some consumption bundles that are attainable if he joins the club, but which were not attainable before.

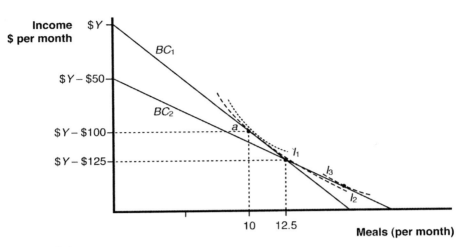

Figure 5.4

Step 2: VERY carefully consider all possible indifference curves that are consistent with the initial consumption bundle.

There are important restrictions on the shape and position of Andy's indifference curves, but there are still a lot of different possibilities. The indifference curve must be drawn so that it is tangent to BC_1 at point *a*. (This is required if Andy is maximizing his utility initially.) It must slope downward, because both income and meals are goods. The curve should show some convexity, since it is doubtful that meals and income are perfect substitutes. One possibility is indifference curve I_1 (drawn with dots). However, another possibility is an indifference curve, like I_2 (drawn with dashes), which does not change its slope so quickly.

Step 3: Decide whether or not he'll go for the meal deal.

If Andy's tastes are like those in indifference curve I_1, then he won't join the club. If Andy's tastes are like those in indifference curve I_2, then he can do better by joining the club, eating more than 10 meals, and reaching a higher indifference curve, like I_3. So, the answer is, "It depends." This is a common answer in economics, because people are not cookie cutter copies of one another.

4. In the text, consumer theory has been applied to choices among products and to choices between goods and leisure. It can also be applied to the allocation of resources over time, intertemporal choice. Shawn Hormsbury earns $50,000 during year one, but he won't be able to work in year two. Shawn cannot borrow, but he can earn 10 percent interest per year. Shawn saves $25,000 of the $50,000 that he earns.

    a. Using budget lines and an indifference curve, show Shawn's decision.

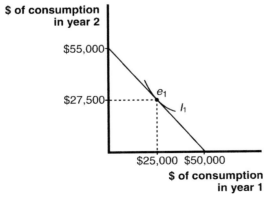

Figure 5.5

Step 1: Construct the budget line.

The key to all consumer analysis is to decide which good to put on each axis and to understand the trade-off between these two goods. Saving does not yield utility directly; it is only a good when consumed in a later period. Therefore, put consumption in year one on one axis and consumption in year two on the other axis. The trade-off between current period and future period consumption is the rate of interest. Shawn can give up $1 in year one consumption and get $1.10 in year two consumption, because the interest rate on savings is 10 percent. Figure 5.5 puts current consumption on the horizontal axis. Notice that the maximum consumption in year one is $50,000—if Shawn spends all his income and saves nothing. Period two consumption is on the vertical axis. The maximum possible consumption in year two is $55,000. If Shawn saves all $50,000, it will earn 10 percent interest, yielding $55,000—($50,000 × (1 + the interest rate))—in period two.

Step 2: Show Shawn's maximizing point.

We assume that the point he chooses is the best possible point for him—a point of tangency between the budget line and the highest indifference curve that he can reach according to the figure. Shawn maximizes by consuming $25,000 and saving $25,000, which allows him to consume $27,500 in period two, at point e_1 along indifference curve I_1.

b. Suppose that the interest rate rises from 10 percent to 30 percent. Will Shawn save more or less when the interest rate rises to 30 percent? Explain by comparing the substitution effect and the income effect.

Step 1: Determine how the increase in the interest rate changes the budget line.

The higher interest rate on savings will not change the maximum amount that he can consume in year one, but it will increase the maximum amount that he can consume in year two. The new maximum is $65,000. Thus the budget line becomes steeper to reflect the increase in the interest rate. Figure 5.6 shows this as the budget line rotates from L_1 to L_2.

Step 2: Determine how he will respond to the new budget line.

As Figure 5.6 shows, there are many potential responses. When the interest rate was 10 percent, Shawn chose point e_1. The new equilibrium point can be at a point like A, where consumption in year one has risen, and therefore, savings has fallen. It could be at a point like B, where savings and year one consumption are unchanged. Or, it could be at a point like C, where consumption in year one falls and savings rises. The indifference curves that are tangent at these points are consistent with the initial indifference curve, I_1.

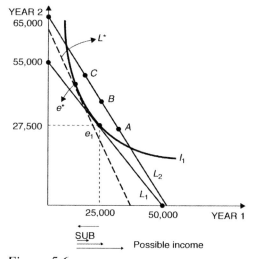

Figure 5.6

Step 3: Show the income and substitution effects of the change in the interest rate.

Remember that the substitution effect identifies how the consumer would move along the initial indifference curve if faced with the new price (interest rate, in this case). Find the point on the initial indifference curve, I_1, that has the same slope as the new, steeper budget line, L_2. This is point e^* in Figure 5.6. (Budget line L^*, which is parallel to L_2, has been drawn in to show that I_1's slope is the same as L_2's at point e^*.) Notice that the substitution effect must have a positive influence on savings—a negative effect on consumption in year one. The relative price of consuming in year one has risen in comparison to the price of consuming in year two. Previously, Shawn had to give up $1.10 in year two if he spent $1 in year one; now he must give up $1.30 in year two if he consumes $1 in year one. For most people, consumption in year one and consumption in year two are normal goods. The interest rate hike makes Shawn richer, so he wants to consume more now and more later. The income effect will counteract the substitution effect, but we cannot predict which one will be stronger. If the income effect is smaller than the substitution effect, Shawn will go to a point like C, and save more as the interest rate rises. If the income effect is larger than the substitution effect, then he will go to a point like A, and save less. Empirical evidence suggests that for most people the income and substitution effects are approximately equal, so they go to point B and do not change their savings as the interest rate on savings rises (or falls).

■ Practice Problems

Multiple-Choice

1. If an individual worker's labor supply curve slopes upward, which of the following is true?
   a. The substitution effect of a wage change is greater than the income effect of a wage change.
   b. The substitution effect of a wage change is equal to the income effect of a wage change.
   c. The substitution effect of a wage change is less than the income effect of a wage change.
   d. The worker is not sensitive to wage changes.

2. Kathleen purchases dental floss and toothbrushes. The price of toothbrushes rises. Kathleen's equivalent variation would measure
   a. the amount of money we would have to take away from Kathleen to make her just as unhappy as the price increase does.
   b. the area under Kathleen's compensated demand curve for toothbrushes.
   c. the amount of money we would have to give Kathleen to keep her just as happy, given the new price of toothbrushes.
   d. the area under Kathleen's ordinary demand curve for toothbrushes.

3. Consumer surplus measures
   a. the utility that a consumer receives from the purchase of a given quantity of goods.
   b. the total value that a consumer receives from the purchase of a given quantity of goods.
   c. the marginal value that a consumer receives from the purchase of a given quantity of goods.
   d. the net benefit, in terms of dollars, that a consumer receives from the purchase of a given quantity of goods.
   e. the net benefit, in terms of utility, that a consumer receives from the purchase of a given quantity of goods.

Fill-in

4. A rising wage causes both an income and a substitution effect. The _____ effect causes people to want to work more hours. In Figure 5.7, the income effect must be stronger than the substitution effect between points _____. The income effect and the substitution effect must be equal between points _____.

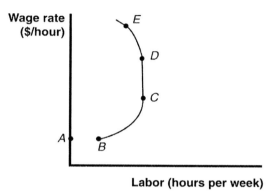

Figure 5.7

5. If the labor supply curve is backward-bending, an increase in the marginal income tax rate will cause an _____ in tax revenues.

True-False-Ambiguous and Explain Why

6. In 2001, Joe earned $20 per hour and subscribed to an Internet provider who charged $1 per hour for access. In 2004, Joe earned $25 per hour. His Internet access fee was cut to $0.25 per hour. Therefore between 2001 and 2004, the cost of an hour of recreational Web surfing fell.

7. Consumers always prefer a gift of cash to an in-kind gift (such as food).

8. If the government wishes to increase the utility of consumers *by a specific amount,* it is less expensive to do that through a cash gift than through a price subsidy on a commonly purchased good (such as food).

Short-Answer

9. Noriko buys paperback books and CDs. Her utility function is $U = 10B^{1/2}C^{1/2}$. The price of a book is $10, and the price of a CD is $10. She currently spends her $200 budget buying 10 books and 10 CDs. When the price of CDs rises to $15, she chooses to buy 10 books and 5 CDs. Find Noriko's equivalent variation, and explain what it means.

10. In Problem 9, you had to find Noriko's equivalent variation. Now find her compensating variation, and explain what it means.

11. Brick Hormsbury's income is enough to allow him to buy Q_1 units of quiz books (if he spends everything on quiz books) or O_1 units of other stuff (if he spends everything on other stuff) and combinations in between. Brick enters and wins the Quiz Bowl sweepstakes. The entry fee is O_2 units of other stuff. The prize allows him to get quiz books at half price. Show Brick's initial and final budget constraints. How much better off does winning the prize make him?

12. Martin has very specific preferences. He likes one slice of toast (T) with one fried egg (E), and no other combination gives him additional utility. Thus his utility function is $U = \min(T, E)$. Currently he spends his $12 breakfast budget buying 6 eggs and 6 slices of toast. Suppose that the price of eggs rises to $2.

   a. Find Martin's new utility-maximizing point.

   b. Find compensating and equivalent variation.

13. Suppose that the law requires that employees receive overtime pay at time-and-a-half after working more than 8 hours in a day, and double-time after 12 hours in a day. Draw a typical worker's budget constraint. Show that a worker with usual-shaped indifference curves over income and leisure may be indifferent between two or three combinations of income and leisure.

14. In many less-developed countries, there are large "informal" sectors of the economy, part of the economy where workers work off the record (and thus are not likely to pay income taxes). Would the existence of a large informal sector make it more or less likely that a tax increase would lower government revenues? Explain.

15. Lizzie Hormsbury has a job that pays $10 per hour, but she must commute for 3 hours a day to get to work. Initially she works 8 hours per day. Draw her budget line. Would she work more hours if her commute fell to 1 hour? Would she consume more or less leisure?

16. Henry Hormsbury has become eligible to receive the negative income tax (NIT). If he earns $0 per day, the NIT provides him with $20 per day. However, every extra dollar he earns reduces his NIT payment by 50 percent. If he earns $40, therefore, he is no longer eligible for the NIT. Before the existence of the NIT he earned $5 per hour and worked 8 hours per day. How will this NIT affect his decision to work? Draw the budget lines he faces before and after the existence of the NIT.

17. Tom's wage is $10 per hour; Sam's is $5 per hour. Tom works 6 hours a day. Sam works 8 hours per day. Is Tom lazier than Sam?

18. Julie must commute 2 hours per day when she works. Based on Figure 5.8, graph Julie's labor supply curve.

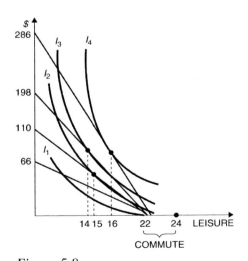

Figure 5.8

19. How would the budget line with food stamps in Figure 5.7 of the text change if there were an illegal market for food stamps in which food stamps sold for 80 cents on the dollar?

20. Describe the labor supply curve of a target earner who will work the maximum number of hours possible if earnings are below $96 per day, but will cut back hours to maintain an income of $96 per day as the wage rate rises. Draw budget constraints and indifference curves that show this and draw the corresponding labor supply curve.

21. At many colleges, seniors are given a specific number of tickets to the graduation ceremony. Since some students want more tickets, and some don't need many at all, usually no one is very happy! Consider three alternative ways of distributing graduation tickets.

    Plan A. Each senior is given 5 tickets and cannot buy or sell any tickets.

    Plan B. No free tickets are given, but you can buy and sell tickets at a price of $20.

    Plan C. Each senior is given 5 free tickets, *and* you can buy or sell tickets at a price of $20.

    a. Draw a budget constraint for each of the plans, putting tickets on the horizontal axis and a composite commodity on the vertical axis. Assume that every student has the same income.
    b. Prove that:
       • not all students will prefer Plan A to Plan B.
       • for every student, Plan C is at least as good as any other plan.

22. You have an income of $500. Currently, you spend all your money on fish and a composite good. The price of fish is $10, and at that price, you choose to buy 25 fish.
    a. You have received a fabulous offer to join the Fish of the Month Club. After paying a membership fee of $100, you will be able to buy fish at a price of $5. Draw your old budget constraint and utility-maximizing point (with an indifference curve), and your new budget constraint if you join the club.
    b. Assuming that you have ordinary, convex preferences, would you be likely to join the Fish of the Month Club? How will this impact your consumption of fish?
    c. The Fish of the Month Club is under new management. Membership is now FREE.

       If you join,
       i. You get a fabulous welcome package that gives you 5 FREE fish from around the world.
       ii. You are obligated to buy a minimum of 10 fish in the current time period at a price of $15/fish.
       iii. After you fulfill your membership agreement, you can buy additional fish at a price of $8.

       Draw your ORIGINAL budget constraint and your new budget constraint. Would you be likely to join the Fish of the Month Club now? Carefully explain. (20 points)

23. Ian's inverse demand curve for amusement park rides is $P = 10 - q$, where q is the number of rides.
    a. If the price of rides is $3, how many rides will he buy, how much money will he spend, and what is his consumer surplus?
    b. If the amusement park changes its admission policy to a $40 entry fee but rides are free, will Ian go? If so, how many rides will Ian go on, and what is his consumer surplus?

24. Suppose that you spend all of your income on Good X and a composite good, Y, and you have ordinary convex indifference curves. The government is considering two tax programs. The first is a per unit sales tax of $t on Good X only. The second is a lump-sum tax of $T. Prove that if the taxes are equivalent (that is, if the taxes are set so that you will pay the same absolute amount of dollars under either program), you will be better of with the lump-sum tax.

25. Consider Problem 24. Show that if Good X and the composite commodity Y are perfect complements, you would be indifferent between the two types of taxes (as long as they are equivalent).

■ Answers to Practice Problems

1. a.

2. a.

3. e.

4. substitution; D and E; C and D

5. increase

6. False. The price of his leisure activity includes the price of time, which rose much more rapidly than the price of Internet access fell.

7. True or ambiguous (in the sense that some consumers will be indifferent between the two programs). See also Solved Problem 2. For consumers who would voluntarily purchase at least the quantity of food given by the government, the two programs are equivalent. Consumers who would choose to purchase less than the gift amount of food are better off with the cash (can reach a higher indifference curve).

8. True or ambiguous (in the unlikely case that some consumers will be indifferent between the two programs if goods are perfect complements). A reduction in the price of food induces both income and substitution effects, and thus consumers buy relatively more food than they did before. A gift of cash has income effects but not substitution effects. See Figure 5.9; Y is a composite commodity, so the vertical axis measures income.

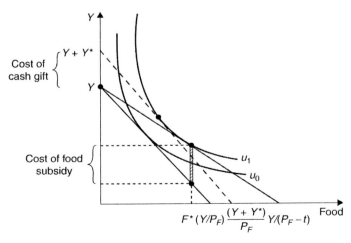

Figure 5.9

9. Noriko's equivalent variation is the amount of money that we would have to *take away* from her to make her just as unhappy as the price increase does. To find this, first note that Noriko's original level of utility was $U_0 = 10(10)^{1/2}(10)^{1/2} = 100$. Her new level of utility is $U_1 = 10(10)^{1/2}(5)^{1/2} = 70.71$. To find what combination of books and CDs Noriko would buy at the *original* price ratio but at the new level of utility, find the first-order condition using the original price ratio.

$$\frac{MU_B}{MU_C} = \frac{P_B}{P_C}$$

$$\frac{\frac{1}{2}B^{-1/2}C^{1/2}}{\frac{1}{2}B^{1/2}C^{-1/2}} = \frac{10}{10}$$

$$\frac{C}{B} = 1$$

$$C = B$$

Now, use the equation of the *new* indifference curve, and solve for B and C.

$$U_1 = 10B^{1/2}C^{1/2} = 70.71$$

$$10(B)^{1/2}(B)^{1/2} = 70.71$$

$$B = C = 7 \text{ (rounded to nearest whole number)}$$

What would it have cost Noriko to buy 7 books and 7 CDs at the old price ratio? Her expenditure would have been $10(7) + $10(7) = $140. Her original income was $200. Thus her equivalent variation is $(200 - 140) = $60. This means that a $60 reduction in income would make her just as unhappy as the rise in price of CDs to $15.

10. Noriko's compensating variation is the amount of money that it would take to restore her original level of utility, given the new price ratio. To find what combination of books and CDs Noriko would buy at her original level of utility but the *new* price ratio, find the first-order conditions using the new price ratio.

$$\frac{MU_B}{MU_C} = \frac{P_B}{P_C}$$

$$\frac{\frac{1}{2}B^{-1/2}C^{1/2}}{\frac{1}{2}B^{1/2}C^{-1/2}} = \frac{10}{15}$$

$$\frac{C}{B} = \frac{2}{3}$$

$$C = \frac{2}{3}B$$

Now, use the equation of the *new* indifference curve, and solve for B and C.

$$U_1 = 10B^{1/2}C^{1/2} = 100$$

$$10(B)^{1/2}(2/3\ B)^{1/2} = 100$$

$$B = 12, C = 8 \text{ (rounded to nearest whole numbers)}$$

What would it cost Noriko to buy 12 books and 8 CDs at the new price ratio? Her expenditure would be $10(12) + $15(8) = $240. Her original income was $200. Thus her compensating variation is (240 − 200) = $40. This means that a $40 increase in income would be required to keep her just as happy as she originally was, given the new price of CDs.

There are two interesting things that can be noted from Problems 9 and 10. One is that compensating and equivalent variation are not, in general, the same amount. The other is that in Problem 10, the amount of income required to compensate Noriko is *less* than it would take for her to buy her original bundle at the new prices. This is one reason why the CPI overstates the effects of inflation, as discussed in Chapter 4. Since Noriko is willing to substitute some books for CDs, it doesn't take as much income to make her just as happy (at the new price ratio) as it would take for her to purchase her original bundle at the new price ratio.

11.   In Figure 5.10, Brick's new budget constraint, BC_2, begins at $O_1 − O_2$ on the vertical axis. This is the maximum amount of other stuff he could originally buy, minus the cost of entering the sweepstakes. The slope of BC_2 is half as steep as BC_1, because Quiz Books are now half-priced. Will he be better off? It depends on his tastes and on the size of the entry fee. If his tastes are like the solid indifference curves, then he is worse off (even though he might be buying more quiz books). If his tastes are like the dashed indifference curves, then he is better off. (Notice that in Figure 5.10 the price of entering the contest is pretty high—it looks as if he has given up about one-sixth of his other stuff just to enter the contest.)

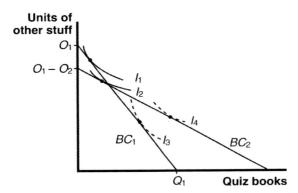

Figure 5.10

12.   a.   The easiest way to solve this is to note that it now costs $3 for Martin's combination. Thus with a budget of $12, he can buy 4 egg-and-toast combinations, so he will buy 4 eggs and 4 slices of toast.

      b.   These goods are perfect complements. Thus there is no substitution effect. To make Martin just as happy as he was originally, given the new prices, he would have to purchase exactly what he bought to begin with. At new prices, it would cost $18 to buy 6 eggs and 6 slices of toast, and thus his compensating variation would be $18 − $12 = $6. Likewise, to find equivalent variation, we need to know what he would purchase at the old price ratio but with his new utility level (which is 4). At *any* price ratio, to achieve a utility level of 4, Martin must buy 4 eggs and 4 slices of toast (since again, he will not substitute). This would cost $8 at the old price ratio. Thus his equivalent variation is $12 − $8 = $4. See Figure 5.11.

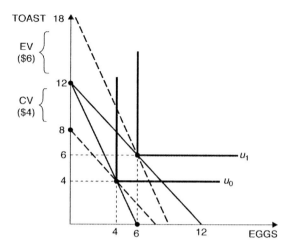

Figure 5.11

13. As Figure 5.12 shows, if the worker's wage is w, then income will be $8w$ after 8 hours. After 12 hours of work, income will be $8w$ for the first 8 hours, plus $1.5w$ per hour for the last 4 hours. Total income will be $14w$. There is a kink in the budget line; at 8 hours of labor (16 hours of leisure), it becomes steeper due to overtime pay. If the worker pulled a 24-hour shift, income would be $14w$ for the first 12 hours and $24w$ for the last 12 hours, so total income would be $38w$. The indifference curve has been drawn so that the worker is indifferent among points A, B, and C on the budget line.

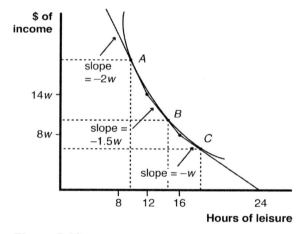

Figure 5.12

14. It is reasonable to assume that a large informal sector means that there is alternative employment available that is untaxed. While wages in these sectors tend to be far lower than in the formal sectors of the economy, if taxes are sufficiently high, these jobs would become more attractive. Thus the elasticity of supply of labor in the formal sector would be relatively larger. As discussed in the chapter, for an increase in taxes to result in a reduction in government revenue, the elasticity of labor supply must be greater than ($\tau/(1 - \tau)$), where τ is the tax rate. Thus numerically, a greater elasticity of labor supply would make it more likely that this condition would be met. Conceptually, with alternative employment available, it would be more probable that an increase in tax rates would cause workers to leave the formal sector, resulting in a reduction in work hours and thus lowering government tax revenues.

15. Lizzie's budget line is given in Figure 5.13. There is a flat section along the bottom because she must give up leisure (commuting) without gaining any income. When the commute is 3 hours, this flat section is 3 hours long and her maximum daily consumption (if she works 21 hours) is $210. As the commute shortens to 1 hour, the flat section shrinks to 1 hour and maximum daily income rises to $230. If both consumption and leisure are normal goods, then she will move to the northeast of her initial point. As she does, she will increase *both* leisure time and work time. (If one of the two is inferior, she could move to a point like *A*, where hours of leisure fall from 13 to 12 and hours worked climb from 8 to 11, or a point like *B*, where hours of leisure climb to 16, but hours of work fall to 7.)

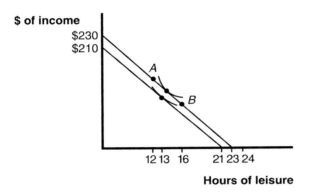

Figure 5.13

16. Figure 5.14 shows Henry's budget lines. L_1 has a slope of –$5 per hour, so it hits the vertical axis at $120 per day. L_2 rises vertically by $20 at 24 hours of leisure. This is the $20 which the NIT provides Henry when his income is $0 per day. The slope of L_2 is only –$2.50 per hour and it joins L_1 at 8 hours of work per day. Henry's initial equilibrium was at e_1, on indifference curve I_1. He can now reach indifference curve I_2 by working fewer hours. The movement from e_1 to e^* is the substitution effect. The movement from e^* to e_2 is the income effect. Both effects cause him to work less.

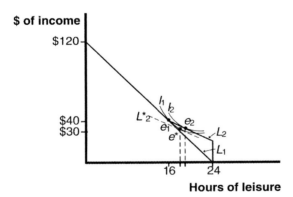

Figure 5.14

17. Figure 5.15 shows the decisions of Tom and Sam. L_T is Tom's budget line; e_T is his equilibrium point. L_S is Sam's budget line: e_S is his equilibrium point. It doesn't seem possible to decide who is lazier. After all, if Tom's wage was only $5 per hour, he might work 8 hours per day, just like Sam. If Sam's wage was $10 per hour, he might work 6 hours per day, just like Tom. Apparently, laziness depends on the contraints one faces. If they both faced the exact same budget constraint and Tom chose fewer hours, then we might be able to say that he is "lazy" compared to Sam.

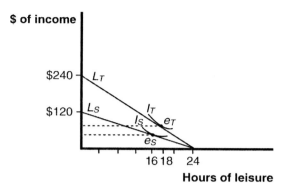

Figure 5.15

18. Using Figure 5.8, we can derive Figure 5.16. To figure out the wage rate in Figure 5.8, divide the end points of each budget line by 22 (since the wage rate × 22 hours gives the maximum she can earn per day). At the lowest wage, $3 per hour, Julie prefers to enjoy 24 hours of leisure per day. At $5 she is indifferent between working 7 hours per day (plus a 2 hour commute) and not working at all. (This wage, the lowest wage at which she is willing to work, is known as the reservation wage.) At $9 per hour, she reaches I_3 and works 8 hours per day. At $13 per hour, she works 6 hours per day.

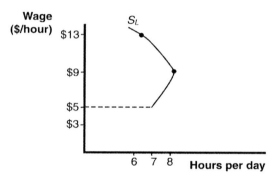

Figure 5.16

19. Figure 5.17 shows how the budget line would change. Because people can sell the $100 in food stamps for $80, the illegal market budget line reaches $Y + 80$. Its slope is −80 cents worth of other goods per every $1 worth of food, until all the food stamps were sold at point *e*. To the right of point *e* the two budget lines are the same.

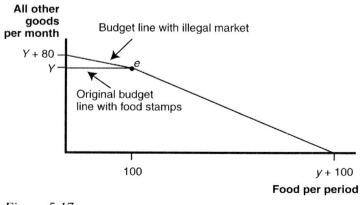

Figure 5.17

20. Figure 5.18(a) shows budget lines and indifference curves for a target earner whose target is $96 per day. Notice that at wages below $4 per hour, the target earner will work 24 hours per day. As the wage rises above $4 per hour, the target earner will reduce hours so that $4 times hours equals $96. Figure 5.18(b) plots the labor supply curve based on the information in Figure 5.18(b).

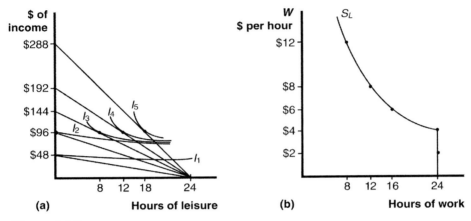

(a)   Hours of leisure   (b)   Hours of work

Figure 5.18

21. a.   See Figure 5.19. Note that Plan A is a single point, since tickets can be neither bought nor sold.

b.   Students with a strong preference for tickets (perhaps those with large and demanding families!) will have indifference curves that are tangent to the budget line at bundles that include more than 5 tickets. Thus they are better off with Plan B than Plan A, even though they must buy all their tickets. Plan C includes the single point in Plan A, and creates a larger opportunity set everywhere else, so every student is at least as well off with Plan C (students who preferred Plan B to Plan A are strictly better off with Plan C).

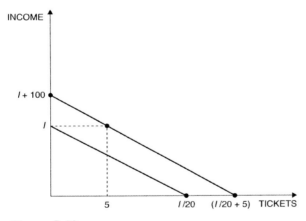

Figure 5.19

22. The equation of your old budget line is: $500 = 10F + I$, where I is other consumption. The equation of your new budget line is $400 = 5F + I$. These lines cross at the point (20, 300). See Figure 5.20(a).

b.   Yes, you will join the Fish of the Month Club. We know this because your original consumption point was rightward of where the budget constraints cross, and thus with convex preferences, you can reach levels of utility that you could not reach before if you join the club. You will also consume more fish (obvious, both because the price of fish fell and because it's the only way that you're better off).

c. Note first that to buy 15 fish before would have cost you $150. Now, you get 5 free fish and have to buy 10 at $15 ... it STILL costs you $150 for 15 fish! After that, you have $350 to spend on fish, and you now can buy another 43.75 fish (call it 44). Thus your maximum fish purchases are 59, the new budget is everywhere either greater than or equal to the old constraint, and anyone who was buying 25 fish before will absolutely join the club now. See Figure 5.20(b).

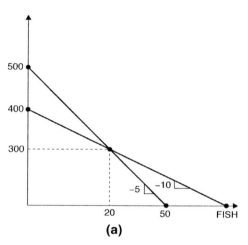

(a)

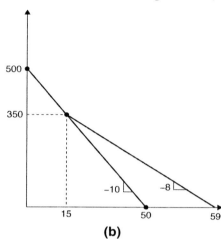

(b)

Figure 5.20

23. a. Ian will buy 7 rides at a price of $3/ride. He spends a total of $(7)(3) = \$21$, and his consumer surplus is $(9 - 3) + (8 - 3) + (7 - 3) + (6 - 3) + (5 - 3) + (4 - 3) + (3 - 3) = \$21$. (You could also assume that the demand curve is continuous; in this case, $CS = \frac{1}{2}(10 - 3)(7) = \$24.50$, but this slightly overestimates CS in this case, and is less correct since demand in this case is discrete; you can't buy something like a half of a ride.)

b. Since there is now no price per ride, Ian will ride 10 rides. The total price that he pays *for rides* is $0, and the total value that he receives is $(9 - 0) + (8 - 0) + (7 - 0) + (6 - 0) + (5 - 0) + (4 - 0) + (3 - 0) + (2 - 0) + (1 - 0) + (0 - 0) = \$45$. Since the admission fee is $40, the total value he receives for the package is greater than the cost of admission, and he will go to the park. His consumer surplus is $5, the difference between the $45 value that he receives from the rides and the $40 admission fee. (This type of pricing structure is called a *two-part tariff.*)

24. The trick to this type of problem is to draw the budget constraints correctly. Start by drawing an initial budget constraint (B_0). Then draw a budget constraint with the *sales* tax. Since only the price of good X changes, this budget constraint rotates inward on the X axis only (budget line B_1). Now draw an indifference curve that is tangent to this budget line. Figure 5.21(a) shows the problem this far. Then note that since the taxes are equivalent, there must be one point at which the consumer can buy the same amount under either program. Thus the budget constraint with the lump-sum tax (B_2) must go through the utility-maximizing point on B_1 but be parallel to B_0. If you drew your indifference curve so that is strictly convex, it is easy to see that the consumer can reach a higher indifference curve with the lump-sum tax than with the sales tax (Figure 5.21(b)). This is because the sales tax has both an income and a substitution effect, while the lump-sum tax has only an income effect.

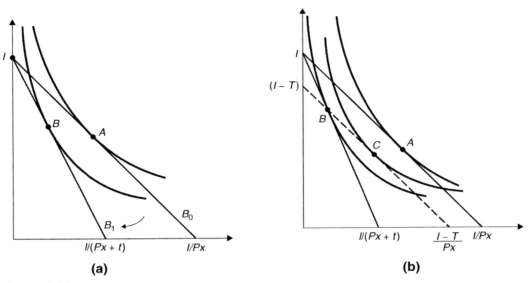

(a)   **(b)**

Figure 5.21

25. In this case, there is no substitution effect. Thus the lump-sum tax and the sales tax will have exactly the same effect, and the consumer would be indifferent between them. See Figure 5.22.

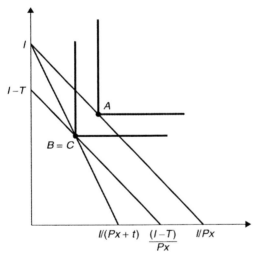

Figure 5.22

■ Exercises

True-False-Ambiguous and Explain Why

1. It is better to receive cash than socks for Christmas, even if you absolutely love socks.

2. Consumer surplus measures the total value that a consumer receives from purchasing a good.

Short Answer

3. Cameron buys cheese (C) and chocolate pudding (P). His utility function is $U = 5C^{1/4}P^{3/4}$. The price of cheese is $1, and the price of chocolate pudding is $2. Cameron's weekly snack budget is $50.

   a. Find Cameron's utility-maximizing point.

   b. Find Cameron's compensating and equivalent variation if the price of pudding falls to $1.

4. Suppose that in 1990, the price of bread was $2 per loaf and the price of milk was $1 per gallon. By 2000, the price of bread rises to $3 per loaf, and the price of milk rises to $2 per gallon. Assume that consumers have convex indifference curves, and that consumer incomes do not change over the time period. The government, concerned about the loss in consumer purchasing power, wishes to subsidize consumers. Prove graphically and explain why it will be less expensive to give consumers enough money to restore their original level of utility than to allow them to purchase their original consumption bundle.

5. Barbara earns $10 per hour at her regular job, where her maximum daily shift is 8 hours. If she wants to earn more (moonlight), she can work as many hours as she wants at $5 an hour. Initially, she works exactly 8 hours per day. Then the wage on her moonlighting job rises to $10 an hour. Show this graphically. Will Barbara work more hours? Is she necessarily better off now?

6. Aaron Hormsbury has a job that pays $10 per hour, but he must pay for child care if he works. The local day care center bills in four-hour increments and charges $10 per four-hour block. Draw his budget line.

7. Unfortunately, Louisa's wage has fallen from $10 to $5 per hour. Fortunately, she has inherited enough money so that she now earns $60 per day even when she works zero hours per day, so her utility is the same as it was before the wage was cut. How will this fall in wages coincident with an increase in non-wage income affect her hours of work? Draw a graph.

8. Sabrina currently works 10 hours per week at a wage of $50 per hour, and receives $1000 per week in investment income. For Sabrina, leisure is a neutral good; that is, an increase in income will not cause her to increase (or decrease) her consumption of leisure. Which would increase her utility by a greater amount, a 10% increase in investment income, or a 20% increase in the wage? Use a graph to prove your answer.

9. Becky's weekly demand curve for drinks is $q = 12 - \frac{1}{2}P$.

   a. The pub on the corner sells drinks for $6. How many drinks will Becky buy, and what is her consumer surplus?

   b. A new bar opens across the street. At the new bar, drinks are $4, but you have to pay a $20 (weekly) cover charge to go into the bar. Will Becky go to the new bar or to her original pub?

   c. Now suppose that the pub closes. Will Becky be willing to go to the bar now?

10. The Ant and the Grasshopper have different intertemporal utility functions. The Ant likes to save for the future, while the Grasshopper prefers to have a good time now. Both can borrow and lend at an interest rate of 5%, and each receives $20,000 income Now and $20,000 income Later.

    a. Graph the budget constraint for each insect, and explain how their consumption choices are likely to be different.

    b. Suppose that the interest rate rises to 10%. Using income and substitution effects, explain the likely effects on the Ant and the Grasshopper's utility.

11. During the 1973–1974 oil crisis, the U.S. government placed a temporary price ceiling on gasoline, resulting in shortages. Some gas stations rationed gas, allowing consumers to buy only a specific amount of gas at a time, such as 10 gallons. How does this quota on gasoline change consumer utility, and would it have been better for the government to let the price rise to its equilibrium level?

12. Grandma Hormsbury entered and won the Food City sweepstakes. This gives the winner $500 in free groceries, provided that they spend $A on groceries at Food City. Would Grandma rather receive $500 in cash or this prize?

Chapter 6
Firms and Production

Chapter Summary

Firms vary from Mom and Pop's neighborhood store to giants like General Motors and WalMart. Despite this variety, they all have a lot in common: All **firms** are organizations that convert inputs into outputs (the goods or services that they sell) in an attempt to earn profits. The vast majority of goods and services produced in developed countries are made by firms. **Sole proprietorships** are firms owned and run by a single individual. **Partnerships** are firms jointly owned and run by two or more people. **Corporations** are owned by shareholders, who elect a board of directors that runs the firm with the help of managers. Corporations have **limited liability**—the owners' personal assets cannot be taken to pay a corporation's debts if it goes bankrupt. While proprietorships are much more numerous, corporations make over 80 percent of all business sales. Economists generally assume that the single goal of firms is to maximize **profit**, π, which equals the difference between revenue and cost. To maximize profits, a firm must produce as efficiently as possible. A firm engages in **efficient production** (or achieves **technical** efficiency) if it cannot produce its current level of output with fewer inputs, given existing knowledge about technology and organization. (Efficient production alone cannot ensure that profit is maximized, however.)

Firms create output from three types of **inputs**—**capital** (buildings and equipment), **labor** (human services provided by employees), and **materials**. The various ways inputs can be transformed into output are summarized in the **production function**—the relationship between the quantities of inputs used and the *maximum* quantity of output that can be produced, given current knowledge about technology and organization. The production function includes only efficient production processes. A firm can vary the amount it produces by varying its inputs. The **short run** is a period in which the firm *cannot* change the level of at least one factor of production—usually capital. In the **long run**, *all* input levels can be varied. In some industries, long-run adjustments can be made in only a few days. In other industries, long-run adjustments can take years or decades.

Our analysis of the short run assumes that capital cannot be varied, while labor can be varied. (Materials are ignored for simplicity.) The **total product** of labor curve plots the relationship between the level of output, q, and the level of labor, L—while all else, especially the level of capital, K, is constant.

$$q = f(L, \overline{K})$$

The **marginal product of labor** (MP_L) is the change in total output resulting from using an extra unit of labor, holding other factors constant.

$$MP_L = \frac{\partial q}{\partial L} = \frac{\partial f(L, K)}{\partial L}$$

The **average product of labor** is the ratio of output to the number of workers used to produce that output. $AP_L = q/L$. The three curves (total, average, and marginal product) are geometrically related. The AP_L curve slopes upward whenever the MP_L is above it and slopes downward whenever the MP_L is below it. This makes intuitive sense: Whenever output from the last worker (the marginal worker) is above average, it must pull up the average. The slope of the total product curve at a given point equals the marginal product of labor. For most production processes, AP_L first rises (due to teamwork and specialization) and then falls as labor increases. This eventual fall in AP_L is due to the **law of diminishing marginal returns**—which states that if a firm keeps increasing an input while all other inputs and technology are constant, then corresponding increases in output will eventually become smaller. This occurs because there is less and less of the second input to be used by each unit of the first input; for example, each worker has fewer tools to use.

In the long run, a firm can produce a given amount of output in a myriad of different ways. An **isoquant** shows the efficient combinations of labor and capital that can produce a single level of output.

$$\overline{q} = f(L, K)$$

Analytically, isoquants are very similar to indifference curves—the farther from the origin, the greater the level of output; they cannot cross; isoquants generally slope downward and are convex to the origin; and isoquants must be thin. Two exceptions to convexity arise when inputs are perfect substitutes (yielding linear isoquants) and when inputs must always be used in the same proportion to one another (yielding L-shaped isoquants). The absolute value of the slope of an isoquant is called the **marginal rate of technical substitution** (*MRTS*).

$$MRTS = \frac{\Delta K}{\Delta L} = \frac{dK}{dL} = -\frac{MP_L}{MP_K}$$

Most isoquants exhibit a diminishing *MRTS*—they become flatter as the input on the horizontal axis increases because it becomes more and more difficult to substitute that input for the other input. The **elasticity of substitution**, σ, measures the ease of substitution.

$$\sigma = \frac{\dfrac{d(K/L)}{K/L}}{\dfrac{dMRTS}{MRTS}} = \frac{d(K/L)}{dMRTS} \frac{MRTS}{K/L}$$

With the exception of **constant elasticity of substitution** (*CES*) production functions, the elasticity of substitution generally varies along an isoquant. Some common examples of *CES* production functions are linear production functions (σ = infinity, since the inputs are perfect substitutes), the Cobb-Douglas production function (σ = 1), and the fixed-proportion production function (σ = 0).

Returns to scale refer to how output changes if *all* inputs are increased by equal proportions. **Constant returns to scale** (*CRS*) occur if output increases at the same rate by which all inputs increase. **Increasing returns to scale** (*IRS*) occur if output increases at a faster rate than inputs. **Decreasing returns to scale** (*DRS*) occur if output increases at a slower rate than inputs. Many production functions have *IRS* for low levels of output, *CRS* for moderate levels of output, and *DRS* for large amounts of output.

Even though all firms may be producing efficiently (getting as much output from their inputs as possible), they won't usually all be equally productive. One firm's best may be better than another firm's best. We measure a firm's relative productivity by expressing its actual output, *q*, as a percentage of the output that the most productive firm could have produced, q^*. **Technical progress** allows a firm to produce more output using the same level of inputs (or to produce the same amount of output using fewer inputs). If the firm experiences **neutral** technical change, it continues to use the original ratio of inputs.

■ Key Concepts and Formulas

- **Short run:** period in which at least one input (usually capital) cannot be varied.
- **Long run:** period in which all inputs can be varied.
- **Total product curve:** plots the relationship between the level of output, *q*, and the level of labor, *L*, while all else (including capital, *K*) remains constant.
- **Average product of labor:** average output of all workers. $AP_L = q/L$.

- **Marginal product of labor:** change in output resulting from a change in the labor input.

$$MP_L = \frac{\partial q}{\partial L} = \frac{\partial f(L,K)}{\partial L}$$

- **Isoquant:** shows efficient combinations of labor and capital that can produce a single level of output.
- **Marginal rate of technical substitution:** the absolute value of the slope of an isoquant $= -\Delta K/\Delta L = MP_L/MP_K$.
- **Elasticity of substitution:** measure of the ease with which one input can be substituted for another.

$$\sigma = \frac{\dfrac{d(K/L)}{K/L}}{\dfrac{dMRTS}{MRTS}} = \frac{d(K/L)}{dMRTS}\frac{MRTS}{K/L}$$

- **Returns to scale:** how output changes if all inputs are increased by equal proportions.

■ Application: Marginal Product of Nineteenth Century Farm Family Members

Before the twentieth century, families acted not just as consumption units; many families also acted as firms. Farm families, for example, brought together capital (buildings, fences, work animals, tools), land, and family labor to produce a wide variety of outputs—food, fibers, shelter, and transportation, plus additional capital. One of the key production decisions for farming couples involved their family size. In 1850, the average American woman gave birth to about six children. (This rate is about three times higher than today.) Why did these couples choose to have so many children? Why did rural families choose to have more children than urban families? Why did families in some regions (e.g., the Midwest) choose to have more children than in other regions (e.g., the Northeast)? One traditional explanation says that farm families had so many children because they could almost immediately be put to work, raising the family's output by a considerable amount.

Question: How productive were farm children (and other family members) in the middle of the last century?

Answer: A recent study by economic historian Lee A. Craig estimates the marginal product of farm family members in the Northern states in 1860. To estimate the productivity, he first tallied up all the different outputs produced on farms and then converted them into a common unit—dollars. Next he measured all the inputs used on the farms—not just workers, but land and capital as well. Both of these sets of numbers were extracted from the census. Finally, he estimated the additional (marginal) output produced each year on farms with extra workers in seven different categories. Using multivariate regression (see Appendix 2A), Craig found the annual marginal products of labor given below.

Category of Labor	Northeast	Midwest	Frontier
Children (age 0–6)	–$ 20.82	$ 8.59	–$ 6.41
Children (age 7–12)	$ 22.81	$ 27.76	$ 27.12
Teenage females	$ 22.95	$ 39.75	$ 17.53
Teenage males	$111.03	$ 47.57	$ 49.03
Adult females	$154.08	$ 70.25	$147.28
Adult males (19–54)	$294.77	$186.44	$193.66
Adult males (55 and older)	$145.95	$121.94	$135.44

Notice that the marginal product of the youngest children is *negative*. This means that the household produced less output when young children were around—probably because others had to spend time giving birth to and caring for them, rather than producing saleable output. The relative marginal product of almost all children is estimated to have been fairly low—even teenage boys had a marginal product that was about 25 percent to 38 percent of adult men. Because physical strength was so important in agriculture in this period, the marginal product of adult women was much lower than that of adult men, also. Interestingly, Craig finds that the relative wage of women to men was about the same as their relative marginal products. (Chapter 15 explains why wages will equal the marginal product of labor in a competitive market.) Finally, we can see that the marginal product of men fell with age. These findings provide little support for the theory that says family size was closely tied to the potential productivity of children on the farm. For example, they cannot explain why family size was smallest in the Northeast. The leading theories of declining fertility focus on opportunities off the farm, the value of adult children to elderly parents, and the opportunity costs of raising children—especially the opportunity cost of women's time.

Source: Lee A. Craig, *To Sow One Acre More: Childbearing and Farm Productivity in the Antebellum North,* 1993.

■ Solved Problems

1. Suppose that the annual production function for soy beans is $q = 4K^{1/2}T^{1/2}L^{1/2}$, where q is hundreds of bushels, K = work years of machine service, T = acres of land, and L = work years of labor. $K = 25$ and $T = 100$. Find and graph the total product, marginal product of labor, and average product of labor.

    Step 1: Find the total product.

    Plug the values for K and T into the equation. This simplifies the equation to $q = 4(25^{1/2})(100^{1/2})$ $L^{1/2} = 200L^{1/2}$.

    Step 2: Find the marginal product of labor.

    Take the derivative of the total product equation with respect to L. $MP_L = dq/dL = 100L^{-1/2}$.

    Step 3: Find the average product of labor.

    $AP_L = q/L = 200L^{-1/2}$.

    These functions are graphed in Figure 6.1. Some things to note when graphing short-run production functions are as follows.

    a. It is customary to graph total product on one graph and marginal and average products on a second graph.

    b. For nearly every production function, the TP curve starts at the origin, because with no labor (or any other required input) there is zero production.

    c. Since marginal product is strictly decreasing in this case, (a) there are diminishing returns to the variable factor everywhere, and (b) the average product curve will always be above the marginal product curve and will always be downward sloping. Since each worker always produces less than the previous worker, average output per worker will always decrease.

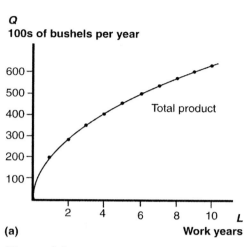

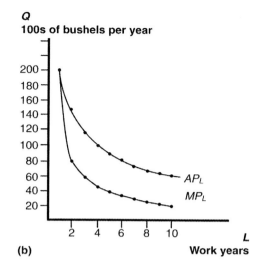

Figure 6.1

2. Draw some representative isoquants for a firm whose production function is $q = 10L^5K^5$. What returns to scale does this production function possess?

    Step 1: Make a graph with capital on one axis and labor on the other, then pick a point and find how much output this combination of labor and capital generates.

    Suppose we pick point a—1 unit of capital and 1 unit of labor. Plugging these numbers into the production function yields 10 units of output ($q = 10L^5K^5 = 10 \times 1 \times 1 = 10$).

    Step 2: Find other points in the graph that will give the same amount of output.

    What other combinations of capital and labor yield 10 units of output? Pick a quantity of one input and solve for the quantity of the other input.

    For example, if $K = 4$, then

    $$10L^5 4^5 = 10$$
    $$10L^2 2 = 10$$
    $$2L^5 = 1$$
    $$L^5 = 0.5$$
    $$L = 0.25$$

Likewise, if $L = 4$, then $K = 0.25$ will yield $q = 10$.

$$\text{If } K = 2, \text{ then}$$
$$10L^5 2^5 = 10$$
$$10L^5(\sqrt{2}) = 10$$
$$\sqrt{2}L^5 = 1$$
$$L^5 = 1/\sqrt{2}$$
$$L = 1/2$$

Notice the pattern: K and L must be the inverses of one another.

Step 3: Connect the dots.

Hook up all the bundles that give the same amount of output. See isoquant $q = 10$ in Figure 6.2.

Step 4: Repeat the process for additional isoquants representing different levels of output. Figure 6.2 shows the isoquant curve for isoquant $q = 20$.

Notice that all three combinations yield $q = 20$.

$$\text{If } K = L = 2, \text{ then } 10 \times 2^{0.5} \times 2^{0.5} = 10 \times 4^{0.5} = 10 \times 2 = 20.$$
$$\text{If } K = 1 \text{ and } L = 4, \text{ then } 10 \times 4^{0.5} \times 1^{0.5} = 10 \times 2 \times 1 = 20.$$
$$\text{If } K = 4 \text{ and } L = 1, \text{ then } 10 \times 1^{0.5} \times 4^{0.5} = 10 \times 1 \times 2 = 20.$$

Step 5: Use Figure 6.2 to find out what type of returns to scale the production function exhibits.

To discover returns to scale, we must increase all inputs proportionately and see if output increases by the same proportion (constant returns to scale), a smaller proportion (decreasing returns to scale), or a larger proportion (increasing returns to scale). The easiest way to do this is to pick an initial combination of inputs and plug these numbers into the production function. Then double the initial input combination and plug these numbers into the production function. In this case, we can use the numbers we've already calculated, found in the isoquants plotted in Figure 6.2. As inputs are doubled (from $K = L = 1$ to $K = L = 2$), output also doubles (from 10 to 20), so we have constant returns to scale. Most production functions exhibit increasing returns in some regions, constant returns in some regions, and decreasing returns in some regions, so it is always a good idea to check more than one point. For example, begin with $K = 4$ and $L = 1$ and double these inputs to $K = 8$ and $L = 2$. We know from Figure 6.2 that $K = 4$ and $L = 1$ produces output of 20. Plugging $K = 8$ and $L = 2$ into the production function yields $q = (10 \times 2^{.5} \times 8^{.5}) = 10 \times 16^{.5} = 10 \times 4 = 40$. Thus, doubling inputs causes output to double from 20 to 40; again we find constant returns to scale.

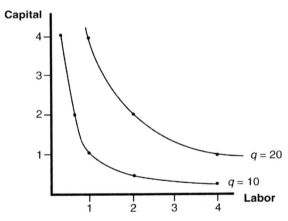

Figure 6.2

■ Practice Problems

Multiple-Choice

1. Which of the following is a firm?
    a. The U.S. Postal Service
    b. United Parcel Service
    c. Harvard University
    d. The University of Maryland

2. The production function $q = KL$ exhibits
    a. decreasing returns to scale.
    b. constant returns to scale.
    c. increasing returns to scale.
    d. decreasing returns to scale in one region and increasing returns to scale in another region.

3. Between points A and B, the total product curve in Figure 6.3 exhibits
    a. increasing marginal returns to labor.
    b. decreasing marginal returns to labor.
    c. an increasing marginal rate of substitution.
    d. a decreasing marginal rate of substitution.

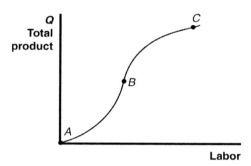

Figure 6.3

4. Between points B and C, the total product curve in Figure 6.3 exhibits
    a. increasing returns to scale.
    b. constant returns to scale.
    c. decreasing returns to scale.
    d. none of the above.

5. At point C in Figure 6.3
    a. the marginal product of labor is greater than the average product of labor.
    b. the marginal product of labor is less than the average product of labor.
    c. the marginal product of labor equals the average product of labor.
    d. one cannot determine whether the marginal product of labor is greater than, less than, or equal to the average product of labor.

6. Moving downward along the isoquant in Figure 6.4,
    a. skilled labor and unskilled labor are perfect substitutes.
    b. the marginal rate of technical substitution between skilled labor and unskilled labor is diminishing.
    c. the ratio of the marginal product of unskilled labor to the marginal product of skilled labor is falling.
    d. both b and c.

7. As we move from point A to point B in Figure 6.4, if the marginal product of skilled labor is 1, then the marginal product of unskilled labor
    a. is 1/2.
    b. is also 1.
    c. is 2.
    d. cannot be determined.

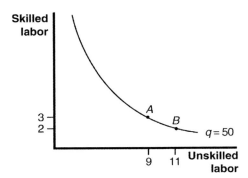

Figure 6.4

Fill-in

8. One big disadvantage of corporations is that their owners must pay additional taxes not paid by sole proprietorships or partnerships. One big advantage is that their owners face _____ for the firm's debts.

9. If Mr. Jones employs 5 workers and 5 tractors on 1000 acres, the output is 1 million bushels. If he employs the same 5 workers and 5 tractors on 1500 acres, the law of diminishing marginal returns says that his output will be _____.

10. _____ technical changes are innovations that alter the proportion in which inputs are used. One example is labor-saving technical change.

True-False-Ambiguous and Explain Why

11. 84% of business sales are made by corporations, even though only 20% of all firms are corporations. This shows that proprietorships and partnerships are less efficient than corporations and should convert into corporations.

12. Technical progress will shift an isoquant outward.

13. As a firm substitutes labor for capital along an isoquant, the elasticity of substitution will decrease.

14. Firms attempt to maximize profits.

15. The law of diminishing marginal returns to labor is caused by the fact that newly hired workers are not as skilled as more experienced workers.

16. You should stop studying for your economics exam once you reach the point of diminishing returns.

■ Short-Answer

17. Draw an isoquant with an *increasing* marginal rate of technical substitution. What would such a curve imply about the productivity of inputs?

18. The firm's production function is $q = 10L^{0.5}K^{0.5}$.
    a. Does this production function exhibit diminishing marginal returns to labor?
    b. Does it exhibit diminishing marginal returns to capital?

19. Calculate the marginal product of labor in Figure 6.5 when $K = 2$, $K = 4$, and $K = 6$. Graph the total product and marginal product of labor curves when $K = 4$. When does the law of diminishing marginal returns set in?

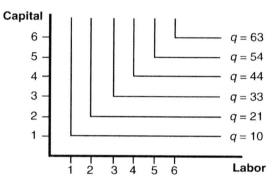

Figure 6.5

20. The firm's production function is $q = 12L^{3/4}K^{1/4}$.
    a. In the short run, $K = 1$. Find total product, marginal product, and average product, and graph the functions.
    b. What can you say about returns to scale for this function?

21. If technology exhibits constant returns to scale, and capital and labor are perfect substitutes with a marginal rate of technical substitution that is always 1, will the production function exhibit a diminishing marginal product of labor?

22. Vertigo Construction, Inc. finds that it can decrease the number of welders needed to construct a 25-story skyscraper, but in doing so, the number of accidents and injuries among welders will rise. Draw an isoquant showing this production function.

23. Podunk, Inc. has been making widgets by hand (using no machinery at all) for years. Their production function has been $q = 0.9L$. Recently, they purchased high-tech machines to aid the workers. Unfortunately, none of the workers can figure out how to use the machines. Sketch Podunk's isoquants.

24. Jan manages a factory with 20 units of capital. Last year, with 20 employees, the factory produced 400 McBoover devices. This year, the work force has expanded to 25 workers and output has climbed to 450 McBoover devices. June, the company's CEO, is all over Jan's case because the average product of labor has fallen from 20 McBoover devices per worker to 18 McBoover devices per worker. She says that Jan's factory is not as efficient as before and Jan had better explain why or she'll be "downsized." Is June correct? Should she fire Jan?

25. At the Bok Chicken Factory, the manager knows that the marginal product of labor increases for each of the first 10 workers hired, is constant for the next 10 workers, and decreases for every additional worker. Draw the general shape of the Bok Chicken Factory's marginal and average product curves.

26. When capital = 10, the production function for lizards at Luke's Lizard Ranch is $q = -8 + 20L - 0.5L^2$. Show the average product of labor and the marginal product of labor. At what level of output is average product of labor the highest?

27. Draw a total product curve to illustrate each of these adages:
    "Too many cooks spoil the broth."
    "That's the straw that broke the camel's back."

28. The production function is $q = 50L^{0.4}K^{0.6}$. Find the marginal rate of technical substitution (*MRTS*) of the isoquant $q = 50$, when $L = 1$.

29. Efficiency, Inc.'s production function takes the standard Cobb-Douglas form, $q = AL^{\alpha}K^{\beta}$. Sluggish Ltd. uses the same technology, but is only 80 percent as efficient as Efficiency Inc. What is the production function for Sluggish Ltd.?

30. The industry leader, Shiny Widget, has a production function $q = 10LK$. Draw one of its isoquants and then draw an isoquant for Rusty Widget, which is only half as efficient as Shiny Widget.

31. Using isoquant curves, show how neutral technical change differs from nonneutral technical change.

32. In Harbor City, the equipment allows one worker to unload 10 cargo containers from a ship for each hour of work. Adding an extra worker will not increase output any and, of course, a worker can only run one crane at a time, so there is always a ratio of one worker per crane. In Port Town, the equipment is different. It takes two workers for each crane—one to run the controls in the crane, the other at work on the ground—but they can unload 10 containers in 45 minutes. Sketch and compare the isoquants at these two unloading facilities, using number of crane hours on one axis and number of labor hours on the other.

33. Ffolrep Corporation's production function is $AL^{\alpha}K^{\beta}$. Will it increase its output more by doubling its inputs or by technical progress that makes it twice as productive?

34. Suppose that your local police department recovers ten tickets to a big NASCAR race in a drug raid. It decides to distribute these tickets to the city resident who can write the best essay explaining why he or she deserves the tickets. Is this an efficient way to distribute the tickets?

■ Answers to Practice Problems

1. b. All of these take inputs and turn them into outputs, but government agencies and nonprofit institutions are not considered firms. Only United Parcel Service has owners who can earn profits.

2. c. To verify that it exhibits increasing returns to scale, plug in any two positive initial values for capital and labor and then increase them by the same proportion (e.g., double them). For example, start with $K = L = 1$. Initially $q = 1$. After doubling the inputs, $K = L = 2$, so $q = 4$, which is more than twice the initial amount of output. Therefore, output has increased at a faster rate than inputs, and the function exhibits increasing returns to scale.

3. a. Because the total product curve becomes steeper, the marginal product of labor curve (which equals the slope of the total product curve) is rising—that is, increasing marginal returns to labor. Note that there is no substitution along this curve since only labor, not capital, varies.

4. d. In Figure 6.3, only labor varies. We need to vary all inputs (labor and capital) to deduce returns to scale.

5. b. The marginal product of labor equals the slope of the total product curve at any point. The average product of labor equals the slope of a ray from the origin to that point. The slope of the ray from the origin to point C is greater than the slope of the curve at point C.

6. d. The slope of the isoquant $= -\Delta\text{rise}/\Delta\text{run} = MRTS = MP_{\text{unskilled}}/MP_{\text{skilled}}$.

7. a. Moving along the isoquant, the output lost by cutting skilled labor must be replaced by increasing unskilled labor—$(MP_S \times \Delta S) + (MP_U \times \Delta U) = 0$, where $S =$ skilled labor and $U =$ unskilled labor. $(1 \times -1) + (MP_U \times 2) = 0$, so $MP_U = 1/2$.

8. limited liability

9. less than 1.5 million bushels

10. Nonneutral

11. False. One firm or type of firm is more efficient than another if it can turn the same amount of inputs into more output or if it can produce the same amount of output with fewer inputs. The problem doesn't give the value of inputs, only the value of outputs, so we cannot make this comparison. There are advantages to incorporating—especially limited liability for debts—but there are also disadvantages—especially the requirement of paying higher taxes on profits. The corporate form is better for owners in some settings, while partnerships and proprietorships are better in other settings.

12. False. The shift is inward because now the firm can produce the same quantity using fewer inputs.

13. Ambiguous. In general, the elasticity of substitution changes along an isoquant. It becomes more difficult to substitute additional units of any given input for the other, and thus the elasticity of substitution decreases (becomes more inelastic) as the capital–labor ratio increases, and vice versa. However, some production functions have a constant elasticity of substitution, such as linear, Cobb-Douglas, and fixed-proportion production functions.

14. Ambiguous. This assumption is almost always used by economists because it yields clear, testable predictions that generally have a better track record than models using other assumptions. However, this does not mean that all firms attempt to maximize profits. In many larger firms, the management may be attempting to maximize its own utility rather than the profits of the owners. (Enron seems to be an example of this. More on this principal-agent problem in Chapter 20.) In smaller firms, especially sole proprietorships, the owner of the firm may try to maximize utility and be willing to trade profits for increased utility. For example, a friend of mine entered a small business and was ready to make a purchase. The owner began telling him an off-color joke. My friend objected to the joke. The owner told my friend that he would have to take his business elsewhere. The owner gave up profits to run the business in a manner that maximized his own utility.

15. False. The law of diminishing marginal returns holds worker quality constant. The law of diminishing marginal returns says that even if new hires are just as skilled and hard-working as their coworkers, the extra output from hiring additional workers will eventually fall if other inputs are held constant.

16. Ambiguous. The point of diminishing returns is the point at which studying an additional hour yields smaller gains than studying during the previous hour (i.e., additional inputs yield a smaller increment to output). To decide whether or not you should stop, however, you'll need to compare the gains from studying to the costs of studying. Even if the gains begin to decline, they may still be greater than the cost (e.g., foregone leisure or gains from studying for another class).

17. Recall that the absolute value of the slope of an isoquant is called the marginal rate of technical substitution (*MRTS*). Typically *MRTS* is decreasing, but in this case, the *MRTS* is increasing so the isoquant is concave to the origin—bowed outward, as in Figure 6.6. The figure implies that 10 workers from group *A* can produce 100 widgets. If we take away one worker from group *A*, we need 9 workers from group *B* to maintain production. Taking away 9 more workers from group *A*, we need to add only 1 worker from group *B* to maintain output at 100 widgets. These workers are not perfect substitutes for one another—a linear isoquant. They are not perfect complements of one another—L-shaped isoquants. And they are not in between these two extremes. Instead, these workers seem to hamper one another. Nine workers from group *A* plus 9 workers from group *B* are only as productive as 10 workers from either group working alone. For example, the workers in these two groups may be on bad terms with one another and so they worry about getting into fights rather than making widgets. On the other hand, the workers in these two groups may be on great terms with each other, so they gossip and flirt instead of paying attention to widget making. (In either case, few employers will want to mix these two groups together.)

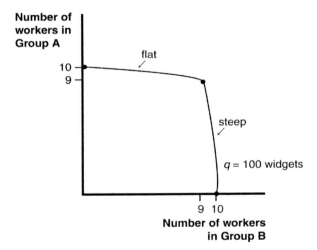

Figure 6.6

18. Yes, the function exhibits the law of diminishing marginal returns for both labor and capital. Find the equation for the marginal product curve—by taking the first derivative of total product with respect to labor. Taking the first derivative of the marginal product of labor curve shows that it is negative. Thus, the marginal product of labor is declining. (A similar procedure could be followed to show that the marginal product of capital is declining.)

$$\partial \text{ (total product) } / \partial L = MP_L = 5L^{-0.5}K^{0.5}.$$

$$\partial \text{ (marginal product of labor) } / \partial L = -2.5L^{-1.5}K^{0.5}.$$

19.

When $K = 2$		When $K = 4$		When $K = 6$	
Labor	**MP_L**	**Labor**	**MP_L**	**Labor**	**MP_L**
1	10	1	10	1	10
2	11	2	11	2	11
3	0	3	12	3	12
4	0	4	11	4	11
5	0	5	0	5	10
6	0	6	0	6	9

Diminishing marginal returns begin when the marginal product of labor begins to fall or whenever the marginal product of labor curve begins to slope downward. This occurs with the addition of the third worker when $K = 2$, and with the addition of the fourth worker when $K = 4$ and $K = 6$. The law of diminishing returns is very strict when $K = 2$ because this figure shows a fixed proportions technology. The third worker does not have any capital to use, so he is completely unproductive. Notice that when $K = 4$ and $K = 6$, diminishing returns begin even before the workers run out of machines to use. Thus diminishing returns can occur for reasons other than lack of other inputs. In addition, notice that Figure 6.5 exhibits increasing returns to scale as inputs rise from $K = L = 1$ to $K = L = 3$; constant returns to scale as inputs rise from $K = L = 3$ to $K = L = 4$; and decreasing returns to scale as inputs rise proportionately beyond $K = L = 4$.

Figure 6.7 graphs the total product and marginal product of labor curves when $K = 4$.

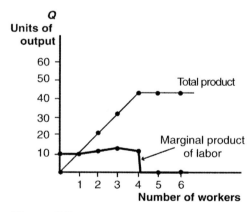

Figure 6.7

20. The firm's production function is $q = 12L^{0.3/4}K^{0.1/4}$.

a. $TP = q = 12L^{0.3/4}$

$MP_L = dq/dL = 9\ L^{-1/4}$

$AP_L = 12\ L^{-1/4}$

These functions are graphed in Figure 6.8.

b. The exponents of this Cobb-Douglas function add up to 1, so it's a constant returns to scale function. You could also find this by choosing some input level like (1,1), doubling it, and seeing what happens to output.

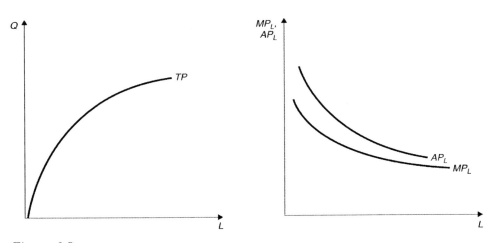

Figure 6.8

21. No. See Figure 6.9. The isoquants are all linear with a slope of −1. The numbers listed with each isoquant are consistent with constant returns to scale; for example, when we double inputs from $K = L = 1/2$ to $K = L = 1$, output doubles from $q = 1$ to $q = 2$. Doubling inputs again to $K = L = 2$ doubles output to $q = 4$. (The production function that is consistent with these isoquants is $q = L + K$.) To find the marginal product of labor, fix the value of capital and measure the change in output as labor is progressively increased by one unit. In Figure 6.8, points are marked for $K = 2$. When $K = 2$, the figure shows that

Labor	Total Product	Marginal Product of Labor
0	2	
1	3	1
2	4	1
3	5	1
4	6	1
5	7	1

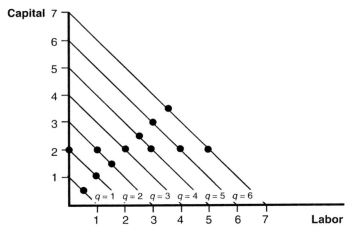

Figure 6.9

Thus, the marginal product of labor is always one. It does not diminish. The law of diminishing marginal returns generally holds because the variable input is spread over smaller and smaller amounts of the fixed input. In this case, however, the variable input is a perfect substitute for the fixed input, so the production function acts as if the fixed input is rising, too.

22. As shown in Figure 6.10, work hours and accidents are both inputs into the production of a 25-story skyscraper. If the number of workers is decreased (from L_1 to L_0), the number of accidents must increase (from A_1 to A_2) to maintain the same level of output. (Point A and point B are both along isoquant $q = 25$ stories.) Likewise, decreasing accidents will necessitate hiring workers for more hours. Thus accidents can be traded off with work hours. In addition, extra accidents yield more output—such as when we move from point A to C and output climbs from 25 stories to 26 stories. The point of this question is to show that all sorts of things can be inputs into production functions— even accidents. For example, a production function for raising children might include units of tough love (hours spent scolding, number of spankings) and soft love (hours spent teaching and playing, number of hugs).

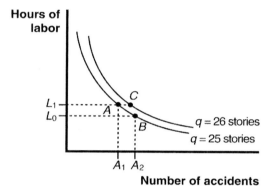

Figure 6.10

23. Figure 6.11 shows the isoquants. The addition of capital does nothing to increase output. Notice that these isoquant curves look just like indifference curves for which one of the goods gives no utility to the consumer.

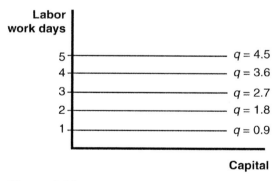

Figure 6.11

24. June's theory that the factory is less efficient implies that it has fallen to a lower total product curve. June's story would be correct if the factory has fallen from TP_1 to TP_2 in Figure 6.12. Jan's theory is that the average product is falling because capital has not increased—that the factory is demonstrating the law of diminishing marginal returns to labor. Jan's theory is correct if the factory has moved along TP_3 in Figure 6.12. We need more information to know who is correct.

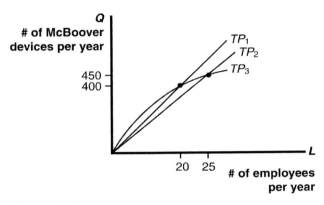

Figure 6.12

25. Figure 6.13 shows one possible version of the marginal and average product curves. The shape of the marginal product curve is correct (but numerical values and steepness would vary if we had an actual function); the exact shape of the AP curve would again depend on the exact function but is roughly correct. The point of this exercise is to show how marginal product tells you the shape of average product curves; if marginal product is rising, it will pull the average up. If marginal product is constant, average product will be roughly constant, once it meets marginal product. If marginal product is falling, it will pull the average down.

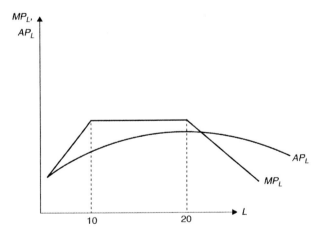

Figure 6.13

26. Average product of labor $= q/L = -8/L + 20 - 0.5L$.

Marginal product of labor $= \delta(\text{total product})/\delta L = 20 - L$.

The table below gives the values for $L = 1$ to $L = 5$.

To find the maximum average product of labor, we can use the fact that $MP_L = AP_L$ at AP_L's maximum.

$$20 - L = -8/L + 20 - 0.5L$$
$$-L = -8/L - 0.5L$$
$$-0.5L = -8/L$$
$$L = 16/L$$
$$L^2 = 16$$
$$L = 4$$

Labor	Total Product	AP_L	MP_L
1	11.5	11.50	19
2	30	15.00	18
3	47.5	15.83	17
4	64	16.00	16
5	79.5	15.9	15

(If you calculate $MP_L = \Delta(\text{total product})/\Delta L$ from the table, rather than using $MP_L = 20 - L$, you will find numbers that are always 0.5 higher than those given in the last column in the table. This is because this method calculates the MP_L halfway between each level of labor.)

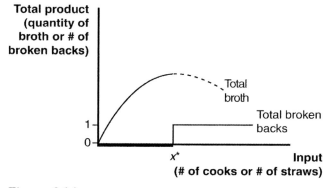

Figure 6.14

27. Figure 6.14 shows both proverbs. The total broth curve rises initially, but once we exceed X^*, cooks' output of broth starts to fall—the spoiled broth must be thrown away. The dashed part of this line indicates that this number of cooks is inefficient and is not part of the production function. The total broken backs curve (output = number of broken camel backs) runs along the horizontal axis, until we reach the critical value, X^*. Then output jumps from 0 to 1 broken back and continues at 1 broken back as we pile more and more straw on the poor, injured beast. The marginal product is zero for every straw, except "the straw that broke the camel's back," which has a marginal product of one broken back.

28. The $MRTS = MP_L/MP_K$. First figure out what K equals at this point.

$$50 = 50 \times 1^{0.4}K^{0.6} \quad \text{or} \quad 50 = 50K^{0.6} \quad \text{or} \quad 1 = K^{0.6}, \quad \text{so} \quad K = 1.$$

Find the MP_L and MP_K by taking the first derivative of the production function with respect to L and then K.

$$MP_L = 20L^{-0.6}K^{0.6}. \quad \text{When } K = L = 1, MP_L = 20.$$
$$MP_K = 30L^{0.4}K^{-0.4}. \quad \text{When } K = L = 1, MP_K = 30, \quad \text{so}$$
$$MRTS = 20/30 = 0.666 \text{ at this point.}$$

29. Sluggish's production function is $q = 0.8AL^{\alpha}K^{\beta}$.

30. Figure 6.15 shows Shiny Widget's isoquant for $q = 40$. Lying right on top of this isoquant is Rusty Widget's isoquant for $q = 20$. Figure 6.13 also shows Rusty Widget's isoquant for $q = 40$. (With the inputs along Rusty's Widget's $q = 40$ isoquant, Shiny Widget could have produced $q = 80$.) Rusty Widget's production function is $q = 5LK$.

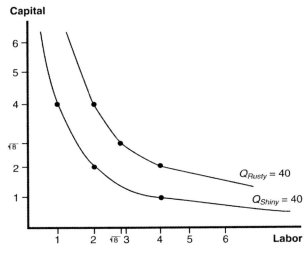

Figure 6.15

31. Figure 6.16(a) shows the case of neutral technical change. Figure 6.16(b) shows nonneutral technical change. The essence of a technical improvement is the ability to produce the same output level with fewer inputs than before or more output with the same inputs. With neutral technical change, more output can be producing using the same ratio of inputs as before. This yields a "parallel" inward shift in the isoquant curves. The points along isoquant curve q_1 initially produced 100 units of output. After the technological change, this same curve produces 150 units. After the technological change, the points along isoquant curve q_2 produce 100 units of output. Comparing q_1 and q_2, we can see that the ratios of inputs are the same as before. One hundred units of output could originally be produced with capital-labor combinations at points A, B, and C and now can be produced at points D, E, and F, each of which has the same ratio of inputs: $K = 2L$ at points A and D; $K = L$ at points B and E; and $K = .5L$ at C and F.

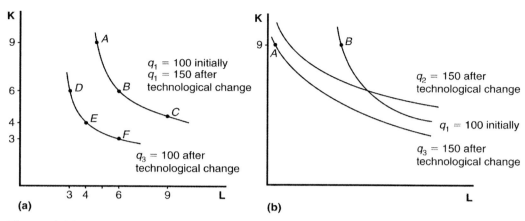

Figure 6.16

With nonneutral technical change, the shapes of the isoquant curves have changed. Figure 6.14(b) shows labor-saving technical change. The isoquant curve that produces 100 units of output shifts inward (from q_1 to q_3) showing that technology has improved, since fewer inputs are needed to produce the same output, but the shift isn't "parallel." In producing the same output level, we can keep the amount of capital used constant, but cut back the amount of labor by a huge amount (compare point A to point B). After the nonneutral technical change, none of the new isoquant curves lie on top of q_1; instead curves like q_2 cross over q_1, because the marginal rate of substitution between labor and capital has changed, so that it is much easier to substitute capital for labor.

32. Figure 6.17 shows the isoquants. Harbor City's isoquants are given by solid lines; Port Town's with dashed lines. Both sets are L-shaped because of the fixed-proportions technology.

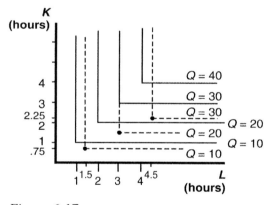

Figure 6.17

33. The technical progress will change its production function from $AL^\alpha K^\beta$ to $2AL^\alpha K^\beta$, giving it twice as much output. Doubling the inputs will make the output increase from $AL^\alpha K^\beta$ to $A(2L)^\alpha (2K)^\beta$ or $A2^{\alpha+\beta}L^\alpha K^\beta$, so it depends on the sum of α and β. If they sum to less than one, output will less than double. If they sum to one, output will double. If they sum to more than one, output will more than double. In other words, if the firm has increasing returns to scale, its output will increase faster by doubling inputs than by doubling A. (A is also called total factor productivity.)

34. Efficiency occurs when output cannot be produced using fewer inputs. In this case *distribution* is the output being produced. This isn't an efficient way to distribute the tickets, since it uses so much time. The time of the city employees who read the essays is being used up (as is the time of those who write the essays) and the tickets could be distributed using much less labor. Perhaps the most efficient way to distribute the tickets is to hand them out unannounced to people walking by—this would take only a minute or two. Alternatively, the city could sell them back to NASCAR and have them distribute the tickets.

■ Exercises

True-False-Ambiguous and Explain Why

1. During the 2005 season, Peyton Manning, star quarterback of the Indianapolis Colts, gained 8.3 yards per pass attempt, while Edgerrin James, star running back of the Colts, gained 4.2 yards per rushing attempt. This implies that the Colts would have made more yardage by passing more often and running less.

2. Rasputin's Sweatshop, Inc. produces shirts in a dark attic in some anonymous city. Rasputin currently employs five workers and rents five sewing machines. Therefore, the marginal product of labor of the sixth worker will be zero.

3. Decreasing returns to scale occur because of the law of diminishing marginal returns.

Short-Answer

4. What are the returns to scale as one proportionately increases the inputs from isoquant $q = 10$ in Figure 6.18?

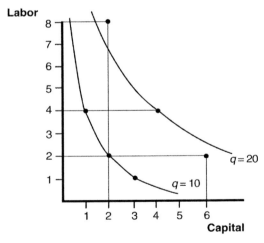

Figure 6.18

5. Suppose we pick a point along isoquant $q = 20$ in Figure 6.18. At this point, the marginal product of labor is 5 units of output and the marginal rate of technical substitution is 2. What must the marginal product of capital be?

6. XYZ Corporation has four alternative methods of producing 1000 widgets. Each method represents different combinations of three factors: labor, lathe time, and raw materials. The inputs required by each method are given in the following table:

Method	A	B	C	D
Labor hours	100	80	90	70
Lathe hours	25	85	70	80
Raw materials (pounds)	160	150	100	120

Which of these could *not* be on XYZ's three-dimensional isoquant?

7. For each of the following production functions, draw at least two isoquants and identify the elasticity of substitution and returns to scale.
   a. $q = \min(\frac{1}{2}K, L)$
   b. $q = L^{1/4}K^{1/4}$
   c. $q = 3K + L$

8. Assume that capital is fixed at 1 in the short run. For each of the following production functions, find total product, marginal product, and average product. Graph your results.
   a. $q = 100L^2K$
   b. $q = K + L$
   c. $q = L^{1/4}K^{1/4}$

9. Based on the following statement, draw the approximate shape of this firm's total, marginal, and average product curves.

   In the short run, this firm has increasing returns to the variable factor, due to gains from specialization. After the 20th worker, diminishing returns set in.

10. Suppose that a firm has a production function with ordinary, convex isoquants. All of the workers are sent to a training program that doubles their productivity. How does the shape of the isoquants change, relative to the original isoquants? How does the change in the productivity of labor change the productivity of capital?

11. A recent report stated that United States workers are the most productive in the world. How could you demonstrate this using production functions?

12. $q = L^2K$. Calculate the elasticity of substitution.

Chapter 7
Costs

■ Chapter Summary

All of microeconomics boils down to a weighing of costs against benefits. To weigh things properly, we need to appropriately measure cost. Economists say that "there's no such thing as a free lunch," because they are careful to consider *all* costs—both **explicit costs** (out-of-pocket payments for inputs) and **implicit costs** (the value of time and the value of other resources used but not purchased in the period). A firm's **economic cost** or **opportunity cost** of producing something is the value of the best alternative use of its resources. Thus, for example, the cost of running your own business includes the opportunity cost of your own time—the highest wage you could have earned working for someone else. Capital is a **durable good**— a product that is useful for years. The economic cost of capital is not the same as the accounting cost, which arbitrarily spreads costs over time according to rules set by the government. The economic cost of capital is its opportunity cost—the amount the firm could receive if it rented out its capital. To maximize profit, a firm must pay attention to the opportunity cost of its capital and *not* what the firm paid for it—its **historical cost**. If a piece of equipment has no alternative use, the historical cost is a **sunk cost**: an expenditure that can never be recovered. In this case, the opportunity cost is zero, so the firm should ignore historical and sunk costs and realize that it costs nothing to use the equipment.

To produce a given level of output in the short run, a firm incurs costs for both its fixed and variable inputs. A firm's **fixed cost** is its production expense that does not vary with output in the short run. This includes the cost of inputs that the firm cannot practically adjust in the short run, especially capital. **Variable cost** is the production expenses that change with the quantity of output produced—the cost of variable inputs, such as labor and materials. **Total cost**, C, is the sum of variable cost, VC, and fixed costs, F. **Marginal cost**, MC, is the amount by which a firm's cost changes if it produces one more unit of output. $MC = dC/dq$ and (because only variable cost changes with output) dVC/dq. Firms pay attention to three average cost measures: **average fixed cost** $(AFC) = F/q$; **average variable cost** $(AVC) = VC/q$; **average cost** or average total cost $(AC) = C/q = AFC + AVC$. (A **transaction cost** is the cost of setting up a deal or making a trade and can include both fixed and variables costs.)

The AFC curve always falls as output increases, approaching zero as output gets large, as fixed cost is spread over more and more units of output. The MC curve is the slope of both the C and the VC curves at a given level of output. Where the MC curve is below the average cost, the AC curve falls with output, because the lower marginal cost pulls down the average cost. Where the MC curve is above the average cost, the AC curve rises. Therefore, the marginal cost curve must intersect the average cost curve at its lowest point. (The same logic holds for the relationship between the marginal cost curve and the AVC curve.) The shapes of the cost curves are inversely related to the shapes of the product curves discussed in Chapter 6. If input prices are constant and labor is the only variable input, then $MC = \Delta VC/\Delta q = w(\Delta L/\Delta Q) = w/MP_L$, where w = wage. Thus, the MC curve eventually slopes upward because the marginal product of labor (MP_L) eventually falls—the law of diminishing marginal returns. $AVC = wL/q = w/AP_L$. Rising input prices or a specific tax shifts up the marginal cost and the average cost curves, but does not affect the output at which the AC curve is minimized. A franchise tax or business license fee affects fixed costs but not variable costs.

An **isocost line** plots all combinations of capital and labor that require the same total expenditure. This cost, C, depends on the price of labor and capital: Along an isocost line, cost is fixed at a particular level, C, so $C = wL + rK$, or $K = C/r - (w/r)L$, where r is the rental rate for capital. The firm has an infinite number of isocost lines—one for each cost level. Isocost lines that are farther from the origin cost more. The slope of all these parallel isocost lines is $-w/r$. To maximize profits, the firm must be **economically efficient**—choosing the lowest-cost way to produce a given level of output. Three different but equivalent approaches can be used to choose the combination of capital and labor that maximizes profits. The **lowest-isocost rule** states that the firm minimizes cost by using the combination of inputs on the isoquant that is on the lowest isocost line touching the isoquant. The **tangency rule** states that in choosing the input combination where the relevant isoquant is tangent to an isocost line, the firm produces a given level of output at the lowest cost. At the point of tangency, the slope of the isoquant (marginal rate of technical substitution) equals the slope of the isocost curve so $MRTS = w/r$. Because $MRTS = MP_L/MP_K$, this implies that $MP_L/MP_K = w/r$ or $MP_L/w = MP_K/r$. This equation is the **last-dollar rule**: cost is minimized if inputs are chosen so that the last dollar spent on labor adds as much extra output as the last dollar spent on capital.

As you did when you found the expenditure function in the consumer theory chapters, the cost-minimizing input combination for a given level of output can be found using the Lagrangian method. The dual of this problem is maximizing output subject to a cost constraint. If factor prices change, the firm minimizes its new cost by substituting away from the input that has become relatively more expensive. As a firm increases its desired level of output, it will move to a new point of tangency. The curve through the tangency points is the long-run **expansion path**—the cost-minimizing combinations of labor and capital at each output level. **Long-run average cost** (*LRAC*) curves are U-shaped for many firms, although not for the reasons that short-run average cost curves are U-shaped. This has nothing to do with the law of diminishing marginal returns and is not due to the presence of fixed costs, since neither of these forces can operate in the long run. Returns to scale play a major role in determining the shape of long-run average and marginal cost curves. When input prices are constant, the firm's long-run average cost curve will be U-shaped if it exhibits first increasing returns to scale, then constant returns to scale, then decreasing returns to scale as output rises. A cost function exhibits **economies of scale** if the long-run average cost of production falls as output expands, and **diseconomies of scale** if *LRAC* rises as output expands. Long-run cost is lower than (or equal to) short-run cost because the firm has more flexibility. In the long run, it can choose the level of capital that minimizes the cost of the corresponding output level. The long-run average cost curve is the lower bound (the **envelope**) of all the short-run average cost curves.

Many firms experience **learning by doing**—when workers and managers become more skilled at their jobs and discover better ways to produce as they gain experience. Learning by doing will shift cost curves downward. If learning by doing depends on cumulative output, firms have an incentive to produce more in the short run than they otherwise would—to lower their costs in the future. **Economies of scope** exist if it is less expensive to produce goods jointly than separately. A measure of the degree of economies of scope, SC, is

$$SC = \frac{C(q_1, 0) + C(0, q_2) - C(q_1, q_2)}{C(q_1, q_2)}$$

where $C(q_1, 0)$ is the cost of producing q_1 units of the first good by itself, $C(0, q_2)$ is the cost of producing q_2 units of the second good by itself, and $C(q_1, q_2)$ is the cost of producing both goods together. If SC is negative, then there are **diseconomies of scope** and the two goods should be produced separately. Economies of scope exist if the **production possibilities frontier** (the maximum amounts of outputs that can be produced from a fixed amount of inputs) for the two goods is concave.

There are important parallels between consumer theory (Chapters 3–5) and the theory of the firm (Chapters 6–7). Examining these parallels will help you better understand both consumers and producers. The table on the following two pages identifies these symmetries.

■ Key Concepts

- **Opportunity cost (economic cost):** value of the best alternative use of resources.
- **Isocost line:** plots capital and labor combinations requiring the same total expenditure.
- **Maximizing profits:** requires economic efficiency, that is, choosing the lowest-cost way to produce a given level of output. Equivalent ways to do this: (1) use the combination of inputs on the isoquant that is on the lowest isocost line touching the isoquant; (2) choose the input combination where the relevant isoquant is tangent to an isocost line; and (3) pick capital and labor so that $MP_L/w = MP_K/r$.
- **Long-run average cost curve:** the lower bound of all the short-run average cost curves. Its shape is tied closely to returns to scale.
- **Economies of scale:** long-run average costs fall as output rises.
- **Diseconomies of scale:** long-run average costs rise as output rises.
- **Economies of scope:** less expensive to produce goods jointly than separately.

■ Summary of Cost Formulas

Term	Symbol	Definition	Formula
Fixed Cost	F	Cost of fixed inputs; cost that is independent of output in the short run	
Variable Cost	VC	Cost of variable inputs; cost that varies with output in the short run	
Total Cost (or Cost)	C	Cost of all inputs	$C = F + VC$
Output	q	Total output produced	
Marginal Cost	MC	Change in total cost resulting from a one-unit increase in output; slope of the total cost curve	$MC = dC/dq$
Average Fixed Cost	AFC	Fixed cost per unit of output	$AFC = F/q$
Average Variable Cost	AVC	Variable cost per unit of output	$AVC = VC/q$
Average Total Cost	AC	Total cost per unit of output	$AC = AFC + AVC$ $AC = C/q$

Consumer Behavior (Demand)	Producer Behavior (Supply)
1. Goal: Maximize utility	1. Goal: Maximize profits
2. Utility function $U = f(\text{goods})$ $U = f(X, Y)$	2. Production function $q = f(\text{inputs})$ $q = f(L, K)$
3. Indifference curve	3. Isoquant
4. Convexity of indifference curve relates to subjective substitutability and complementarity among goods and services	4. Convexity of isoquant relates to objective substitutability and complementarity among inputs
5. Perfect substitutes Perfect complements	5. Perfect substitutes Fixed proportions

(Continued)

Consumer Behavior (Demand)	**Producer Behavior (Supply)**
6. Marginal rate of substitution (*MRS*) = slope of indifference curve	6. Marginal rate of technical substitution (*MRTS*) = −slope of isoquant
7. $MRS_{YX} = \Delta Y/\Delta X = -MU_X/MU_Y$	7. $MRTS_{KL} = -\Delta K/\Delta L = MP_L/MP_K$
8. MU_X is subjective, not measurable	8. MP_L is objective, measurable
9. Income and relative prices	9. Costs
10. Budget line	10. Isocost line
11. $MRS_{YX} = -p_X/p_Y$ Consumer's equilibrium condition	11. $MRTS = w/r$ Firm's equilibrium condition
12. $MU_A/P_A = MU_B/P_B$	12. $MP_L/w = MP_K/r$
13. Diminishing marginal utility	13. Diminishing marginal returns
14. Change in tastes	14. Change in technology
15. Income–consumption curve	15. Long-run expansion path

■ Application: Agriculture in Europe and America

European visitors to America during the colonial and early national period often commented disparagingly about American agricultural practices. They were shocked by the haphazard and wasteful behavior of American farmers. American farmers let their hogs run wild, fencing in their crops rather than their animals. Their fields were full of stumps, which farmers plowed around rather than removing. Their barns and other buildings were hastily constructed. They never spread manure on their fields. In Europe, things were done differently—animals were fenced in, stumps were removed, buildings were made of stone, and manuring was common. Yet the visitors commented that everyone was always busy on American farms, land was very cheap, and the output per worker and agricultural wages were enviably high. Visitors also noticed that American colonists used their land and labor much differently and much more productively than did Native Americans.

Question: Can economic analysis explain the differing agricultural practices of Europe and America?

Answer: Isoquants and isocost lines can be used to explain why Europeans and Americans used drastically different methods to produce the same goods. In Figure 7.1, the isoquant shows that many different combinations of land and labor can be used to produce 100 bushels of grain. In America, land was very inexpensive and labor was relatively scarce and therefore expensive. Isocost lines in America, such as $C_{America}$, were very steep. $C_{America}$'s slope is $-w/p_{Land}$, which is high because wages were high in America and the price of land was low. Isocost lines in Europe, such as C_{Europe}, were very flat, because wages were relatively low there and the price of land was relatively high. Because their isocost lines had such dramatically different slopes, American farmers and European farmers chose dramatically different ways of producing 100 bushels of grain. American farmers chose a point like *A*, using a large amount of land, T_A, and a small amount of labor, L_A, while European farmers chose a point like *E*, with a small amount of land, T_E, and a large amount of labor, L_E. Thus, Americans could afford to "waste" land by leaving stumps in the ground and allowing their hogs to roam in uncultivated lands, but they couldn't afford to waste labor time in building high-quality structures and hauling manure to their fields. Notice that both methods produce 100 bushels of grain, so each worker in America has a much higher average product of labor than in Europe.

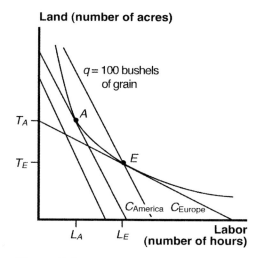

Figure 7.1

Figure 7.2 demonstrates the total product curves for American and European farms of the same size. Because there are fewer workers per acre in America, the American workers' marginal product, MP_{LA}—the slope of the total product curve at point A—is higher than the marginal product of labor for the European worker, MP_{LE}.

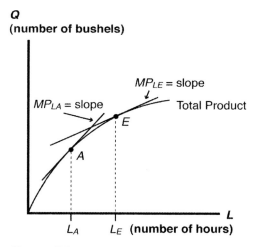

Figure 7.2

Figure 7.3 compares the food production of Native Americans and colonial Americans. The isoquant for one unit of food is much closer to the origin for colonial Americans than it was for Native Americans. Colonists were able to produce food using less of both inputs because they had superior technology and were better organized. Before the arrival of the colonists, Native Americans had no metal tools (such as axes, shovels, plows, and guns), no horses, and poorly developed trade networks and markets. In practice, the colonists worked as much or more hours per day, used about one one-thousandth as much land as Native Americans (who used about 1000 to 2000 acres per person), and were able to enjoy a much higher standard of living than the Native Americans. (See John McCusker and Russell Menard, *The Economy of British America: 1607–1789,* Chapel Hill, NC, 1985, pp. 305–308; Stanley Lebergott, *The Americans: An Economic Record,* New York, 1984, pp. 14–17.)

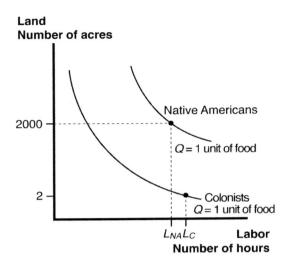

Land
Number of acres

Figure 7.3

■ Solved Problems

1. The Bok Chicken Factory is trying to figure out how to minimize the cost of producing 12,000 units of chicken parts. The production function is $q = 100L^{1/2}K^{1/2}$. The wage rate is $9 per hour, and the rental rate on capital is $4 per machine hour.
    a. Find the minimum cost of producing 1200 units.
    b. Find the maximum output that can be produced for a total cost of $720.
    c. Graph your results.

    Step 1: If you know how to do expenditure function problems, the good news is that you already know how to do this problem!

    Think of the cost function as expenditure for the firm, and minimize cost subject to a quantity constraint.

    $$\text{Min } C = 9L + 4K$$
    $$\text{subject to: } 1200 = 100L^{1/2}K^{1/2}$$

    1: Write the Lagrangian function.

    Again, the Lagrangian function consists of two parts: what you are trying to optimize and a constraint. In this case, the constraint is the production level that the company wishes to produce.

    $$\mathbf{L} + = (\text{function to be minimized}) + (\mathbf{L})$$
    $$= 9L + 4K + \lambda(1200 - 100L^{1/2}K^{1/2})$$

    2: Take partial derivatives with respect to q_1, q_2, and λ, and set the partial derivatives equal to zero.

    $$\frac{\partial \mathbf{L}+}{\partial L} = 9 - 50\lambda L^{-1/2}K^{1/2} = 0$$

    $$\frac{\partial \mathbf{L}+}{\partial K} = 4 - 50\lambda L^{1/2}K^{-1/2} = 0$$

    $$\frac{\partial \mathbf{L}+}{\partial \lambda} = 1200 - 100L^{1/2}K^{1/2} = 0$$

3:   Use the first two equations to find a relationship between the two factors of production.

$$\frac{K}{L} = \frac{9}{4}$$

$$K = \frac{9}{4}L$$

The relationship you have just found is also the equation of the **expansion path.**

4:   Substitute into the original constraint.

Substitute into the original production constraint and solve for K and L.

$$1200 = 100L^{1/2}K^{1/2}$$

$$12 = L^{1/2}\left(\frac{9}{4}L\right)^{1/2}$$

$$12 = \left(\frac{9}{4}\right)^{1/2}L$$

$$L = 8$$

$$K = 18$$

$$E = 9(8) + 4(18) = \$144$$

In order to produce 1200 units at the <u>least cost</u>, the Bok Chicken Factory must spend \$144 and purchase 8 units of labor and 18 units of capital. There are other ways that the firm could produce this amount, but they would cost more. (This is the answer to part a of the problem.)

Step 2: Find maximum production for a cost of \$720.

Maximizing production subject to a cost constraint is the *dual* of the cost minimization problem that you just did.

$$\textbf{Max } q = 100L^{1/2}K^{1/2}$$

$$\textbf{subject to: } 720 = 9L + 4K$$

In this problem, you are maximizing output rather than minimizing cost, so the objective function is the production function and the constraint is the cost function.

1:   Write the Lagrangian function.

Again, the Lagrangian function consists of two parts: what you are trying to optimize and a constraint. In this case, the constraint is the production level that the company wishes to produce.

$$\textbf{L}+ = (\text{function to be maximized}) + (\textbf{L})$$

$$= 100L^{1/2}K^{1/2} + \lambda(720 - 9L + 4K)$$

2:   Take partial derivatives with respect to q_1, q_2, and λ, and set the partial derivatives equal to zero.

$$\frac{\partial\textbf{L}+}{\partial L} = 50L^{-1/2}K^{1/2} - 9\lambda = 0$$

$$\frac{\partial\textbf{L}+}{\partial K} = 50L^{1/2}K^{-1/2} - 4\lambda = 0$$

$$\frac{\partial\textbf{L}+}{\partial \lambda} = 720 - 9L - 4K = 0$$

3: Use the first two equations to find a relationship between the two factors of production.

$$\frac{K}{L} = \frac{9}{4}$$

$$K = \frac{9}{4}L$$

The relationship you have just found is also the equation of the **expansion path**, AND it is the same equation that you found in part a of this problem.

4: Substitute into the original constraint.

Substitute into the original production constraint and solve for K and L.

$$720 = 9L + 4K$$

$$720 = 9L + 4\left(\frac{9}{4}L\right)$$

$$720 = 18L$$

$$L = 40$$

$$K = 90$$

$$q = 100L^{1/2}K^{1/2} = 6000$$

For a total cost of $720, the most output that the Bok Chicken Factory can produce is 6000 units. (This is the answer to part b of the problem.)

Step 3: Graph your results.

Figure 7.4 shows a graphical representation of this problem. Be sure to label everything on your graph!

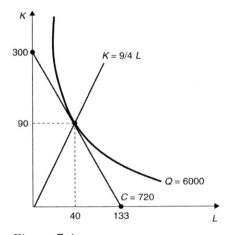

Figure 7.4

2. Assume that the Bok Chicken Factory has purchased 90 units of capital and intends to produce 6000 units of output, as you found in part b. of Problem 1. Suddenly demand conditions worsen, and management decides to produce 4800 units of output. Graphically and mathematically show the firm's short-run and long-run adjustment to the change in demand conditions, using an isoquant map.

Step 1: Find the new short-run input combination.

In the short run, the Bok Chicken Factory cannot change the amount of capital that it has; it is stuck with 90 units. Thus it cannot adjust optimally. To find the best short-run input combination, use the production function to solve for the required amount of labor.

$$4800 = 100L^{1/2}K^{1/2}$$
$$4800 = 100L^{1/2}(90)^{1/2}$$
$$L = 25.60 \cong 26$$
$$C = 9(26) + 4(90) = \$594$$

Thus in the short run, the Bok Chicken Factory will use 26 units of labor and 90 units of capital, for a total cost of $594. This is *not* an optimal long-run position, as we see in the next step, because the firm is unable to adjust the amount of capital in the short run.

Step 2: Find the new long-run input combination.

In the long run, the firm moves along its expansion path. Thus at every point, $K = 9/4L$, as you found in the earlier problem. To find the optimal input combination, simply substitute this relationship into the production function.

$$4800 = 100L^{1/2}K^{1/2}$$
$$48 = L^{1/2}\left(\frac{9}{4}L\right)^{1/2}$$
$$L = 32$$
$$K = 72$$
$$C = 9(32) + 4(72) = \$576$$

When the firm can adjust all inputs optimally, it uses relatively LESS capital as it reduces output and relatively MORE labor than it would in the short run. (Note that this would be the opposite if the firm was expanding.) Long-run total cost is less than short-run total cost.

Step 3: Graph your results.

Figure 7.5 shows the original position of the firm, the short-run expansion path (after the purchase of 90 units of capital), the short-run cost of producing 4800 units, and the long-run cost (on the long-run expansion path).

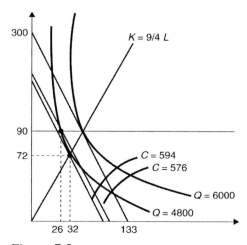

Figure 7.5

3. Using the information in Solved Problems 1, find the Bok Chicken Factory's short and long-run total cost, marginal cost, and average cost functions and graph them, using them to show all the points that you found in Solved Problem 2.

Step 1: Find the long-run cost functions.

When you are trying to find cost functions, the most important thing to remember is that a cost function is a function of <u>quantity</u>, not inputs. Thus you have to take the isoquant form ($C = 9L + 4K$) of the total cost function and turn it into a function of q. In order to do this, you need to rearrange the production function so that q is a function of one input, using the expansion path relationship that you found in Solved Problem 1, $K = 9/4L$.

$$q = 100L^{1/2}K^{1/2}$$

$$q = 100L^{1/2}\left(\frac{9}{4}L\right)^{1/2} = \frac{300}{2}L$$

$$L = \frac{q}{150}$$

Now take the relationship between L and q and substitute into $C = 9L + 4K$. You also have to use the expansion path equation again to make C a function of L alone.

$$C = 9L + 4K$$

$$C = 9L + 4\left(\frac{9}{4}L\right) = 18L$$

$$C(q) = 18\left(\frac{q}{150}\right)$$

$$C(q) = \frac{27}{100}q = 0.12q$$

From the total cost function, you can find marginal and average cost.

$$MC = \frac{dC}{dq} = 0.12$$

$$AC = \frac{C}{q} = 0.12$$

Step 2: Find the short-run cost functions.

Finding the short-run cost curves is exactly like finding the long-run cost curves, except that capital is fixed at some given level (in this case, 90, in the initial problem). First find q as a function of L.

$$q = 100L^{1/2}K^{1/2} = 100L^{1/2}(90)^{1/2}$$

$$q \cong 949L^{1/2}$$

$$L \cong \frac{q^2}{900,000}$$

Now substitute into $C = 9L + 4K$, and find C, MC, ATC, and AVC.

$$C = 9L + 4(90)$$

$$C = 9\left(\frac{q^2}{900,000}\right) + 360 = \frac{q^2}{100,000} + 360$$

$$MC = \frac{q}{50,000}$$

$$ATC = \frac{q}{100,000} + \frac{360}{q}$$

$$AVC = \frac{q}{100,000}$$

Step 3: Graph and interpret your results.

The question just asks you to graph the functions, but let's also think about what you found. First, this is a constant returns to scale production function, and thus the long run total cost curve must be a straight line. Long-run marginal and average cost curves are constant. These curves are the *envelope* of the short run curve, the lower boundary, as you can see in the graph. They represent the least cost of producing any given level of output, given that all inputs can be optimally adjusted.

In the short run, capital is fixed, and thus there is a fixed cost and a variable cost. The short-run total cost function is quadratic, and short-run marginal costs are increasing. Even though the long-run cost function is linear, the fixed capital input means that marginal costs increase in the short run (since not all inputs can be adjusted optimally). This short-run cost function is specific to the fixed level of capital; a different level of capital would result in a different short-run total cost curve (with the same general shape but a different intercept).

Figure 7.6 shows the general shape of the short- and long-run cost curves.

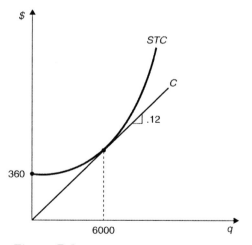
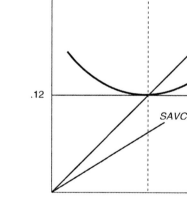

Figure 7.6

Figure 7.7 shows the points from Solved Problem 2, including the new short-run cost curve, after the firm adjusts to a lower level of capital (72). The equation of this curve is

$$C = \frac{q^2}{100,000} + 288$$

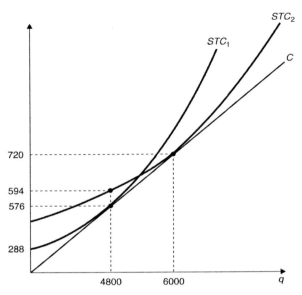

Figure 7.7

4. The Kardbored Box company can make its boxes out of either recycled newspaper or wood pulp. In fact, one pound of recycled newspaper and one pound of wood pulp are perfect substitutes for one another. The company wishes to produce 100 boxes. Show how changes in the price of wood pulp will affect its decision about how to produce the 100 boxes.

    Step 1: Draw Kardbored's isoquant, $q = 100$.

    Because they are perfect substitutes, the isoquant is linear. Its slope is −1. We don't know exactly how many pounds of the two inputs are needed, so we cannot label the axes precisely, but we do know that the points where it hits the axes must be equal. In Figure 7.8, $N_1 = W_1$.

    Step 2: Draw an isocost line facing the company and determine how a profit-maximizing (cost-minimizing) firm would respond.

    The isocost line is linear. Its slope depends on the relative prices of the two inputs—recycled newspaper and wood pulp. For example, we could have drawn in the dashed isocost line, C_x. Obviously, the firm can do better than to produce along this isocost line, at point X. Its goal is to minimize costs, and it can produce $q = 100$ at a lower cost. Draw in the lowest isocost line that allows the firm to produce $q = 100$ and that reflects the same prices as isocost line C_x. Isocost line C_1 is this line. The company will produce 100 boxes at the lowest cost by using nothing but recycled newspapers.

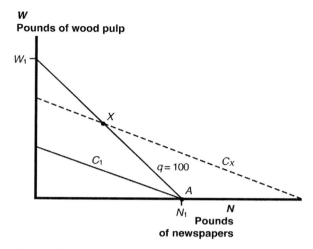

Figure 7.8

Step 3: Change the price of wood pulp and determine how a profit-maximizing firm would respond.

Figure 7.9 shows the isoquant $q = 100$ (the dark line) and isocost line C_1 from Figure 7.4. Increasing the price of wood pulp will cause the isocost line to rotate toward isocost line C_0. The company will continue using only newspaper (point A). Cutting the price of wood pulp by a small amount will cause the isocost line to rotate to isocost line C_2. Again, the firm will minimize costs at point A. If the price of wood pulp falls even more, the isocost line could have the same slope as the isoquant line. In this case, the firm can pick any point along the isoquant. (If newspaper and wood pulp have the same price per pound, the company does not care which one it uses.) Finally, if the price of wood pulp falls below that of newspapers, we'll have isocost lines with a slope like that of C_3 and C_4. The firm will choose point B, along isocost line C_4, because this costs less than any point along C_3. Thus the firm will use newspaper whenever newspaper is cheaper and wood pulp whenever wood pulp is cheaper.

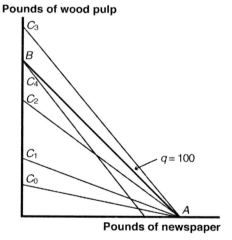

Figure 7.9

5.   Using the information from the isoquants and isocost lines in Figure 7.10, derive the firm's long-run average total costs, average fixed costs, average variable costs, marginal costs, and short-run average total costs. All the isocost lines have the same slope. The capital rental rate is $10 per hour.

Step 1: Calculate the cost associated with each isocost line.

Along any isocost line, cost, C, equals $wL + rK$. We don't know the wage rate, w, but we can calculate the cost at the end point where no labor is used. Along the isocost that is closest to the origin, C_1, cost must be $C_1 = (w \times 0) + (\$10 \times 8) = \$80$, because 8 units of capital are used at point A and $r = \$10$ per hour. Therefore, wage must be $20 per hour, since cost is $80 at point B and 4 hours of labor are used (with no capital). Knowing that $w = \$20$, it follows that $C_2 = \$160$ and $C_3 = \$240$.

Step 2: Calculate the long-run average cost.

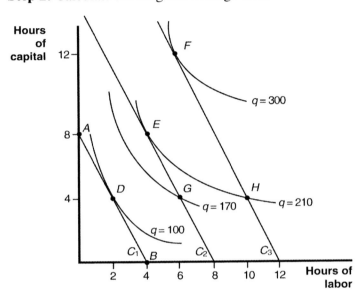

Figure 7.10

In the long run, both capital and labor can adjust, so the firm will produce any quantity at the cost-minimizing point—at the point of tangency between the isoquant and the lowest possible isocost line. Three points on the long-run average cost curve are at D, E, and F. Average cost = Cost/Quantity, so

Point	Long-run Average Cost
D	$80/100 = $0.80
E	$160/210 = $0.76
F	$240/300 = $0.80

This long-run average cost curve is U-shaped because the production function first exhibits increasing returns to scale (output more than doubles as inputs double between D and E) and then decreasing returns to scale (output rises at a slower rate than inputs between points E and F).

Step 3: Calculate the short-run costs.

In the short run, capital is fixed. There are an infinite number of short-run average, variable, fixed, and marginal cost curves—one for each level of capital. Figure 7.6 allows us to calculate the short-run cost curves for $K = 4$. To expand output in the short run, the firm will move from point D to G to H.

Fixed cost = rK, or $10 \times 4 = 40$ in all cases.

Variable cost = wL. $w = \$20$ and we can find the amount of labor from Figure 7.6.

Total cost = Fixed cost + variable cost.

Marginal cost = Δtotal cost/Δoutput.

Point	Output q	Fixed Cost F	Variable Cost VC	Total Cost C	Marginal Cost MC
D	100	$40	$20 × 2 = $40	$80	
G	170	$40	$20 × 6 = $120	$160	$80/70 = $1.14
H	210	$40	$20 × 10 = $200	$240	$80/40 = $2.00

Point	Output	Average Fixed Cost AFC = F/q	Average Variable Cost AVC = VC/q	Average Cost AC = C/q
D	100	$0.400	$0.400	$0.800
G	170	$0.235	$0.706	$0.941
H	210	$0.190	$0.952	$1.143

■ Practice Problems

Multiple-Choice

1. A lump-sum tax (franchise fee) will cause a parallel upward shift in
   a. the marginal cost curve.
   b. the average fixed cost curve.
   c. the average variable cost curve.
   d. the average cost curve.
   e. none of the cost curves.

2. The minimum point on a short-run average cost curve will also be on the long-run average cost curve if the long-run average cost curve exhibits
   a. economies of scale.
   b. constant returns to scale.
   c. diseconomies of scale.
   d. economies of scope.

Fill-in

3. Miracle Drug, Inc. has spent $100,000,000 on research in developing its product, Elixir of Life, which it hopes will add years to the average life span. So far, the company has not discovered anything that is commercially valuable. The $100,000,000 is a _____.

4. The wage rate is $10 per hour and the marginal product of labor is 50 widgets per hour; therefore, the marginal cost of a widget is _____.

5. A cost-minimizing firm faces $w = \$5$ and $r = \$50$. If it selects labor and capital so that $MP_L = 4$, then $MP_K = $ _____.

6. One reason that a buyer may prefer shopping at the mall rather than driving all over town is that even if the prices are a bit higher, the _____ costs are lower.

True-False-Ambiguous and Explain Why

7. A U-shaped long-run average cost curve initially slopes downward because it hasn't experienced the law of diminishing marginal returns at this output level.

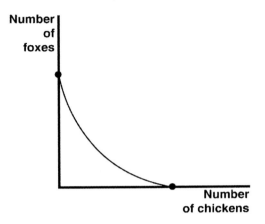

Figure 7.11

8. The firm whose production possibilities frontier is shown in Figure 7.7 has economies of scope in the production of foxes and chickens.

9. The minimum point of a short-run average cost curve will be on the long-run average cost curve.

10. The minimum point on a firm's average variable cost curve can occur at the same output level as the minimum point on the firm's average total cost curve.

Short-Answer

11. A firm's total cost function is $C = 100 + 40q + 5q^2$. Give equations for its fixed cost, variable marginal cost, average fixed cost, average variable cost, and average total cost.

12. A firm's total cost function is $C = 600 + 50q + 6q^2$. Its marginal cost function is $MC = 50 + 12q$.
    a. At what output does it minimize short-run average total cost?
    b. At what output does it minimize short-run average variable cost?

13. Draw isocost lines for a company that bids up the wage rate as it employs more workers.

14. Draw a firm's long-run cost curve, long-run average cost curve, and long-run marginal cost curve if its input costs are constant and it experiences increasing returns to scale at all output levels.

15. Joe and Marcy are at the video store. Marcy suggests that they rent the movie they've both been dying to see, *Walk the Line*. Joe says, "No can do. We rented that one last week for $5, but got too busy to see it and paid $10 in late fines. Rerenting is a waste of money." All the movies in the video store cost $5. With whom would an economist side? Explain why.

16. Would a firm ever hire Tom, a worker whose marginal product of labor is zero for every hour he works? Explain using isoquant–isocost analysis.

17. Why does marginal cost equal the slope of both the variable cost curve and the total cost curve?

18. What is the difference between increasing returns to scale and economies of scale?

19. Robert went to the Immigration History Research Center and began entering data from the records of the First Catholic Slovak Fraternal Union. In the first hour he entered 100 pieces of data. In the second hour he entered 150 pieces of data. In the third hour he entered 170 pieces of data. What explains his increased marginal product of labor per hour?

20. Radio station WFAN purchased two tickets to the Super Bowl at $50 each. Mr. Lucky, CEO of Lucky Enterprises, won the tickets when he was randomly approached and answered WFAN's daily trivia question correctly. Mr. Lucky decided to take a corporate client to the big game. As they left the parking lot, a scalper offered Mr. Lucky $250 for each ticket. What was the cost to Mr. Lucky of taking his client to the Super Bowl?

21. A firm's cost function is $C = 200 - 5q + q^2 - 0.2LBD$, where q = output in the current period and LBD is the total amount of learning by doing in the firm's history—that is, its cumulative output in past years. The firm has produced 100 units during its history. Draw its average cost curve for this year and its average cost curve for next year, assuming that it produces 50 units this year.

22. Figure 7.12 shows the situation facing Alejandro, a farmer who raises cotton. Faced with the price ratio in isocost line C_1 and desiring to produce 100 bales, he selects L_1 units of labor and P_1 units of pesticides. The next year a war breaks out, the government begins using pesticides to defoliate enemy jungles, and rations pesticides to farmers. Now Alejandro cannot use more than P_1 units of pesticides. Show the lowest isocost line that allows Alejandro to produce 200 bales of cotton after the war begins.

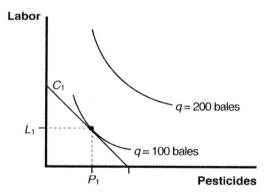

Figure 7.12

23. The total cost of producing cat food is

$$C_{CF} = 30 + q_{CF}.$$

The total cost of producing dog food is

$$C_{DF} = 30 + q_{DF}.$$

The total cost of jointly producing cat food and dog food is

$$C_{Joint} = 50 + q_{CF} + q_{DF}.$$

Does the production of cat food and dog food exhibit economies of scope?

24. The total cost of producing cat food is

$$C_{CF} = 30 + q_{CF}.$$

The total cost of producing dog food is

$$C_{DF} = 30 + 0.5q_{DF}.$$

The total cost of jointly producing cat food and dog food is $C_{\text{Joint}} = 70 + q_{CF} + 0.25q_{DF}$.

Does the production of cat food and dog food exhibit economies of scope?

25. Melvin claims that his firm's average total cost and average variable cost schedules are given below. Do you believe him? Explain.

q	AC	AVC
1	10	8
2	8	6
3	7	5
4	8	6
5	9	7

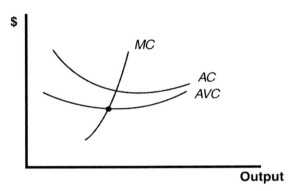

Figure 7.13

26. Now Melvin claims that his firm's cost curves are given in Figure 7.13. Do you believe him this time? Explain.

27. The Hormsbury Corporation produces yo-yos at its factory. Wages are $12 per hour and yo-yo making equipment (a computer-controlled plastic extruding machine) rents for $4 per hour. The production function is $q = 40K^{0.25}L^{0.75}$, where q = boxes of yo-yos per week, K = hours of yo-yo equipment use, and L = hours of labor.

   a. Determine the cost-minimizing capital–labor ratio.

   b. Graph the company's isoquant for $q = 1000$ and the isocost line tangent to this isoquant. What is the minimum cost of producing 1000 boxes of yo-yos?

   c. Show the firm's expansion path.

   d. Suppose that capital is fixed at the level that minimizes the cost of producing 1000 yo-yos. Explain what the firm would do in the short run in order to produce 1500 boxes of yo-yos per week. Give the new input mix and cost of production.

e. Leopard Hormsbury is in charge of long-term planning. He knows that the prices of inputs won't change if the firm expands and believes that the firm should increase the scale of output to tap into economies of scale. Is he correct? Explain.

f. Draw the long-run and short-run average cost curves for this firm.

28. Figure 7.14 gives the initial equilibrium for a firm making 100 widgets per hour. Then, the wage rate doubles. Draw the new $C = \$1,000$ isocost line facing the firm and show how it responds to the doubling of the wage in the short run and in the long run, if it wishes to continue making 100 widgets per hour. What are the short-run and the long-run costs of making 100 widgets after the wage rate doubles?

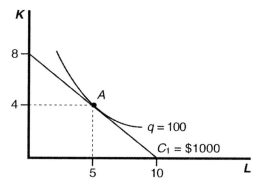

Figure 7.14

29. Suppose that a firm's production function is $q = 4KL$. In addition, the price of capital is $2 per machine hour, the price of labor is $10 per hour, and capital is fixed at 5 machine hours. Graph the fixed cost, variable cost, total cost, average fixed cost, average variable cost, average total cost, and marginal cost curves when output equals 10, 20, 30, and 40.

30. Jackson discovers that he can produce 200 pounds of pork by feeding his hogs the following combinations of feed:

Combination	Quantity of Corn (pounds)	Quantity of Potatoes (pounds)
A	500	1650
B	550	1460
C	600	1280
D	650	1120
E	700	1060
F	750	1020

If the price of a pound of potatoes is half the price of a pound of corn, and corn sells for P dollars per pound, what is the cost of each combination? What is the minimum-cost combination? Plot isocost curves and the isoquant, showing the cost-minimizing combination.

31. Suppose that Kyle is taking two courses during summer school—Economy and History. Tomorrow he has final exams in both classes and he has decided to devote ten hours to studying. Below are listed the grades on the final exam that he can receive in each class. Of course, the grades are tied to how much he studies for each class. Draw a production possibilities frontier showing the trade-off involved in studying for each subject. Derive a marginal cost curve for studying history for Kyle.

Hours Spent Studying for Class	Grade on Final Exam	
	Economy	History
0	50	50
1	57	58
2	63	66
3	69	73
4	74	80
5	79	86
6	84	91
7	88	95
8	92	97
9	95	99
10	97	100

32. Dynamic Industries, whose total product of labor curve is given in Figure 7.15, faces a wage rate of $10 per hour and a capital cost of $5 per day. They have 7 pieces of capital in operation. Use this information to calculate the firm's daily variable costs, total costs, marginal costs, average variable costs, and average total costs.

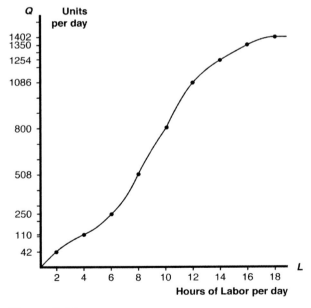

Figure 7.15

33. Figure 7.16 shows the expansion path of McFly Industries. The wage rate is $20 per hour. Draw McFly's long-run average cost curve. In what regions are there economies of scale and/or diseconomies of scale? What do we know about McFly's returns to scale?

34. How would Figure 7.16 change if McFly's production process underwent a neutral technological change that increased productivity by 30 percent?

35. How would Figure 7.16 change if McFly's production process underwent a labor-saving technological improvement?

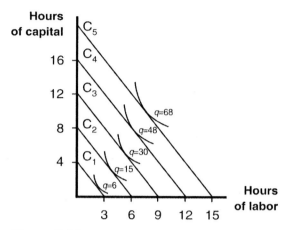

Figure 7.16

36. A firm has the production function $q = K^{1/2}L^{1/2}$. The wage rate and the rental rate on capital are both equal to \$1. The firm would like to know the minimum cost of producing 1000 units of output. Find the combination of inputs that minimizes the cost of producing 1000 units, the total cost, and identify the expansion path. Graph your results.

37. The firm described in Problem 36 would like to know how much output it can produce for a cost of \$5000. Find the output-maximizing input combination and the maximum output that can be produced.

38. The firm described in Problem 36 has decided to purchase 1000 units of capital. Derive the firm's short- and long-run cost curves.

39. The firm described in Problem 36 planned to produce an output of 1000, and thus purchased 1000 units of capital. An unexpected increase in demand has made it desirable to produce 1500 units instead.
    a. Find the firm's cost minimizing choice of inputs in the short run, and the short-run total and average total cost of producing 1500 units.
    b. Find the firm's long-run choice of inputs and the long-run total cost of producing 1500 units.
    c. Carefully graph your results, both as an isoquant map and as a graph of short- and long-run total cost curves.

40. Based on the following statement, draw the short-run marginal product, average product, and total product curves AND the total cost, variable cost, marginal cost, average variable cost and average total cost curve.

    "The firm initially experiences increasing returns to the variable factor. After the 50th worker, the marginal product of labor is constant until the firm reaches the 100th worker. After that point, there are diminishing returns."

■ Answers to Practice Problems

1. e. The average fixed cost curve and the average cost curve will shift upward, but the shift will not be parallel.

2. b.

3. sunk cost.

4. $0.20 per widget. $MC = w/MP_L$.

5. $MP_K = \$40$. Assuming that the firm is at a point of tangency, then equilibrium implies that $w/r = MP_L/MP_K$.

6. transactions

7. False. The law of diminishing marginal returns only holds in the *short run*. The long-run average cost curve's shape is determined by returns to scale and the prices of inputs.

8. False. Economies of scope exist when the production possibilities frontier is concave to the origin. This *PPF* is convex. It is more expensive to produce foxes and chickens together—probably because the foxes keep raiding the hen house.

9. Ambiguous. The minimum point of a short-run average cost curve may be on the long-run average cost curve, but it often is not. The minimum point on a short-run average cost curve shows the output level that minimizes the cost of producing when capital is at a certain level. There may be a way of producing this level of output more cheaply by changing the level of capital.

10. True. This will occur if and only if the firm has no fixed cost. In that case, the average variable cost curve and the average total cost curve are exactly the same. Otherwise, the *AVC* minimum must be at a lower output than the *AC* minimum. $AC = AVC + AFC$. Since the *AFC* is declining everywhere, the *AC* curve must be sloped downward when the *AVC* curve is at its minimum point. Since the *AC* is sloped downward at the *AVC*'s minimum point, the *AC*'s minimum point must come at a higher output level.

11. Fixed cost, $F = 100$.

    Variable cost, $VC = 40q + 5q^2$.

    Marginal cost $= 40 + 10q$

    Average fixed cost, $AFC = F/q = 100/q$.

    Average variable cost, $AVC = VC/q = 40 + 5q$.

    Average total cost $= AC = C/q = 100/q + 40 + 5q$.

    We could also calculate the marginal cost function, $MC = 40 + 10q$, which can be derived by taking the first derivative of the total cost function.

12. Because the marginal cost curve cuts through both the average total cost and the average variable cost curves at their minimum points, all we need to do is find the intersections.

$$AC = C/q = 600/q + 50 + 6q.$$
$$VC = 50q + 6q^2.$$
$$AVC = VC/q = 50 + 6q.$$

a.   At the minimum average cost, $AC = MC$:

$$Ac = 600/q + 50 + 6q = 50 + 12q = MC$$
$$600/q = 6q$$
$$600 = 6q^2$$
$$100 = q^2$$

$q = 10$ is the output that minimizes average cost.

b.   At the minimum average variable cost, $AVC = MC$:

$$AVC = 50 + 6q = 50 + 12q = MC$$
$$6q = 12q$$

$q = 0$ is the output that minimizes average variable cost.

13. Figure 7.17 gives an example. If the firm hires more than five workers, the wage rate rises. The dashed section of isocost line C_1 shows what the isocost cost line would look like if the wage rate did not rise. Because the wage rate rises, C_1 is kinked and is inside the dashed isocost line—less input can be hired at a cost of C_1 than if the wage rate did not rise. Because the wage rate depends on the quantity of labor hired, C_1 and C_0 have their kinks at the same level of labor ($L = 5$).

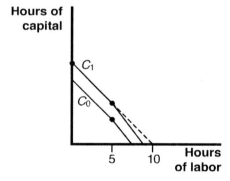

Figure 7.17

14. Increasing returns to scale means that output rises faster than inputs. Since the question assumes that input prices are constant, costs will rise at the same rate as inputs, so output rises faster than costs. As Figure 7.18(a) shows, this means that the long-run cost curve gets flatter and flatter as output rises. The long-run average cost can be found as the slope of a ray from the origin to a point on the long-run cost curve. The long-run marginal cost curve can be found as the slope of the long-run cost curve. Figure 7.18(b) is derived from 7.148(a) and shows that if returns to scale are always increasing, then the long-run average cost curve is always sloping downward, with the long-run marginal cost curve always below it.

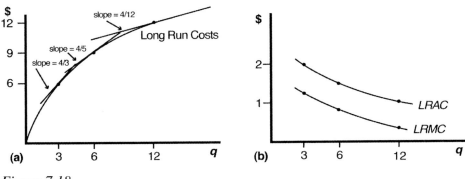

Figure 7.18

15. The economist sides with Marcy. The marginal cost of all the movies is the same, $5. The $15 that has already been spent on *Walk the Line* is a sunk cost and should be ignored.

16. Figure 7.19 shows the firm's isoquant. It is a horizontal line because extra hours of Tom's labor yield no extra output. If the price of Tom's labor is positive, as it is for isocost line C_1, then the firm will have a corner solution and won't hire Tom. The firm would gain by hiring him if his wage were negative (i.e., someone *paid* them to use the worker). This might happen if the government is paying the firm to train the worker. It might also happen if the firm is not trying to maximize profits—hiring the boss's incompetent son. It might also happen if the firm has a very restrictive contract mandating a certain level of employment. The isocost line would look like C_2—lying on top of the isoquant curve until H_{min}. For example, when railroads were switching from steam to diesel locomotives, their contracts with the unions mandated that each crew have a fireman (whose job it was to stoke the fire in the locomotive's boiler). Since the new diesel engines had no boiler to stoke, the fireman was redundant. This practice was known as featherbedding, because there were stories about idle firemen bringing featherbeds onto the train, so they could nap on the job.

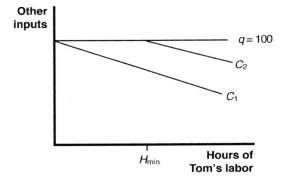

Figure 7.19

17. Because they have the same slope. Total cost = variable cost + fixed cost. Since fixed cost is a constant, the total cost curve is parallel to the variable cost curve.

18. Increasing returns to scale is a production relationship—it compares the rate of change of all inputs to the rate of change of output, keeping the ratio of inputs constant. If output rises at a faster rate than do inputs, then the production function exhibits increasing returns to scale. Economies of scale is a cost relationship—it compares the rate of change of costs to the rate of change of output. If costs rise more slowly than output, then long-run average costs fall and the cost function exhibits economies of scale. If input prices (wages, rental rate for capital, etc.) are constant, then increasing returns to scale will cause economies of scale. Since input prices are not always constant, and because the production function may be such that different levels of output are produced most efficiently with different ratios of inputs, there is not a one-to-one correspondence between increasing returns to scale and economies of scale.

19. This appears to be a case of learning by doing. Learning by doing occurs when workers become more skilled at their jobs and discover better ways to produce as they gain experience. It causes average costs to fall. For example, if Robert's time was worth $20 per hour, the cost of data fell from 20 cents per piece of data to 11.7 ¢ per piece of data.

20. $250 (plus any transportation, parking fees, etc.). Cost = opportunity cost, the best alternative use of a resource. In this case, the best alternative is to sell the client's ticket to the scalper and gain $250.

21. Figure 7.20 shows the average cost curves, $AC_{This\ Year}$ and $AC_{Next\ Year}$. Cumulative output in past years, LBD, enters as a constant in each year's annual cost function, so learning by doing shifts the cost curve down from $C = 180 - 5q + q^2$ to $C = 170 - 5q + q^2$. The average cost curve falls from $AC = 180/q - 5 + q$ to $AC = 170/q - 5 + q$.

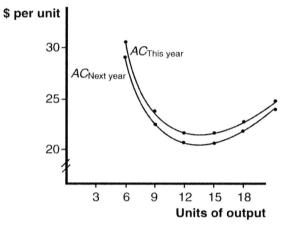

Figure 7.20

22. Figure 7.21 shows the new isocost line that allows him to produce $q = 200$ bales. The maximum amount of pesticides that he can buy is P_1, so the isocost line cannot go beyond P_1. (It is as if the price of pesticides becomes infinite when more than P_1 is purchased.) Notice that the isocost line is not tangent to the isoquant.

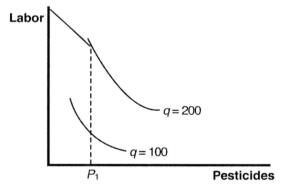

Figure 7.21

23. Use the Scope Coefficient formula

$$SC = \frac{C(q_1, 0) + C(0, q_2) - C(q_1, q_2)}{C(q_1, q_2)}$$

where $C(q_1, 0)$ is the cost of producing q_1 units of the first good by itself, $C(0, q_2)$ is the cost of producing q_2 units of the second good by itself, and $C(q_1, q_2)$ is the cost of producing both goods together.

$$SC = (30 + q_{CF} + 30 + q_{DF} - (50 + q_{CF} + q_{DF}))/(50 + q_{CF} + q_{DF}).$$

$$SC = 10/(50 + q_{CF} + q_{DF}) > 0, \quad \text{so economies of scope exist.}$$

We could have noticed this without using the formula. By producing the two products together, the fixed cost of production fell from 60 to 50. This savings of fixed costs generated the economies of scope.

24. $SC = (30 + q_{CF} + 30 + 0.5q_{DF} - (70 + q_{CF} + 0.25q_{DF}))/(70 + q_{CF} + 0.25q_{DF})$

$\qquad = (-10 + 0.25q_{DF})/(70 + q_{CF} + 0.25q_{DF})$

This expression can be either greater or less than zero.

It is greater than zero if $-10 + 0.25q_{DF} > 0$, or if $q_{DF} > 40$.

25. Melvin must have made a mistake. $AC = AVC + AFC$. This table implies that AFC is always 2, but since $AFC = F/q$, it cannot be a constant—it must decline as q rises. If $AFC = 2$ when $q = 1$, then $F = 2$. If $AFC = 2$ when $q = 2$, then $F = 1$. Both of these cannot be true, because C does not vary as q changes.

26. Poor Melvin cannot be correct about his marginal cost curve. It must pass through the minimum point on the AVC curve and the minimum point on the AC curve. It obviously does not pass through the minimum point of the AC curve in Figure 7.13.

27. a. To minimize cost, the firm picks K and L so that $w/r = MP_L/MP_K$ (this is also the first-order condition from a cost-minimization problem and is the expansion path). $MP_L = 30K^{0.25}L^{-0.25}$ and $MP_K = 10K^{-0.75}L^{0.75}$. Substituting in the information from the problem:

$$12/4 = 30K^{0.25}L^{-0.25}/10K^{-0.75}L^{0.75}$$

$$3 = 3K/L$$

$$K = L.$$

b. Figure 7.22 shows isoquant $q = 1,000$. To find the tangency point, substitute $K = L$ for K and then solve for L. $q = 1,000 = 40L^{0.25}L^{0.75} = 40L$, so $L = 25$ and $K = 25$. Find other points by picking a level for K and solving for L.

For example, when $K = 40$, $q = 1000 = (40 \times 40^{0.25}L^{0.75}) = (40 \times 2.514867 \times L^{0.75})$

$$1000/100.595 = L^{0.75}$$

$$(9.9408)^{4/3} = (L^{3/4})^{4/3}$$

$$L = 21.375.$$

Likewise, if $L = 40$, then

$$q = 1000 = (40 \times K^{0.25} 40^{0.75})$$

$$= (40 \times 15.905 \times K^{0.25})$$

$$1000/636.2 = K^{0.25}$$

$$(1.5718)^4 = (K^{1/4})^4$$

$$K = 6.104.$$

Isocost line C_1 is tangent to $q = 1000$ at $K = L = 25$, so the cost along this isocost line is $C = wL + rK = (\$12 \times 25) + (\$4 \times 25) = \$400$. The minimum cost of producing 1000 boxes of yo-yos is $400.

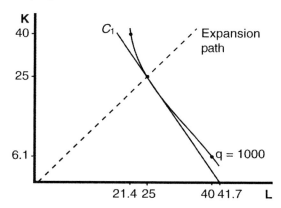

Figure 7.22

c. Figure 7.22 shows the firm's expansion path. In part *a* of this problem, we found that when $w/r = 3$, the firm will select $K = L$. This holds for all levels of output.

d. In the short run, the firm cannot increase capital, but can only increase labor. To find out how much labor is needed to produce $q = 1500$ boxes of yo-yos, substitute in $K = 25$ and solve for L. $q = 1500 = (40 \times 25^{0.25} L^{0.75}) = (40 \times 2.236 L^{0.75})$

$$1500 / 89.44 = L^{0.75}$$

$$(16.771)^{4/3} = (L^{3/4})^{4/3}$$

$$L = 42.928.$$

The cost of making 1500 yo-yos in the short run, when $K = 25$, is $C = (\$4 \times 25 + \$12 \times 42.928) = \$615.14$.

e. Leopard Hormsbury is incorrect. The firm does not enjoy economies of scale because it has constant returns to scale. (We know that if $K = L = 25$, then $q = 1000$. If $K = L = 50$, then $q = (40 \times 50^{0.25} \times 50^{0.75}) = (40 \times 50^{(0.25 + 0.75)}) = 40 \times 50 = 2000$. Therefore, the firm has constant returns to scale.) Any time the exponents in a Cobb-Douglas production function add up to 1, the production function has constant returns to scale. If the exponents' sum is greater than one, it has increasing returns to scale. If the exponents sum to less than one, it has decreasing returns to scale.

f. Figure 7.23 shows the long-run and short-run average cost curves. We have already found one point on the long-run average cost curve. In part b we found that the minimum cost of producing 1000 boxes is $400, or $0.40 per box. We can quickly find other points by calculating other quantities along the expansion path in Figure 7.22. For example, where $K = L = 37.5$, the output is $q = 40 \times 37.5^{0.25} \times 37.5^{0.75} = (40 \times 37.5) = 1500$. The cost of producing 1500 boxes is $C = (12 \times 37.5) + (4 \times 37.5) = 600$, so the average cost is $C/q = 600/1500 = \$0.40$. Thus, the average cost is the same whether producing 1000 or 1500 boxes. The long-run average cost curve is flat, as we would expect since in part e of this question, we determined that this production function exhibits constant returns to scale.

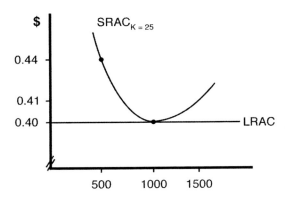

Figure 7.23

We already have enough information to calculate two points on one of the short-run average cost curves—the one where $K = 25$. As calculated in the previous paragraph, the average cost of making 1000 boxes when $K = 25$ is $0.40 per box. From part d of this problem, we know that the cost of making 1500 boxes is $615.14 when $K = 25$. Therefore, the average cost is $C/q = \$615.14/1,500 = \$0.4101$. The figure also plots the short-run average of producing 500 boxes with $K = 25$, which is $0.438 per box. (You could also find all the cost curves as shown in the Solved Problems.)

28. Figure 7.24 shows that the isocost lines become twice as steep. The firm can no longer produce 100 widgets for $1000. In the long run, it will substitute away from labor and toward capital—moving from point A to point B. In the short run the firm cannot change its level of capital and must continue making the widgets in the same way—at point A. We can deduce the costs of these two points. The endpoint of isocost C_1 says that 8 units of capital cost $1000. Therefore, capital costs $125 per unit. Likewise, the wage rate must initially be $100, but it climbs to $200.

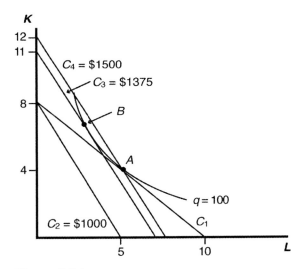

Figure 7.24

According to the figure, the endpoint of isocost C_3 is at $K = 11$. If so, it costs $1375 everywhere along C_3. C_4 goes through the initial point, thus its cost must be $125 \times 4 = \$500$ for capital and $200 \times 5 = \$1000$ for labor—i.e., it costs $1500 everywhere along C_4. The firm must spend $125 more to make the 100 widgets in the short run. This is the cost of not being able to adjust capital to reach the point of tangency at B.

29. Figure 7.25(a) plots the fixed cost, variable cost, and total cost from the table below. Figure 7.25(b) plots the average fixed cost, average variable cost, average total cost, and marginal cost curves. First plug $K = 5$ into the production function, $q = 4KL$ and solve for the quantity of labor needed to produce each output level. For example, $q = 10 = (4 \times 5 \times L)$, so $L = 0.5$. Then remember the following:

Fixed costs, F, equal K times the price of capital. Since K always equals 5 and the price of capital is $2 per machine hour, $F = \$10$.

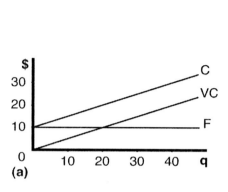

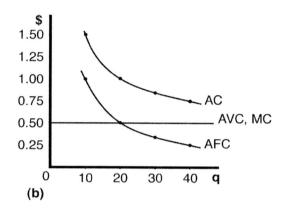

Figure 7.25

Variable costs, VC, equal L times the wage rate ($10 per hour).

$$C = F + VC,$$
$$AFC = F/q,$$
$$AVC = VC/q,$$
$$AC = C/q,$$

$MC = \Delta C/\Delta q$, which is always $0.50 here because costs rise by $5 for every 10 extra units produced.

K	L	q	F ($)	VC ($)	C ($)	AFC ($)	AVC ($)	ATC ($)	MC ($)
5	0.5	10	10	5	15	1.00	0.50	1.50	0.50
5	1.0	20	10	10	20	0.50	0.50	1.00	0.50
5	1.5	30	10	15	25	0.33	0.50	0.83	0.50
5	2.0	40	10	20	30	0.25	0.50	0.75	0.50

30. The table below gives the costs of the various combinations. Note that cost $= (P \times \text{Quantity of Corn}) + (0.5P \times \text{Quantity of Potatoes})$

A. $1325P$ D. $1210P$
B. $1280P$ E. $1230P$
C. $1240P$ F. $1260P$

The cheapest combination of inputs that produces 200 pounds of pork for Jackson is combination D, which costs $1210P$.

Figure 7.26 shows the isoquant and two of the isocost lines. Notice that the isocost lines have the same slope, reflecting the fact that the price of potatoes is half that of corn.

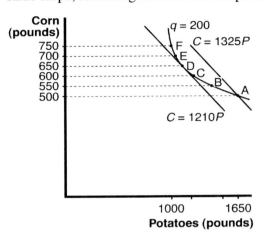

Figure 7.26

31. Figure 7.27 shows the joint production of exam scores on history and economics finals. Notice that it is bowed outward from the origin, indicating some economies of scope.

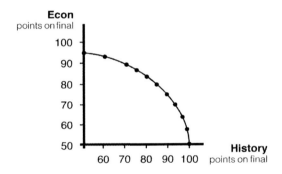

Figure 7.27

The marginal cost of studying for history can be expressed in points lost on the economics test. For each hour spent on history one less hour is spent on economics, and the economics grade falls, so this is the opportunity cost of studying history.

Hours Spent on History	Grade in Economics	Marginal Cost (Economics Points Lost)
0	97	
1	95	2
2	92	3
3	88	4
4	84	4
5	79	5
6	74	5
7	69	5
8	63	6
9	57	6
10	50	7

32.

L	q	VC (w × L)	TC (VC + FC)	MC ΔTC/q	AVC VC/q	ATC
0	0	0	35			
				20/42 = 0.476		
2	42	20	55		0.476	1.310
				20/68 = 0.294		
4	110	40	75		0.364	0.682
				20/140 = 0.143		
6	250	60	95		0.240	0.380
				20/258 = 0.078		
8	508	80	115		0.157	0.227
				20/292 = 0.068		
10	800	100	135		0.125	0.169
				20/286 = 0.070		
12	1086	120	155		0.110	0.143
				20/168 = 0.119		
14	1254	140	175		0.112	0.140
				20/96 = 0.208		
16	1350	160	195		0.119	0.144
				20/52 = 0.385		
18	1402	180	215		0.128	0.153

33. The long-run average cost curve comes from finding the cost minimizing combinations of labor and capital for each output level. These will be the points of tangency between the firm's isocost lines and its isoquant curves shown in Figure 7.16. We are given the quantities, and the costs for each isocost curve can be found by multiplying the wage rate by the quantity of labor where the isocost meets the horizontal axis. (The cost of capital must be $15 per hour.) The table below uses this information to calculate the (long-run) average cost.

Quantity	Cost	Average Cost = C/q
6	$ 60	$10.00
15	$120	$ 8.00
30	$180	$ 6.00
48	$240	$ 5.00
68	$300	$ 4.41

The long-run average cost curve is shown in Figure 7.28. McFly has economies of scale throughout this range, since the long-run average costs fall with rising output. We cannot tell much about the returns to scale, however. Returns to scale compare the rate of increase in output to the rate of increase of inputs, when all inputs are increased by the same proportion. In Figure 7.16, the ratio of capital to labor changes all along the expansion path—the capital and labor are never increased by the same proportion—so it is impossible to determine the returns to scale.

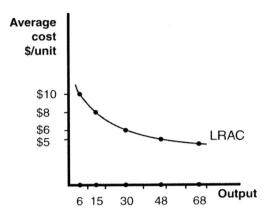

Figure 7.28

34. The only change to the diagram would be that the numbers associated with each isoquant curve would be 30% higher. Notice that this also changes the long-run average cost curve.

Old Quantity	New Quantity (After Technology Change)	Cost	Old *AC*	New *AC*
6	7.8	$ 60	$10.00	$7.69
15	19.5	$120	$ 8.00	$6.15
30	39	$180	$ 6.00	$4.61
48	62.4	$240	$ 5.00	$3.85
68	88.4	$300	$ 4.41	$3.39

35. A labor-saving technological improvement would reduce the ratio of labor to capital used to produce a given level of output. In Figure 7.12 it takes 7.5 hours of labor and 10 hours of capital to make 68 units of output. (Note that (7.5 hours of labor × $20 per hour) + (10 hours of capital × $15 per hour) = $300 and the cost all along C_5 is $300.) A labor-saving change would mean that the ratio of labor to capital would fall below the 7.5–10 ratio. For example, only 4.5 hours of labor might be needed to run the capital for 10 hours in making 68 units of output, as is the case at point *A* in Figure 7.25. The isoquant curves would move inward and somewhat to the left so that the expansion path would be to the left of the current expansion path. Figure 7.25 shows the general pattern.

36. To solve this problem, set up the cost minimization problem and then follow the steps in Solved Problem 1.

$$\text{Min } TC = L + K$$
$$\text{Subject to: } 1{,}000 = K^{1/2}L^{1/2}$$

After setting up the Lagrangian, you find $K/L = 1$ (or $K = L$) This is the first-order condition and the *expansion path*. Substitute into isocost constraint, and solve. $K = 1000$; $L = 1000$; $TC^* = \$2000$.

37. You can solve this problem by setting up the output maximization problem, but since you have already found the expansion path, the easy way to do this is to use that relationship. $5{,}000 = K + L$, so (substituting in the expansion path relationship) $5{,}000 = 2L$, and $L = 2{,}500$. Thus $K = 2{,}500$, and $Q = 2{,}500$.

38. Short-run costs:

$K = 1000$

$Q = (1000)^{1/2} L^{1/2}$

$L = 2250$

$STC = 1*1000 + 1*[Q^2/(1000)] = 1000 + Q^2/1000$

$SMC = Q/500$

$SAVC = Q/1000$

$SATC = 1000/Q + Q/1000$

Long-run costs:

$Q = K^{1/2}L^{1/2}$

$Q = L^{1/2}L^{1/2}$ (from the expansion path)

$Q = L$

$TC = L + K = 2L$

$TC = 2Q$

$MC = 2$

$AC = 2$

39. a. Short run:

$STC = 1000 + (1500)^2/1000 = \$3250$

$SMC = Q/500 = 3$

$SAVC = Q/1000 = 1.5$

$SATC = 1000/Q + Q/1000 = 2.16$

  b. Long run:

  Using the expansion path, $K = L = 1500$, and $TC = \$3000$. $AC (= MC) = 2$

  c. See graphs.

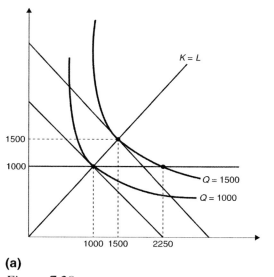

(a)

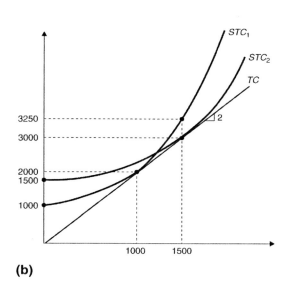

(b)

Figure 7.29

40. Figure 7.30 shows the approximate shape of all curves. The *exact* shape of these curves depends on the underlying mathematical functions, and the average marginal and variable cost curves will approach but are unlikely to meet the related marginal cost curves.

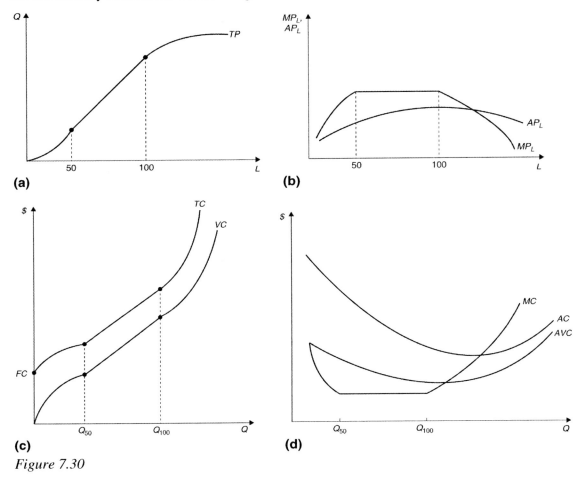

Figure 7.30

■ Exercises

Fill-in

1. The marginal rate of technical substitution at point *A* in Figure 7.31 is _____.

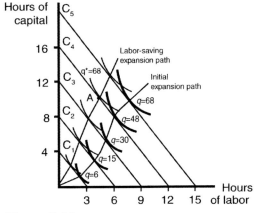

Figure 7.31

True-False-Ambiguous and Explain Why

2. The firm in Figure 7.32 sees both of its input prices double. If it wishes to produce 100 units of output, it will continue to use 3 units of labor and 3 units of capital.

3. The firm in Figure 7.32 experiences a neutral technological improvement. If it wishes to produce 100 units of output, it will continue to use 3 units of labor and 3 units of capital.

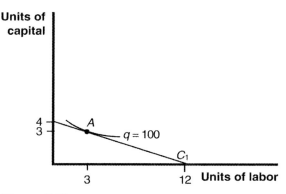

Figure 7.32

Short-Answer

4. The short-run cost function for Jim and Huck's Raft Company is $C = 50 + 20q + 4q^2$, where $C =$ dollars per day, and $q =$ ton-miles of cargo hauled. Find the marginal, average total, average variable, and average fixed costs, and graph them accurately.

5. Ace's Dog Yummies produces dog treats and toys. The production function for dog treats is $q = 500K^{3/4}L^{1/4}$. The rental cost of capital is $9 per hour, and the wage rate is $3 per hour. Find the cost-minimizing choice of inputs and cost of producing 24,000 dog treats.

6. Assuming that Ace's Dog Yummies purchases the level of capital that you found in Exercise 6, find the short and long-run cost curves.

7. One stop on the Aging Stones' latest concert tour is Gigantic Stadium, which seats exactly 100,000. (The fire marshall will not allow them to seat even one more customer.) For every 500 customers, the stadium needs to hire one security guard, one ticket taker, and one parking lot attendant. Each can be hired for $50 for the night of the concert. Draw the stadium's short-run marginal cost curve.

8. Dane decides to give up a job as a pricey $200,000-a-year lawyer and convert the duplex that he owns (and had been renting out for $10,000 a year) into a UFO Museum. His expenses include $20,000 per year paid to his assistant and $5000 per year for utilities. In addition, he must cash in his $100,000 in government bonds (which could be earning 5 percent interest a year) to buy extraterrestrial paraphernalia. What is his annual cost of running this business?

9. Lengthy Limos, Inc. has two gas stations next to its headquarters. At the Jiffy Mart, gasoline sells for $1.10 per gallon. At the SuperSlug, gas sells for $1.00 per gallon. At each station, it takes one minute to pump a gallon of gas. At the Jiffy Mart, you can pay at the pump, but at the SuperSlug, you need to wait in line to pay and this always takes 10 minutes. To which gas station should Lengthy Limos send it employees? Draw a graph showing the average cost of gasoline at the two stations, assuming that employees earn $6 per hour (10 cents per minute). How would the graph differ if the wage rate of the employees rose?

10. Figure 7.33 contains the average variable cost curve and a fragment of the average cost curve for a firm. Based on this information, complete the firm's *AC* curve and draw its marginal cost curve. What is the firm's fixed cost?

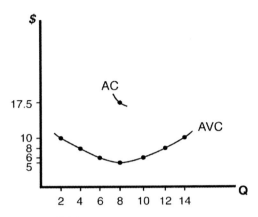

Figure 7.33

11. Draw an isoquant–isocost line graph to illustrate the following situation. Carbon, Inc. can rent mining machines for $200 per day and hire workers for $100 per day. It can minimize the cost of producing 50 tons of coal per day by using five machines and ten workers at a total cost of $2000. It can minimize the cost of producing 110 tons per day by using 10 machines and 20 workers at a total cost of $4000. And, it can minimize the cost of producing 150 tons per day by using 15 machines and 30 workers at a total cost of $6000. Draw Carbon's expansion path and (on another graph) its long-run average cost curve. Discuss the economies and diseconomies of scale that it possesses.

12. Suppose that a firm experiences decreasing returns to scale at all levels of production. Draw the approximate shape of the long-run total, marginal, and average cost curves.

Chapter 8
Competitive Firms and Markets

■ Chapter Summary

The behavior of firms depends on market structure: the number of firms in the market, the ease with which firms can enter and leave markets, and the ability of firms to differentiate their products. In a competitive market, each firm is a **price taker**. It cannot significantly affect the market price for its output (or inputs). A price taker faces a horizontal (or nearly horizontal) demand curve at the market price. It can sell as much as it wants at the market price, so it has no incentive to cut its price, and it cannot raise its price because no one will buy its output if it charges more than the going rate. Firms are likely to be price takers in markets that have some or all of these traits: (1) consumers believe that all firms sell identical products; (2) firms freely enter and exit the market; (3) buyers and sellers know the prices charged by firms; and (4) transactions costs are low. If maximizing consumers know your product is no better than other firms' products, if they know that you are attempting to charge more than other sellers, and if they can easily switch sellers, then they will not buy from you. If all four of the conditions hold exactly, the market is perfectly competitive. Even if some of these conditions are violated, firms may still be price takers. Many markets closely match this description. A individual firm's demand curve is called the **residual demand curve**, the market demand not met by other sellers at any given price, or $D'(p) = D(p) - S(p)$. For a competitive firm, the residual demand curve must be highly elastic (since there are many firms in the market selling identical products, and thus the firm is a price taker).

A firm's **economic profit**, π, is the difference between its revenue, R, and its opportunity cost, C. (Opportunity cost is the best alternative use of any asset the firm uses and includes both explicit and implicit costs.) Economic profit is generally smaller than **business profit**—revenue minus explicit cost. Earning zero economic profit is okay. It means the firm is doing as well as it could be doing if it used its assets in any other manner. To maximize profit, any firm (regardless of the market structure) must select the correct level of output—which may be zero. The **output rules for profit maximization** say that a firm must pick output so that **marginal cost** (MC) equals **marginal revenue** (MR), or in other words, marginal profit is zero. MR is the extra revenue that a firm earns from selling one more unit of output, dR/dq. If a firm is making a loss, it may continue to produce in the short run. The **shut-down rule** for profit maximization says that a firm must **shut down** (produce nothing) if it can reduce its loss by doing so—if its revenue is less than its variable cost at all levels of output.

In competitive markets, $MR \equiv p$ (since the price does not change as the firm sells more units), so the profit-maximizing rules imply that a competitive firm will pick its output where $MC = p$. This condition corresponds with the output rules described above; marginal profit must be equal to zero. (Second-order conditions also require that the second derivative of the cost function be positive.) It will shut down if its revenue is less than its variable cost: $R = pq < VC$. This occurs when the market price is less than the minimum of its short-run average variable cost curve: $p < AVC(q)$.

To derive the competitive firm's supply curve, we must see how it reacts to different price levels. The output and shut-down rules imply that the **competitive firm's short-run supply curve** is its marginal cost curve above its minimum average variable cost. The **market supply curve** horizontally sums the supply curves of all the individual firms in the market. The more identical firms producing at a given price, the more elastic is the short-run market supply curve any given price. When firms' costs differ, only the low-cost firm supplies at relatively low prices. As the price rises, higher-cost firms start supplying, creating a stair-like market supply curve. Together, the short-run market supply curve and the market demand curve determine the short-run competitive equilibrium and the price that all the firms must take.

A **competitive firm's long-run supply curve** is its marginal cost curve above its minimum long-run average cost. The firm chooses a plant size to maximize its long-run economic profit based on its beliefs about the future. The long-run market supply curve depends on the entry and exit of firms and how input prices vary with output. In the long run, firms enter a market if they can earn profit by doing so. These profits must take into account any entry or exit costs. Entry occurs until the last firm to enter the market—the **marginal firm**—makes zero long-run profit. Exit occurs when price falls and firms with minimum average cost above the new price leave. Firms making zero long-run profit are indifferent between staying and leaving. The long-run market supply curve is horizontal at the minimum long-run average cost if: (1) firms can freely enter and exit; (2) all firms have identical costs; and (3) input prices are constant. If entry is limited (by regulations, lack of resources, or costly entry), the long-run market supply curve will slope upward. If there are a limited number of the lowest-cost firms, the long-run market supply curve will slope upward. If input prices rise as output rises (an **increasing-cost market**), then the long-run market supply curve will slope upward. However, if input prices fall as output rises (a **decreasing-cost market**), the long-run market supply curve can slope downward. If the long-run competitive market supply curve is horizontal, then a shift in demand affects only the equilibrium output level and the number of firms, not the price.

In an importing country, the long-run supply curve equals the domestic supply curve plus the world's **residual supply curve**—which equals the quantity the market supplies that is not consumed by *other* demanders at any given price. The elasticity of residual supply, η_r, facing a given country is $\eta_r = (\eta/\theta) - ((1 - \theta)/\theta)\varepsilon_0$, where η is the market supply elasticity, ε_0 is the demand elasticity of the other countries, and $\theta = Q_i/Q$ is the importing country's share of the world's output. Thus if a country imports a small fraction of the world's supply, it will face an almost perfectly elastic, horizontal residual supply curve.

In competitive markets, profits are driven to zero, so any firm that does not maximize profit will lose money and be forced to exit. In long-run competitive equilibrium, profit must be zero, and price must be equal to long-run average cost. Thus the existence of profits in the short run causes entry, increasing supply and reducing prices, until profits equal zero. Losses in the short run cause exit, reducing supply and increasing prices, until profits equal zero.

■ Key Concepts and Formulas

- **Price taker:** a firm that can't significantly affect market price for its output or inputs.
- **The market is competitive and firms are price takers when:** (1) consumers believe that all firms sell identical products; (2) firms freely enter and exit the market; (3) buyers and sellers know the prices charged by firms; and (4) transactions costs are low.
- **Rules for maximizing profit:** (1) pick output so that marginal cost = marginal revenue and (2) shut down if revenue < variable cost (i.e., price < AVC curve's minimum).
- **Competitive firm's short-run supply curve:** its marginal cost curve above the minimum of its average variable cost.
- **Competitive firm's long-run supply curve:** its marginal cost curve above the minimum of its long-run average cost.
- **Long-run market supply** curve is horizontal at the minimum long-run average cost if firms have free entry/exit; all firms have identical costs; and input prices are constant.
- **Residual supply curve:** the quantity that the market supplies that is not consumed by other demanders at any given price.
- **Increasing-cost market:** input prices rise as output rises.

■ Application: Survival of the Fittest

Economists and managers have found it very difficult to estimate cost functions. We often do not have enough data to measure *economic* costs properly. In addition, the linear regressions (see Appendix 2A) used in most studies generally assume that cost functions are very smooth, but often they are not.

Question: How can we use the theory of competitive markets to estimate the output at which firms minimize costs?

Answer: The theory of competitive markets makes the prediction that firms with higher costs will earn negative economic profits and be induced to cut these costs or be forced to exit from the market. Thus firms that are operating on a scale that is too large (in the sense that average cost is higher than those of other firms) must shrink or they will be driven out of business. Firms that are operating on a scale that is too small (in the sense that average cost is higher than those of other firms) will need to scale up or they will be driven out of business. Entering firms, even if they do not know much about economies and diseconomies of scale in the market, will copy the practices of the successful firms—those with the lowest average costs. Thus the model predicts that in competitive markets, a larger and larger share of output will be produced by firms that are the optimal size—the size that minimizes average cost. Knowing this, the economist can examine firm output levels and see which type of firms are becoming more numerous and which are becoming less numerous. (Entry and exit occur in the long run, so it can take years for this process to work itself out.) Studies using this technique generally show that the efficient scale is fairly wide, suggesting that long-run average cost curves in many competitive industries have flat bottoms. (This method can also be used to track the evolution of optimum sizes over long periods of time.)

In Figure 8.1(a), the intersection of the long-run market supply curve, S, and the industry demand curve, D, occurs where price is p. (This must be a constant-cost market, so the long-run supply curve is horizontal and equals the minimum long-run average cost.) Any firm producing output between q^* and q^{**} in Figure 8.1(b) will have an average cost of p and will earn an economic profit equaling zero. These firms will remain in the industry and will have no incentive to change their output level. A firm whose output is q_2 is too large—its average costs are above the price, so its profits are negative. A firm whose output is q_1 is too small—its average costs are above the price, so its profits are negative, too. The firm producing q_1 has average cost equaling C_1, so its loss is $(C_1 - p)q_1$, which is labeled in Figure 8.1(b).

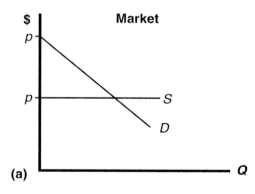
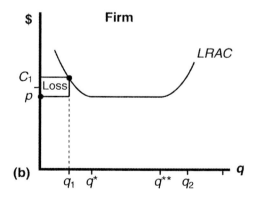

Figure 8.1

■ Solved Problems

1. In a perfectly competitive, constant-cost industry, demand is given by $Q = 2000 - 2P$. The short total cost function (at the scale of production that minimizes long-run costs for each identical firm) is $TC = 1000 + 100q + 10q^2$.

    a. What will the long-run price be in this industry? How many firms will there be in long-run equilibrium?

    b. What is the equation of the short-run supply curve if the industry is in long-run equilibrium?

    c. Suppose that demand in this industry increases to: $Q = 4000 - 2P$. What will the new LONG RUN price be in this industry, and how many firms will there be?

    d. Describe how the industry will adjust to reach the new long-run equilibrium (this should include finding the short-run price and quantity, and the quantity and profit of the firm), and illustrate your answer by drawing a graph of the firm and a graph of the industry, showing everything that you found in *a–c*.

Step 1: Find the long-run industry price.

In long-run equilibrium, profits must be zero, and in a constant-cost industry, in which every firm is identical, every firm must be operating at the minimum point on its average total cost curve. To find the minimum point, set marginal cost equal to average total cost.

$$MC = 100 + 20q$$
$$ATC = 1000/q + 100 + 10q$$
$$100 + 20q = 1000/q + 100 + 10q$$
$$q = 10$$
$$P = \$300$$
$$Q = 2000 - 2(300) = 1400$$
$$1400/10 = 140 \text{ firms}$$

Thus the long-run price in this industry will be $300, and there will be 140 firms.

Step 2: Find the short-run supply curve, given that there are 140 firms.

First, recall that the firm's short-run supply curve is the marginal cost curve above the shutdown point.

$$MC = 100 + 20q$$
$$AVC = 100 + 10q$$

Thus minimum average variable cost (the shutdown point) is at a quantity of zero and a price of $100. The firm's short-run supply curve is $P = 100 + 20q$ (this is the *MC* curve with *P* substituted for *MC*).

The short-run industry supply curve is the sum of the short-run marginal cost curves for each firm in the industry. To sum the supply curves, recall that you must add quantities, not prices, so rearrange the equation so that quantity is on the left-hand side. Then sum over the 140 firms in the industry.

$$q = -5 + 1/20P$$
$$Q_s = \Sigma q_i = \Sigma(-5 + 1/20P) = -700 + 7P$$

Step 3: Find the new long-run equilibrium.

Since there has been no change in costs and firms are identical, the long-run price will not change.

Long-run price = $300

$Q = 4000 - 2(300) = 3400$

$3400/10 = 340$ firms

Short-run price:

$-700 + 7P = 4000 - 2P$

$P = \$522.22$

$Q = 2956$

$q = 21$

Profit of each firm $= (522.22 * 21) - (1000 - 100 * 21 - 2 * 21^2) = \$7042.59$

Step 4: Explain and graph your results.

Higher demand causes industry price and quantity to rise, and each firm will produce more and make a profit. In the long run, profits attract entry, and so more firms will come into the market (shifting the short-run supply curve), lowering price and increasing industry quantity. In long-run equilibrium, each firm returns to the original quantity and makes a profit of zero. See Figure 8.2.

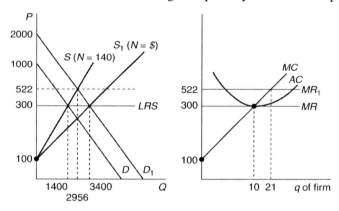

Figure 8.2

2. How will a firm's output decision change in the short run if the government levies a 50 percent tax on economic profits?

Step 1: Show the firm's profit-maximizing output decision before the tax is in place.

Figure 8.3 shows the total cost and total revenue curves for a typical firm. The firm maximizes profit at q_1.

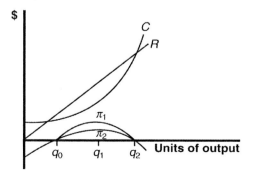

Figure 8.3

Step 2: Show the firm's profit-maximizing output decision after the tax is in place.

The tax on profits alters neither the firm's costs nor its revenues. Instead, it alters the profit curve. When profits are less than zero, no tax is collected. When profits are above zero, the profit curve shifts down by 50 percent from π_1 to π_2. The profit curve still reaches its maximum at q_1, so the tax does not affect the firm's output level. Any tax on profits will not affect the firm's output decision—unless it is a 100 percent tax, which would make the firm indifferent among all the points between q_0 and q_2. (Note that you could also show this problem using a *MR/MC* graph.)

Step 3: Consider the case where the firm shuts down.

In this case, the firm's profits are below zero, so the profit tax will not affect it. A profit tax should not affect a firm's long-run decision, either. If profits are negative, the tax has no effect. If profits are positive, the tax will lower, but not eliminate, the profit. Entry will still occur and will continue until the marginal firm earns zero economic profit—at which point the profit tax has no effect.

3.   A new hybrid seed is developed that costs as much as the old seed, but doubles crop yields. Assuming that the market is initially in long-run equilibrium, that the market is competitive, and that input prices do not rise, how will the new hybrid seed affect the profits of firms growing the crop? How will it affect the price of the crop? How will it affect the number of firms growing the crop?

Step 1: Show how the hybrid seed affects average costs.

Figure 8.4 shows how the hybrid shifts the average total cost curve. Originally, the average cost of growing q^* units of output was $2p$. Now it costs the same to grow $2q^*$, so the average cost of $2q^*$ is half as much, or p. Notice how the points on AC_0 and AC_1 correspond with one another: Point A_0 corresponds with point A_1, point B_0 corresponds with point B_1, and point C_0 corresponds with point C_1.

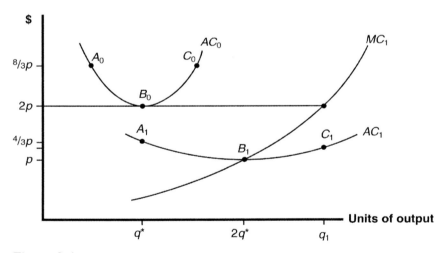

Figure 8.4

Step 2: Show what happens when the first firm adopts the hybrid.

When only one firm has adopted the hybrid, its average costs are lower than those of the other firms. The price will stay at the initial level, $2p$, and the firm will earn high profits. It will produce q_1 units— the point on its marginal cost curve at $2p$ in Figure 8.4, so its total profits will be the rectangle $(2p - 4/3p)q_1$ or $2/3pq_1$. These high potential profits will attract more and more firms to follow the lead, but as they do, total market output will rise enough so that the market price is pushed down. Once the price starts to fall, lagging firms, who haven't yet adopted the hybrid, will earn negative profits.

Step 3: Show what happens when all the firms have adopted the hybrid seed.

In a competitive constant-cost market, the long-run market supply curve is a horizontal line at the minimum point on the firms' long-run average cost curves. The adoption of the hybrid seed pushes down this minimum point and causes the long-run market supply curve to shift down from $2p$ to p, as shown in Figure 8.5. When the price has fallen to this level, firms using the hybrid will earn zero economic profit and will produce $2q^*$. The market output will rise as consumers move down along the demand curve. If the demand for the crop is elastic, output will rise at a greater rate than the rate at which the price falls. If Q_1 is more than twice as large as Q_0, then firms must enter the industry, since the existing firms will only produce $2Q_0$ when price is p. If the demand is inelastic, market output will less than double. Since all the firms have doubled their output, some of the firms will need to exit the market.

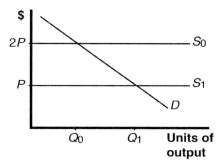

Figure 8.5

4. The insignificant little penny has been at the center of a heated debate. Many observers say that its value has fallen so much that it should be withdrawn from circulation and bills should be rounded to the nearest nickel. (Thus, if you bought a couple of snacks at a convenience store and your sales total was $2.78, your bill would be rounded to $2.80. If the bill came $2.82, it would also be rounded to $2.80.) One school of thought, however, says if the penny were to be eliminated more bills would be rounded upward than downward, enriching convenience stores with higher profits. Another school of thought says that the elimination of the penny would drive up convenience store costs because workers will have to be retrained, employee theft will be easier, and customers will switch to more expensive non-cash payments. With profit margins razor-thin in the convenience store industry, eliminating the penny could either enrich or impoverish convenience store operators according to these lines of reasoning. (See, for example, Raymond E. Lombra, "Eliminating the Penny from the U.S. Coinage System: An Economic Analysis," *Eastern Economic Journal,* Vol. 27, No. 2, Fall 2001.)

Will eliminating the penny yield higher or lower profits in the convenience store industry in the long run?

Step 1: Determine the market structure of the convenience store industry.

An industry is perfectly competitive if consumers believe that all firms in the market sell identical products, firms can freely enter and exit the market, buyers and sellers know the prices charged by firms, and transactions costs are low. The convenience store industry isn't perfectly competitive, but it is very close. So this model is probably a good one to use to analyze it.

Step 2: Decide whether the convenience store industry is a constant-cost, increasing-cost, or decreasing-cost market.

A constant-cost market is one where firms can freely enter and exit, all firms have identical costs, and input prices are constant as the industry increases output. Again, this fits the convenience store industry pretty well. Firms enter and exit this market quite easily and frequently. Likewise, all firms have approximately identical costs because they pay about the same to rent buildings in similar locations, pay suppliers the same for the items they sell, pay their employees about the same, and use about the same technology. Finally, collectively these firms buy a small fraction of the land, labor, capital, and other inputs in each market, so when they expand they do not noticeably bid up input prices.

Step 3: Determine the shape of the long-run supply curve in this industry.

If the industry is competitive and constant-cost, the long-run supply curve will be a horizontal line whose height equals the minimum point of the firms' average cost curves.

Step 4: Analyze the impact that eliminating the penny would have if it leads prices to be rounded up in favor of the convenience stores.

As explained in step three, in a perfectly competitive constant-cost industry the supply curve is horizontal and prices will equal the minimum point on the average cost curve. In this scenario, because costs haven't changed, prices won't change. Even though convenience stores may have the opportunity to round prices upward, they won't do it because of competitive pressures. They don't want to charge more than the competition, therefore they'll adjust their prices so that after rounding, prices will average exactly what they were before rounding to the nearest nickel. If our assumptions about this market are correct, rounding to the nearest nickel will have no net effect on customers or on the convenience stores.

Step 5: Analyze the impact that eliminating the penny will have if doing so increases convenience stores' costs.

Again, in a perfectly competitive constant-cost industry prices will equal the minimum point on the average cost curve. In this scenario, because average costs have risen, prices will rise by the exact same amount. However, this will not reduce the profits of firms in the industry. Both before and after the penny is eliminated, prices equal average costs so—because of the competitive entry and exit in this market—economic profits are zero either way.

Step 6: Generalize.

This logic holds for a perfectly competitive constant-cost industry and it holds for any change that affects all participants—not just eliminating the penny but imposing a new tax or regulation, the introduction of a new technology, or a shift in demand. If the industry is far from being perfectly competitive, profit levels may change and sellers may have room to increase prices above costs. However, in most urban and suburban areas this industry is notoriously competitive, so my bet is that our conclusions are correct.

■ Practice Problems

Multiple-Choice

1. A firm in a perfectly competitive market
   a. is a price taker.
   b. faces a perfectly elastic demand curve.
   c. faces a demand curve that is horizontal at the market price.
   d. All of the above are correct.

2. The shutdown rule for a price-taking firm says
   a. shut down if price is less than average variable cost at all output levels.
   b. shut down if revenue is less than variable cost at all output levels.
   c. shut down if revenue is less than total cost at all output levels.
   d. both a and b.

3. In a competitive market, a short-run equilibrium cannot persist in the long run if
    a. the firms are earning zero economic profits.
    b. the firms are earning positive economic profits.
    c. the firms are earning negative economic profits.
    d. both b and c.

4. Which of these products is least likely to be sold in a perfectly competitive industry?
    a. 87-octane gasoline
    b. fast food burgers
    c. wheat
    d. industrial benzene

Fill-in

5. In the long run in a competitive market, economic profits will be _____, while business profits will be _____.

6. In some markets, there are no barriers or fixed costs to entry and exit. Firms can engage in _____ entry and exit: They enter the market whenever they can make a profit and exit when they cannot.

7. In Figure 8.6, the firm's supply curve is _____. The firm's shutdown price is _____. At a price of p_1, the firm will produce _____.

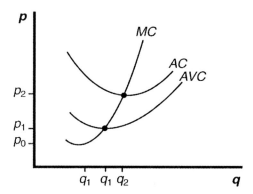

Figure 8.6

8. If the market in Figure 8.5 consists of many firms with identical costs, and input prices are not affected by the level of output, then the long-run market supply curve will be _____.

9. The price of the good in Figure 8.7 is _____.

True-False-Ambiguous and Explain Why

10. The firm whose cost, revenue, and profit curves are shown in Figure 8.7 operates in a competitive market.

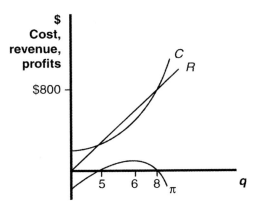

Figure 8.7

11. The cost and revenue curves shown in Figure 8.7 represent a long-run competitive equilibrium.

12. The love of money is the root of all evil.

13. If all the firms in a market record accounting profits of $1 million per year, other firms will desire to enter this market.

14. If all the firms in a market earn economic profits of $1 million per year, other firms will desire to enter this market.

15. The long-run supply curve for widgets slopes upward.

16. A farmer who owns her own land cannot come out ahead when the price of her output rises in a perfectly competitive market, since economic profits are driven to zero.

17. A price-taking firm's average revenue equals its marginal revenue.

18. Racial discrimination is more likely to be practiced in competitive markets than in noncompetitive markets.

19. If a city's population jumps by 50 percent over a period of 10 years, the rising demand will push up the price of dry cleaning in the city.

Short-Answer

20. Kim's company makes dachshund refrigerator magnets. The total cost function is $C = 9 + 3q + q^2$, where q = packets of magnets. The market price is $11.
    a. How many packets will she supply in the short run?
    b. How much profit will she earn?
    c. What is Kim's shut-down point?
    d. Draw a graph showing her short-run supply curve and the demand curve that she faces.
    e. Is the price likely to stay at $11 in the long run? What will be the price in the long run if this is a constant-cost market?

21. Below is production information for the Hormsbury Corp., which operates in a perfectly competitive market with hundreds of identical firms.

	Output				
L	if K = 1	if K = 2	if K = 3	if K = 4	if K = 5
1	8	12	15	16	18
2	15	18	22	26	28
3	18	24	28	30	32
4	20	26	31	34	36
5	21	28	32	36	38

Capital and labor are the only inputs; output = 0 when K or $L = 0$; $r = \$3$ and $w = \$2$.

a. In the short run when $K = 3$ and $p = \$0.666$, how many units does the firm produce and what is its profit?

b. If there is free entry and exit for this market, will the price rise, fall, or stay the same in the long run? Explain.

c. What will price be in the long run—assuming a constant cost for inputs and no entry barriers?

22. If one firm in a competitive industry is unionized and the union drives up wages, how will this affect the firm and the market?

23. Bob's Boats & Tours, Inc. (BB&T) is situated in a resort where the number of visitors fluctuates greatly from month to month. The boat touring industry is very competitive at this resort and Bob is a price taker.

Bob's monthly fixed cost (overhead) is $2000. His variable costs are:

Quantity of Boat Tours per Month	Variable Cost
100	$ 700
200	$1500
300	$2400
400	$4000
500	$5800
600	$7800

Since Bob is a price taker, he must charge what everybody else in the market charges. The market price varies from month to month as shown below.

Month	Market Price
January	$ 5
March	$10
May	$15
July	$19
September	$17

a. Give the profit-maximizing output of this firm and calculate its profits in each of these months.

b. Will firms enter or exit this market in the long run?

c. How would the firm's output decisions differ if fixed cost were $1000 per month?

24. Suppose there are five firms for which $C = 10 + 3q + q^2$. There are five other firms for which $C = 15 + 4q + q^2$. What is the short-run market supply curve?

25. The housing industry is usually considered to be a good example of an increasing cost industry, because expansion in the industry drives up the demand for lumber, a relatively scarce resource.
    a.   Assume that the industry is currently in long-run equilibrium. Draw a graph showing the short-run effect of an increase in demand, and explain your graph.
    b.   Show and explain how the industry will adjust in the long run.

26. Use the information in Figure 8.8 to answer the following, assuming that the firm operates in a perfectly competitive market.
    a.   What is the firm's shutdown price?
    b.   If the price of output is $23, what is the maximum profit that the firm can earn?

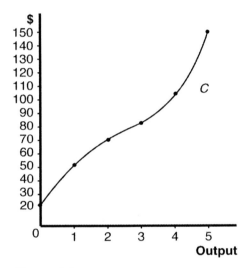

Figure 8.8

27. A firm in a perfectly competitive industry has the short run marginal cost curve, $MC = 50 + 5q$. If the price of the product is $100, how many units will this firm produce in the short run and what profit will it earn?

28. A firm's short-run total cost function is $C = 500 + 50q + 5q^2$. If the price of the product is $200, how many units will the firm produce in the short run, and what profit will the firm earn? Illustrate your answer using a graph of marginal revenue and marginal cost.

29. What would the firm described in Problem 28 expect to see happen in its industry over time?

30. In the world market for oranges, ε_o, the demand elasticity of the other countries, equals –0.5. The residual supply elasticity facing the European Union is 14.5 and its share of world orange consumption is 10 percent. What must the world market supply elasticity for oranges?

■ Answers to Practice Problems

1. d.

2. d.

3. d. Positive economic profits will prompt entry, which will cause prices to fall. Negative economic profits (economic losses) will prompt exit, which will cause prices to rise.

4. b. Perfect competition requires that products are believed to be identical and that buyers know the prices. Wheat and industrial benzene are bought and sold as commodities on national exchanges, where everyone knows the going price. One batch of benzene is chemically identical to another and one farmer's wheat is virtually identical to another's. Gasoline differs somewhat from seller to seller—some include additives and others don't, but these differences are pretty minor and prices are very well known, because in most places sellers are required by law to post prices on a large sign visible from the road. If the Shell station posts a price a couple of cents a gallon more than the Exxon across the street, people will know and the Shell will lose almost all of its customers. Gasoline may not be perfectly competitive, but it comes close. On the other hand, burgers differ considerably from one fast food joint to another—some are square, some have special sauce, some have puffier buns— customers' taste buds know that these burgers are not identical, so the market is furthest from being perfectly competitive.

5. zero; greater than zero. Entry and exit will drive economic profits to zero. Business profit calculations ignore implicit opportunity costs, so they will be greater than zero. The median return on capital (business profit) for all markets was about 9.4 percent in the early 1990s.

6. hit-and-run

7. the marginal cost curve (MC) above p_1; p_1; either 0 or q_1.

8. a horizontal line at or below p_2. The supply curve will be at p_2 if the minimum point on the short-run AC curve shown in Figure 8.7 is also the minimum point on the long-run average cost curve.

9. $100. To find this, divide total revenue by output. $800/8 = $100.

10. True. The total revenue curve is linear. Therefore, the marginal revenue is a constant equal to the price. This can only occur in a competitive market.

11. False. Figure 8.7 shows that economic profit is above zero. Above-normal profits will attract entry to the market. Due to entry, supply will grow and prices will fall—rotating the revenue curve clockwise until profits are driven to zero.

12. Ambiguous. Loving money can lead people to do unscrupulous things, such as theft or even murder. However, the models in this chapter show the love of money, if channeled into the desire to maximize profits in a competitive market, can lead to a number of virtuous outcomes (as suggested by G. B. Shaw in the chapter's opening quote). Profit maximization leads to an attempt to produce output at the lowest cost, which saves on society's scarce resources. These cost savings are then passed along to customers in the form of lower prices, as Solved Problem 3 shows.

13. Ambiguous. A business profit of $1 million per year could be consistent with economic profit below or greater than zero.

14. Ambiguous. If there are other firms that can produce at the same cost as the initial firms, and if these firms expect this economic profit to continue, they will enter (assuming there are not any barriers). If the economic profit was due to a temporary force, then they will not want to enter the market. Suppose that economic profit is initially zero, then demand suddenly surges and pushes price and profits up. However, the demand is expected to drop back to the initial level, so no firms will enter the market. For example, a flood makes half the population of East Podunk homeless. They crowd into hotels and motels in West Podunk, driving demand up. The industry price rises, the profits of a typical firm climb. However, no one builds new hotels and motels because they know that demand will soon return to the original level and economic profits will soon return to zero.

15. Ambiguous. The long-run supply curve of widgets might slope upward, but it need not. Many manufacturing markets have flat long-run supply curves, and long-run supply curves can even slope downward—in a decreasing cost market. A recent study that found that 3 of 26 American manufacturing industries have downward-sloping long-run supply curves. (See John Shea, "Do Supply Curves Slope Up?" *Quarterly Journal of Economics,* 108(1), February 1993:1–32.)

16. False. Economic profits *are* driven to zero because of rising rents. But because the farmer owns the land, she earns high rents and "comes out ahead."

17. True. Revenue = pq. So, average revenue = R/q or pq/q, which equals p. For price takers, $MR = p$ also.

18. False. An employer who practices racial discrimination would refuse to hire a worker from a disfavored group even though he can hire the worker for less than other workers with the same level of productivity. Thus the employer fails to minimize the cost of production. In a competitive market, those who fail to minimize costs must earn negative economic profits and will be driven out of business in the long run. Discriminating firms that fail to minimize costs need not be driven out of business in noncompetitive markets.

Studies of the American South after the Civil War show that the power of market competition forced racist employers to forgo much of their desire to practice discrimination. In most competitive industries, black workers were paid about the same as white workers of the same skill levels. Unfortunately, racist whites were able to go outside the market and use the power of the government (Jim Crow laws) and illegal means to practice discrimination.

Moreover, discrimination was not driven out of markets because customers and other employees were willing to pay to practice it. (See Robert Higgs, *Competition and Coercion: Blacks in the American Economy, 1865–1914,* University of Chicago Press, 1980, who argues that "competitive forces profoundly influenced black economic life . . . competition played an important part in protecting blacks from the racial coercion to which they were peculiarly vulnerable" (p. ix).)

19. Ambiguous. It depends on how elastic the long-run supply is. If firms can freely enter the dry-cleaning industry, input prices (such as labor, dry-cleaning equipment, and commercial real estate) are constant, and old firms don't have better technology or lower costs than new firms, then the long-run average cost curve won't rise and the long-run market supply curve will be horizontal. If so, the price won't rise. Entry into dry cleaning is pretty easy, the technology is such that new firms or new locations should be just as productive as older ones, and most of the input prices are unlikely to rise. Dry cleaners are probably price takers in the labor market and can buy dry cleaning equipment in a national market without driving up its price. Only the price of real estate is likely to rise any, but if the city expands, new roads are built, and new land is zoned for commercial development, its price may be unchanged, as well.

20. a.   Find output by finding the point where $p = MC$. $MC = 3 + 2q$.

$$11 = 3 + 2q$$
$$8 = 2q$$
$$q = 4.$$

b.   Profit $= R - C = (11 \times 4) - (9 + (3 \times 4) + 4^2) = 44 - 37 = \$7$.

c.   Kim's shutdown point is the minimum point on her average variable cost curve. $VC = 3q + q^2$, so $AVC = 3 + q$, whose minimum is at \$3. When price falls below \$3 per packet of magnets, she will shut down.

d.   Her short-run supply curve is her marginal cost curve above the minimum point on the average variable cost curve. As Figure 8.10 shows, the MC curve is always above the AVC curve, so her supply curve is her entire marginal cost curve. The demand curve facing her is a horizontal line at \$11, since she is a price taker.

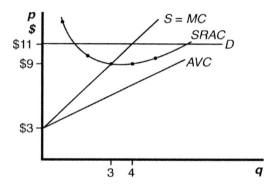

Figure 8.10

e.   A price of \$11 generates economic profits, so there will probably be entry (unless there are barriers), which will drive down the price. If the market has constant costs, the long-run price will be the minimum of the long-run average total cost curve. We cannot find this without more information, but we can find the minimum of this short-run average cost curve. The minimum of the long-run average cost curve will be as low or lower than the minimum of this particular short-run average total cost curve. $AC = C/q = 9/q + 3 + q$. To find its minimum, you could plug in some numbers and create a table:

q	AC
1	13
2	9.5
3	9
4	9.25
5	9.8

or, realizing that $MC = AC$ at AC's minimum, we can set these equations equal to each other and solve for q. $9/q + 3 + q = 3 + 2q$

$$9/q = q$$
$$9 = q^2$$
$$q = 3.$$

Thus the price will fall to at least \$9 in the long run. Figure 8.9 shows the short-run AC curve.

21. a. The table below uses the information in Problem 18 to derive total cost, average total cost, variable cost, and marginal cost when $K = 3$.

Cost = $C = rK + wL = (\$3 \times 3) + \$2L$ and $VC = wL = \$2L$.						
L	q	C	VC	$MC = \Delta C/\Delta q$	$AC = C/q$	$AVC = VC/q$
1	15	11	2	2/15 = 0.133	11/15 = 0.733	2/15 = 0.133
2	22	13	4	2/7 = 0.286	13/22 = 0.591	4/22 = 0.182
3	28	15	6	2/6 = 0.333	15/28 = 0.536	6/28 = 0.214
4	31	17	8	2/3 = 0.667	17/31 = 0.548	8/31 = 0.258
5	32	19	10	2/1 = 2	19/32 = 0.594	10/32 = 0.313

The firm will not shut down because price is above the minimum AVC. The firm will supply 31 units because at this level of output $MC = p$.

Profit = revenue − cost = $pq − C = (\$0.667 \times 31) − \$17 = \$20.667 − \$17 = \$3.667$.

(Actually, the firm is indifferent between producing $q = 28$ and $q = 31$, since the profit for both is the same. Its marginal profit for the last three units of output is zero.)

b. Since profit is greater than zero, there will be entry into the market.

c. In the long run in a constant-cost, competitive market, the price will equal the minimum average total cost. The table below calculates average total cost for each input combination.

L	$K = 1$	$K = 2$	$K = 3$	$K = 4$	$K = 5$
1	5/8	8/12	11/15	14/16	17/18
2	7/15	10/18	13/22	16/26	19/28
3	9/18	12/24	15/28	18/30	21/32
4	11/20	14/26	17/31	20/34	23/36
5	13/21	16/28	19/32	22/36	25/38

The lowest number in the table is when $K = 1$ and $L = 2$, average total cost = \$0.467. In the long run, firms will scale down or smaller firms will enter, driving the price to \$0.467 per unit.

22. The unionized firm will have higher costs than other firms. In the long run it will be driven out of business. The exit of this firm will not influence the overall market price. In Figure 8.11, $LRAC_U$ represents the long-run average cost of the unionized firm and $LRAC_N$ represents the long-run average cost of the nonunionized firms. (The output level that minimizes cost may change as wages rise, but it is assumed that they haven't in Figure 8.11.) The unionized firm will lose $(p_1 − p_0)q$ per period and will be forced to exit. This example demonstrates why it has been historically difficult for unions to organize and increase wages in competitive markets; doing so is a long-run death sentence for the unionized firm and will cost the workers their jobs. On the other hand, if the whole industry is unionized, all the firms' cost curves rise and the price would rise to p_1. In this case there is still a loss of jobs as firms substitute away from labor, and output declines as consumers buy less due to the price increase. As product markets have become increasingly competitive in the United States (due partly to deregulation and international trade), unions have had a harder time organizing firms and increasing members' wages above the competitive level.

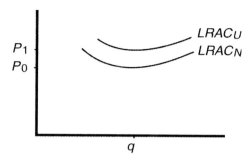

Figure 8.11

23. a.   Calculate marginal cost and average variable cost so that we can use the output rule and the shut-down rule. These are costs given below.

Output	Variable Cost	Marginal Cost $(MC = \Delta VC/\Delta q)$	Average Variable Cost $(AVC = VC/q)$
100	$ 700	$ 7	$ 7.00
200	$1500	$ 8	$ 7.50
300	$2400	$ 9	$ 8.00
400	$4000	$16	$10.00
500	$5800	$18	$11.60
600	$7800	$20	$13.00

Use the shut-down rule and the output rule to calculate how much the firm will produce.

The shut-down rule states that the firm will produce zero if the price is below the minimum point on the average variable cost curve. From above, we can see that the minimum point on the AVC curve is $7. Since the price is below this in January, BB&T will shut down (produce zero) in that month. (Perhaps Bob takes a vacation.)

In months when $p > \$7$, the output rule states that the firm should produce output whenever $p > MC$ and up to the point where $p = MC$.

Thus in March, when $p = \$10$, the firm will produce 300 units (i.e., will give tours to 300 people). Producing the 300th unit brings in $10 in additional revenue, but the marginal cost is only $9. Producing the 400th unit would cause profits to fall since it brings in $10 in additional revenue but marginal cost is a $16. (The table doesn't give marginal cost for values between 300 and 400, so marginal cost might exactly equal $10 at a level between 300 and 400. In this case, output will be somewhat higher than 300. To make things easier, we'll stick with the round numbers in the table.)

Following this logic, the output decision for each month is:

Month	Price	Output
January	$ 5	0
March	$10	300
May	$15	300
July	$19	500
September	$17	400

Calculate the firm's profits.

Profit $= R - C = pq - (F + VC)$. Put the numbers that have been calculated in step two into this formula. The table below does this.

Month	Price	Output	Revenue	Cost	Profit
January	$ 5	0	$ 0	$2000	−$2000
March	$10	300	$3000	$4400	−$1400
May	$15	300	$4500	$4400	$ 100
July	$19	500	$9500	$7800	$1700
September	$17	400	$6800	$6000	$ 800

b. Over the course of these months, it looks like poor Bob has lost money, as the losses in January and March ($3400) exceed the gains in the other three months ($2600). If Bob thinks that these short-run losses are likely to persist into the long run, he would exit the market. If there are other firms with similar costs and similar losses, they would exit in the long run, too.

c. Short-run output levels would not change at all if fixed cost was $1000 per month instead of $2000, since fixed cost affects neither average variable cost nor marginal cost. However, the firm's profit would be $1000 greater in each month. The average monthly profit rate would be positive, and if the firm thought these positive profits were likely to persist into the long run, then it would stay in the industry. (In addition, if barriers to entry are low, long-run positive profits will induce other firms to enter the industry.)

24. First calculate marginal costs for each type of firm. Then, each firm's supply curve is its marginal cost curve above the minimum point on its average variable cost curve. $AVC = C/q = 3 + q$ and $4 + q$ for these two types of firms. Therefore their marginal costs are always above average variable costs. Figure 8.12(a) plots the supply curve for one of the first five firms. The profit-maximizing firm sets $p = MC$ and solves for q at each price. $p = 3 + 2q$. If $p = 3$, then $q = 0$. If $p = 5$, then $q = 1$. If $p = 7$, then $q = 2$, and so on. Market supply for the first five firms is 5 times higher at each price. As shown in Figure 8.12(b), the market supply is the horizontal sum of the marginal cost curves for firms 1 through 5. Figure 8.12(c) shows the market supply of the second five firms. Figure 8.12(d) shows the market supply of all 10 firms.

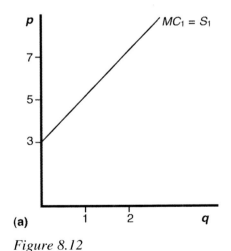
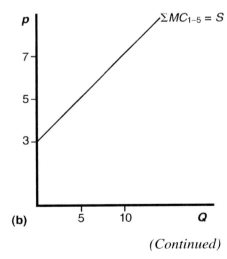

(a)

(b)

Figure 8.12   (Continued)

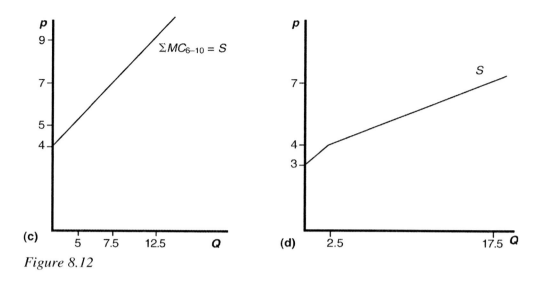

Figure 8.12

25. a. See Figure 8.13. An increase in demand with cause price to rise along the short-run supply curve. Industry output will rise, and existing firms will make positive profits.

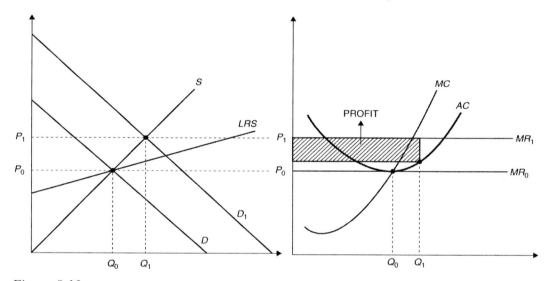

Figure 8.13

b. The increase in economic profits will cause firms to enter in the long run. As the industry expands, costs increase for all firms, and thus marginal and average costs increase for the representative firm. Firms enter until profit returns to zero, which must be at a price (P_2) that exceeds the original price (P_0) but is less than the short-run price (P_1). The industry quantity will be higher, but firm quantity is likely to be lower (because costs have risen so firms break even at a lower level of output).

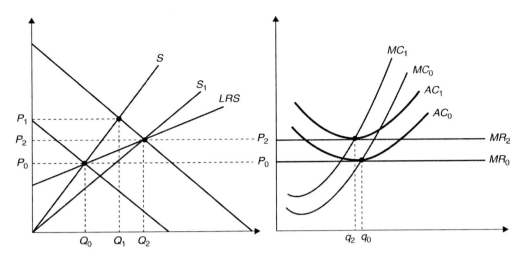

Figure 8.14

26. a. To find the shutdown price, we need to find the minimum point on the firm's average variable cost curve. First find variable costs by subtracting fixed cost (which is $20 here) from the cost curve, *C*. Then find $AVC = VC/q$. The values from Figure 8.7 are given below. The minimum *AVC* is $21, so the firm shuts down if the price falls below $21.

    b. Since $23 is above the shutdown price, the firm should produce additional units as long as the marginal revenue from doing so exceeds the marginal cost. Because this is a perfectly competitive market, the firm's *MR* equals the price. *MC* is calculated below. The firm will produce three units of output. The fourth unit costs $25 but only yields $23 in additional revenue, so the firm does not produce it. Its profit is $pq - C$ or $(\$23 \times 3) - \$83 = \$69 - \$83 = -\$14$. This loss is smaller than the loss from shutting down, since fixed cost is $20.

q	C (dollars)	VC (dollars)	AVC (dollars)	MC (dollars)	Profit (dollars)
0	20	0			−20
1	52	32	32	32	−29
2	70	50	25	18	−24
3	83	63	21	13	−14
4	108	88	22	25	−16
5	150	130	26	42	−35

27. If $P = \$100$, $MR = MC$ at a quantity of 10. However, all this tells us is what quantity the firm will product *if it wishes to produce at all*. Since we have no information on variable or total costs, we cannot tell if the firm should shut down, and we cannot tell if the firm is making a profit . . . only that the highest profit at an output greater than zero will be when the firm produces 10 units.

28. $C = 500 + 50q + 5q^2$, so $MC = 50 + 10q$, $SAVC = 50 + 5q$, and $SAC = 500/q + 50 + 5q$. Set $MR = MC$.

$$200 = 50 + 10q$$
$$q = 25$$
$$\pi = (200*25) - 500 - 50(25) - 5(25^2) = \$125.$$

Since profit is positive, the firm is clearly above its shutdown point. Note that $SAC = \$195$; on the graph (Figure 8.15), profit is the shaded area.

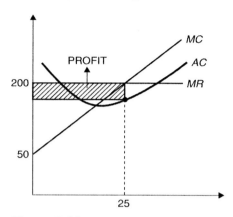

Figure 8.15

29. Since profit is (slightly) positive, the firm should expect that over time, prices in this industry will fall until profits equal zero.

30. Recall that the elasticity of residual supply, η_r, facing a given country is $\eta_r = (\eta/\theta) - ((1-\theta)/\theta)\varepsilon_0$, where η is the market supply elasticity, ε_0 is the demand elasticity of the other countries, and $\theta = Q_r/Q$ is the importing country's share of the world's output. We know η_r, ε_0 and θ and must solve for η.

$$14.5 = \eta/0.1 - [(0.9/0.1) \times -0.5] \quad \text{or}$$
$$14.5 = \eta/0.1 + 4.5 \quad \text{or}$$
$$10 = \eta/0.1, \quad \text{so} \quad \eta = 1$$

■ Exercises

True-False-Ambiguous and Explain Why

1. The Hormsbury Corp. reports that it costs them $3 to raise a chicken, but they sell their chickens for only $2. Therefore, the Hormsbury Corp. is not maximizing profits.

2. Suppose that there are many identical firms in the roofing market that have earned negative profits for several years due to a slump in the construction of new homes. In the long run, prices must rise so that the firms can make positive profits to offset their earlier losses.

3. In a decreasing-cost competitive market, the long-run market supply curve will slope downward.

4. Poindexter is such a great manager that he can get his employees to produce twice as much as employees do at other companies. Therefore, Poindexter's employer will earn higher profits than its competitors.

Short-Answer

5. You are a highly paid consultant to firms in competitive markets. Your clients present you with sets of partial market information upon which you are to base your recommendation to each about what they should do. You can recommend one of the following courses of action:

    a. The firm is currently in the correct position and therefore should not change.
    b. The firm should increase output and sales.
    c. The firm should decrease output and sales.
    d. The firm should shut down.

    Given the following data, make one of the above recommendations for the short run to each of the following three customers, each of whom sells a different product. Make sure to explain your recommendation. Fill in the missing data that can be derived from the information given.

Firm	p	q	TR	TC	F	VC	AC	AVC	MC
A	$3.00		$6,000	$8,000				$3.50	$3.50
B			$9,000	$9,000	$3,000			$1.50	$MC = AC$
C		1,000	$5,000			$1,500	$6.50		$MC < AVC$

6. How will a per-unit tax affect a perfectly competitive market in which firms can freely enter and exit, all firms have identical costs, and input prices are constant? Show using supply and demand curves.

7. For years, the *XYZ* Corporation has been generating its own electricity, and its short-run cost function for producing widgets (not electricity) has been $C = 100 + q + q^2$. Now the company has decided to sell its electricity-generating capital and buy electricity from a local supplier. This switch has reduced the company's total costs, but increased its marginal costs. Show how this will affect its output and profit.

8. Meghan operates a bakery selling chocolate chip cookies and is the only retailer located within city limits. However, she faces considerable competition from sellers located out of town and regards the market as perfectly competitive with a price per cookie of $0.20. Her total cost function is

    $$C = 20 + 0.05q + 0.00005q^2,$$

    where q = cookies per week.

    a. Calculate the profit-maximizing output for Meghan. What is her profit?
    b. The town council has voted to impose a tax of $0.10 per cookie sold in the town, hoping to raise revenue. Calculate her new short-run and long-run profit-maximizing output. What is her profit? How much revenue does the town council collect in the short run and in the long run?
    c. Draw a graph showing Meghan's supply curve, the demand curve facing her, and the tax.

9. Suppose there are 20 firms whose long-run cost curves are like $LRAC_1$ and $LRMC_1$ in Figure 8.16. In addition, there are an unlimited number of potential firms whose long-run cost curves are like $LRAC_2$ and $LRMC_2$ in Figure 8.16. Draw a graph showing the long-run market supply curve.

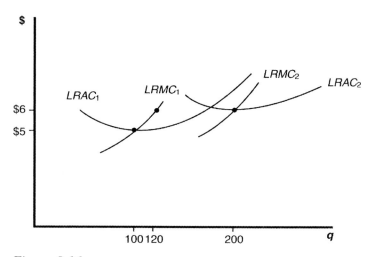

Figure 8.16

10. Suppose that a decreasing cost industry is in long-run equilibrium. Show and explain the short- and long-run effects of an increase in demand on both the industry and on a representative firm.

11. In a perfectly competitive, constant-cost industry, demand is given by $Q = 2000 - P$. The short total cost function (at the scale of production that minimizes long-run costs for each identical firm) is $TC = 500 + 10q + q^2$.

  a. What will the long-run price be in this industry? How many firms will there be in long-run equilibrium?

  b. What is the equation of the short-run supply curve if the industry is in long-run equilibrium?

  c. Suppose that demand in this industry decreases to: $Q = 1000 - P$. What will the new LONG RUN price be in this industry, and how many firms will there be?

  d. Describe how the industry will adjust to reach the new long-run equilibrium (this should include finding the short run price and quantity, and the quantity and profit of the firm), and illustrate your answer by drawing a graph of the firm and a graph of the industry, showing everything that you found in *a–c*.

Chapter 9
Properties and Applications of the Competitive Model

■ Chapter Summary

Competition, which has been denounced for millennia as a destructive force, has some amazing powers. In Chapter 8, we learned how competition causes producers to pass along cost reductions to consumers as it drives producers' economic profits to zero. In this chapter, we learn that competition causes the efficient amount of goods to be produced, maximizing one important measure of societal well-being. In the next chapter, we'll learn that *any* efficient allocation of goods can be obtained using competition.

As discussed in the previous chapter, in long-run equilibrium in perfectly competitive industries, firms will earn zero economic profit—the same return that they would earn in their next best alternative, or a *normal* profit. A firm earning a zero business profit would not be earning a normal rate of return, economic profit would be less than zero, and the firm would exit the industry given sufficient time. In competitive markets where entry is limited, firms bid up the price for scarce inputs, driving up input prices until their own profits are zero. The owners of the scarce inputs (e.g., skilled workers or landlords) earn economic **rents**—payments to an input's owner above the minimum needed to supply the input. Even if the firm owns the scarce resource, it doesn't earn economic profits; as the market value of its resources rises, its opportunity cost of using the resources rises.

In Chapter 5, we discussed **consumer surplus**, the difference between what a consumer is willing to pay for the quantity of the good purchased and what the good actually costs the consumer. Because the demand curve is the consumer's marginal willingness to pay curve (and thus, a marginal value curve), consumer surplus can be calculated as the area under the demand curve and above the market price up to the quantity the consumer buys. A supplier's gain from participating in the market is measured by its **producer surplus**—the difference between the amount for which a good sells and the minimum amount necessary for the seller to be willing to produce it. Graphically, total producer surplus is the area above the supply curve and below the market price up to the quantity actually produced. Alternatively, producer surplus equals revenue minus variable cost—$PS = R - VC$, which can be found by integrating the difference between the firm's demand function and its marginal cost function. In the short run, producer surplus minus fixed cost equals profit. In the long run, profit and producer surplus are the same.

One commonly used measure of the **welfare** of society is the sum of consumer surplus and producer surplus: $W = CS + PS$. This measure implicitly weights the well-being of each consumer and each producer equally. Producing the competitive output level (where the supply and demand curves cross) maximizes this type of welfare. Actions that move the market away from its competitive equilibrium cause a **deadweight loss** to society—a net reduction in welfare from losses of surplus by one group that are not offset by gains to another group. When more than the competitive output level is produced, a deadweight loss occurs because consumers value the last units of output less than the marginal cost of producing them. When less than the competitive output level is produced, a deadweight loss occurs because consumers value additional output more than the marginal cost of producing it, and yet it is not produced. Competition maximizes welfare because marginal benefit equals marginal cost at the competitive equilibrium.

Many governmental policies shift the supply curve leftward, lowering consumer surplus and welfare. Some policies directly restrict the number of firms—such as limits on the number of taxis in a city. This creates an economic rent for permit holders. If a particular group is excluded from a market, the favored group can often benefit, while consumers are harmed. Examples of practices that exclude certain groups are unions, guilds, and discriminatory laws and practices. A long-run **barrier to entry**—an explicit governmental restriction or a cost that applies only to potential new firms and not to existing firms—may stop firms from responding to profit opportunities, allowing the equilibrium price and firms' profits to remain high forever. In the short run, exit barriers, which make it harder to go out of business, can keep the number of firms in a market relatively high, but in the long run, they may limit the entry of firms to a market.

Many governmental policies create a gap between the supply and demand curves—blocking the market from reaching the competitive equilibrium. Sales taxes reduce producer and consumer surplus by more than the amount of the tax revenue. A **subsidy** is the opposite of a tax. It causes a wedge between supply and demand to the right of the initial equilibrium point and a drop in overall welfare, because the gains in both consumer and producer surplus are smaller than the government's expenses. In some markets, the government creates a **price floor** or **price support** by promising to buy as much output as needed to drive the price up to the price floor. These can create massive deadweight losses—partly due to excess production that must be stored, destroyed, or sold elsewhere. Agricultural markets have been full of government price supports, quotas, and subsidies that benefit producers at the expense of consumers and taxpayers. Price ceilings reduce producer surplus and help some consumers, but cause a deadweight loss.

If a government reduces imports of a good, the domestic price rises, domestic producer surplus increases, and domestic consumer surplus falls by more. **Tariffs**—taxes levied only on imported goods—cause a deadweight loss in two parts. The first part equals the extra cost of producing more of the good domestically when foreign firms have lower costs. The second part equals the loss from domestic consumers who consume too little of the good. A **quota**—a statutory limit on the amount imported—can cause even larger losses to a society than a tariff. The gain to producers and loss to consumers is the same as with an equivalent tariff, but the government receives no tariff revenue. In practice, nontariff barriers can have a much bigger impact than do tariffs or quotas. Trade barriers exist, despite reducing overall welfare, because the gains from them are concentrated on a few producers, while the losses are spread out across many consumers. Efforts and expenditures, such as lobbying for a tariff, whose purpose is to gain a rent or profit from government actions, are called **rent seeking**. Rent seeking uses up many resources, so deadweight loss estimates for trade barriers understate the true loss to society.

■ Key Concepts and Formulas

- **Economic rent:** payments to an input's owner above the minimum needed to supply the input.
- **Consumer surplus:** the difference between what consumers are willing to pay and the price they pay for it. Calculated as the area under the demand curve and above the market price up to the quantity consumers buy.
- **Producer surplus:** the difference between the amount for which a good sells and the minimum amount necessary for sellers to be willing to produce the good.
- **Deadweight loss:** a net reduction in welfare from losses of surplus by one group that are not offset by gains to another group.
- **Tariff:** a tax levied on imported goods.
- **Quota:** a statutory limit on the amount imported.
- **Rent seeking:** effort and spending done to gain rent or profit from government action.
- **Subsidy:** a payment for the purchase of a good; the opposite of a tax.

■ Application: The Adoption Market

Adoption laws in the United States and many other developed countries allow couples to pay numerous fees and charges in order to adopt a baby—charges have recently averaged about $25,000. However, the laws do not allow birth mothers to sell their babies.

Question: What would happen if the laws were changed so that birth mothers could sell their newborn babies in a competitive market? Who would win and who would lose? (Do you favor such a policy?)

Answer: Figure 9.1 depicts the forces at work. The quantity supplied is positive even when the price paid to a birth mother is $0. Allowing this price to rise to the competitive equilibrium level will increase the quantity supplied from Q_0 to Q_E. The increase in quantity also induces a movement along the demand curve, with the price falling from $25,000 to p_E. The buyers (adoptive parents) gain surplus of $A + B$. The sellers (birth mothers) gain surplus of $C + D$. Currently adoptive parents pay $A + C$, but these payments go to middlemen (adoption agencies), not birth mothers. The figure implies that these middlemen will be driven out of the market.

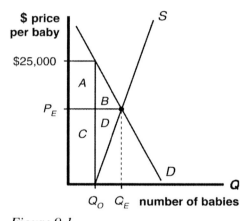

Figure 9.1

Proponents of this proposal argue that there are many winners and few losers from the policy. The adoptive parents pay less and more children are put into loving homes. The birth mothers who put their babies up for adoption (a group which is typically poor) see their incomes rise. The babies are better off, they argue, because they go from a home in which they are little desired into a home where they are greatly desired. The pregnant women may pay more attention to the health of their unborn children and curb destructive habits (e.g. smoking, excessive alcohol use, and drug use), knowing that this will increase the market price of their babies. Some women who may have opted for abortions will give birth because of the monetary payoff. Only the rent-seeking middlemen will lose. This model and argument is presented in Donald Boudreaux, "A Modest Proposal to Deregulate Infant Adoptions" *Cato Journal*, Vol. 15, no. 1 (Spring/Summer 1995).

Critics of the proposal argue that the gains to the adoptive parents are good, but that the birth mothers should not be rewarded for their behavior. It's OK to reward producers of most products—cars, haircuts, food, etc.—because these producers deserve to be rewarded. Sellers of other things—e.g., addictive drugs, sex, or babies—don't deserve to be rewarded. In the case of babies, bearing a child brings the responsibility of caring for and raising that child, not selling it to make a profit. Doing so is simply immoral. Other critics point out that the market doesn't always reach equilibrium. The workings of supply and demand are fine for most goods because there's not a huge problem if the excess inventory goes unsold. Obviously, it is different for babies. Babies unsold in the adoption market go into foster care, which is less than ideal, or stay in homes where they aren't really wanted. In addition, critics point out that the model oversimplifies by assuming that babies are identical. The high prices are only for "in-demand" babies—healthy, cute, etc. Other babies are not "in demand"—e.g., minority babies—and some of these already languish in foster care because supply currently exceeds demand. If the proposal increases the quantity supplied of "in-demand" babies and drives down their prices, it will decrease the demand for other babies, increasing this surplus. This is a thought-provoking proposal, so you may be able to think of additional arguments for or against it.

■ Solved Problems

1. What are the welfare effects of conscription? In particular, what are the welfare effects of a law that requires suppliers to sell the equilibrium output to the government at a price that is lower than the market price?

    Step 1: Show the initial welfare level of producers.

    Without conscription the market moves to equilibrium, where supply equals demand, at p_1 and Q_1 in Figure 9.2. Producer surplus is the area above the supply curve, up to the price line—areas B and C. Consumer surplus is A.

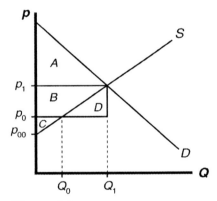

    Figure 9.2

    Step 2: Show the welfare of producers when conscription takes place.

    The government "purchases" the initial quantity, Q_1, but forces suppliers to accept a below-equilibrium price, p_0. Because the price is so low, the producers don't want to produce more than Q_0. (If price is lower than p_{00} they won't want to sell anything.) However, they are forced to produce Q_1, all of which goes to the government. The low-cost producers still receive some producer surplus, area C, but the higher-cost producers are paid less than their costs (which equal the supply curve). Those who produce units between Q_0 and Q_1 have losses equal to area D—their producer surplus is negative. Consumers don't get to buy any output, since it all goes to the government, so their consumer surplus is zero.

    Step 3: Compare the initial and final surplus.

    In a competitive market the producer surplus is $B + C$. With conscription, producers' "surplus" is $C - D$. Actually, this is a loss, since $D > C$. The change in producer surplus is $-C - D$. Consumer surplus drops from A to 0. The consumers' and producers' losses are the government's gain. In this case there is no deadweight loss because the efficient quantity is still produced. (Examples of conscription are common in wartime, including the use of a military draft. Presumably the government has a really good reason for using conscription, such as a national emergency, since the impact is essentially the same as that of theft. The government can reduce its budgetary costs through conscription, but it cannot reduce the overall cost of the output. By conscripting, rather than purchasing, it shifts the costs from itself (or taxpayers) to consumers and producers of the product.)

2.   Show that consumers' willingness to accept a price ceiling depends on the elasticity of supply.

Step 1: Show the effect of a binding price ceiling.

As Figure 9.3 shows, a binding price ceiling shifts neither the supply curve, S_1, nor the demand curve, D, but keeps the price below the equilibrium level. D and S_1 intersect at p_E and Q_2. The price ceiling, p_C, is below the equilibrium price, p_E, causing the quantity supplied to fall to Q_1 and the quantity demanded to rise to Q_3, thus creating a shortage.

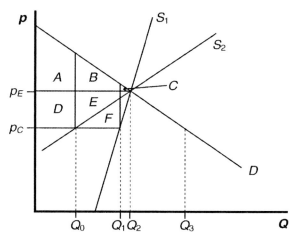

Figure 9.3

Step 2: Show the effect of the same price ceiling when the supply and demand curves have the same intersection but the supply curve has a different elasticity.

S_2 is more elastic than S_1 and still intersects D at p_E and Q_2. The price ceiling now causes a larger shortage because the quantity supplied drops to Q_0 instead of Q_1.

Step 3: Find the welfare of consumers in the absence of the price ceiling, when the supply curve is less elastic (S_1) and when it is more elastic (S_2).

	No Price Ceiling	**Price Ceiling**	
		S_1	S_2
Consumer Surplus	$A + B + C$	$A + B + D + E + F$	$A + D$

When there is no price ceiling, consumer surplus is $A + B + C$.

When there is a price ceiling and the supply curve is less elastic, S_1, output is Q_1, so consumer surplus (the area between the demand curve and the price out to Q_1) is $A + B + D + E + F$.

When the supply curve is more elastic, S_2, output is Q_0, so consumer surplus is $A + D$.

Thus the more elastic the supply curve becomes, the smaller will be consumer surplus when there is a price ceiling. If the supply curve had been even more elastic, area D would be even smaller. If area D is small enough, consumer surplus without the price ceiling ($A + B + C$) will be larger than consumer surplus with the price ceiling ($A + D$), since area D will become smaller than $B + C$. Conclusion: Consumers may be better off or worse off because of a price ceiling.

3. The quantity supplied of Bitty Baby Toys is $Q_s = -1,000,000 + 600,000p$. Initially, the quantity demanded is $Q_D = 6,000,000 - 800,000p$. Then Bitty Babies become the hottest fad in elementary schools across America and the quantity demanded jumps to $Q_D = 13,000,000 - 800,000p$. How does this soaring popularity for Bitty Babies affect welfare?

Step 1: Graph the supply curve and the two demand curves, finding each equilibrium.

Figure 9.4 shows the supply and demand curves. Price has risen from \$5 to \$10, while quantity has risen from 2,000,000 to 5,000,000.

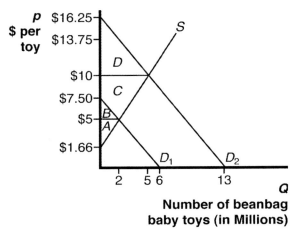

Figure 9.4

$$\text{Initially } -1,000,000 + 600,000p = 6,000,000 - 800,000p$$
$$1,400,000p = 7,000,000$$
$$p = \$5$$
$$Q = 2,000,000$$
$$\text{Later, } -1,000,000 + 600,000p = 13,000,000 - 800,000p$$
$$1,400,000p = 14,000,000$$
$$p = \$10$$
$$Q = 5,000,000$$

Step 2: Calculate the consumer and producer surplus in each case.

The initial producer surplus is area A.

The initial consumer surplus is area B.

After the demand curve shifts, producer surplus rises to area $A + B + C$, and consumer surplus becomes area D. The area of a triangle is base times height times one-half, so initial producer surplus is $2,000,000 \times \$3.33 \times 0.5 = \$3,333,333$, area A. Initial consumer surplus is $2,000,000 \times \$2.50 \times 0.5 = \$2,500,000$, area B. Final producer surplus is $5,000,000 \times \$8.33 \times 0.5 = \$20,833,333$, area $A + B + C$. Final consumer surplus is $5,000,000 \times \$6.25 \times 0.5 = \$15,625,000$, area D. (If the supply and demand curves were not linear, you would need to integrate to find these areas.)

Step 3: Compare the consumer and producer surplus in each case.

Producer surplus rises by \$17,500,000.

Consumer surplus rises by \$13,125,000.

Notice that the rise in consumer surplus was driven mostly by the fact that consumers increased their desire for these toys. The first 2,000,000 Bitty Babies initially generated $2,500,000 in consumer surplus. Now consumers are willing to pay $13.75 for the 2,000,000th toy (find this by solving for price when the second quantity demanded equation equals 2,000,000). Therefore, after the demand curve shifts, the consumer surplus from the first 2,000,000 toys averages $5.00 per toy ($6.25 for the first, $3.75 for the 2,000,000th) and the total consumer surplus from the first 2,000,000 toys is $10,000,000. Thus the consumer surplus from the first 2,000,000 toys has risen by $7,500,000 solely because consumers want the toys more than they used to. Consumer surplus, like consumer welfare and utility in general, is largely in the mind of the consumer.

■ Practice Problems

Multiple-Choice

1. In Figure 9.5, the deadweight loss would be highest if output is
    a. 0.
    b. 10.
    c. 20.
    d. 30.

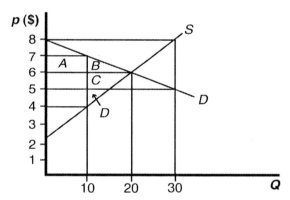

Figure 9.5

2. In Figure 9.5, the deadweight loss is zero if price is
    a. $2.
    b. $4.
    c. $6.
    d. $8.

3. In Figure 9.5, the deadweight loss from the 30th unit is
    a. $0.
    b. $3.
    c. $8.
    d. $15.

4. In Figure 9.5, suppose that the government sets a quota at 10 units of output, and the price rises to $7. In comparison to a competitive market, the consumer surplus would fall by
   a. $0.
   b. $10.
   c. $15.
   d. $20.

5. In Figure 9.5, suppose that the government sets a quota at 10 units of output, and the price rises to $7. In comparison to a competitive market, the producer surplus would rise by
   a. $0.
   b. $10.
   c. $15.
   d. $20.

6. In Figure 9.5, suppose that the government pays a subsidy of $3 per unit. This would cost the government
   a. $60.
   b. $90.
   c. $120.
   d. $240.

7. In Figure 9.5, suppose that the government pays a subsidy of $3 per unit. The subsidy will create a deadweight loss of
   a. $0.
   b. $10.
   c. $15.
   d. $30.

8. Rent seeking
   a. occurs when a firm attempts to increase its profits by selling its products cheaper than its competitors' products.
   b. occurs when a firm uses advertising to increase demand for its product.
   c. causes the deadweight loss calculations from tariffs and quotas to overstate the true loss to society.
   d. will increase production costs.

Fill-in

9. The Hormsbury Corp. is in a competitive market and sells 10 Megazappers for $1,000,000 each. Their *MC* for the first 5 Megazappers is $500,000 and the *MC* for the next five is $900,000. Their variable cost of producing Megazappers is _____. Their producer surplus from selling 10 Megazappers is _____. The marginal cost of producing the eleventh Megazapper must be _____.

10. A new law is passed requiring employers to pay workers $50,000 when they are permanently laid off. This law creates a barrier to _____ in the short run.

True-False-Ambiguous and Explain Why

11. A firm's producer surplus equals its profit.

12. Discriminatory laws (such as the apartheid laws once used in South Africa) that ban a certain group from producing a good in a competitive market will shift the supply curve, causing a rise in price, a drop in quantity, and a deadweight loss.

13. A binding price ceiling will always cause a deadweight loss.

Short-Answer

14. In Figure 9.6, what is the total consumer surplus of all consumers in this unregulated competitive market? How much consumer surplus is gained from 100th unit? From the 200th unit?

15. In Figure 9.6, what level of output maximizes welfare? At what prices would a market failure arise?

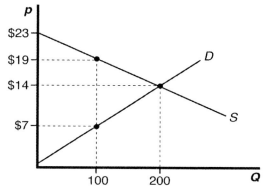

Figure 9.6

16. The cost of a physical exam is $50 ($25 for the physician's labor, $25 for use of the equipment and tests), but the Hormsbury family is eligible for Medicaid health insurance, so they pay nothing for the procedure and can have as many exams as they desire. Draw the supply curve facing the Hormsbury family and a hypothetical Hormsbury family demand curve for physical exams (number of exams per year). Label the graph and show the added consumer surplus they receive because they don't pay for exams. Does insurance lead them to consume an efficient amount of physical exams? Explain any deadweight loss that may arise.

17. Who benefits in the long run from technological improvements in a constant-cost perfectly competitive industry with unlimited entry? (An example would be when bioengineering produces a crop that grows faster.) Draw a graph showing the change in consumer surplus and other welfare effects.

18. Show how welfare changes in the short run if technological progress occurs when the government has a price support program that supports an above-equilibrium price floor by buying up excess supply (as in Figure 9.8 of the text).

19. What are the welfare effects of a quota on imports if the government auctions off the quota to the highest bidder? (Use Figure 9.10 from the textbook.)

20. In Figure 9.7, if the price equals p_0, then what is consumer surplus when

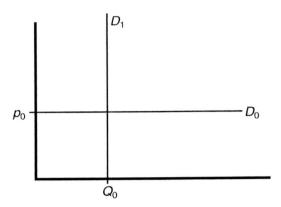

Figure 9.7

   a. the demand curve is D_0?
   b. the demand curve is D_1?

21. The domestic demand for almonds is $Q_D = 20{,}000{,}000 - 500{,}000p$. The domestic supply is $Q_s = -2{,}000{,}000 + 600{,}000p$, where quantity is in crates per year and $p =$ price per crate. The world price is $15 per crate.
   a. Suppose that the country initially has no restrictions on trade and then imposes an import quota of 3,000,000 crates per year. How will this affect the price and the quantity imported? What are the welfare effects?
   b. Suppose that the country initially has no restrictions on trade and then imposes an import quota of 7,000,000 crates per year. How will this affect the price and quantity imported? What are the welfare effects?
   c. How much should the quota be if the government wants to increase the price of almonds to $18 per crate?

22. The equilibrium wage for housekeepers is $4 per hour, but the government is about to increase the minimum wage from $5 per hour to $6 per hour. Show the welfare effects of this increase in the minimum wage in the market for housekeepers.

23. Figure 9.8 shows a budget line, L, and indifference curves for Andy, who currently buys 10 meals per month at the Boar's Head Inn. How much consumer surplus does he get from these meals?

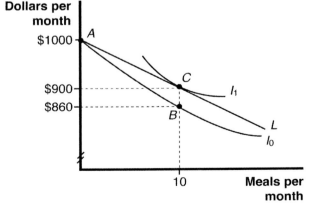

Figure 9.8

24. Gilda buys cat food for 25 cents per can. Cat food makers switch from cans that require can openers to easy-opening pop-top cans. How will this affect Gilda's consumer surplus from cat food?

25. Murdoch has $5 to spend at lunch. Based on the information below, should he go to the Burger Barn or the Chicken Roost?

Burger Barn			Chicken Roost		
Item	Price	Willingness to Pay	Item	Price	Willingness to Pay
Pepsi	$1.00	$1.10	Pepsi	$1.00	$1.10
Root Beer	$1.00	$1.50	Ginger Ale	$1.00	$0.80
Deluxe Burger	$2.00	$2.50	Super Chicken	$2.00	$2.85
Medium Fries	$1.00	$1.25	Curly Fries	$1.00	$1.35
Salad	$1.00	$1.15	Salad	$1.00	$1.25
NASCAR poster	$1.00	$0.50	Mr. T Figure	$1.00	$1.05

26. The initial demand for bottled water is $Q_{DI} = 300 - 200p$. The supply of bottled water is $Q_S = -100 + 600p$, where quantity is gallons per day and $p =$ dollars per gallon. Then a hurricane hits and the demand for bottled water climbs to $Q_{DH} = 500 - 200p$. Which policy is in the best interest of consumers as a group, setting a price ceiling at the old equilibrium price or allowing the price to rise to the new equilibrium?

27. A report examining underage drinking says the following. "The costs of underage drinking are numerous—automobile accidents, lower grades, poor health, broken relationships, increased likelihood of pregnancy—the list is long. The benefits from underage drinking are few—only the revenue that the industry earns." Using the tools developed in this chapter, what flaws do you see in this analysis?

■ Answers to Practice Problems

1. a. With an output of zero, all consumer and producer surplus will be lost. (The deadweight loss would be even bigger if a very large amount, much greater than 30, were produced.)

2. c. When price equals $6, output is 20 units and there is no deadweight loss.

3. b. The cost of making the 30th unit is $8, but its value to consumers is only $5, so there will be a deadweight loss of $3 if it is produced.

4. c. Lost consumer surplus is area A + area B. Area A = $10 (base × height = 10 × $1). Area B = $5 (1/2 × base × height = 0.5 × 10 × $1).

5. a. The gain in producer surplus from a higher price (area A) is completely offset by a loss in producer surplus due to lower sales (area $C + E$).

6. b. The subsidy creates a wedge between supply and demand, so that supply is greater than demand by the amount of the subsidy. At an output of 30, the supply curve is $3 above the demand curve, so output is 30. With a subsidy of $3 per unit and sales of 30, the total cost expenditures by the government are $90.

7. c. As the previous answer explains, the subsidy increases output to 30. The deadweight loss is area
       F, the amount by which marginal cost (given by the supply curve) exceeds marginal benefit
       (given by the demand curve) for each unit above the efficient quantity (which is 20, where supply
       equals demand). The area of F is $0.5 \times \$3 \times 10 = \$15$.

8. d. Rent seeking refers to attempts to use the government's actions to gain additional profits. This
       rules out choices *a* and *b*. Rent seeking uses firms' resources to influence others (e.g., hiring
       lobbyists) rather than to produce output. It uses up real resources, so it increases costs and any
       deadweight loss estimates.

9. VC = the sum of MC = \$7,000,000; PS = Revenue − VC = \$3,000,000; greater than \$1,000,000—
    otherwise the Hormsbury Corp. would have produced the eleventh Megazapper.

10. Exit. In the long run, it may act as a barrier to entry.

11. Ambiguous. Profit = revenue − (fixed cost + variable cost). Producer surplus = revenue − variable
    cost. If the firm has fixed costs, then its profit will be smaller than its producer surplus. In the long
    run, no cost is fixed; therefore in the long run, profit = producer surplus.

12. Ambiguous. In the short run, if certain producers are banned from the market, the supply curve will
    shift inward since the market supply curve is the sum of all the firm's supply curves and there are
    now fewer firms. In the long run, however, the supply curve may or may not shift inward. For example,
    if the market has constant input prices and each potential firm has the same costs, then the supply
    curve is horizontal. If certain firms are banned from the market, then other firms will enter and the
    supply curve will still be horizontal at the old price. If, however, the replacement firms have higher
    costs than the banned firms, then the supply curve will shift inward, prices may rise, and a deadweight
    loss may exist. In Figure 9.9, banning firms that supply output equaling $Q_4 − Q_1$ will cause an inward
    shift in the supply curve from S_0 to S_1. If the demand is low, D_0, there will be enough remaining firms
    at the lowest cost to keep price at p_0. However, if demand is high relative to supply, D_1, then the price
    will rise to p_1, output will fall from Q_3 to Q_2, and a deadweight loss of A will occur.

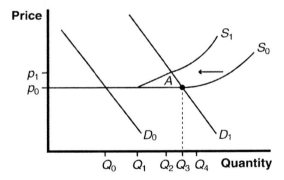

Figure 9.9

13. False. If the supply curve is perfectly inelastic, as in Figure 9.10, the total surplus will remain the same, so there will be no deadweight loss. At the equilibrium price, p_E, the consumer surplus is A and the producer surplus is $B + C$ (all producer revenue is surplus, since producers are willing to supply Q_0 at price = zero). At the price ceiling, p_C, the consumer surplus is $A + B$ and the producer surplus is C. Thus, total surplus is $A + B + C$ in both cases.

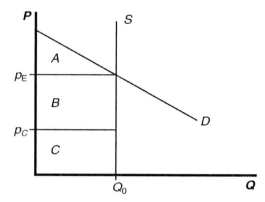

Figure 9.10

14. The total consumer surplus is the area of the triangle beneath the demand curve and above the equilibrium price, $14. Area = (height × base × 0.5) = ($9 × 200 × 0.5) = $900.

    The 100th unit gives $19 − $14 = $5 of consumer surplus. The 200th unit gives zero dollars in consumer surplus.

15. Welfare is maximized when the sum of consumer surplus and producer surplus is maximized. This occurs at the intersection of the supply and demand curves—at an output of 200. Market failure occurs when the price is at a level that does not maximize total welfare. Thus, any price other than $14 will cause a market failure.

16. Figure 9.11 shows a typical (downward-sloping) demand curve for physical exams and the supply curve facing the family—which is horizontal at $50 per exam. If the family had no insurance, they would pay for Q_1 examinations per year. Because exams are free, the family consumes Q_3 examinations per year. The family's consumer surplus rises from A to $A + B + E$. Unfortunately, the marginal cost exceeds the marginal benefit for all units past Q_1, so the program creates a deadweight loss of $C + D$. Presumably, the backers of Medicaid (a federal program giving free health care to the poor) believe that the demand for health care among the poor is too low (because of low incomes), so the subsidy is designed to increase their consumption of health care. Since policy makers wish to reduce the potential deadweight loss, they usually place a limit on free goods that are available. For example, placing a limit at Q_2 would reduce the deadweight loss by D, while reducing consumer surplus by only E.

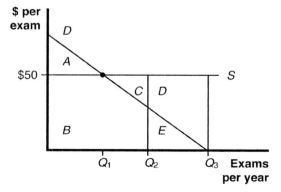

Figure 9.11

17. As Figure 9.12 shows, the long-run supply curve in a constant-cost perfect competitive industry with unlimited entry is horizontal (at the minimum point on each firm's long-run average cost curve). The technological improvement shifts the long-run supply curve down from p_1 to p_2. Consumer surplus rises from A to $A + B$. Producer surplus (which equals profits in the long run) is zero before and after the improvement. Thus producers in this type of market compete away all their gains, and only consumers come out ahead.

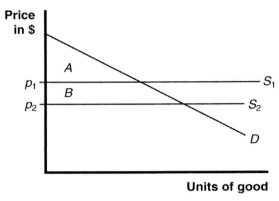

Figure 9.12

18. Figure 9.13 shows the effect of the price support at p_0. The supply curve shifts outward from S_1 to S_2 due to the technological progress.

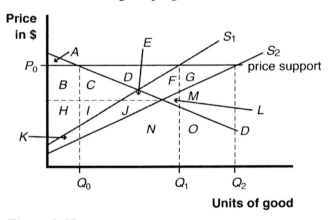

Figure 9.13

This has no effect on consumer surplus because consumers still pay p_0 to buy Q_0. Consumer surplus is A.

Producer surplus was initially $B \mu C + D + H + I$. As the supply curve shifts downward while price stays at P_0, the producer surplus grows to be $B + C + D + H + I$ (the initial producer surplus) plus the area between the two supply curves, $K + J + E + F + G$.

Government payments climb from $p_0(Q_1 - Q_0)$ to $p_0(Q_2 - Q_0)$, i.e., they rise by $G + M + O$.

Change in total surplus $= \Delta CS + \Delta PS - \Delta(\text{Government Expense})$.

$$\Delta CS = 0$$
$$\Delta PS = K + J + E + F + G.$$
$$\Delta(\text{Government Expense}) = G + M + O.$$
$$\Delta \text{Welfare} = K + J + E + F - M - O.$$

In this case, because of the price support, all of the gains go to the suppliers; yet the taxpayers pay more, and society as a whole can end up worse off: if $K + J + E + F < M + O$.

19. Figure 9.14 is the same as Figure 9.10 from the textbook. A quota of 2.8 million barrels of oil per day has the same impact on price, domestic production, imports, and domestic consumption as a tariff of $5 per barrel. The tariff and the quota have the same effects on consumer surplus and domestic producers' surplus, but the tariff brings in governmental revenue equaling area *TR*, while a freely granted quota yields no revenue to the government. How much revenue will the government gain if it auctioned off the quota to the highest bidder? Foreign producers will be willing to pay for the right to export to the U.S. market because they can sell there for $5 more than they can in the world market. In fact, any business can buy oil on the world market at $14.70 and turn around and resell it in the U.S. market at $19.70 (ignoring any shipping costs, as does the discussion in the text). A firm could earn $14 million per day ($5 per barrel × 2.8 million barrels per day). Thus a firm will be willing to bid up to $14 million per day for the right to fill the U.S. quota. If there are no barriers to entering the auction, there will be many bidders and they will drive the price of the right to import up to approximately $14 million per day. Thus auctioning the right to import will yield the same revenue as does a tariff.

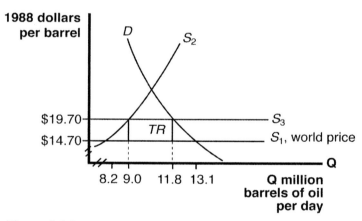

Figure 9.14

20. a. If the demand curve is horizontal, consumer surplus is 0. The consumers are indifferent between buying and not buying the good at price $= p_0$.

  b. If the demand curve is vertical, it would never hit the vertical axis, so the area "below" it would be infinite. (Obviously, this is impossible. People cannot pay an infinite amount for a good, since they don't have an infinite amount of income. A demand curve can be vertical only within a certain price range.)

21. a. Figure 9.15 shows the domestic demand, D_D, the domestic supply, S_D, and the world supply, S_w. If there are no restrictions on trade, then the price is the world price, domestic production is 7,000,000 crates, domestic consumption is 12,500,000 crates, and imports are 5,500,000 crates.

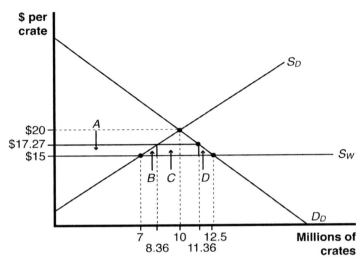

Figure 9.15

To find the impact of a 3,000,000 crate quota, find the price where $Q_S + 3,000,000 = Q_D$.

$$-2,000,000 + 600,000p + 3,000,000 = 20,000,000 - 500,000p.$$
$$1,100,000p = 19,000,000$$
$$p = \$17.2727$$

At this price, $Q_D = 11,363,636$, $Q_S = 8,363,636$, so imports are 3,000,000.

The quota increases domestic producer surplus by A. The area of a trapezoid is (height × average length), so this area is ($2.27 × (8,363,636 + 7,000,000)/2) = $17,458,677.

The quota reduces domestic consumer surplus by $A + B + C + D$ or ($2.27 × (12,500,000 + 11,363,636)/2) = $27,117,768.

Foreign producers gain C or ($2.27 × 3,000,000) = $6,818,181.

Deadweight loss equals $B + D$ or $27,117,768 − $17,458,677 − $6,818,181 = $2,840,910.

b. If the quota is set at 7,000,000 crates per year, it will have no effect at all. Importers will be unwilling to import more than 5,500,000 crates, so the quota is unfilled.

c. At $18, domestic producers desire to sell −2,000,000 + (600,000 × 18) = 8,800,000 crates.

Domestic consumers wish to buy 20,000,000 − (500,000 × 18) = 11,000,000 crates. Thus the quota must be 11,000,000 − 8,800,000 = 2,200,000 crates to drive the price to $18 per crate.

22. Figure 9.16 shows that raising the minimum wage from $5 to $6 per hour will reduce employment from L_1 to L_2. When the minimum wage is $5, consumer surplus is $E + F + G$. At $5 per hour, the economic rent of housekeepers is $A + B + C + D$. (This is economic rent rather than producer surplus, since the payment is to labor, rather than a firm.) When the minimum wage is $6, consumer surplus falls to G, and economic rent becomes $A + C + E$. Thus

$$\Delta CS \qquad\qquad -E - F$$
$$\Delta \text{Economic Rent} \qquad E - D - B$$
$$\Delta \text{Total Surplus} \qquad -B - D - F$$

Some housekeepers gain economic rent, but others lose their jobs and the economic rent that went with the jobs. Those who keep the jobs gain E. Those who lose their jobs lose B and D.

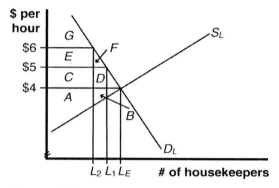

Figure 9.16

23. As Figure 9.8 shows, Andy is indifferent between bundle A ($1000 per month with no meals at the Boar's Head) and bundle B ($860 per month with 10 meals at the Boar's head). Therefore he is willing to pay $140 for the 10 meals. However, because meals only cost $10 each, he spends only $100 on the 10 meals. His consumer surplus (willingness to pay minus amount paid) is $40.

24. As Figure 9.17 shows, the improvement in quality will shift Gilda's demand curve (marginal benefit curve) to the right since she is now willing to pay more for a can of cat food than she did before. The demand curve shifts from D_0 to D_1. If the price stays at 25 cents, her consumer surplus will rise from $A + B$ to $A + B + C + D$. If the price rises to, say, 30 cents, consumer surplus will change from $A + B$ to $A + C$. If $C > B$, then she gains. If $B > C$, then she loses. Figure 9.18 is drawn so that $C > B$, but if the demand curve shifted out by less, then B could be greater than C.

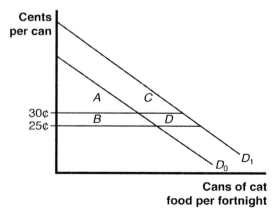

Figure 9.17

25. Murdoch wants to maximize his well-being and can do this by gaining the most consumer surplus from spending his $5. At the Burger Barn, he would spend his $5 on root beer, a deluxe burger, medium fries, and a salad. He wouldn't buy the NASCAR poster, because he isn't willing to pay $1 for it, and he won't buy the Pepsi because his last $1 would be more wisely spent on a salad, for which he is willing to pay $1.15—greater than the $1.10 that he's willing to pay for the Pepsi. Adding things up, he's willing to pay $6.40 for the root beer, burger, fries, and salad and it only costs him $5, so his consumer surplus is $1.40 at the Burger Barn. Meanwhile, over at the Chicken Roost, he can gain the most by buying a Pepsi, a super chicken, curly fries, and a salad. His willingness to pay for this combination is $6.55. Thus he can gain more consumer surplus from buying a lunch at the Chicken Roost.

26. To answer, we need to compare the consumer surplus under the two policies. Figure 9.18 shows the supply curve, S, and the demand curve, which shifts outward from D_I to D_H. The initial equilibrium price is $0.50 per gallon. ($Q_{DI} = 300 - 200p = Q_S = -100 + 600p$, or $400 = 800p$, so $p = 0.50$.) At this price producers are willing to sell $Q_S = 200$ gallons. After the hurricane, the demand rises, pushing the equilibrium price up to $0.75 per gallon. ($500 - 200p = -100 + 600p$, or $600 = 800p$, so $p = 0.75$.) The new equilibrium quantity is 350 gallons. (Plug $0.75 into either the supply or the hurricane demand curve: $Q_S = -100 + (600 \times 0.75) = 350$.) Thus if the price is allowed to rise to $0.75 per gallon, the quantity supplied will rise to 350 gallons and the consumer surplus will be area ($A + B + C + D$) in Figure 9.18. This triangle's area is $(350 \times \$1.75 \times 0.5) = \$306.25$. If the price ceiling at the old price, $0.50 per gallon, is adopted, only 200 gallons will be supplied, so the consumer surplus will be area ($A + B + C + E + F$). $A = (200 \times \$1 \times 0.5) = \$100$. Rectangle $B + C + E + F = (200 \times \$1) = \$200$. Thus the consumer surplus with the price ceiling is $300. Therefore, the consumers gain more surplus without the price ceiling than they do with the price ceiling.

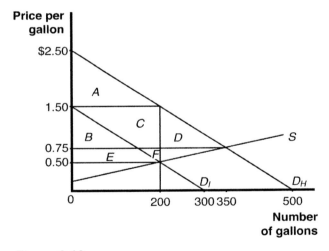

Figure 9.18

27. The article has done a poor job in analyzing the benefits from underage drinking. Revenue is a *cost* to consumers, so a better way to analyze the net benefits is to look at producer surplus, which equals revenues minus variable costs. Even more importantly, the article has omitted what may be the primary benefit of underage drinking—or any act of consumption—the consumer surplus that arises. This consumer surplus is likely to be very large. When a student of mine proposed the idea of a drinking license for 18, 19, and 20 year olds, I asked the class how much they would be willing to pay for such a license. Many were willing to pay $100 per year or more, so clearly they perceive considerable consumer surplus from the ability to consume alcohol.

■ Exercises

True-False-Ambiguous and Explain Why

1. A per-unit tax will always cause a deadweight loss.

2. Everyone wins when a product is freely traded.

3. Tom's demand curve for carnival ride tickets is given in Figure 9.19. If the carnival only sells tickets in packs of 15 and the price of tickets is $0.60 each, then Tom will buy 45 tickets.

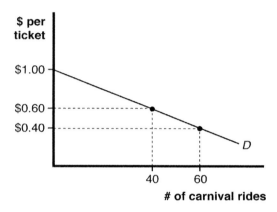

Figure 9.19

Short-Answer

4. Tom's demand curve for haircuts is given in Figure 9.20. Haircuts cost $6 each. Tom's mom forces him to get six haircuts per year. How much consumer surplus does he get from the money he spends on haircuts?

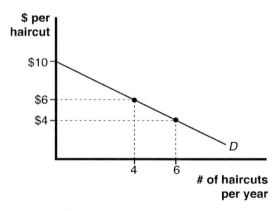

Figure 9.20

5. The annual demand for *Study Guide to Accompany Microeconomics* is $Q_d = 100,000 - 5,000p + 4Y$, where $p =$ the price per study guide, which is initially $15, and $Y =$ parents' average income, which is initially $40,000. How would consumer surplus from the study guide change if the price dropped to $10? How would consumer surplus from the study guide change if the price was still $15, but average income rose to $50,000? Draw a graph and explain.

6. Currently about 5 billion pounds of apples are consumed annually in the United States and growers are paid an average of $0.50 per pound. The government establishes a price support program with a price of $1.00 per pound.

   a. Could this program cost the government more than $5 billion per year? Under what conditions? Could it cost less than $5 billion per year? Under what conditions? Use graphs in your explanation.

   b. What is the maximum amount of surplus that the producers could gain from the price support program? What is the minimum amount? Use a graph in your explanation.

   c. What is the most consumer surplus that could be lost due to this program? The least? Use a graph in your explanation.

7. The domestic demand for almonds is $Q_D = 20,000,000 - 500,000p$. The domestic supply is $Q_S = -2,000,000 + 600,000p$, where quantity is in crates per year and p = price per crate. The world price is $15 per crate.

   a. Suppose that the country initially has no restrictions on trade and then imposes a tariff of $2 per crate. How will this affect the price and the quantity imported? What are the welfare effects?

   b. Suppose that the country initially has no restrictions on trade and then imposes a tariff of $8 per crate. How will this affect the price and quantity imported? What are the welfare effects?

8. In the market for chicken $Q_d = 200,000 - 2,000p_C$, $Q_s = -100,000 + 3,000p_C$, where the quantity is tons per week and p_C is price in cents per pound of chicken. In the market for barbecue sauce, $Q_d = 130,000 - 300p_B - 1,000p_C$, $Q_s = -20,000 + 200p_B$, where quantity is cases per week and p_B is price in dollars per case of barbecue sauce. Avian flu sweeps through the chicken coops of America, causing the chicken supply curve to shift to $Q_s = -200,000 + 3,000p_C$. How does this affect consumer surplus, and surplus among chicken and barbecue sauce producers? What is the overall change in welfare?

9. Suppose that the market for eye examinations has the following supply and demand curves: $Q_d = 100,000 - 2000p$ and $Q_s = -20,000 + 4000p$, where Q = visits per month and a = dollars per visit. The market equilibrium output of 60,000 visits is considered too low, so the government decides to subsidize eye examinations. How big of a subsidy will be needed to boost the number of exams to 80,000 per month?

10. Vespuccia is a small country that trades with the world. It can buy or sell as much as it wants at the world price.

$$Q_{Dworld} = 1,000,000 - 50,000p$$
$$Q_{Sworld} = 100,000 + 40,000p$$
$$Q_{Ddomestic} = 2000 - 100p$$
$$Q_{Sdomestic} = -100 + 320p,$$

   where Q is in pounds and p is in dollars per pound.

   a. Based on the world demand and supply and the domestic demand and supply of the mystery good, determine whether Vespuccia imports or exports this good and how much.

   b. What would be the change in consumer surplus, producer surplus, and deadweight loss if Vespuccia stopped trading with the rest of the world?

11. Suppose that the market for milk has the following presubsidy supply and demand curves:

$$Q_D = 100,000 - 2000p$$

$$\text{and } Q_s = -40,000 + 4000p,$$

where Q = cups per month and p = cents per cup.

The government wants to boost consumption because milk's calcium helps prevent osteoporosis. It decides to subsidize milk producers by 5 cents per cup. What is the economic impact of this subsidy in terms of consumer surplus, producer surplus, deadweight loss and government spending?

Chapter 10
General Equilibrium and Economic Welfare

■ Chapter Summary

This chapter is as easy as pie. Well, actually, it's one of the most abstract, difficult chapters in the text, but it *is* all about pie—how competition can be used to get the most valuable economic pie possible with the available resources, and the potential to use competition to divide the pie in exactly the way society desires.

Partial-equilibrium analysis examines equilibrium in one market in isolation. Often, partial-equilibrium analysis makes valid predictions, but when there are important interactions (spillover effects) among markets, we need to use **general-equilibrium analysis**: the study of how equilibrium is determined in all markets simultaneously. One example of general-equilibrium analysis is interrelated markets, in which a change in the price of one good has an effect on the demand for another good, and vice versa. For example, if a shift in the demand for one product causes its price to change, this will cause a shift in the demand and/or supply of a related good, causing the second good's price to change. The price change in the second market can feed back into the first market, causing supply and demand to shift there and setting off continuing rounds of adjustments across the two markets, which general-equilibrium analysis can trace out. General-equilibrium analysis often involves solving systems of equations for supply and demand in many markets.

Another application of general-equilibrium analysis is trading between people. An **Edgeworth box** illustrates trade between two people with a **fixed endowment**—an initial allocation—of two goods. The height of the box equals the sum of the two people's endowments of one good. The length equals the sum of the endowment of the other good. Measuring from the lower-left corner, the endowment point tells how much of the two goods the first person has. Measuring from the upper-right corner, the same endowment point tells how much the second person has. If we assume that each person maximizes utility, has usual-shaped indifference curves, has positive marginal utility for each good (nonsatiation), and that neither person's utility depends on the other's consumption, then two people whose indifference curves cross each other at the endowment point can gain from trading with each other. Any point inside the football-shaped area that lies between the two indifference curves passing through their endowment point is preferred by both to the endowment point. The **contract curve** contains all the points within the Edgeworth box at which the indifference curves of the two people are tangent. At points off the contract curve, both parties can gain from trade because their **marginal rates of substitution**—the rates at which each is willing to trade off the two goods—differ. For example, the first person is willing to give the second more of good A than the second person needs to trade away one unit of good B, while the second person is willing to give the first more of good B than the first person needs to trade away a unit of good A. Along the contract curve, the marginal rate of substitution (*MRS*) of each person is the same, so there are no more gains from trade. Because bargaining abilities differ, we cannot predict which point the two traders will pick, but it must be a point along the contract curve that makes them both better off. The contract curve is the set of all consumption bundles that are **Pareto-efficient**—goods cannot be reallocated so as to make one person better off without harming another person.

When two large groups of people trade, they will reach a competitive equilibrium, so we can predict the final allocation and price. The **First Theorem of Welfare Economics** shows that the competitive equilibrium is efficient. The **Second Theorem of Welfare Economics** shows that all possible efficient allocations can be obtained by competitive exchange, given an appropriate initial allocation of goods. (These theorems assume that everyone knows the preferences of all traders, there are no transactions costs, and indifference curves have the usual shapes.) In a competitive two-good market, members of each group will be willing to trade until their own *MRS* is the same as the price ratio. At most price ratios, however, the desired trades of the two groups will be incompatible, so the relative price must adjust until the quantity of each good supplied equals the quantity of each good demanded. This can only occur where the indifference curves of the two groups are tangent because at this point MRS_{Group1} = price ratio = MRS_{Group2}. The marginal rates of substitution of the two groups are equal only along the contract curve. Thus, competitive trading brings society to the contract curve—to an efficient allocation of goods. This same chain of reasoning implies that any Pareto-efficient Bundle *x* can be obtained as a competitive equilibrium if the endowment lies on a price line through *x*, where the slope of the price line equals the *MRS* of the indifference curves that are tangent at *x*. In essence, the first welfare theorem says that society can achieve efficiency by allowing competition. The second welfare theorem says that society can obtain the particular efficient allocation it prefers if it can costlessly redistribute endowments.

This model can be expanded to include production by assuming that each trader has an endowment (labor) used to produce the two goods. The **production possibilities frontier** (*PPF*) shows the maximum combinations of the two goods that a person can produce from a given amount of input. The slope of the *PPF* is the **marginal rate of transformation** (*MRT*), which tells how much of one good can be produced if production of the other good is reduced by one unit. Someone with a lower opportunity cost of producing a good than someone else has a **comparative advantage** in producing that good. People can benefit from trade if they have a different *MRT*. They do better if they trade because each person uses his comparative advantage, specializing in the good that he makes at the lowest opportunity cost. Competition will push the market to an efficient product mix—where each consumer's marginal rate of substitution equals the price ratio, which equals the economy's marginal rate of transformation. By combining the *PPF* and the Edgeworth box, we can show the competitive equilibrium for both production and consumption. The two welfare theorems still hold in an economy with production.

Virtually every governmental activity redistributes wealth. Many economists make the value judgment that government should use the **Pareto principle** and prefer allocations in which someone is made better off if no one else is harmed—allowing voluntary trades, encouraging competition, and trying to prevent forces that reduce efficiency. Most government policies create winners and losers, but many of these could be turned into **Pareto-superior allocations** (where no one loses) if the winners compensate the losers. Fairness or **equity** is based on value judgments that can be summarized in a **social welfare function**—which is something like a utility function for society as a whole. The **utility possibility frontier** is the set of utility levels corresponding to the Pareto-efficient allocations along the contract curve. In principle, a society could pick the point on the utility possibilities frontier that reaches the highest level of social welfare. In practice, this is more difficult. Majority voting does not always work very well because the resulting social ordering of allocations is not generally transitive. The **Arrow Impossibility Theorem** proves that it is impossible to find a social-decision-making rule that always satisfies the four criteria for a socially desirable decision-making system: (1) that social preferences be complete; (2) that if everyone prefers allocation *A* to allocation *B*, then *A* should be socially preferred to *B*; (3) that society's ranking of *A* and *B* should depend only on individuals' ordering of these two allocations, not on how they rank other alternatives; and (4) that dictatorship is not allowed. Determining how much weight to give to the preferences of various people in society is a key step in determining the social welfare function. **Egalitarianism** suggests that everyone be given the exact same bundle. **Utilitarianism** argues that we should try to maximize the sum of the utilities of all members of society. Philosopher John Rawls argues that if everyone picked the decision rule before they knew to which group they would belong, then society would maximize the well-being of the worst-off member of society. Serious objections to all of these rules have been raised by critics.

A competitive equilibrium may not be very equitable even though it is Pareto-efficient. However, in practice, attempts to achieve greater equity generally reduce efficiency because redistribution (tax and transfer programs) eats up resources and puts in place incentives that cause people to use their resources less efficiently than otherwise (deadweight losses). However, removing existing taxes, transfers, and other programs that change economic incentives may not improve efficiency (unless *all* such distortions are eliminated). A competitive economy with no distortions at all is called a *first-best equilibrium*—any distortion will reduce efficiency. But if there is more than one market distortion, the **Theory of the Second Best** states that correcting a single distortion may increase or decrease social welfare. In other words, if the best equilibrium occurs where there are no restrictions, it does not necessarily follow that removing a subset of restrictions will lead to a relatively "better" equilibrium.

■ Key Concepts and Formulas

- **Partial-equilibrium analysis:** the study of how equilibrium is determined in one market in isolation.
- **General-equilibrium analysis:** the study of how equilibrium is determined in all markets simultaneously.
- **Contract curve:** contains all the points within the Edgeworth box at which the indifference curves of the two people are tangent. It is the set of all consumption bundles that are Pareto-efficient.
- **Pareto-efficient:** an allocation in which goods cannot be reallocated so as to make one person better off without harming another person.
- **First Theorem of Welfare Economics:** any competitive equilibrium is efficient.
- **Second Theorem of Welfare Economics:** all possible efficient allocations can be obtained by competitive exchange, given an appropriate initial allocation of goods.
- **Production possibilities frontier (*PPF*):** shows the maximum combinations of the two goods that can be produced from a given amount of inputs.
- **Marginal rate of transformation:** the slope of the *PPF*; the opportunity cost of producing one more unit of a good.
- **Comparative advantage:** having a lower opportunity cost of producing a good than someone else.
- **Social welfare function:** a utility function for society as a whole.
- **Theory of the Second Best:** if an economy has more than one market distortion, removing a subset (but not all) of the distortions may either increase or decrease social welfare.
- **Utility possibility frontier:** the set of utility levels corresponding to the Pareto-efficient allocations along the contract curve.

■ Application: General Equilibrium Analysis of the Flat Tax

Nearly every taxpayer and politician complains about the U.S. tax code. It is said to be unfair, economically inefficient, overly complicated, and difficult to enforce. Recently, many economists and politicians have touted the flat tax as a better way to go. The most popular flat tax proposals (such as the one put forward by Robert Hall and Alvin Rabushka) would modify the current system by: (1) taxing business and wage income at the same (flat) tax rate (while exempting people with low incomes from income taxes altogether); (2) eliminating tax breaks for fringe benefits (such as health plans) and eliminating virtually every tax break in the individual income tax code (such as deductions for mortgage interest payments, earnings from municipal government bonds, and donations to charity); and (3) eliminating taxation of earnings from savings (thus taxing only consumption).

Question: Would a flat tax improve the efficiency of the U.S. economy? Would a flat tax be fairer than the current tax system?

Answer: Because the tax system impinges on nearly every aspect of the economy, partial-equilibrium analysis is too simple to answer these questions. We must turn to general-equilibrium analysis. Advocates of the flat tax argue that it will enhance economic efficiency in a number of ways. For example, the current tax deduction for mortgage interest cuts the cost of borrowing money to buy a home, inducing more people to buy homes and encouraging them to buy bigger homes than they otherwise would. Normally, people spend money on housing until the last dollar spent yields as much utility as the last dollar spent on other goods. However, the tax break means that the consumer pays the marginal cost minus the tax rate. A person in the 28 percent tax bracket spends $1 on mortgage interest and receives 28 cents back from the government due to the tax deduction. Figure 10.1 shows the impact of the housing tax break on one person. This person consumes housing until the marginal benefit from the last unit is only 72 cents, while the marginal cost of building this unit of housing is $1, at Q_T. The efficient amount to consume is Q_E, so the tax break creates a deadweight loss to society—area A in Figure 10.1. Eliminating these tax breaks will generally reduce spending on items currently encouraged by the tax code—such as housing, health insurance, and charity, while it will increase the demand for goods that do not currently receive special tax breaks. The quantity of housing demanded could fall dramatically, drastically lowering the price of houses. Estimates vary because there are disagreements about the size of the demand effects and the shape of the supply of housing curve.

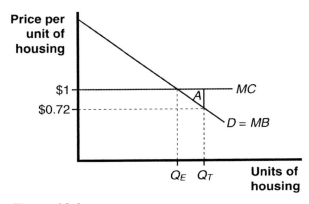

Figure 10.1

Advocates of the flat tax argue that the zero tax rate on the returns from saving will eliminate the deadweight loss from the existing tax on saving, boost the quantity of savings (and investment), and reduce the interest rate charged to borrowers. As Figure 10.2 shows, when there is no tax on savings, savers earn an interest rate of r_E, the investors who borrow the savings pay r_E, and total investment is I_E. If the saving supply is somewhat elastic, S_E, then the tax lowers the return for savers to r_s and raises the rate paid by investors to $r_s + t$, as total savings and investment fall to I_T. The tax creates a deadweight loss—triangle A in Figure 10.2. If the tax is removed, total investment will rise, and capital will become cheaper, making it cheaper to produce a whole range of goods. The cheaper capital will reduce the costs of producing goods for which capital is an input, such as automobiles. As Figure 10.3 shows, cheaper capital will shift out the supply of autos, from S_0 to S_1. The demand for autos may also shift out, from D_0 to D_1, as income previously spent on goods with tax breaks is reallocated. If we knew more about these shifts, we could predict the impact on the price of autos. This drop in interest rates will boost the demand for housing—offsetting some or all of the effect of ending the mortgage interest deductions. Figure 10.4 shows how the flat tax may affect the housing market. The demand for housing falls from D_0 to D_1 (due to the termination of the mortgage interest deduction), but it rises from D_1 to D_2 (due to the lower interest rates). Some supporters of the flat tax argue that D_2 will be in the same position as D_0, so the price of houses (a vital concern of home owners) will not change from p_0. You can see why a detailed general-equilibrium assessment is both very important to decision makers (including voting homeowners) and very complex, since there may be a wide range of spillovers among markets.

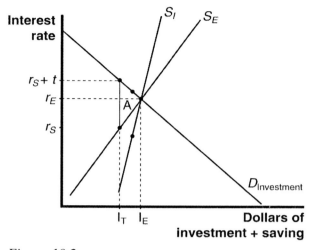

Figure 10.2

Finally, flat-tax supporters argue that because the marginal tax on wages will fall for most workers (while rising for some), the deadweight loss in the labor market will be reduced, more labor will be supplied, and the economy and average incomes will grow. Rising income will shift the demand curve for any good that has an income elasticity not equal to zero. In sum, analysts need to trace the impact of the flat tax through a wide range of output markets and input markets, they need to estimate the elasticities of supply and demand in these markets, they need to estimate the cross-price elasticities among these markets, and they need to estimate income elasticities in these markets. Hall and Rabushka project a 3 percent increase in total output from increased total work and an additional increase of 3 percent due to added capital formation and improved entrepreneurial incentives (Robert E. Hall and Alvin Rabushka, *The Flat Tax,* 2nd edition, Stanford, 1995, p. 89). Others say the impact will be much smaller (if any) because, among other things, the savings supply curve is fairly inelastic. Examining Figure 10.2 shows that if the savings supply curve is very inelastic, S_I, the tax on savings reduces investment by a very small amount and creates a small deadweight loss.

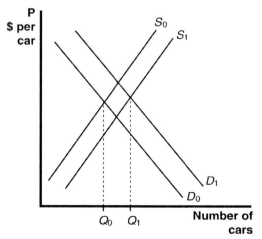

Figure 10.3

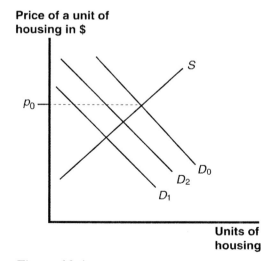

Figure 10.4

Assessing the fairness of a move to the flat tax is even more complex. First, analysts must discern who actually bears the tax. (Recall that the incidence of a tax is determined by the relative elasticities of supply and demand of the good or input.) Second, analysts must use general equilibrium analysis to predict how incomes and prices will change. Table 10.1 gives estimates (from the U.S. Department of Treasury, Office of Tax Analysis) of the average tax rates currently paid by people in a range of income groups. Is this current tax system fair? The table also gives projections (based on general-equilibrium analysis) of the average tax rates under three different flat tax proposals. Are any of the alternative taxes more fair? The answer to these questions depends on your own sense of fairness—which differs greatly from person to person. According to the estimates, all of the flat tax proposals will increase the average tax rate for the lower and middle income groups, while cutting the average tax rate for the richest. If these predictions are correct, it is unlikely that any of these variants of a flat tax will be passed—since the number of losers is so much greater than the number of winners. Note, however, that these projections assume that the flat tax will bring no improvement in economic efficiency and no economic growth. If flat-tax advocates are correct, there should be more winners and fewer losers than the table shows.

TABLE 10.1

Family Income	Average Tax Rates (percent)			
		(1)	(2)	(3)
Percentile Rank	Current Personal & Corporate Income Taxes	20.8% Flat Tax, $31,400 Exemption, No EITC	17% Flat Tax, $15,000 Exemption, No EITC	22.9% Flat Tax, $35,750 Exemption, Keep EITC
0 to 20%	−2.4	3.8	4.6	1.5
21 to 40%	2.0	6.7	8.3	3.1
41 to 60%	7.1	9.5	10.9	8.5
61 to 80%	9.3	11.2	12.3	11.1
81 to 90%	10.8	12.9	13.1	13.2
91 to 95%	12.8	14.2	13.5	14.6
96 to 99%	15.7	14.8	13.2	15.0
Top 1%	22.4	13.5	11.3	14.3

Note: Each flat tax plan is estimated by the Treasury to be revenue-neutral, assuming no induced economic growth. They assume that the burden of labor taxes falls on workers, and the burden of business taxes falls on capital income generally.

Source: Joel Slemrod and Jon Bakija, *Taxing Ourselves: A Citizen's Guide to the Great Debate Over Tax Reform* (Cambridge, MA: MIT Press, 1996), p. 222.

■ Solved Problems

1.   Huck and Jim are floating down the Mississippi River. Huck finds a raft with 20 pounds of coffee and 10 pounds of salt pork. Jim finds a raft with 30 pounds of coffee and 30 pounds of salt pork. Draw an Edgeworth box showing the initial allocation of coffee and salt pork for Huck and Jim.

Step 1: Construct the Edgeworth box.

The length of the Edgeworth box is the sum of the endowments of the first good. Since Huck has 20 pounds of coffee and Jim has 30 pounds of coffee, the length of the box is 50 pounds of coffee.

The height of the Edgeworth box is the sum of the endowments of the second good. Since Huck has 10 pounds of salt pork and Jim has 30 pounds of salt pork, the height of the box is 40 pounds of salt pork.

Next, label the lower left corner as the zero point for one of the people and the upper right corner as the zero point for the other.

Figure 10.5 measures Huck's quantities beginning at the lower left corner and Jim's quantities beginning at the upper right corner.

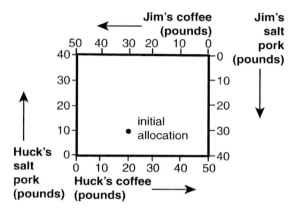

Figure 10.5

Step 2: Plot the endowment point (the initial allocation).

The point must be 20 pounds of coffee to the right of Huck's zero point and 10 pounds of salt pork above Huck's zero point. Likewise, the point must be 30 pounds of coffee to the left of Jim's zero point and 30 pounds of salt pork below Jim's zero point.

2. What is the general equilibrium impact of a boost in the minimum wage? Assume that all workers are covered by the minimum wage, but that there are two types of labor that can be substituted for each other—less-skilled workers whose equilibrium wage is below the minimum and more skilled workers whose equilibrium wage is above the minimum.

    Step 1: Analyze the impact of the minimum wage in the market for unskilled workers.

    Figure 10.6(a) shows the market for less-skilled workers. It is identical to the standard model. The employment of less-skilled workers falls from L_0 to L_M when the minimum wage rises to w_{MIN}, which is above their equilibrium wage, w_0.

    Step 2: Analyze the impact of the minimum wage in the market for skilled workers.

    Figure 10.6(b) shows the market for more-skilled workers. The minimum wage is below their initial equilibrium wage, w_1. Because more-skilled workers are substitutes for less-skilled workers, the rise in the wage of less-skilled workers (from w_0 to w_{MIN}) increases the demand for more-skilled workers—shifting the demand curve from D_0 to D_1. This increases the wages of more-skilled workers (from w_1 to w_2) and increases their employment (from L_1 to L_2). Thus, an increase in the minimum wage increases the employment of one group of workers but decreases the employment of the other group. Factors such as these make estimating the impact of minimum wage laws very tricky. In a recent paper, economists David Neumark and William Wascher estimate that a 21 percent increase in the minimum wage (such as the increase enacted between 1996 and 1998) would have a big effect on teen employment and school enrollment. They estimate that it would increase the number of teens (age 16 to 19) who were not employed and not in school by 17 percent. These are mostly the unskilled teens from

Figure 10.6(a). However, the minimum wage increase also would decrease the group that was in school and employed (about 10 percent) while increasing the group who are employed and not in school (by 4 percent). They estimate that more skilled teens will be pulled out of school by the wage increase shown in Figure 10.6(b). (See David Neumark and William Wascher, "Minimum Wage Effects on Employment and School Enrollment," *Journal of Business and Economic Statistics,* Vol. 13, no. 2, 1995).

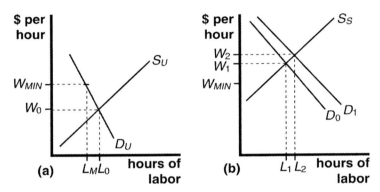

Figure 10.6

Step 3: Examine the chain of spillovers that reverberate between the more-skilled labor market and the less-skilled labor market.

Because the wage of more-skilled workers has risen, the demand for less-skilled workers will rise a little; this pushes up employment of less-skilled workers. Because the equilibrium wage in this market is still below the minimum, the wage of less-skilled workers will not rise, so the chain of reverberations between the two labor markets ends here.

Step 4: Examine the impact of the rise in the minimum wage in the product market.

The rise in the minimum wage will increase the marginal and average cost of production of goods made by less-skilled workers. In the short run, the supply curve (marginal cost curve) in these markets will shift upward, causing price to rise, from p_0 to p_1, and quantity demanded to fall, from Q_0 to Q_1. See Figure 10.7(a), which represents one market with many less-skilled workers—the fast food market. (In the long run, the supply curve will not rise as much, because the firms can adjust capital, so prices won't rise as much and quantity won't fall as much.)

Because of the rising price of fast food, the demand will rise for substitutes to fast food. Figure 10.7(b) shows the demand for food in higher quality restaurants whose workers earn more than the minimum wage. Demand will rise in these markets—but less so in the long run.

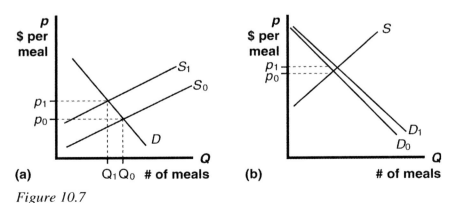

Figure 10.7

Step 5: Examine the impact of the rise in the minimum wage on other input markets.

As the minimum wage rises, producers will substitute away from labor and toward certain types of capital—such as automatic french fry machines.

3. Using a production possibilities frontier and an Edgeworth box, show how a technological improvement in the production of one of the two goods affects the competitive equilibrium.

Step 1: Show how the technological improvement changes the production possibilities frontier.

Figure 10.8 (on page) shows the production possibilities frontier from Figure 10.10 of the textbook. Technological improvements make it easier to produce firewood than before. The *PPF* shifts outward, from PPF_1 to PPF_2, so that the maximum amount of firewood that can be produced rises from 70 cords to 105 cords. The maximum amount of candy bars that can be produced stays the same. PPF_2 is drawn with a dashed line.

Step 2: Show how the change in the shape of the production possibilities frontier will affect the consumer and producer equilibrium.

Equilibrium requires that prices adjust so that the marginal rate of substitution (*MRS*) between firewood and candy bars for both people is equal to the ratio of prices $(-p_c/p_w)$ which is also equal to the marginal rate of transformation (*MRT*). The economy will most likely move to a point where the price of firewood is relatively lower than before, since at any output level it is cheaper to produce (in terms of candy bars) than it was before. Thus, $-p_{c1}/p_{w1}$, the slope of the new price line, is steeper than $-p_{c0}/p_{w0}$, the slope of the initial price line. Without knowing the utility functions of consumers we cannot tell the exact equilibrium, but Figure 10.8 shows a representative case. The new price line must be tangent to the *PPF* and tangent to both indifference curves within the Edgeworth box. The dimensions of the Edgeworth box are determined by the point chosen along the *PPF*. All of the new curves and lines are drawn with dashes in Figure 10.8. In this example, both consumers buy more firewood and fewer candy bars—the allocation shifts from point A to point B.

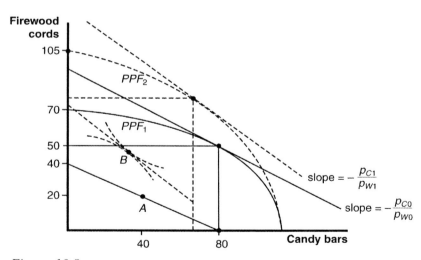

Figure 10.8

4. In a simple exchange economy with two goods, cola(C), and pizza (P), Samantha's utility function is $U(C, P) = 10CP$. Josie's utility function is $U(C, P) = C^{1/2} P^{1/2}$.

   a.   Find the equation of the contract curve.

   b.   If Samantha's initial endowment is $200C$ and $100P$, and Josie's initial endowment is $200C$ and $300P$, draw the Edgeworth box for this economy, identify the initial endowment and the contract curve. What trades are feasible in this economy? Which are efficient?

   c.   Show a Pareto-efficient allocation for this economy.

Step 1: Find the equation of the contract curve.

To find the equation of the contract curve, first find the *MRS* for each person. The *MRS* is equal to the ratio of the marginal utilities, so for Sabrina,

$$MRS_S = \frac{\dfrac{\delta U}{\delta C_S}}{\dfrac{\delta U}{\delta P_S}} = \frac{10 P_S}{10 C_S} = \frac{P_S}{C_S}$$

For Josie,

$$MRS_J = \frac{\dfrac{\delta U}{\delta C_J}}{\dfrac{\delta U}{\delta P_J}} = \frac{\dfrac{1}{2} C_J^{-1/2} P_J^{1/2}}{\dfrac{1}{2} C_J^{1/2} P_J^{-1/2}} = \frac{P_J}{C_J}$$

Thus to find the contract curve, set Samantha's *MRS* equal to Josie's *MRS*. Since the total endowment of each good is 400, we can substitute $(400 - P_s)$ for Josie's amount of pizza and $(400 - C_s)$ for Josie's cola.

$$MRS_S = MRS_J$$

$$\frac{P_S}{C_S} = \frac{P_J}{C_J}$$

$$\frac{P_S}{C_S} = \frac{(400 - P_S)}{(400 - C_S)}$$

$$P_S = C_S$$

Thus the contract curve is a straight 45-degree line through the origin. (See also Solved Problem 10.3 in the text.)

Step 2: Draw the Edgeworth box and the initial endowment point.

The total endowment in this economy is $400 q_1$ and $400 q_2$, so the box is a square. The contract curve, as described above, is a 45-degree line through the origin. If we make the lower corner Samantha's origin, then the endowment point is as shown in Figure 10.9. We can also draw the initial indifference curves.

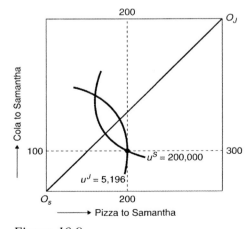

Figure 10.9

Note that the initial endowment point is not on the contract curve. Thus Samantha and Josie can trade, and any bundle inside the lens formed by the initial indifference curves is feasible, in the sense that both Samantha and Josie are better off than they were in the initial allocation. Although we don't know exactly what point they will end up at, the equilibrium allocation must be on the segment of the contract curve inside the lens formed by the initial indifference curves; these points are both feasible and Pareto efficient. This segment is usually called the *core* of this economy. These areas are shown in Figure 10.10.

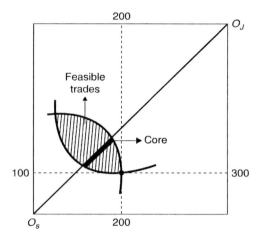

Figure 10.10

Step 3: Show a Pareto-efficient allocation for this economy.

While we do not know at what point Sabrina and Josie will end up, because it depends on their individual bargaining skills, Figure 10.11 shows a possible Pareto-efficient allocation. This point could be anywhere that is in the lens that you found in Step 2 and is also on the contract curve. The graph also shows a possible price ratio that is consistent with this allocation.

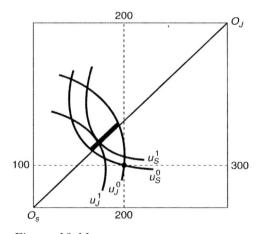

Figure 10.11

■ Practice Problems

Multiple-Choice

1. Suppose that Curly's marginal rate of substitution of meat for potatoes is –4, while Larry's marginal rate of substitution of meat for potatoes is –1. We can conclude that in a market, Curly and Larry
   a. choose not to trade.
   b. trade, but Larry is made worse off.
   c. trade, but Curly is made worse off.
   d. trade from their initial allocation to a point on the contract curve.

2. A voluntary trade that results in a move from a point off the contract curve to a point on the contract curve
   a. makes someone better off, but others worse off.
   b. makes someone better off without making anyone worse off.
   c. is possible only if initial endowments are unequal.
   d. is possible only if preferences are different.

3. If Ariel and Ursula are at point *A* in the Edgeworth box in Figure 10.12, then
   a. the allocation is efficient.
   b. Ariel and Ursula have the same marginal rate of substitution between clams and shrimp.
   c. Ariel and Ursula cannot work out any mutually beneficial trades.
   d. all of the above are true.

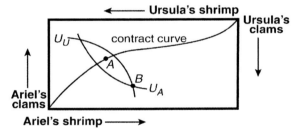

Figure 10.12

4. If Ariel and Ursula are at point *B* in the Edgeworth box in Figure 10.12, then moving to point *A*
   a. moves them along the utility possibility frontier.
   b. makes both of them worse off.
   c. makes both of them better off.
   d. makes one of them better off, but the other worse off.

5. Ariel and Ursula are at point *B* in the Edgeworth box in Figure 10.12. If Ursula loses 10 shrimp and Ariel finds them, then
   a. the Edgeworth box gets wider.
   b. the Edgeworth box gets taller.
   c. they will no longer be able to reach the contract curve by trading.
   d. the new endowment point will be to the right of its initial position.

Fill-in

6. In Figure 10.12 at point *A*, Ariel is willing to trade one shrimp for one clam. Therefore, at point *A*, Ursula is willing to trade one shrimp for _____.

7. According to the First Theorem of Welfare Economics, any competitive equilibrium is _____ and lies on the _____.

8. The government desires to achieve the equilibrium at point *A* in Figure 10.13. According to the Second Theorem of Welfare Economics, the government can achieve this Pareto-efficient equilibrium by redistributing endowments from point *B* to _____.

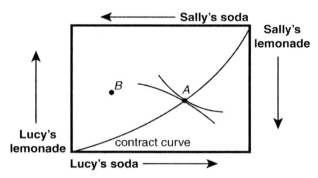

Figure 10.13

True-False-Ambiguous and Explain Why

9. If there are gains that could be made from trade, then the marginal rate of substitution between good *Y* and good *X* will be the same for all consumers.

10. If an economy has taxes on both movies and concerts, removing the tax on movies will bring the economy closer to a Pareto-efficient allocation of resources.

11. Robinson Crusoe is the only person on a deserted island. In one hour he can harvest 10 pounds of bananas or catch 5 pounds of fish. Therefore, his comparative advantage is in harvesting bananas.

Short-Answer

12. There are two goods in the economy—food and clothing. Initially the allocations of food and clothing are unequal. Then the government adopts an egalitarian plan, decreeing that it will equalize all allocation differences. For example, if someone has less than the average amount of food, then food will be taken from others who have more than average and given to the person with less than average. If that person has more clothing than average, he must give his clothing to those with less than average. Is this an efficient policy? Discuss the case of a two-person economy with no production and an economy with production.

13. Should it be the responsibility of the government to reduce the differences in income between people with high incomes and those with low incomes?

14. Draw a set of indifference curves that are consistent with the contract curve shown in Figure 10.14.

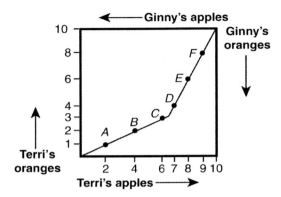

Figure 10.14

15. Tonya's utility function is $U = 2(\min(C, S))$. Derek's utility function is $U = 3(C + S)$, where C is pounds of coffee, and S is pounds of sugar. Initially Tonya has 12 pounds of coffee and no sugar, while Derek has 12 pounds of sugar and no coffee. Draw the contract curve for Tonya and Derek.

16. Tonya's utility function is $U = 2(\min(C, S))$. Derek's utility function is $U = 3(C + S)$. Draw the utility possibilities frontier for Tonya and Derek.

17. Which point on Tonya and Derek's utility possibilities frontier is favored by a utilitarian? Which point is favored by an egalitarian? Which point is favored by a Rawlsian?

18. What do Rawlsian isowelfare curves look like in a two-dimensional graph? What do utilitarian isowelfare curves look like?

19. Francis (who is a real saint) is altruistic. If someone else is poor, Francis feels worse off, so he prefers to give away some of his food and/or clothing to the poor person. When the person is rich enough he no longer feels better by giving away things to this person. Using an Edgeworth box, draw Francis's indifference curves.

20. Guyana can produce 10 units of clothing per day or 5 units of food per day (or any linear combination), while Suriname can produce 8 units of clothing per day or 2 units of food per day (or any linear combination). What should Suriname export to Guyana? Explain.

21. Latvia can produce 10 units of clothing per day or 8 units of food per day (or any linear combination), while Estonia can produce 8 units of clothing per day or 4 units of food per day (or any linear combination). Which country has a comparative advantage in producing clothing? What should Latvia export to Estonia?

22. If a curved production possibilities frontier shifts out so that it is "parallel" to its original position, will the price change? Use a diagram to explain.

23. For some goods, a person needs a minimum amount before the good is of much use. For example, one Lego is pretty useless, since it has nothing to connect with. Likewise, one or only a few Lincoln Logs are pretty useless—you need a bunch of them before you can build anything. Suppose that Jon and Zach each has an endowment of 10 Legos and 10 Lincoln Logs. Draw an Edgeworth Box showing their endowment, their indifference curves, and the trade they are likely to work out. (Hint: Their indifference curves are not convex.)

24. The table below gives the utilities of Ginny and Terri at points, *A, B, C, D, E,* and *F* in Figure 10.14. Which of these points is favored by a utilitarian? Which is favored by a Rawlsian?

Point	Ginny's Utility	Terri's Utility
A	38	17
B	36	25
C	33	30
D	30	33
E	25	36
F	17	38

25. Figure 10.15 shows the preferences of three people in one Edgeworth box. Mary has been trading with Peter, but he's gone away on a long voyage and now she trades with Paul. Mary's indifference curves are labeled *IM*, Peter's are labeled (starting at the opposite end of the box) *IT*, and Paul's are labeled *IL*—Paul's are drawn with dashed lines. Three initial endowments *A, B,* and *C* are given. Does Mary's trading partner matter? Do her final consumption bundle and the contract curve depend on whom she trades with?

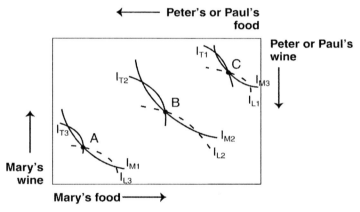

Figure 10.15

26. A group of students is voting on which university is the best. Their preferences are given below. Compare the outcomes of the elections under these voting procedures:

a. majority/plurality voting for top choice.

b. plurality voting with a run-off between the top two finishers.

c. Borda voting (3 votes for first place, 2 for second, 1 for third).

d. voting in rounds with Wake Forest vs. Maryland in the first round and the winner against Penn in the second round.

Number with Preference	Top Choice	Second Choice	Third Choice
4	Penn	Maryland	Wake Forest
5	Maryland	Wake Forest	Penn
7	Wake Forest	Penn	Maryland

■ Answers to Practice Problems

1. d. People will trade whenever their marginal rates of substitution differ. Since trade is voluntary, it must be beneficial to both.

2. b. If someone was made worse off, the voluntary exchange would not take place.

3. d.

4. c. Both can reach a higher indifference curve.

5. d.

6. 1 clam. All along the contract curve, the marginal rate of substitution is the same for the two traders.

7. Pareto-efficient; contract curve.

8. any point along the price line that goes through point A and has a slope equaling the marginal rate of substitution of the indifference curves that are tangent at A.

9. False. Consumers can only gain from trading if their indifference curves are not tangent—that is, when the consumers don't have the same marginal rate of substitution.

10. Ambiguous. According to the Theory of the Second Best, removing one but not all of the taxes will not necessarily improve the efficiency of the economy. For example, suppose that the economy has the same percentage tax rate on both goods. The existence of the tax creates a deadweight loss in both markets, but since the relative price does not change, consumers have no incentive to change the relative share of each good in their consumption bundles. Removing the tax on movies reduces the deadweight loss due to the tax in the movie market, but also causes consumers to substitute from concerts to movies, since the relative price has changed. This substitution effect may worsen social welfare by a greater amount than the improvement from the removal of the tax, and thus the economy may be less efficient, not more.

11. False. Comparative advantage compares the opportunity cost of production across two (or more) people.

12. Figure 10.16 shows the case of an economy without production. The egalitarian scheme requires that the final allocation be in the exact center of the Edgeworth box, point C, where Ginger's food level is the same level as Fred's food level and her clothing level is the same as Fred's clothing level. This type of redistribution can only be efficient if point C is on the contract curve. In most cases, because the preferences of people vary so much, the egalitarian point will not lie on the contract curve. (Imagine getting the average amount of everything—for example, you don't smoke but get the average amount of cigarettes, you love to read but get the average amount of books, and so on.) Thus, it is unlikely that the egalitarian policy will be efficient.

    If Ginger and Fred's initial endowment is at a point such as A, they will trade until they reach a point on the contract curve that lies between their initial indifference curves, such as point B. In this case, the egalitarian point will make them both worse off than point B. (If the government does not stop them, they are likely to trade back to point B, away from the egalitarian point.) If Ginger and Fred's initial endowment is at a point such as D, they will trade until they reach a point on the contract curve such as point E. In this case, the redistribution to the egalitarian point will make Ginger better off and Fred worse off. (Again, they'll want to trade away from point C to a point such as B.)

In a market with production, egalitarianism would be devastating to an economy. A hard-working person will quickly learn that hard work does not pay off. If she earns enough to buy more than the average amount of a good, then the extra portion will be taken away by the government. Likewise, risk taking, innovative thinking, and thrift will not pay off. On the other hand, even if she loafs and earns nothing, she will be given goods to pull her consumption up to the average. Unless people like to work for the sake of working, are altruistic, or face some social sanction for not working hard, they are likely to cut back on their work effort tremendously. All the shares of the economic pie will be equal, but the size of the pie will shrink away toward nothing. Society will end up in the interior of the production possibilities frontier.

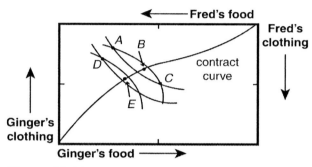

Figure 10.16

13. The answer to this question, of course, depends on your beliefs about fairness. You need to compare the income distribution when government does not redistribute income with all the possible income distributions that the government could achieve by redistributing income from those with high incomes to those with low incomes. Assuming that the competitive market generates an efficient distribution, if you feel the initial distribution is most fair, then you will not want the government to redistribute income. If you think the government could generate a fairer distribution, then you will weigh the benefits of this redistribution against the costs of achieving it. Despite the Second Theorem of Welfare Economics, there are almost always efficiency losses in the process of redistribution. Resources are used by the government and incentives to produce must be weakened.

In addition, many people who favor the goal of a different income distribution will object to certain means of achieving it. For example, many people favored the goal of equalizing land ownership among Russian and Chinese peasants, but objected to the violent means used to achieve this by Stalin and Mao. Others point out that taxation itself is a coercive use of state power and are willing to use this power only if the gains in fairness are very large. The bottom line is that most people care as much about the process by which the income distribution is generated as they do about the final distribution itself.

A series of international polls show that Americans are unusual. They are much less likely to think that it is the responsibility of government to redistribute income.

"Do you agree/strongly agree that it is the responsibility of the government to reduce the differences in income between people with high incomes and those with low incomes?"

	All	Low Income	High Income
United States	29%	42%	17%
Switzerland	43		
Australia	44	51	31
West Germany	61	72	50
Great Britain	64	67	52
Netherlands	65	78	37
Hungary	80		
Austria	81	88	72
Italy	82	90	75

Source: "America: A Unique Outlook?" *The American Enterprise,* Vol. 1, no. 2, March/April, 1990, pp. 113–117.

14. Figure 10.17 shows a set of indifference curves for Ginny and Terri that are consistent with this contract curve. The important feature is that Ginny's and Terri's indifference curves are tangent to one another at points along the contract curve.

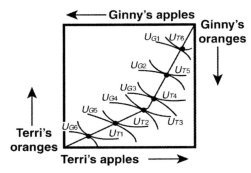

Figure 10.17

15. As Figure 10.18 shows, Derek regards sugar and coffee as perfect substitutes, so his indifference curves are linear, with a slope of −1. Tonya regards sugar and coffee as perfect complements, so her indifference curves have right angles where the amounts of coffee and sugar are equal. The efficient points occur where Tonya's indifference curves touch Derek's indifference curves (rather than crossing through them). The contract curve is a 45-degree diagonal line. For example, moving from point E, Tonya can only reach a higher utility if she gets more of both goods, but this will make Derek worse off, so this is an efficient point.

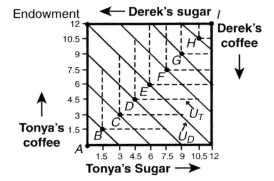

Figure 10.18

16. The utility possibility frontier is the set of utility levels corresponding to the Pareto-efficient allocations along the contract curve. Points *A* through *I* from Figure 10.18 are along the contract curve, and the table below calculates the utility of Tonya and the utility of Derek at each of these points. The information in the table is graphed in Figure 10.19.

Point	Tonya's Allocation Coffee (pounds)	Sugar	Tonya's Utility $U = 2(\min(C, S))$ (pounds)	Derek's Allocation Coffee (pounds)	Sugar	Derek's Utility $U = 3(C + S)$ (pounds)
A	0	0	0	12	12	72
B	1.5	1.5	3	10.5	10.5	63
C	3	3	6	9	9	54
D	4.5	4.5	9	7.5	7.5	45
E	6	6	12	6	6	36
F	7.5	7.5	15	4.5	4.5	27
G	9	9	18	3	3	18
H	10.5	10.5	21	1.5	1.5	9
I	12	12	24	0	0	0

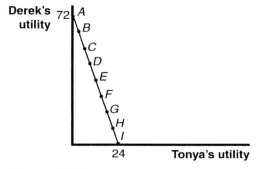

Figure 10.19

17. The utilitarian prefers the point where the sum of utility is maximized. In this case, he would prefer that all of the goods go to Derek. At point A in Figure 10.19, the sum of utility equals 72. At no other point does it equal or exceed this. For example, at point *B*, the sum of utility is 66. This shows a possible shortcoming of utilitarianism. Because Derek is so efficient at producing utility, he ends up with all the goods. (Another shortcoming is that it isn't generally possible to measure and compare utility.)

The egalitarian favors point *E*, where Tonya and Derek have the same consumption bundle.

The Rawlsian wants to maximize the minimum utility level and would favor point *G*. At this point both Tonya and Derek have 18 units of utility. As we move in either direction along the utility possibilities frontier, the lowest level of utility falls. At point *F*, Tonya's utility falls to 15, so the minimum utility level is lower than at point *G*. At point *H*, Derek's utility level falls to 9, so the minimum utility level is lower than at point *F*. Notice a shortcoming of the Rawlsian approach. Because she is so inefficient at producing utility, Tonya ends up with three times as much coffee and sugar as Derek.

18. Beginning at a point where the utility of the two people is equal, the Rawlsian welfare function does not rise if one person gains utility, but the other's utility is unchanged. Thus, Rawlsian isowelfare curves look like the indifference curve for perfect complements—forming a right angle at the point at which the utility of one person equals the utility of the other person, as in Figure 10.20. The Utilitarian isowelfare curves are linear, with a slope of −1. (The slope may differ if individuals are not weighted equally.)

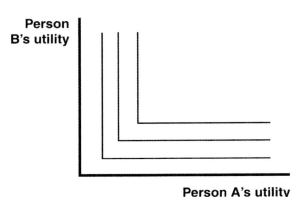

Figure 10.20

19. Figure 10.21 shows the Edgeworth Box. In the lower left corner, the other person is fairly rich, so Francis's indifference curves look like standard indifference curves. In the upper right corner, the other person is poor. In this range, Francis moves to a higher indifference curve when he gives some food and clothing away to the poor person. Starting at point *A*, Francis is better off if he gives some food and clothing away—moving to point *B*. He doesn't get too much utility from consuming the last few units of food and clothing, but gets more utility from knowing that he has made the poor person better off. Francis is indifferent between point *A* and point *D*. He loses utility from not consuming the food and clothing himself, but gains an equal amount of utility from knowing that he has made the poor person quite a bit better off. Francis prefers *A* to *E*. If he gives this much away, his own consumption falls by a lot, but he is beginning to spoil the other person whose consumption is now about as high as his own. The allocation that gives Francis the most utility is point *C*.

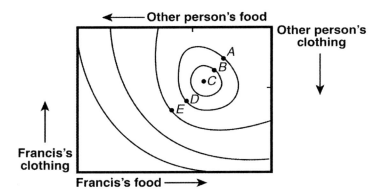

Figure 10.21

For simplicity, the text assumes that "neither person's utility depends on the other's consumption." This assumption is violated when people are altruistic and it is also violated when the opposite occurs—when people are envious. Surveys suggest that many people are envious, and because of this, they may reject what appear to be Pareto-superior outcomes in which everyone ends up with larger allocations. For example, in a 1990 survey, residents of New York City and Moscow were asked, "Suppose the government wants to undertake a reform to improve the productivity of the economy. As a result, everyone will be better off, but the improvement in life will not affect people equally. A million people (people who respond energetically to the incentives in the plan and people with certain skills) will see their incomes triple, while everyone else will see only a tiny income increase, about 1 percent. Would you support the plan?" 55 percent of the Moscovites and only 38 percent of the New Yorkers said they would support the plan! Envy is a green-eyed monster. (See Robert Shiller, Maxim Boycko, and Vladimir Korobov, "Popular Attitudes toward Free Markets: The Soviet Union and the United States Compared," *American Economic Review,* June 1991.)

20. In Guyana, the cost of 1 unit of clothing is 0.5 units of food. In Suriname, the cost of 1 unit of clothing is only 0.25 units of food. Therefore, the cost of clothing is lower in Suriname, so it should export clothing. (Alternatively, we could calculate the cost of food in terms of clothing. In Guyana, the cost of 1 unit of food is 2 units of clothing. In Suriname, the cost of 1 unit of food is 4 units of clothing. Therefore the cost of food is higher in Suriname, and it should import food.) One exception to this trading pattern occurs when people in each country don't care much for one of the goods. In this case, they might consume only food or only clothing and there will be no room for trade.

21. Neither country has a comparative advantage, because they have the same opportunity cost. There are no gains from trade, so Lavtia doesn't export anything to Estonia.

22. Figure 10.22 shows a parallel outward shift in the production possibilities frontier. Competition will push the market to a new efficient product mix—where each consumer's marginal rate of substitution equals the price ratio, which equals the economy's marginal rate of transformation. Because we do not know the shapes of the indifference curves, we cannot predict the new prices. The larger *PPF* is like an increase in income to consumers. If the income elasticities of demand for both products are the same, then the price will stay the same. But if, for example, one good is normal and the other is inferior, the larger Edgeworth box will induce consumers to switch away to the normal good, driving up its price relative to the inferior good. Figure 10.19 shows this case. Oatmeal is inferior; steak is normal. The consumption point shifts from A to C. The production point shifts from B to D. The price ratio goes from p_{O1}/p_{S1} to p_{O2}/p_{S2}.

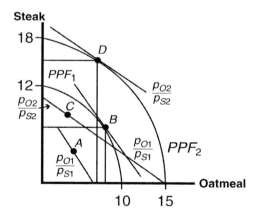

Figure 10.22

23. Figure 10.23 shows the Edgeworth box, endowment, and indifference curves for Zach and Jon. The Edgeworth box is 20 by 20, because there are 20 Legos and 20 Lincoln Logs altogether. The endowment point is at *E*, in the middle of the box. Point *E* is a point of tangency, but Zach and Jon can do better than this point. Zach can climb from I_{z_1} to I_{z_2} and Jon can climb from I_{J_1} to I_{J_2} by trading to either point *A* or point *B*. At both of these points, one of them has all of one good and the other has all of the other good. This unusual result occurs because the indifference curves are concave to the origin (bowed outward from the origin, just like a production possibilities frontier). Thus Jon can use all the Legos together to build a robot and Zach can use all the Lincoln Logs together to build a log fort—or vice versa.

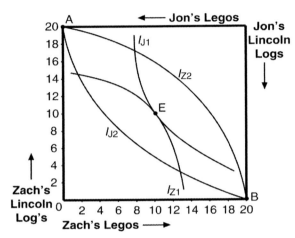

Figure 10.23

24. The goal of the utilitarian is to maximize the sum of utility. The goal of the Rawlsian is to maximize the utility of the worst-off person. These are given below for the points *A*, *B*, *C*, *D*, *E*, and *F*.

Point	Sum of Ginny's and Terri's Utilities	Minimum of Ginny's and Terri's Utility
A	55	17
B	61	25
C	63	30
D	63	30
E	61	25
F	55	17

Thus both the Rawlsian and the utilitarian are indifferent between points *C* and *D*. This result is much different than in Problem 16, when the utilitarian and the Rawlsian preferred significantly difference points on the utility possibility frontier.

25. Figure 10.24 reproduces Figure 10.15 but fills in the two potential contract curves—points where Mary's indifference curves are tangent to each of her trading partner's indifference curves. Beginning at each of the three labeled endowments, Mary trades with each partner to a point inside the football-shaped zone. In Peter's case it is the football with solid lines on each side, and in Paul's case it is the football with one dashed line. Who she trades with matters a lot. Because Peter and Paul have fairly different tastes, Mary ends of with considerably different bundles in each case. If she trades with Peter, she ends up consuming points like *D*, *E*, and *F*. If she trades with Paul, she ends up consuming points like *G*, *H*, and *I*—even though she begins with the same endowments in both cases.

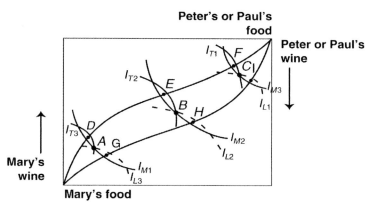

Figure 10.24

26. a.   The plurality of top choice votes goes to Wake Forest (7 votes), with Maryland in second (5 votes).

   b.   In a run-off between Wake Forest and Maryland, Maryland wins, since 9 prefer it to Wake Forest and only 7 prefer Wake Forest to Maryland.

   c.   Borda voting (similar to what is used in college football and basketball rankings) yields the result below—Wake Forest wins again.

	First Place × 3	Second Place × 2	Third Place × 1	Total
Wake Forest	7 × 3	5 × 2	4 × 1	35
Maryland	5 × 3	4 × 2	7 × 1	30
Penn	4 × 3	7 × 2	5 × 1	31

   d.   In round 1 Maryland is selected over Wake Forest (just like the run-off in part b), but when Maryland is pitted against Penn, Penn whips Maryland 11 to 5. Suppose that a crafty Penn fan was in charge of deciding on the voting procedure. She could pick this procedure, ensuring a win for Penn. This is known as agenda setting. The person who controls the agenda (including what will be voted on and when) can wield a lot of power. In this case, she could have tilted the results so that her favorite would win, even though it would have lost under more commonly used procedures.

■ Exercises

True-False-Ambiguous and Explain Why

1.   If initial endowments are the same, indifference curves are convex, and preferences are the same, then trade will not occur.

2.   According to the Second Theorem of Welfare Economics, the government can achieve any final equilibrium by redistributing endowments and allowing competition to set prices.

3.   Tom has 8 red M&Ms and 2 blue M&Ms, and Nina has 4 red M&Ms and 2 blue M&Ms. If Tom and Nina trade, the equilibrium price ratio must be between 4 and 2 red M&Ms per blue M&M.

4.   Reducing the number of market distortions, such as taxes and subsidies, in a competitive economy will increase social welfare.

Short-Answer

5. The supply of land on two islands is fixed. East Island has 100 acres. West Island has 200 acres. The demand for land on East Island is $Q_D = 300 - 2p_E + p_W$. The demand for land on West Island is $Q_D = 500 - 3p_W + p_E$ where the quantity is in acres; p_E = the price of land on East Island in thousands of dollars per acre; and p_W = the price of land on West Island in thousands of dollars per acre. What is the equilibrium price of land on the two islands?

6. There are two types of jobs in town, truck driving and factory work. Initially, the wage of truck drivers equals that of factory workers. Then the government passes a law saying that to cut down on accidents, all truck drivers must have graduated from high school and be fluent in English. Describe the general-equilibrium impact of this law in these labor markets.

7. There are two equal-sized groups of prisoners of war in Stalag 13. The British soldiers receive a Red Cross package containing 10 servings of tea. The French soldiers receive a Red Cross package containing 10 servings of coffee. The soldiers trade so that each group ends up with 5 servings of both tea and coffee. Draw an Edgeworth box that shows this case, and give a hypothetical contract curve. All of a sudden, the French Red Cross package begins to include 20 servings of coffee. Show how this affects the allocation of goods. Who is better off because of the larger French Red Cross ration?

8. Figure 10.25 gives a contract curve for Person A and Person B. Several indifference curves are labeled with the amount of utility the person receives at all points along the indifference curve. Use this information to construct the utility possibilities frontier for Person A and Person B. Which point along the utility possibilities frontier would be selected by a utilitarian? By a Rawlsian?

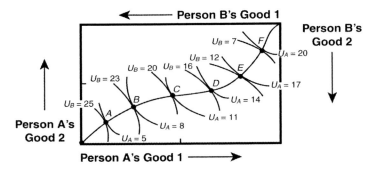

Figure 10.25

9. The production possibilities frontiers for Charlie and Rose are given in Figure 10.26. What is their joint production possibilities frontier?

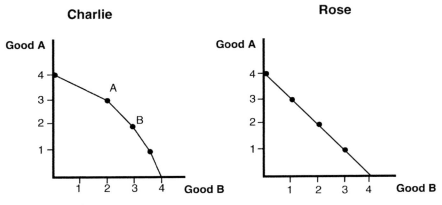

Figure 10.26

10. Elmo, Big Bird, and Oscar find $3 and have decided to vote on how to spend the money. The price of a movie ticket is $1 and the price of an ice cream cone is $1. Willingness to pay for each item is given below. Is majority voting efficient? Is it fair? What's the best solution?

	Movie	Ice Cream
Elmo	$1.50	$1
Big Bird	$1.50	$1
Oscar	$1	$3

11. The supply for new shirts in the U.S. is characterized by a perfectly elastic supply curve that equals the long-run average cost of a shirt, which is $10 for both men's and women's shirts. The demand for new shirts in the U.S. is

$$Q_{DNewWomen} = 300,000 - 6000p \text{ and}$$
$$Q_{DNewMen} = 150,000 - 600p.$$

Most men wear their shirts until they are worn out, so the supply of used men's shirts shipped to poorer countries equals $Q_{SUsedMen} = 0.2Q_{NewMen}$. Most women don't wear their shirts until they are worn out, so the supply of used women's shirts shipped to poorer countries is $Q_{SUsedWomen} = 0.5Q_{NewWomen}$. The demand for women's and men's shirts in poor countries is exactly the same:

$$Q_{DUsedWomen} = Q_{DUsedMen} = 160,000 - 40,000p.$$

How will a tax of 10 percent on shirts in the U.S. change the price and quantity in each of these four markets?

12. In a simple exchange economy, there are only two people, Meep and Bok, and only two goods, hamburgers (H) and potatoes (P). Meep likes 1 hamburger with potato, and likes no other combination; his utility function is $U(H, P) = min(H, P)$. Bok has the following utility function: $U(H, P) = H^{1/2}P^{1/2}$. Meep has 200 hamburgers and 400 potatoes, and Bok has 300 hamburgers and 100 potatoes.

   a. Draw the Edgeworth box, indifference curves for the two people, and show the contract curve for this economy.
   b. What is the equation of the contract curve?
   c. Show the feasible trades for this economy.

13. In a simple exchange economy, Bob's utility function is $X^{1/2}Y^{1/2}$. Stephanie's utility function is $X^{2/3}Y^{1/3}$. Initially, Bob has 300 units of X and 900 units of Y, and Stephanie has 300 units of X and 600 units of Y.

   a. Find the equation of the contract curve.
   b. Find the equilibrium price ratio.

Chapter 11
Monopoly

■ Chapter Summary

A monopoly is an industry with only one firm; it faces no competition. Unlike a competitive firm, the monopolist gets to choose its price: It is a price maker. If a monopoly wants to increase its sales, it has to cut its price. Therefore the extra revenue collected from a one-unit increase in sales is smaller than the price at which the unit sells. In other words, marginal revenue for a monopolist is less than price. Like a competitive firm, a monopoly wants to make its economic profits as large as possible. To maximize its profits, the monopolist determines the output where marginal revenue equals marginal cost and then charges the highest price it can get away with. This price is determined by market demand or, to put it in somewhat mechanical terms, price is read off the market demand curve.

Because the monopolist sets output equal to marginal revenue and marginal cost, and marginal revenue is less than price, the monopolist winds up charging a price above marginal cost. Just how much a monopoly marks up its price above marginal cost depends on the amount of **market power** it has. One convenient way to measure this level of market power is through the Lerner index. The Lerner index is inversely related to the price elasticity of demand, so that we expect a higher markup in markets with less elastic demand, all else equal.

Now, just because the monopoly has found this profit-maximizing price doesn't mean it will stick with it forever. A monopolist will adjust its output (and thus the price it charges) if it is confronted with a change in marginal cost. In isolation, an increase in marginal cost will cause the monopoly to cut back on production, a decision that will generate an increase in price. Similarly, an outward shift in market demand raises marginal revenue, which pushes up production. While the increase in output tends to depress price, the outward shift in demand tends to push equilibrium price up. So, while output is sure to rise, the net effect on price is ambiguous (price could rise or fall).

While this profit-maximizing arrangement is great for the monopolist, it's not so hot for society. As a general rule, society benefits from any transaction where the buyer's value exceeds the seller's opportunity cost. In market terms, such a transaction occurs when price exceeds marginal cost. Since the monopoly charges a price above marginal cost, some potential welfare gains aren't realized. In other words, there is a **deadweight loss** associated with the monopolist's profit-maximizing choice. The magnitude of this welfare loss depends on the degree to which the monopoly reduces output below the level where price equals marginal cost, and the amount by which price exceeds marginal cost.

But how did we wind up with this monopoly in the first place? One possible reason is that the monopoly is just more efficient than other firms. Perhaps the firm's owner was smart enough to identify a promising market before anyone else, or maybe the firm is just better at making the product in question. If it is better at producing this good, it enjoys a **cost advantage**. A cost advantage not only creates the opportunity to capture a market in the first place, it also makes it hard for other firms to get into the action later on. Because a monopoly can't remain a monopoly unless there is something that prevents other firms from entering, there must be some barriers to entry. Examples of barriers to entry include a cost advantage, control of a key resource, or patent protection. If the monopoly's cost advantage is large enough so that no other firm can make a profit, there is a *natural monopoly*.

Patents are a prime example of a **government policy that creates a monopoly**. Another example is the granting of a license, as is common with local cable companies, power utilities, and local phone service. In each case, a regulatory authority prevents competitors from entering the monopoly's market.

There is usually a flip side to these types of agreements: In exchange for granting a monopoly position, the regulatory authority gets to limit the monopolist's actions. This control might take the form of restricting the price charged, or it can show up as a restriction on the types of inputs used. Even in markets where there is no regulatory authority, **government can take actions that limit monopoly power**. In most industrialized countries, there are antitrust laws prohibiting the procurement of monopoly power.

Now, most firms don't seem to be monopolies. (How many pizza joints are there in your town?) But think about this: In scores of small American towns, air service is provided by only one carrier. In other countries, especially ones with smaller or more sparsely distributed populations, monopolies are not at all uncommon. Along the west coast of the South Island of New Zealand, for example, you are typically offered one option for petrol and one option for lodging. Pay up! All these facts suggest a subtle but absolutely crucial issue: How do we figure out when one seller of a particular product really has a monopoly? Often, this depends on the *real* market of interest. Is it airplane flights between your town and the large metropolitan airport over 100 miles away, or is it transportation to that airport? Because it is often hard to establish monopoly power without defining the market very narrowly, antitrust challenges to alleged monopolies are relatively uncommon.

■ Key Concepts and Formulas

- Monopoly leads to deadweight loss by reducing output below the level where $p = MC$, and charging a price that exceeds MC.
- Government can mitigate this deadweight loss by regulating price at a level below the profit-maximizing level, although this can lead to other problems if this price is less than long-run average cost. In such a case, the regulation would lead to exit.
- $MR = MC$: the rule that determines the monopoly's profit-maximizing output.
- $MC = dC(Q)/dQ$: the rule for determining marginal cost from the cost function.
- $MR = d(p \times Q)/dQ = p + Q(dp/dQ)$: the rule for determining marginal revenue from the demand curve.
- $MR = p(1 + 1/\varepsilon)$: a way of relating marginal revenue to price elasticity.
- $L = (p - MC)/p$: the Lerner index, a way of measuring market power; it equals $-1/\varepsilon$ at the profit-maximizing output.

■ Application: Microsoft and the Department of Justice

One of the most dramatic antitrust cases in recent memory concerns Microsoft Corporation. The U.S. Department of Justice (DOJ) alleged that Microsoft held a monopoly in the sale of operating systems for personal computers. Nineteen states joined with DOJ in bringing the antitrust suit. U.S. District Judge Thomas Penfield Jackson, who presided over the case, found that Microsoft did in fact hold a monopoly, and that its conduct hurt consumers. Despite these facts, some experts do not believe Microsoft should be broken up, in part because they believe Microsoft is more efficient than any potential competitors.

Question: What are the potential problems associated with Microsoft's monopoly? What conditions would make Microsoft position beneficial to society at large? Could society do even better?

Answer: One problem with Microsoft's monopoly is that there may be a deadweight loss at the present price. Consider Figure 11.1, which plots the market demand for operating systems. To simplify the discussion a bit, let's assume Microsoft's marginal costs are constant at MC. To maximize its profits, Microsoft chooses the output Q_M, where its marginal costs (MC) equal its marginal revenue (MR). It then determines price from the market demand curve as p_M. To calculate the deadweight loss at this output, we first find Q_C, the output that would be obtained if Microsoft chose a price just equal to its marginal cost. This is the output that maximizes welfare (the sum of consumer surplus and producer surplus). Graphically, this is located where *MC* crosses market demand. Deadweight loss is the difference between welfare at Q_c and welfare at Q_M. So we need to identify consumer surplus and producer surplus at each of the outputs. Consumer surplus can be measured by the area below market demand and above price, out to the production level in question. So for output Q_M, consumer surplus is the area *A*. Producer surplus is the area above marginal cost and below price, out to the production level in question. For output Q_M, producer surplus is the area *B*, and so welfare is equal to the sum of areas *A* and *B*. At output Q_C, price equals marginal cost. Because marginal cost is constant, there is no area between price and marginal cost; that is, producer surplus equals zero. So welfare is equal to consumer surplus, which is the sum of areas *A*, *B*, and *C*. Comparing these two levels of welfare, deadweight loss is the area *C*.

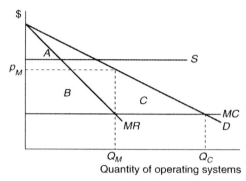

Figure 11.1

Even though Microsoft's production level leads to deadweight loss, society might not be better off by disbanding it. We need to know what the alternative is. If Microsoft has a distinct cost advantage over potential competitors, then prices could be lower with a Microsoft monopoly than with a competitive market. In Figure 11.1, the potential competitors' marginal cost curve is *S*. These marginal costs are also constant, but much larger than Microsoft's. Because Microsoft's cost advantage is so large, an industry made up solely of these other firms would lead to higher prices than Microsoft charges, with a smaller quantity of operating systems sold. The combination of higher prices and lower quantity sold reduces consumer surplus; consumers would be worse off without Microsoft. Of course, Microsoft may not really be so much more efficient (see Practice Problem 14). In this case, dissolution of Microsoft could conceivably lower market price. Regardless of whether Microsoft is much more efficient than the potential competition, society is still worse off at the monopoly price than at the price where demand equals Microsoft's marginal cost. Getting Microsoft to operate at that lower price is the real trick.

■ Solved Problems

1.   Suppose a monopolist faces a demand curve with constant price elasticity of −2, and that the monopolist's marginal costs equal $10 for all output levels. Determine the profit-maximizing output and the associated price the monopolist will charge.

Step 1: Describe the monopolist's marginal revenue. For a price elasticity of ε, the monopolist's marginal revenue can be written as $MR = p\,(1 + 1/\varepsilon)$. If the price elasticity is constant and equal to −2, the monopolist's marginal revenue is $p \times (1 + 1/{-2}) = p \times 1/2$.

Step 2: Describe the monopolist's profit-maximizing output choice. The monopolist maximizes profit by setting marginal revenue equal to marginal cost: $MR = MC$. Since $MC = 10$ and $MR = p \times 1/2$, at the profit-maximizing output $10 = p \times 1/2$.

Step 3: Determine the price at which the monopolist maximizes profit. As $10 = p \times 1/2$, we conclude that the price charged by the monopolist at its profit-maximizing output is $p = 20$.

2. The United States Postal Service (USPS) has a monopoly on the delivery of addressed third-class mail. Other carriers may deliver unaddressed mail, but they are excluded from delivering addressed pieces. Suppose the marginal cost for the USPS is constant at 12.3 cents per piece, that the USPS charges 16.7 cents per piece, and that 49.8 (billion) units are sold. Suppose the demand for third-class mail is linear, with $p = a - bQ$, and that the price elasticity of demand is -0.625 at the price currently charged by the USPS. What are producer surplus, consumer surplus, welfare, and deadweight loss at the monopoly profit-maximizing price and quantity?

    Step 1: Use the information on the price elasticity of demand to identify the market demand curve. The formula for price elasticity of demand is

    $$\varepsilon = (dQ/dp)(p/Q).$$

    The part in parentheses, dQ/dp, is the inverse of the slope of the demand curve. Since demand is linear, it has a constant slope ($dp/dQ = -b$) and so $dQ/dp = -1/b$. Inserting this into the formula for elasticity and rearranging, we get

    $$b = -p/(\varepsilon Q).$$

    We are told that currently the USPS is setting $p = 16.7$ and $Q = 49.8$, and that at this combination $\varepsilon = -.625$. Combining all these facts, we find that $b = .537$. Because the current price and output determine a point on the demand curve, we infer that

    $$16.7 = a - .537 \times 49.8,$$

and so $a = 43.44$.

    Step 2: Using this demand curve, find the profit-maximizing monopoly output and price. The profit-maximizing output for monopoly sets marginal revenue equal to marginal cost. One of the key facts for monopoly is that $MR = p + Qdp/dQ$. Since $dp/dQ = -b$, we get

    $$MR = p - bQ.$$

    Now insert the formula for demand ($p = a - bQ$) to get

    $$MR = a - 2bQ.$$

    Since $a = 43.44$ and $b = .537$, we find the monopoly profit-maximizing output (Q_M) by setting $MR = MC$:

    $$MR = 43.44 - (2 \times .527) \times Q_M = 12.3 = MC,$$

    or $Q_M = 28.99$ billion. To determine the monopoly price (p_M), insert this output into the equation for market demand: $p_M = 43.44 - .537 \times 28.99 = 27.87$.

Step 3: Calculate producer surplus, consumer surplus, and welfare. Producer surplus is

$$PS = \int_0^6 [p^* - MC(Q)]dQ = \int_0^6 [12 - Q]dQ = (12Q - \tfrac{1}{2}Q^2)\big|_0^6 = 54.$$

Since output is measured as billions of units and prices are given in pennies, the value for PS is in billions of cents. (Put into billions of U.S. dollars, $PS = 4.5137$.) Consumer surplus is

$$CS = \int_0^6 [p(Q) - p^*]dQ = \int_0^6 [18 - Q - 12]dQ = (6Q - \tfrac{1}{2}Q^2)\big|_0^6 = 18.$$

Welfare is the sum of CS and PS, or $W = 677.06$.

Step 4: Identify deadweight loss. For this part, we first need to determine welfare at the output where price equals marginal cost. This output, call it Q_c, generates the largest possible value of welfare. Algebraically, Q_c sets price equal to marginal cost ($p = MC$):

$$p = 43.44 - .537 \times Q_c = 12.3 = MC,$$

or $Q_c = 57.99$. At this output, welfare is the area of the triangle with height $43.44 - 12.3 = 31.14$, and base 57.99. So, $W = 0.5 \times 57.99 \times 31.14 = 902.90$. Deadweight loss is the difference between this maximum value and welfare at the monopoly output, or $902.90 - 677.06 = 225.84$ billion cents.

3. Suppose the demand for chocolate crickets is given by $p = 24 - Q$, and that Jiminy's, Inc. is the sole producer of chocolate crickets. As a monopoly, Jiminy's marginal revenue curve is $MR = 24 - 2Q$. Imagine that Jiminy's costs are $C(Q) = \tfrac{1}{2}Q^2$. The local government is thinking about placing a $6-per-unit tax on Jiminy's, but there is some opposition. One outraged citizen has the goofy idea that such a tax will fall disproportionately on consumers, while another makes the daffy argument that such a tax would have less of an impact on consumers than it would if Jiminy's operated as a competitive firm (producing where price equaled marginal cost). Which one of these characters is correct?

Step 1: Find the monopoly price before any tax is imposed. To do this, we first we determine the profit-maximizing output. This is the output where $MR = MC$. Now, $MR = p + dp/dQ = 24 - Q - Q = 24 - 2Q$; $MC = dC(Q)/dQ = 2 \times \tfrac{1}{2}Q = Q$. Thus the monopoly output solves

$$24 - 2Q_M = Q_M,$$

or $Q_M = 8$. Plugging this output into demand ($p = 24 - Q$), we find that Jiminy's sells chocolate crickets at a price of $16 each.

Step 2: Determine the price if there is a tax. With a $6-per-unit tax, Jiminy's marginal cost rises to $MC = Q + 6$. This lowers his profit-maximizing output to Q_M^t, which equates marginal revenue with marginal cost after the tax:

$$24 - 2Q_M^t = 6 + Q_M^t,$$

or $Q_M^t = 6$. At this new output, Jiminy's price becomes $18.

Step 3: Calculate the tax incidence borne by consumers. The tax incidence is the increase in price paid by consumers, which is $2 in this example ($18 - $16). This increase in price represents only one-third of the tax, so the goofy character is wrong.

Step 4: Find the competitive price before any tax is imposed. At this output, which we will call Q_C, price equals marginal cost. This output is determined by

$$24 - Q_c = Q_c,$$

which means that $Q_c = 12$. Plugging this output into demand, we get a price of $12.

Step 5: Determine the competitive price if there is a tax. As in step 2, the tax raises marginal cost by $6. The competitive output with a tax, let's call it Q_C^t, sets price equal to this new marginal cost. We find this output by solving

$$24 - Q_C^t = 6 + Q_C^t,$$

which gives $Q_C^t = 9$. The competitive price with the tax is thus $15.

Step 6: Determine the tax incidence on consumers. Again, the tax incidence is the increase in price paid by consumers. The competitive price rises by $3 (from $12 to $15). This increase in price represents *one-half* of the tax.

Step 7: Compare the tax incidence under monopoly with the tax incidence under competition. The tax incidence is larger if Jiminy's acts as a competitive firm than if Jiminy's acts as a monopolist ($3 vs. $2). So we see that the daffy character was correct. The general principles at work here are illustrated in Figure 11.2. Since the marginal revenue curve is commonly steeper than market demand, an increase in marginal cost (because of a tax) induces a smaller reduction in output for a monopolist than it would if the firm were perfectly competitive. Thus price rises less as well—less of the tax is paid by customers of a monopoly.

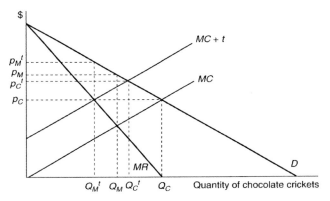

Figure 11.2

■ Practice Problems

Multiple-Choice

1. Which of the following would explain the presence of a monopoly?
   a. control of a key input
   b. a patent for the production process
   c. significant economies of scale
   d. All of the above are correct.

2. Imagine that Fred's Turbo is a monopolist in the fast gas market. Fred can sell 9 units of fast gas at a price of $6, but to sell 10 units he must lower his price to $5.50. Marginal revenue for the 10th unit is then
   a. $0.50.
   b. $1.00.
   c. $5.00
   d. $5.50.

3. Inspector Gadget is the only producer of gadgets. The marginal cost of every unit Inspector Gadget produces is $2 (that is, his *MC* curve is constant at $2). If the market demand for gadgets is given by $p = 14 - Q$, then how many gadgets will Inspector Gadget sell?
   a. 6
   b. 8
   c. 12
   d. None of the above.

4. In Question 3, what price will Inspector Gadget charge?
   a. 2
   b. 6
   c. 8
   d. None of the above.

5. Which of the following is an important complication in effectively regulating a monopolist?
   a. Regulators rarely know the firm's true costs.
   b. Using optimal price regulation on a natural monopoly can lead to exit.
   c. Employees at the regulating agency may be inclined to protect the firm, especially if they think they might work for it later in life.
   d. All of the above are true.

Fill-in

6. Imagine that the only firm in the local cable market is Terrible Communications Associated (TCA). The demand curve in the local market can be described by $p = 18 - Q$, where p and Q are the price charged and the quantity of cable subscriptions sold locally. TCA's costs are $C(Q) = 50 + \frac{1}{2}Q^2$.
   a. Marginal revenue for the local market is $MR =$ _____ .
   b. TCA's profit-maximizing output is _____ units.
   c. TCA's profit-maximizing price is _____.
   d. At the profit-maximizing price and output, TCA's profits are _____.
   e. At TCA's profit-maximizing output, welfare is _____ .
   f. At TCA's profit-maximizing output, deadweight loss is _____.
   g. If TCA were forced to set a price equal to marginal cost, deadweight loss would be_____.

True-False-Ambiguous and Explain Why

7. In order to raise sales, a monopolist must lower its price.

8. Suppose that Harry is the only seller of banana boats, and that he is currently maximizing profits. If the price elasticity of demand for banana boats is −3 and price is $24, then the marginal cost of the last banana boat Harry sold is $16.

9. In Solved Problem 1, we assumed the price elasticity of demand is −0.625 at the current price charged by USPS. If this were the true level of price elasticity, the USPS would increase its revenues if it lowered its price.

10. A profit-maximizing monopolist will always operate in the elastic region of demand.

Short-Answer

11. Calculate the Lerner index at the profit-maximizing output from Solved Problem 1, and use it to infer the price elasticity of demand.

12. Cross-Country Ken sells ski gear. Ken's regular price is p_0, and his marginal cost is $p_0/2$ (i.e., he marks up his price 100 percent over cost). One day, Ken decides to have a sale. In the sale he cuts his prices by 10 percent, and he finds that his sales rise by 30 percent.
    a. What is Ken's marginal revenue at his regular price?
    b. Is Ken maximizing his profit at the regular price? Explain.

13. Perloff and Wachter (1984) show that USPS workers are paid wages 21 percent higher than other workers with similar jobs. Suppose these higher labor costs imply a 21 percent higher marginal cost than the value included in Solved Problem 1. What would be the profit-maximizing output and price for the USPS?

14. Reconsider the questions in the Microsoft–DOJ application assuming that Microsoft's potential competitors' marginal costs (p_s) are smaller than p_M, as in Figure 11.3. Why might Microsoft retain a monopoly in this situation?

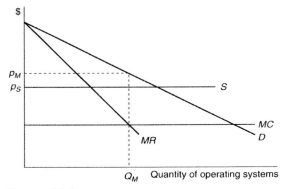

Figure 11.3

15. Imagine that the market demand for commotion is $p = 24 − Q$, that Sam is the sole supplier of commotion, and that Sam's costs are $C(Q) = Q^2$.
    a. Graph market demand, marginal revenue, and Sam's marginal cost curves.
    b. Show Sam's profit-maximizing output and price.
    Now imagine that Sam's demand curve shifts to $p = 18 − 0.5Q$.
    c. Graph the new demand and the marginal revenue curves.
    d. Show Sam's new profit-maximizing output and price.

16. Chef K is a monopolist in the gumbo market. The market demand for gumbo may be characterized by $P = 24 - 2Q$, where Q is the number of (massively large!) bowls of gumbo K sells, and P is the market price of a bowl of gumbo. Chef K's costs are $C(Q) = 48 + Q^2$. Determine K's profit-maximizing output, the corresponding price, and its profit; graph this situation.

17. Suppose, in the context of the Microsoft–DOJ application, that we decided to allow Microsoft to retain its monopoly position but restricted the price it could charge. What difficulties are likely to emerge if we forced Microsoft to set a price that equals its marginal cost?

18. In the analysis of the Microsoft–DOJ application, we assumed both Microsoft and the potential competition had constant marginal costs. Suppose now that both Microsoft's marginal cost curve and the supply curve for the potential competitors are upward sloping. Compare the monopoly regime with the potential competitive market, using both a written explanation and appropriate graphs.

19. From 1977 to late 1983, the GlaxoSmithKline product Tagamet was the only anti-ulcer drug of its kind. Suppose that during this period, GlaxoSmithKline ran a series of ads that changed the demand curve for Tagamet. Imagine that these ads convinced consumers that there really was no substitute for Tagamet, and so the new demand curve is less elastic than the old demand curve. However (and this is the odd part), the new demand curve passes through the point on the old demand curve that GlaxoSmithKline had originally selected as its profit-maximizing price and output for Tagamet. What effect will this change have on GlaxoSmithKline's price, output, and profits?

■ Answers to Practice Problems

1. For a monopoly to exist, there must be important barriers to entry. Examples include control of a key input, patent protection, or natural monopoly (which often occurs when there are significant economies of scale). Thus, all of a, b, and c are viable explanations: The best answer is d.

2. Recall that $MR = p + Q(dp/dQ)$. To add an extra sale, Fred must cut price by 50 cents, so $dp/dQ = -0.5$. He initially sells 9 units, so the contribution from the second term is $-\$4.50$. The tenth unit sells for $p = \$5.50$, so the marginal revenue for Fred's tenth unit is $\$5.50 - \$4.50 = \$1$: Answer b is correct.

3. As demand is $p = 14 - Q$, $MR = 14 - 2Q$. Inspector Gadget maximizes profit by setting this equal to $\$2$, his MC; this gives an output of 6 gadgets: answer a. Note that answer c is the result of setting marginal cost equal to price, not marginal revenue.

4. In light of the answer to Question 3, market price is $p = 8$: Answer c is correct.

5. Effective regulation requires that the regulator know the firm's costs and market demand, the regulated firm is able to earn at least normal profits, and the regulator's incentives be aligned with those of society. Thus, a, b, and c are all correct responses, so answer d is best.

6. Answers and brief explanations follow.
    a. $MR = p - Q \times dp/dQ = 18 - 2Q$.
    b.   The profit-maximizing output, Q^*, solves $18 - 2Q^* = Q^*$, so $Q^* = 6$.
    c.   Insert Q^* into the demand equation to get $p = 12 (= 18 - 6)$.
    d.   Total revenue is $6 \times 12 = 72$. Total costs are $50 + \frac{1}{2} \times 6^2 = 50 + 18 = 68$. Hence TCA's profit is 4.

e. $PS = \int_0^6 [p^* - MC(Q)]dQ = \int_0^6 [12 - Q]dQ = (12Q - \frac{1}{2}Q^2)\big|_0^6 = 54$; $CS = \int_0^6 [p(Q) - p^*]dQ$

$= \int_0^6 [18 - Q - 12]dQ = (6Q - \frac{1}{2}Q^2)\big|_0^6 = 18$.

Hence $W = 72$.

f.   If TCA set output where $p = MC$, it would produce $Q_c = 9$. At this output, $p = 9$ as well, so $TR = 81$, so that

$$PS = \int_0^9 [9 - Q]dQ = (9Q - \frac{1}{2}Q^2)\big|_0^9 = 40.5; \quad CS = \int_0^6 [18 - Q - 9]dQ = (9Q - \frac{1}{2}Q^2)\big|_0^9 = 40.5$$

as well, which gives $W = 81$. Deadweight loss is the difference between this amount and 72 (the amount we found in part e), or 9.

g.   This one is a bit sneaky. In the short term, setting $P = MC$ eliminates deadweight loss. The problem is that TCA will lose money: The producer surplus we found in part f, 40.5, is smaller than the fixed costs (50). So, this regime will force TCA to bear losses. These losses may ultimately cause TCA to exit the industry, in which case welfare falls to zero and deadweight loss becomes 81.

7.   Ambiguous. Since monopoly is a market structure with only one seller, its demand curve equals the market demand curve. As a general rule, we expect market demand to be downward sloping, but if demand is perfectly elastic the monopolist would be able to increase sales without lowering its price.

8.   True. Since Harry is maximizing profit, we know marginal cost of the last unit produced equals marginal revenue. One way to express marginal revenue is by relating it to price elasticity: $MR = p[1 + (1/\varepsilon)]$. We know that $p = 24$ and $\varepsilon = -3$, from which we determine that $MR = \$24(1 - 1/3) = \$16$.

9.   False. Since $\varepsilon = -0.625$, demand is inelastic. This means marginal revenue is negative. Hence an increase in output lowers revenues. As a decrease in price will raise sales, this means that the USPS will *lower* its revenues if it cuts price.

10. True. To maximize profit, a monopolist selects that output with $MR = MC$. Since MC is generally positive, and most certainly is not negative, this means that marginal revenue will be positive at the profit-maximizing output. But for MR to be positive, demand must be elastic.

11. The Lerner index is $L = (p - MC)/p$. Based on the information in the USPS example, the profit-maximizing price is $p = 27.87$ and $MC = 12.3$; this gives $L = (27.87 - 12.3)/27.87 = .5587$. Since we are looking at the profit-maximizing output and price, $L = -1/\varepsilon$. Hence, $\varepsilon = -1/L = -1/.5587 = -1.79$.

12. Marginal revenue can be expressed as $MR = p(1 + 1/\varepsilon)$, where is the price elasticity of demand. The price elasticity of demand is the percentage change in quantity divided by the percentage change in price.

a.   Starting from his regular price, *a* 10 percent price cut raises Ken's sales by 30 percent, so his price elasticity of demand is $30/(-10)$, or -3. Thus, Ken's marginal revenue at his regular price is $p_0 \times (1 + (1/-3))$, or $MR = 2/3 \times p_0$.

b.   As $MC = 1/2 \times p_0$, Ken's marginal cost is less than his marginal revenue. Ken can raise his profits by selling more ski gear, which he affects by lowering his price. Since Ken can earn larger profits at a different output and price, he is not maximizing his profits at his regular price.

13. If the USPS marginal cost is 21 percent higher than the figure quoted in Solved Problem 1, which was 12.3, their marginal cost is 14.88 (to two decimal places). Using the information on demand and marginal revenue, we have $p = 43.44 - 0.537 \times Q$ and $MR = 43.44 - 1.074 \times Q$, where p is the price charged for third-class mail and Q is the number of units delivered. To maximize its profits, the USPS would select the output Q'_M that sets MR equal to MC, so $43.44 - 1.074 \times Q'_M = 14.88$. This relation gives $Q'_M = 26.59$. Plugging Q'_M into the formula for market demand, we find that USPS should charge $P'_M = 29.16$.

14. Since Microsoft's potential competitor's marginal costs are less than the monopoly price, dissolving Microsoft is likely to lead to lower prices. Replacing the monopoly with a competitive market will lead to market supply S, so that the competitive price would be p_s in Figure 11.3. Microsoft could retain a monopoly even with $p_M > p_s$ if there are other barriers to entry, which is a concern that Microsoft's detractors often express.

15. First, use the information on demand to derive marginal revenue. As demand is $p = a - bQ$, $MR = p - Q \times dp/dQ = a - 2bQ$. In part a, this gives $MR = 24 - 2Q$; in part c we have $MR = 18 - Q$. These curves are plotted in Figure 11.4. To answer parts b and d, set $MR = MC$ ($MC = Q$ for each part). The monopoly output is 6 for both parts b and d. The monopoly price in part b is 18 (= 24 − 6), and 15 (= 18 − 0.5 × 6) in part d.

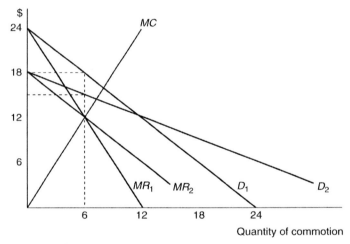

Figure 11.4

16. Since demand is linear, marginal revenue has the same intercept (24) and twice the slope (−4): $MR = 24 - 4Q$. To maximize profits, Chef K's selects the output Q_M that sets marginal revenue equal to marginal cost, $24 - 4Q_M = 2Q_M$. Rearranging, we find $24 = 6Q_M$, or $Q_M = 4$. At this output, the appropriate price is $P_M = 24 - 2 \times 4 = \$16$. With this combination, Chef K's earns revenues of $64 (= 4 \times 16)$. The average cost associated with this output is $48/4 + 4$, or $16. Thus, its costs are also $64; it makes zero economic profit. The situation is graphed in Figure 11.5.

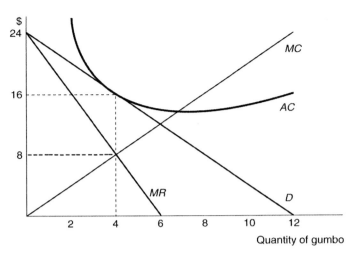

Figure 11.5

17. In the Microsoft–DOJ application, we assumed marginal cost was a constant—call it *m*. That means total cost has to equal $mQ + F$, where *F* is fixed costs. Because optimal price regulation sets price equal to marginal cost, revenues would wind up as mQ; if Microsoft has any fixed costs (i.e., if *F* is positive), they wind up with negative economic profits. But if Microsoft were to earn negative profits it would have no incentive to produce anything in either the short run (where they lose the same amount whether they produce or shut down) or the long run (where they are strictly better off by exiting).

18. There are two ways to think about this one. One possibility is that Microsoft's marginal cost curve lies below the potential competitor's supply curve at Q_M, Microsoft's profit-maximizing output. In this case, the competitive equilibrium output, Q_C, is less than Q_M. This means that, as in the discussion of the application, dissolving Microsoft makes consumers worse off. See Figure 11.6. The second possibility is that Microsoft's marginal cost curve lies above the potential competitor's supply curve at Q_M. In this case, we need to know if there are some sort of costs that keep the potential competitors out of the market. If there are costs that keep the potential competitors out of the market, dissolving Microsoft will lower price, as in Figure 11.7.

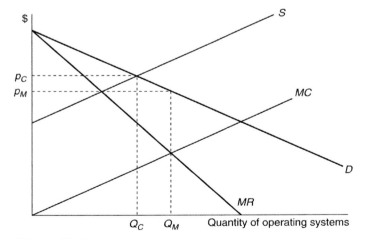

Figure 11.6

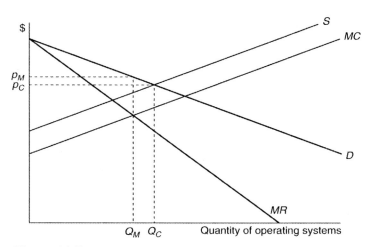

Figure 11.7

If potential competitors can enter the market costlessly, then we have to use the dominant firm–competitive fringe model to find the equilibrium. In this situation, Microsoft's profit-maximizing price is smaller than the competitive price (that's the only way Microsoft gets any sales). It follows that dissolving Microsoft will raise price. See Figure 11.8.

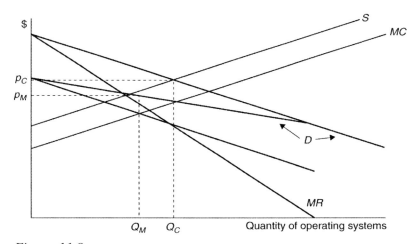

Figure 11.8

19. Let's call the old profit-maximizing output Q_0, and call the associated price p_0. We know that the new demand curve is less elastic at output Q_0 (and price p_0). This means that the new marginal revenue at Q_0—call it MR_1—is less than the old marginal revenue at Q_0—call it MR_0. (Let ε_0 be the old price elasticity and ε_1 the new elasticity; since demand is now less elastic at p_0, $\varepsilon_0 < \varepsilon_1 < 0$, which means that $MR_1 = p_0(1 + 1/\varepsilon_1) < p_0(1 + 1/\varepsilon_0) = MR_0$.) But for Q_0 to maximize profits, MC at $Q_0 = MR_0$. Since $MR_1 < MR_0$, we conclude that marginal cost exceeds the new marginal revenue at Q_0. So GlaxoSmithKline can do better by lowering their output from Q_0 to Q_1. With this reduction in output, the price of Tagamet rises from p_0 to p_1. See Figure 11.9. Since the combination of Q_0 and p_0 lies on both demand curves, GlaxoSmithKline can always do at least as well on the new demand curve as on the old curve (just by leaving price at p_0). Since they adjusted their output, and thereby raised profits, they must be earning higher profits with the new demand curve.

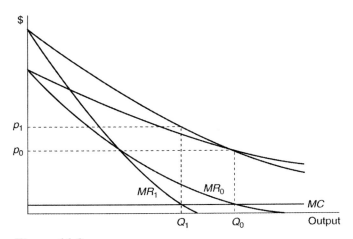

Figure 11.9

■ Exercises

Multiple Choice

1. Joe's Jazz is a monopoly in the sax market, but not a natural monopoly. Which of the following describes the best way to deal with Joe's?

   a. Impose a regulated price where $D = MC$.

   b. Impose a regulated price where $D = AC$.

   c. Impose a tax on Joe's production.

   d. None of the above.

Fill-in

2. Suppose that Mickey is a monopolist in the market for stale cheese. The demand for stale cheese is given by $p = 40 - 1/2Q$. (As W.C. Fields said, there's a sucker born every minute!) Imagine that Mickey's marginal cost is constant at $10, and that he has decided to charge a price where the Lerner index equals 50 percent.

   a. Mickey's current output must be _____.

   b. At Mickey's current output, his marginal revenue is _____.

   c. To maximize his profits, Mickey should produce _____ units of stale cheese, and sell them for a price of _____ each.

   d. At this combination, the Lerner index is _____.

True-False-Ambiguous and Explain Why

3. In Solved Problem 1, we assumed the price elasticity of demand is −0.625 at the current price charged by the USPS. If this were the true level of price elasticity, USPS profits would increase if they raised their price.

4. An increase in demand will always cause a monopolist to raise output.

5. Imposing optimal price regulation on a natural monopolist will surely eliminate any deadweight social welfare loss in both the short and long run.

Short-Answer

6. Calculate the Lerner index at the profit-maximizing output from Solved Problem 2, when Jiminy's, Inc. is not regulated, and use it to infer the price elasticity of demand.

7. Aficionados of oddball music recordings recognize that there is only one Spike Jones. Suppose that Don has obtained the rights to all of Jones's recordings, and so has a monopoly in the market for this music. It turns out that the market demand for Spike Jones's records is given by $p = 120 - 0.2Q$, where p is market price and Q is quantity demanded. Production of these recordings requires paying a fixed cost of $1,000 to rent certain machinery, plus a per-unit payment of $20 (which includes royalties to Jones's estate, and other variable costs). Thus Don's costs are $1,000 + 20Q$.

   a. Determine Don's profit-maximizing output and price.

   b. Determine Don's profits, total consumer surplus, and the social deadweight loss at this output and price.

8. Every fall, squirrels start running around like crazy in Laramie. Ultimately, many of them wind up flattened on city streets. In an attempt to create an innovative new industry, High Flyin' Hatty has convinced the Laramie city council to grant her an exclusive license to collect, clean, and skin these defunct rodents this upcoming fall. Amazingly enough, it seems the fur extracted in this manner makes superb material for producing fishing flies, so good that every Orvis shop in America is clamoring for some. (Orvis is an elite purveyor of hunting, camping, and fishing gear.) Hatty realizes that she has stumbled onto a gold mine, since there is no serious competition to her enterprise. On recognizing this fact, Hatty does a bit of research, and determines that the market demand for one-ounce bags of dead squirrel fur can be expressed by $p = 2 - Q/60$, where p is the dollar price of a bag and Q is the number of bags Hatty sells. With all that fur lying around, Hatty can process these things for next to nothing, so let's suppose her only costs are the $100 fee she paid to the city council to buy her license—in particular, she has no variable costs. How many bags should Hatty produce? Was it worth buying the license?

9. The discussion of the Botox application in the text suggests a demand curve for Allergan, the maker of Botox, that can be written as $p = 775 - 375Q$, along with a constant marginal costs of $MC = 25$, where Q represents millions of vials. Its profit-maximizing output based on this information is 1 million vials, which are sold at a price of $400. Suppose an ad valorem tax of 20% is imposed. Determine Allergan's new optimal production, price, and profits, as well as tax revenues collected by the government.

10. King Cones, located in beautiful Pinedale, is the only roadside hamburger stand for at least 50 miles in all directions. Their most popular feature is the "road kill" burger. (There really is such a place, and they really do sell a road kill burger.) Every day, Elvis, the owner of King Cones, drives out of town looking for the day's raw ingredients. As it turns out, he has to drive 1 mile to collect enough meat for one road kill burger, an additional 2 miles to collect material for a second burger, a further 3 miles for a third, and so on. (All these distances are one way.) Suppose that the price of gas is such that it costs him 20 cents for fuel for each mile traveled, and that the opportunity cost of his time represents an additional 30 cents per mile. If the market demand for road kill burgers is characterized by $Q = 24 - 4p$, how many burgers should Elvis produce each day, and what price should he charge?

11. As it turns out, the demand given in Exercise 10 is only valid during Elvis' busiest season. In the off-season, demand falls to $Q = 8 - p$. It also turns out that his off season costs are $C(Q) = F + Q^2$, where F are Elvis' fixed costs. If Elvis decides to close during the off season, he doesn't have any costs. If Elvis stays open in the off season, what output and price should he set? How small must his fixed costs be if he is to remain open in the off season?

12. A monopoly produces a good with a network externality at a constant marginal and average cost of 4. In the first period, its inverse demand curve is $p = 12 - Q$. In the second period, its demand is $p = 12 - Q$ unless it sells at least $Q = 10$ units in the first period. If it meets or exceeds this target, then the demand curve in its inverse demand curve in the second period is $p = 20 - Q$. The monopoly knows that it can sell no output after the second period. The monopoly's objective is to maximize the sum of its profits over the two periods. Determine the profit-maximizing output and price for each period.

13. Suppose that the demand for caffe-super-double-mocha-lattes on your campus is given by $p = AQ^{-\eta}$. The well-known purveyor of caffeine, Moonbucks, has obtained the sole right to sell such drinks.

   a. Give a formula for the price elasticity of demand in terms of the parameters.

   b. Give a formula for marginal revenue in terms of the parameters.

   c. Determine Moonbucks' profit-maximizing output if $MC = Q$.

   d. Determine Moonbucks' profit-maximizing output if $MC = m$, an arbitrary constant.

14. There is no better trout fishing in the world than one finds in New Zealand, and the crème de la crème is to be found in the headwaters of the Mohaka River. Unfortunately, to get there, one must walk through dense bush for days, or take a helicopter ride into the river on Sika choppers. For those who do not want to walk, Sika has a monopoly. The demand for these chopper rides, as it turns out, can be expressed as $Q = 20 - p^{1/2}$ (for prices greater than \$400, $Q = 0$). Sika's costs are $c(Q) = 120Q - 12Q^2 + Q^3$. Determine Sika's profit-maximizing price and output, and the resultant level of profits.

Chapter 12
Pricing and Advertising

■ Chapter Summary

Firms in noncompetitive markets often have substantial power to influence price. In such cases, it can sometimes pay the firm to charge different prices to different groups. For example, movie theaters regularly charge less for admission by senior citizens, students, and youths than for adults. When a firm charges different prices to different groups, they **price discriminate**. Price discrimination is commonly profitable, because it lets the firm raise sales (by adding customers from the lower price group) without cutting price to everybody. However, to price discriminate, the firm must accomplish three things: It needs to be able to raise its price without losing all its sales, it has to distinguish the group that would pay higher prices from the group that is less willing to pay higher prices, and it needs to prevent those who buy at the low price from purchasing extra units and then selling these to the group who would pay the higher price. For the first feature, it is enough that the firm has some market power. Thus we could see price discrimination by any imperfectly competitive firm (monopoly or oligopoly), but not by a perfectly competitive firm. The second feature is often accomplished by linking price to some simply observed trait, such as age ("we give a 10 percent senior citizen discount"), education status ("show me your student ID and you get a discount"), or gender (ladies night at the local tavern). The third element is the ability to prevent resale. For some products or services this is simple (can you imagine reselling surgery?), while for others it is not so easy.

In the extreme, the firm may be able to charge exactly the highest price each customer is willing to pay. If so, the firm is able to **perfectly price discriminate**. A grueling 3-hour session haggling over the price of a new car might convince you that car dealers come very close to achieving perfect price discrimination. The additional revenue a perfectly discriminating firm collects from selling an extra unit is the price for that unit. Therefore the perfectly discriminating firm maximizes profit by producing where demand equals marginal cost. As with perfect competition, the efficient level of output results. Unlike perfect competition, each customer pays exactly what he or she is willing to pay, and so there is no consumer surplus.

One particularly easy way to price discriminate is by using **quantity discrimination**. Many firms grant quantity discounts, charging less to customers who buy large amounts than to customers who buy small amounts. If those customers who buy large amounts are relatively more sensitive to price, then quantity discrimination allows the firm to charge a higher price to customers who are less price sensitive, just as with price discrimination. The **two-part tariff** is a special form of quantity discrimination. Membership clubs like Sam's Club use a two-part tariff, charging an annual membership fee (an access fee), followed by a per-unit-price. One way to think of such schemes is that the first unit costs the buyer the per-unit-price *plus* the access fee, while the price of all additional units is just the per-unit-price.

A second simple way to price discriminate is to use **multi-market price discrimination**, wherein the firm charges different prices to different markets. Now, just because a firm charges different prices to different customers does not mean it is price discriminating. While one almost always pays more for gasoline in rural areas than in urban areas, it is more expensive to distribute the fuel to the rural markets. Price discrimination means charging different prices that are not based on different costs.

A final technique that a firm can employ to extract more money from its customers is to use **tie-in sales** or **bundling**. Maybe you just bought a vehicle that came complete with air conditioning and four-wheel drive. If you live in Alaska you probably weren't all that interested in getting air conditioning, but the extra traction of four-wheel drive will come in handy. If you live in Florida the air conditioning could be a lifesaver, but there aren't too many places where you'll need four-wheel drive. The two groups' demands for four-wheel drive and air conditioning are negatively correlated—they go in opposite directions. If the manufacturer sold a vehicle that came with neither air conditioning nor four-wheel drive and then offered each option separately, Alaskans would buy four-wheel drive while Floridians would opt for air conditioning. By selling the vehicle complete with both options, the manufacturer gets car buyers to pay more for the option the buyer really wants.

■ Key Concepts and Formulas

- **Differentiated products:** goods or services that consumers *believe* are different.
- **Block pricing:** a pricing scheme where the firm charges one price for the first block of units, a second price for the second block of units, and so on.
- To maximize profits, the price-discriminating firm must choose outputs for the different groups that equate their marginal revenues to marginal cost.
- The price-discriminating firm charges a higher price to consumers with less elastic demand and lower price to consumers with more elastic demand.
- $MR_1 = MR_2$: the rule for determining outputs in each of two markets, 1 and 2, under multimarket price discrimination.

■ Application: Internet Bundling

Thanks to the internet, our society has entered the age of the information superhighway. There are Web pages for vendors selling just about everything, from flowers to fly rods, from nature walks to news. Internet news services provide an interesting alternative to the traditional pleasure of the morning paper. Like the hard copy alternative, virtual news is delivered as a package. You buy access rights to the source, and may then download as many stories as you like. It is easy to see why traditional newspapers sell you a bundle of stories—imagine trying to get the *San Francisco Chronicle* to deliver a handful of articles to your house each day. The extra costs associated with tailoring such a package to each customer's desires would be prohibitive. But virtual newspapers can provide such a tailored service at very low cost: You could agree to pay a fixed charge for every story you access. There are similar examples in other lines of commerce. Suppose you surf through a virtual travel agent's Web page. Such services often provide "special deals" for members. The membership fee is an annual charge; you benefit from these special deals whether you fly a little or a lot.

Question: Why don't we see more newspapers providing articles on a per-unit fee basis? Why don't Internet travel agents charge a service fee on each transaction?

Answer: One possible explanation for the widespread use of one-time fees by Internet merchants is that they are selling a bundle. Perhaps newspaper customers vary widely in their tastes; some folks like to read about current events, while others care only about sporting events. The amount the first group might be willing to pay per story is probably different from the amount the second group would pay per story, so the news service would like to price discriminate. If each type of reader has some, albeit smaller, interest in the other set of stories, then news readers' demands for current events and sporting events are quite likely to be negatively correlated. By selling news as a package, the virtual paper can charge a higher price per story than they would otherwise. Sports readers get consumer surplus from reading more sports stories, so they are willing to "pay" for current events as part of the package deal. Internet travel agents are playing a similar angle, though they use a different ruse. Booking a flight is not costly, so the virtual travel agent's marginal cost is pretty small. Traditional travel agents get a small commission on each sale (usually in the range of 8 percent to 10 percent). By discounting tickets, Internet travel agents give back a portion of the commission (which is quite like offering their service at lower cost than the traditional agent). These discounts raise the number of sales per customer, and also raise the typical customer's consumer surplus. Judicious use of the membership fee appropriates some of this consumer surplus.

■ Application: Discount Theater Tickets

The theater district in London is rightly famous for its brilliant productions. Some shows have successful runs for years, or even decades. These shows attract tourists by the score, many of whom pay 40 pounds (the equivalent of $70) or more for their seats. But savvy theatergoers know that last-minute discounts are available at a number of outlets in Leicester square. These discount seats, which generally become available only hours before a performance, can be had for up to 50% below the regular price. The trick is, if the show you are interested in is sold out, or close to sold out, you may be left without any tickets at all.

Question: Why are such dramatic discounts available, and why doesn't everyone try to cash in on them?

Answer: Many potential theatergoers are tourists, and have a relatively inflexible schedule. They may have only one or two nights free to see the show they are interested in. Such customers would presumably be willing to pay a premium to ensure availability on the date they are hoping to attend. In other words, these consumers' demand is relatively less elastic. On the other hand, those with more flexible schedules can wait for another date, or perhaps substitute a different show. These consumers' demand is more elastic. For a theater to price-discriminate, they need a simple means of identifying whether a particular consumer has relatively less elastic or relatively more elastic demand. Because those with relatively more elastic demand are willing to wait to the last minute, while those with less elastic demand are not, distinguishing between the two cohorts is a fairly simple process: set a high regular price, and offer last-minute discounts.

■ Solved Problems

1. Kiwi Woolens provides superb sweaters to frostbitten foresters in New Zealand. Their clientele is incredibly loyal, so much so that Kiwi Woolens is a monopolist in New Zealand. Quite recently, these sweaters have been brought to America, where there is an abundance of very close substitutes. In fact, Kiwi Woolens is content to take the American price as given, just as if they were a competitive firm. Since making extra sweaters requires shearing extra sheep, a process that is both exhausting and unenjoyable, Kiwi Woolens reckons its marginal cost curve is upward sloping. Determine the profit-maximizing volume of sweaters, the number to be delivered to each market, and the associated prices Kiwi Woolens can charge.

Step 1: Determine the best market in which to sell an additional sweater. Since Kiwi Woolens is a monopolist in New Zealand, if they sell one more sweater on the New Zealand market the additional revenue they receive is determined by the New Zealand market marginal revenue curve (MR_{NZ}). If Kiwi Woolens sells one more sweater in the American market, the additional revenue they earn is the market price for sweaters in the United States (p_{US}). If the marginal revenue in New Zealand exceeds the price in the United States ($MR_{NZ} > p_{US}$), Kiwi Woolens will sell the next sweater in New Zealand; otherwise, they will sell the next sweater in the United States.

Step 2: Determine the total amount that Kiwi Woolens should produce to maximize its profit. Kiwi Woolens must find the level of output whose marginal cost (*MC*) just equals its marginal revenue. If the marginal cost of the monopoly output in New Zealand is larger than p_{US}, Kiwi Woolens sells only in New Zealand, and the amount they sell is the monopoly output. See panel (a) of Figure 12.1. On the other hand, if the marginal cost of the monopoly output in New Zealand is smaller than p_{US}, Kiwi Woolens sells sweaters in both markets, and the total amount produced sets marginal cost equal to p_{US}. See panel (b) of Figure 12.1.

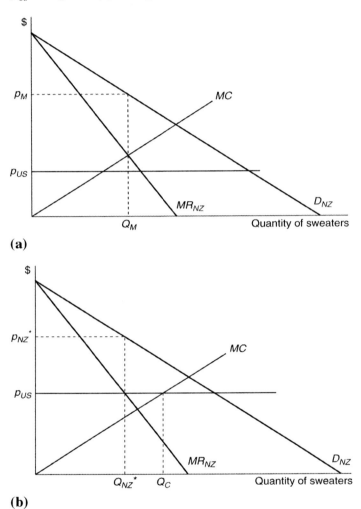

(a)

(b)

Figure 12.1

Step 3: Determine the profit-maximizing level of sales in each market. In panel (a), Kiwi Woolens sells nothing in the American market; they sell the monopoly output in the New Zealand market (Q_M) at the monopoly price (p_M). In panel (b), Kiwi Woolens sells Q_C total units. They split this output between the two markets so that the last unit sold in New Zealand delivers the same marginal revenue as the last unit sold in the United States, which is p_{US}. First, they find the level of sales in New Zealand where marginal revenue equals p_{US}, which is Q_{NZ}^*. Kiwi Woolens sells this amount to New Zealand, and they sell the reminder, $Q_C - Q_{NZ}^*$, to the United States.

Step 4: Determine the prices Kiwi Woolens charges in each market. We already know the price Kiwi Woolens charges in the American market—they charge p_{US} (since they are taking this price as fixed). The price Kiwi Woolens charges in New Zealand is read off the New Zealand demand curve at the output sold there (Q_{NZ}^*). Referring to panel (b) of Figure 12.1, Kiwi Woolens charges the price p_{NZ}^* in New Zealand.

2.   Suppose that Mickey's, Inc. is a monopolist in the Hula Hoop market. Market demand for Hula Hoops is given by $p = 120 - 0.2Q$, where p is market price and Q is quantity demanded. Mickey's marginal cost is $MC = 20$. Mickey knows there are 100 consumers who have identical preferences, but Mickey cannot price discriminate. If Mickey uses a two-part tariff, what price will he charge, and what access fee will he levy?

Step 1: Determine market consumer surplus. If Mickey sells a certain amount Q_0, the resultant market price is $p_0 = 120 - Q_0/5$. Market consumer surplus is

$$\int_0^{Q_0}[p(Q) - p_0]dQ = \int_0^{Q_0}[120 - Q/5 - (120 - Q_0)/5]dQ = \int_0^{Q_0}[Q_0/5 - Q/5]dQ$$
$$= (QQ/5 - \tfrac{1}{2}Q^2/5)\Big|_0^{Q_0} = Q_0^2/10.$$

Step 2: Determine the consumer surplus each buyer will receive. Since there are 100 identical consumers, each buyer gets the same amount of consumer surplus—an amount equal to the market consumer surplus divided by 100. Each buyer's consumer surplus is $Q_0^2/1000$.

Step 3: Determine Mickey's total revenue. If Mickey charges the price p_0, he could also levy an access fee equal to each buyer's consumer surplus, or $Q_0^2/1000$. The total revenue Mickey collects with this two-part tariff is then the product of price and quantity demanded, plus the revenues from the access fee:

$$TR = p_0 \times Q_0 + 100 \times Q_0^2/1000$$
$$= 120 \times Q_0 - Q_0^2/10$$
$$= [120 - Q_0/10] \times Q_0.$$

Step 4: Determine Mickey's profit-maximizing output. To maximize his profit, Mickey sets this marginal revenue equal to his marginal costs. The expression for Mickey's that we found in Step 3 is exactly the same as the revenue Mickey would collect if he faced a demand curve given by $p = 120 - Q_0/10$, so his marginal revenue from the two-part tariff is

$$MR = 120 - Q_0/5.$$

Mickey's marginal costs are \$20. Thus, Mickey maximizes profit at an output of 500 (where $MR = 120 - 500/5 = 20 = MC$).

Step 5: Determine Mickey's profit-maximizing price and access fee. At an output of 500, Mickey's price is $p = 120 - 500/5 = 20$: Mickey sets his price equal to his marginal cost! At this price, each buyer's consumer surplus is $500^2/1000 = \$250$. Mickey sets the access fee equal to each buyer's consumer surplus, or \$250.

■ Practice Problems

Multiple-Choice

1. Relative to a monopolist that does not price discriminate, which of the following are likely to be associated with a price-discriminating monopolist?
   a. larger output
   b. some consumers pay a smaller price
   c. some consumers get less consumer surplus
   d. All of the above are correct.

2. A firm that practices multimarket price discrimination is likely to
   a. charge a higher price to the less elastic market.
   b. sell a larger amount to the more elastic market.
   c. sell a smaller amount to the more elastic market.
   d. charge a lower price to the less elastic market.

3. For a firm to profit from price discrimination, which of the following must be true?
   a. Some consumers must be willing to pay very high prices.
   b. Some consumers must have very inelastic demand.
   c. No consumer can purchase from the firm, and then sell to other consumers.
   d. All of the above are correct.

4. A firm can increase its profits by bundling products A and B (a pair of goods) together if
   a. buyers willing to pay more for product A are also willing to pay more for product B.
   b. buyers willing to pay more for product A aren't willing to pay as much for product B.
   c. all of the firm's customers are willing to pay a lot of money for product B.
   d. None of the above are correct.

Fill-in

5. Remember Terrible Communications Associated (TCA), the cable company from Chapter 11? Along with the local market (whose demand curve is given by $p = 18 - Q_L$, where Q_L represents sales to the local market), it seems they can now serve a nearby community (whose demand curve is $p = 20 - 2Q_N$, where Q_N represents sales to the nearby market). As in Chapter 11, TCA's costs are $C(Q) = \frac{1}{2}Q^2$, but now the total output produced by TCA is the sum of the outputs in the two markets ($Q = Q_L + Q_N$).
   a. Marginal revenue for the local market is _____.
   b. Marginal revenue for the nearby market is _____.
   c. TCA's marginal costs are _____.
   d. To maximize its profits, TCA should set Q_L and Q_N so that _____.
   e. TCA's profit maximizing outputs are _____ in the local market and _____ in the nearby market.
   f. If TCA produces the outputs you identified in part e, and price discriminates between the two markets, it will charge a price of _____ to the local market and _____ to the nearby market.

True-False-Ambiguous and Explain Why

6. Welfare under a price-discriminating monopolist is larger than welfare under a monopolist who does not price discriminate.

7. Fly-by-Night Novels sells racy romance stories. They have two types of customers, those who can't wait to get their hands on the next tale of wanton lust, and those who are content to wait, in hopes that the price will drop. Fly-by-Night should reduce the price of each novel it sells a few months after its release.

8. If a monopolist knows that its customers have very similar preferences, it can raise its profit by using a two-part tariff.

Short-Answer

9. Using the information from Practice Problem 5, graphically describe TCA's profit-maximizing multi-market price discrimination scheme.

10. Suppose that Allergan, the seller of Botox, is able to distinguish cosmetic purchasers from crosseyed purchasers, and can prevent resale between the two groups. Suppose further that cosmetic customers (group 1) are so desperate to acquire Botox (to keep their pretty faces wrinkle free!) that the demand for this group equals market demand for prices at and above $400. The demand for crosseyed purchasers (group 2) equals market demand for prices below $400. Determine Allergan's profit-maximizing prices and outputs for each group, and the net impact on total output of price discriminating between the two types of purchasers.

11. Using the information from Solved Problem 2, show the sales revenue and access fees that Mickey's, Inc. collects at the price that is part of the two-part tariff problem. Compare these values to the simple monopoly price and the access fees that Mickey's, Inc. could collect if it charged the monopoly price.

12. There are two types of beer drinkers, chuggers and sippers. Chuggers slam back their brew so fast they can hardly enjoy it, and so they are only willing to pay $0.50 per can. Sippers take their time, savoring every drop. They really enjoy their beer, and so are willing to pay $1 per can. Suppose there are 100 chuggers and 50 sippers in the town of Sudsville, and that each beer drinker is willing to buy up to 6 cans per day. Unfortunately for our beer-drinking buddies, the only place to buy beer in the town of Sudsville is Brewski's. Each can costs Brewski's exactly $0.40 to supply. If Brewski's cannot distinguish between chuggers and sippers, how many beers will they sell, and what price(s) will they charge?

13. Continuing on with Brewski's pricing problem, suppose that Brewski's is able to distinguish chuggers from sippers (as it turns out, chuggers have pudgy noses, while sippers always look down their noses at the clerk). Let's also assume that sippers refuse to have anything to do with chuggers. Now how many beers will Brewski's sell, and what price(s) will they charge?

■ Answers to Practice Problems

1. A non-price-discriminating monopolist sets his output at a point where price exceeds marginal cost because adding sales requires that he cut his price on all units, not just the next unit. A price-discriminating monopolist, on the other hand, does not have to lower price to all customers to encourage extra sales, he only has to lower price to some customers. The result is that his marginal revenue is commonly larger than that of a non-price-discriminating monopolist, so that he usually produces more. If he produces more, someone has to be paying less (since the monopolist's demand curve is downward sloping). One also expects that the price-discriminating monopolist will charge some consumer *more* than a non-price-discriminating monopolist would do; such consumers must then receive less consumer surplus from a price-discriminating monopolist. All of answers a, b, and c are correct; answer d is best.

2. To be profitable, price discrimination requires equating marginal revenues from different groups. The marginal revenue from group i can be written as $p_i(1 + 1/\varepsilon_i)$, where p_i is the price charged to group i and ε_i is the elasticity for group i. If different prices are charged to two groups 1 and 2, the groups' marginal revenues must satisfy $MR_1 = MR_2$. Correspondingly, the prices and elasticities for these two groups are related by

$$p_1(1 + 1/\varepsilon_1) = p_2(1 + 1/\varepsilon_2), \text{ or}$$
$$p_1/p_2 = (1 + 1/\varepsilon_2)\,\varepsilon\,(1 + 1/\varepsilon_1).$$

So, if $p_1 > p_2$ then $1 + 1/\varepsilon_1 > 1 + 1/\varepsilon_2$, which in turn requires that $\varepsilon_1 > \varepsilon_2$. Since both elasticities are negative numbers, we conclude that ε_1 is closer to zero, which means that it is smaller in magnitude. In other words, the demand for group 1 is less elastic; answer a is correct. Because group 2 could be either larger or smaller than group 1, there is no way to know if the price-discriminating monopolist sells more or less to them than to group 1.

3. To benefit from price discrimination, the monopolist needs to identify multiple groups with differing demand elasticities. While he will do particularly well if one of the groups has very inelastic demand or is willing to pay exceptionally high prices, successful price discrimination does not require either feature. (Think of your local movie theater; they are likely to price discriminate between students and adults, but neither group pays an outrageously high price, and both groups are likely to have relatively elastic demand curves.) Whether the groups have very inelastic demands or not, successful price discrimination requires the prevention of resale. Answer c is correct.

4. By setting a price for the bundle that doesn't exceed the sum of the amount each buyer would pay for A and B, the firm is able to sell to several different buyers. This strategy can raise the firm's profits if the demands for the two products are negatively correlated, that is, if the firm's customers who are willing to pay more for good A wouldn't pay as much for good B. Answer b is best. Note that it really doesn't matter if the customers are willing to pay a lot of money for one of the goods, if everyone would pay the same exorbitant price. The firm uses bundling as a way to get every customer to implicitly pay more for one of the goods (say product B) than they would otherwise do, while charging less for the other good (product A) than the customer would be willing to pay.

5. Answers and brief explanations follow.

   a. $MR_L = 18 - 2Q_L$.

   b. $MR_N = 20 - 4Q_N$.

   c. TCA's marginal costs are $dC(Q)/dQ = Q$.

   d. To maximize profits, TCA should solve $MR_L = MC = MR_N$. From parts a, b, and c, and noting that Q (total output) equals Q_L plus Q_N, the profit-maximizing conditions can be written as $18 - 2Q_L = Q_L + Q_N$ and $20 - 4Q_N = Q_L + Q_N$. Doubling both sides of the first relation and combining with the second relation yields $36 - 4Q_L + (20 - 4Q_N) = 2(Q_L + Q_N) + Q_L + Q_N$; combining terms in $Q_L + Q_N$ then gives $56 = 7(Q_L + Q_N)$, or $Q_L + Q_N = 8$.

   e. Substituting the answer from part d) into the profit-maximizing relations gives $18 - 2Q_L = 8$, or $Q_L = 5$; and $20 - 4Q_N = 8$, or $Q_N = 3$.

   f. Since $P_L = 18 - Q_L$ and $Q_L = 5$, the profit-maximizing price in the local market is $P_L = \$13$. As $P_N = 20 - 2Q_N$ and $Q_N = 3$, the profit-maximizing price in the nearby market is $P_N = \$14$.

6. Ambiguous. If the monopolist has constant marginal costs and discriminates between two markets, he winds up charging the same price and producing the same amount in each market as would be the case if he served that market in isolation. Such price discrimination generates the same level of welfare as two monopolists (one for each market) who did not price discriminate. If the monopolist perfectly price discriminates, the resultant level of output sets marginal cost equal to demand; it mimics a perfectly competitive market. So perfect price discrimination clearly raises welfare (although it redistributes all the welfare to the monopolist). Finally, a monopolist that price discriminates between two markets and that faces an *upward sloping* marginal cost curve will sell less in each market than would a non-price-discriminating monopolist. (For example, consider the first solved problem.) Such price discrimination surely lowers welfare.

7. True. Fly-by-Night has two identifiable groups of customers, impatient ones and patient ones. Impatient ones are willing to pay more than patient ones. If the low price is offered later and impatient customers buy now at the higher price, resale is impractical. Thus by charging a higher price early and a lower price later, Fly-by-Night is able to price discriminate.

8. True. Since the monopolist's customers have similar preferences, they demand similar amounts at the monopoly price, and they obtain similar levels of consumer surplus. This value of consumer surplus is roughly equal to market consumer surplus divided by the number of consumers, and so is positive. Since the typical customer gets positive consumer surplus, she would be willing to pay a fee for the right to purchase as many units as she liked at the monopolist's price. Without changing his price at all, the monopolist can raise his revenues. Because he didn't change his output, he didn't change his costs. Thus his profits must have gone up.

9. See Figure 12.2.

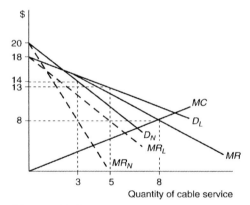

Figure 12.2

10. From Chapter 11, we know that the inverse demand for Botox is given by $p = 775 - 375Q$, so $Q = (775/375) - (1/375)p$. The only purchasers at prices of \$400 and higher are in group 1, so inverse demand for this group is $p_1 = 775 - 375Q_1$ where p_1 is the price charged to cosmetic customers and Q_1 is the quantity purchased by cosmetic customers. The only purchasers at prices below \$400 are in group 2, so their inverse demand is $p_2 = 400 - 375Q_2$. These curves are linear for both groups; we know from Chapter 1 that the marginal revenue curve associated with linear demand has the same intercept as inverse demand with twice the slope, so that $MR_1 = 775 - 750Q_1$ and $MR_2 = 400 - 750Q_2$. To maximize profits, Allergan should choose the outputs that set each marginal revenue equal to marginal cost, or 25. Accordingly we find Q_1^* solves $775 - 750Q_1^* = 25$, or $Q_1^* = 750/750 = 1$ (million vials). Similarly, Q_2^* solves $400 - 750Q_1^* = 25$, or $Q_2^* = 375/750 = 1/2$ (million vials). In the application discussed in the text, the profit maximizing output was 1 million vials; when Allergan is able to price discriminate it sells this much to cosmetic customers and an additional 500,000 vials to crosseyed customers. That is, its total output rises by 500,000 vials (or 50 percent).

11. See Figure 12.3. If Mickey's charges a price of $20, its revenues are the sum of areas R_2 and R_3; it collects access fees equal to consumer surplus, which equals the sum of areas CS_1, R_1, and CS_2. To find the simple monopoly price, we first determine marginal revenue based on the market demand curve $p = 120 - 0.2 \times Q$. This curve has the same intercept and twice the slope as demand: $MR - 120 - 0.4 \times Q$. Setting marginal revenue equal to marginal cost ($120 - 0.4 \times Q = 20$), we find the monopoly output is 250. At this output, market price is $70. Revenues would be areas R_1 and R_2, while access fees would equal consumer surplus (area CS_1).

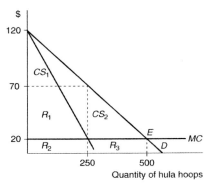

Figure 12.3

12. Since there are two types of consumers, Brewski's only needs to consider two prices. If they charge $1/can, they will sell six cans to each sipper and nothing to chuggers, for a total of 300 cans. Total revenue would be $300, while total costs would be $120 (= $0.40 × 300). If Brewski's charges $0.50 per can, they will sell six cans to everyone, for a total of 900 cans. Total revenue would be $450 and total costs would be $360. If they can sell at different prices, they will charge sippers $1 and chuggers $0.50. At these prices, they sell 300 cans to sippers and 600 cans to chuggers, so total output is again 900 cans, and total costs are $360. Since Brewski's cannot tell the difference between the two groups, they must charge the same price to everyone. Their choices are $1/can, which gives profits of $180 (= $300 − $120) or $0.50/can, which gives profits of $90 (= $450 − $360). They charge $1/can and sell 300 cans, only to sippers.

13. Now Brewski's can price discriminate. They can identify two different groups that have different demands, and they can prevent resale. They charge sippers $1/can, selling 300 cans and collecting revenues of $300. They sell 600 cans to chuggers, collecting revenues of $300. Their total revenue would be $600. With 900 cans sold, total costs are $360, so profit is $240.

■ Exercises

Fill-in

1. X-rocks rents copying machines to two local businesses. One of these businesses, Bert's, would use their machine to make 1,000 copies in a typical month. The other business, Ernie's, would use their machine to make 10,000 copies in a typical month. Suppose that X-rocks can't determine which of the two companies is the heavier user. But X-rocks has arranged their rental agreements so that both customers must buy copying paper from X-rocks (otherwise the rental agreement will be terminated). Suppose the competitive price for copying paper is $0.02 per piece. X-rocks is considering three policies: (A) renting their machines at $500/month and charging $0.02 per piece of copying paper; (B) renting their machines at $400/month and charging $0.04 per piece of paper; and (C) renting their machines at $325/month and charging $0.05 per piece of paper. Finally, assume that both Bert's and Ernie's would be willing to rent under any of the three agreements.

   a. Under policy A, X-rocks will collect _____ from Bert's and _____ from Ernie's.
   b. Under policy B, X-rocks will collect _____ from Bert's and _____ from Ernie's.

c. Under policy C, X-rocks will collect _____ from Bert's and _____ from Ernie's.

d. X-rocks will maximize its profits by using policy _____.

e. What alternative strategy could X-rocks use if it could determine which company was the heavier user? _____.

True-False-Ambiguous and Explain Why

2. Welfare under a monopolist who uses a two-part tariff is larger than welfare under a monopolist who does not use a two-part tariff.

3. If Allergan can discriminate between purchases by medical clients (those treating crosseyes) and cosmetic customers as in Practice Problem 10, welfare will necessarily go up.

4. In many relatively small, more rural areas across America, small air carriers provide connecting service to major hub airports. Often, these connecting flights are short—100 miles or less—and fares can vary quite dramatically. Purchases made within a week of departure are often more than double the cost of more advance purchases. Why do fares vary so dramatically?

Short-Answer

5. Back in Sudsville, the 100 chuggers have had a slight change of heart. Now they are willing to slam down up to 16 cans of beer per day, if the price is $0.50 or less. The 50 Sippers still will buy up to 6 cans if the price is $1. But all this beer drinking has had an effect on sippers' appearance, so Brewski's can no longer tell the groups apart just by looking at them. Explain how they can still get sippers to pay $1/can, while letting chuggers pay $0.50/can, on average.

6. The heyday of beer drinking for chuggers is over. No longer can they afford to drink 16 cans per day; they are back to their old 6 cans per day ritual. As in Exercise 12, Brewski's cannot tell chuggers from sippers when they walk in the door. However, it turns out that both sippers and chuggers like Bob's Big Bag o' Popcorn, which Brewski's can sell on the side. It costs Brewski's $1.50 for each bag they sell. Sippers will pay up to $2 per bag, as long as they are also drinking beer. Chuggers would pay $2 per bag just to eat the popcorn, but they are willing to pay $4 per bag if they buy the popcorn to eat while they drink beer. Can Brewski's profit from bundling beer with popcorn? Explain why. Would your answer change if popcorn cost Bob's $2 per bag? Would your answer change if popcorn cost Bob's $4 per bag?

7. For this final part of Brewski's pricing problem, suppose that sippers are happy to drink with chuggers (and to buy beer from them, if a good deal comes along). How might Brewski's create a scheme that results in the same volume of sales and profits as in part b? (*Hint:* Figure out a way that Brewski's can prevent resale.)

8. Each spring, Cross-Country Ken (from Chapter 11) has a "countdown" sale. Each day of this sale, prices throughout the store are lowered by a fixed percentage: on the first day, prices are cut 10% from the regular level, on the second day they are reduced 20% below the regular level, on the third day, 30% below the regular level, and prices are slashed 40% on the fourth and final day. Suppose Ken's regular price is $100 and that his marginal cost is $25. At this price, Ken sells 40 units. On the first day of the sale, Ken's sales rise by 15 units. Sales rise an additional 20 units on the second day, and then 25 units more on the third day. On the final day, Ken is overwhelmed by a virtual avalanche of sales, with 130 units sold. Base on this information, Ken asks your advice. Is this sale profitable? Is there anything he can do to improve the sale?

9.   Out in deep space, dilithium crystals are the fuel of choice. Two types of interstellar travelers demand this fuel: Romulans and Klingons. At first blush, these two humanoids look and act the same, but on more careful inspection we see that the Klingons' demand for dilithium crystals is Q_K, given by

$$p_K = 30 - Q_K,$$

where p_K is the price Klingons pay. The Romulans' demand for dilithium crystals is Q_R, given by

$$p_R = 30 - 2Q_R,$$

where p_R is the price Romulans pay. The only place to buy these crystals is on the planet Vulcan, and there is only one firm (named Spock's Crystal Palace) that sells the crystals. Spock's costs of producing an amount Q of crystals are $c(Q) = 100 + Q^2$.

If Spock's cannot distinguish between Romulans and Klingons, or if they can't prevent resale, what prices will they charge each type of alien, how much will each type of alien buy, and what are Spock's profits?

If Spock's can distinguish between Romulans and Klingons and they can prevent resale, what prices will they charge each type of alien, how much will each type of alien buy, and what are Spock's profits?

Chapter 13
Oligopoly and Monopolistic Competition

■ Chapter Summary

In many markets, firms have some ability to mark up price above their marginal cost. If you want to fly from San Francisco to Chicago, for example, there are only a few airlines from which to choose. Suppose that you decide to stop for a quick burger on the way to the airport. While there may be many fast food joints from which to choose, they don't all sell the same burger (or at least that's what their ads claim). In both examples, firms need not passively accept market price. In the first case, since there are only a small number of sellers, each carrier knows it has some market power. As shown with monopoly in Chapter 11, this allows the firm to mark up price above marginal cost. Markets like this, where the number of sellers is relatively small, are called **oligopolies**. In the second case, where there are lots of sellers but products are not identical, each seller's product is somewhat different from all other sellers' products. Again, this gives the seller some market power, although perhaps not quite as much as in an oligopoly. Markets with many sellers but differentiated products are called **monopolistically competitive**.

When a firm's price exceeds marginal cost, there is generally a deadweight loss. The magnitude of this loss depends on the firm's ability to exploit market power, which is commonly linked to institutional features of the market. Industries with a small number of firms selling distinct products in the presence of large entry barriers are likely to yield greater markups than industries with more firms selling quite similar products in the face of small entry barriers. Industry size, the degree of product differentiation, and the size of entry barriers are typically very important predictors of a firm's ability to mark up price; we refer to these features collectively as **market structure**. The third feature can influence the first feature. As a general rule, oligopolies occur in markets where entry barriers are large. On the other hand, monopolistic competition occurs in markets with no entry barriers but heterogeneous products.

Oligopoly is trickier to analyze than either perfect competition or monopoly. Competitive firms take price as given; they don't worry about how they affect other firms. A monopoly has no rivals to worry about, so it doesn't care about other firms (unless it is trying to prevent entry, as we shall see in the next chapter). But oligopolists know they can influence price, and that this will impact other firms' actions. Careful analysis of oligopoly must therefore pay attention to this strategic interaction. **Game theory** is a modeling approach that focuses on this strategic interaction by using information on the participants' possible actions and incentives to predict the likely pattern of behavior. A key notion in forming this prediction is the **Nash equilibrium**, a combination of strategies where no player would unilaterally alter its behavior. If we think the oligopoly firms are quantity choosers—they each select an output, and market price is then based on the sum of these production levels—then the game theory approach leads us to the **Cournot model of noncooperative oligopoly**. The outcome from this model is a Nash equilibrium where firms' strategies are the output levels they select. One important element of this model is the timing of output choices—all firms choose at the same time. If one firm is able to select its output before anyone else and the rival firms observe the first firm's production, they will adjust their outputs accordingly. Knowing this, the first firm can influence rival behavior to its advantage. This is the **Stackelberg model of noncooperative oligopoly**. The same type of result can emerge in the Cournot model if each firm's profits can be influenced by some government agency, and one of these governments can commit to actions before outputs are selected. For example, the Australian government imposes an enormous tariff on imported Japanese vehicles. The Japanese auto producers compete with Holden, the domestic Australian producer. By imposing tariffs, the Australian government effectively commits Holden to relatively larger outputs.

The Nash equilibrium prediction is not the only possible outcome. It is entirely possible that firms will act jointly to maximize industry profits. If firms can succeed in this endeavor, they will ultimately mimic the behavior of a monopoly (with individual outputs summing to the monopoly level). This is the **cooperative oligopoly model** of behavior. Firms that cooperate in this fashion are said to *collude;* colluding firms are collectively called a *cartel.* On a certain level, the Cournot model is empirically appealing. One often hears of a firm's desire to raise market share, which can only occur if it wrestles sales away from some other firm. Even so, there are some well-known examples of cartels. OPEC, for example, has flexed its muscles over the price of crude oil for decades. On a national level, there were allegations relatively recently that the airline industry used its advance reservation system to facilitate collusion. At the state level, there are concerns that petroleum refiners in California are fixing prices.

It is usually straightforward to compare prices across the four output choice models. Collusion is designed to restrict output to the monopoly level, and so this yields the highest possible price. In the Cournot model, firms do not collaborate to maximize industry profits, which means the collusive price is higher than the Cournot price. If one firm can choose output before anyone else (the Stackelberg leader), it raises its production above its Cournot level. This increase causes the rival firms to collectively lower their output, by an amount that is smaller than the first firm's increase. The new regime is the Stackelberg equilibrium. Since the Stackelberg leader's output rises by more than the other firms' outputs fall, market output is larger at the Stackelberg equilibrium than at the Cournot equilibrium. Thus the Stackelberg equilibrium is smaller than the Cournot price. Even so, it still exceeds marginal cost. Therefore the competitive price is smaller still than the Stackelberg, Cournot, and collusive prices.

In many markets, it appears that firms decide on a price to charge, as opposed to selecting quantities. Say you want to buy a stereo, and there are only two stores in town. One shop sells Pioneer, the second shop sells Denon. The price for each shop's stereo is clearly indicated at the store; if 10 people come into the Denon store one day, the shop owner will sell 10 units. Since there are only a few stores in this example, the market for stereos in your town is an oligopoly. These oligopolists, however, are choosing their price, not their quantity. Their interaction results in a **price-setting** equilibrium. As a general rule, the prices we observe in a price-setting equilibrium differ from the prices that would occur had firms been competing in output. Whether oligopoly firms interact by choosing prices or quantities depends on a number of features, including the similarity of the products. If Pioneer and Denon stereos were virtually indistinguishable, the two shops in our hypothetical example above would find themselves in brutal, almost cutthroat competition. Such competition seems implausible, since the firms could make more money by agreeing to choose quantities instead of prices. But if the two stereos differ in important ways, then price competition is more likely to occur.

■ Key Concepts and Formulas

- **Nash equilibrium:** a behavioral prediction where each firm tries to make itself as well off as possible, taking other firms' actions as fixed.
- **Best-response curve:** a relation between rivals' outputs and the firm's profit maximizing output; also known as a *reaction curve.*
- **Profit matrix:** a way of representing possible combinations of firms' strategies and the resulting profits they each earn.
- **Game tree:** a way of representing the sequence of decisions firms can make and the resulting profits they each earn along each potential path of play.

■ Application: Cartel Formation by Local Physicians

From the Utah state line to the Rocky Mountain High of Aspen, and from New Mexico to Wyoming, the sparse population of western Colorado is scattered over hundreds of square miles. The largest town in this region, Grand Junction, lies near the geographic center of this wide space. If you live in western Colorado, chances are you do a fair bit of your shopping in Grand Junction, whether it is for macaroni or medical services. And if you are looking for medical help, you are most likely to come into contact with the Mesa County Physicians Independent Practice Association (MCPIPA)—over 70 percent of the area's physicians are members of this association. With those numbers, there is a concern that members are acting jointly to raise their profits, for example, by forcing HMOs to pay higher prices for medical service. It was fear of such price fixing that lead the Federal Trade Commission (FTC) to bring suit against MCPIPA in 1996, alleging violations of antitrust statutes that prohibit price fixing. Recently, MCPIPA and the FTC reached an agreement that resulted in the abandonment of the antitrust case. The settlement calls for MCPIPA to stop negotiating with insurers and HMOs on behalf of member physicians.

Question: Will the negotiated agreement between FTC and MCPIPA lead to increased price competition?

Answer: In the initial arrangement, physicians use MCPIPA to negotiate with insurance companies and HMOs, which has two crucial effects. The first effect is that it reduces the potential gains to any individual physician from defecting. Suppose Dr. Jones wants to cut a special deal with insurance company SF for a certain patient, maybe because the patient is relatively poor. Realizing that Dr. Jones is willing to undermine MCPIPA's role as sole negotiator, SF will demand similar concessions on all Jones's patients. But Jones will want to avoid this, and so he refuses to deal with SF directly. The second effect is that detecting defectors becomes relatively simple. When Jones cuts this deal with SF, and winds up doing all his business with SF in this manner, all the other physicians will notice that she no longer uses MCPIPA in her dealings with SF. They will conclude that she either has decided to stop doing business with patients who are insured by SF, or that she has cut a special deal with SF. Assuming some of these other doctors deal with SF, they will know if SF has become unwilling to deal with MCPIPA. Assuming this is not true, it will be apparent that Jones has cut a special deal with SF. For a cartel to succeed, each participant must believe that the gains from defection outweigh the costs. The gains are based on the extra sales that can be realized by chiseling on price, and the period of time that will pass before this defection is noticed. The costs are the end of the comfortable profits associated with the cartel. The structure of MCPIPA serves to lower the gains from defection, which enhances the chance it will be a successful cartel. If MCPIPA agrees to stop negotiating for member physicians, the cooperative oligopoly model would no longer describe the market for medical services in western Colorado. In its place, we might anticipate the Cournot model of noncooperative oligopoly to provide a reasonable description of behavior. Because of this, a plausible prediction is that prices will fall.

■ Solved Problems

1. Each Friday evening, *Time* and *Newsweek* select a cover story for their weekly news magazines. This week, there are three good stories available: They can discuss a recent minor breakthrough in AIDS research, the debate over current budget impasse, or a major flood that has just ravaged the Midwest. In choosing between the three cover stories, each magazine would like to distinguish itself from its rival. Suppose the payoff table for *Newsweek* and *Time* is as follows (the first number in each cell represents *Time*'s profits—in millions of dollars—and the second number is *Newsweek*'s profits):

Newsweek's choice

		AIDS	Budget	Flood
Time's Choice	AIDS	1, 1	3, 7	2, 6
	Budget	10, 2	1, 1	4, 3
	Flood	8, 3	7, 2	1, 1

What covers will each magazine select?

Step 1: Determine *Time*'s best responses—the cover choice *Time* would want to make for each possible cover choice by *Newsweek*.

To determine *Time*'s best responses, pick a choice for *Newsweek*. This determines a column in the payoff table. For example, if *Time* thought *Newsweek* would pick Budget, *Time* would expect to get payoffs from the second column. The possible payoffs are 3 (if *Time* picks AIDS), 1 (if *Time* picks Budget), and 7 (if *Time* picks Flood). The largest of these payoffs, 7, determines *Time*'s best response—Flood. Likewise, if *Time* thought *Newsweek* were going to pick AIDS, *Time* would select Budget. *Time* would also select Budget if they thought *Newsweek* were going to pick Flood.

Step 2: Determine *Newsweek*'s best responses—the cover choice *Newsweek* would want to make for each possible cover choice by *Time*.

To determine *Time*'s best responses, pick a choice for *Time*. This determines a row in the payoff table. For example, if *Newsweek* thought *Time* would pick AIDS, *Newsweek* would expect to get payoffs from the first row. The possible payoffs are 1 (if *Newsweek* picks AIDS), 7 (if *Newsweek* picks Budget), and 6 (if *Newsweek* picks Flood). The largest of these payoffs, 7, determines Newsweek's best response—Budget. Likewise, if *Newsweek* thought *Time* were going to pick Budget, *Newsweek* would select Flood. If they thought *Time* was going to pick Flood, *Newsweek* would select AIDS.

Step 3: Find a pair of cover choices, one for *Time* and one for *Newsweek,* such that neither magazine would wish to alter its cover in light of the other magazine's choice.

At this combination, *Time*'s choice will be a best response to *Newsweek*'s choice, and *Newsweek*'s choice will be a best response to *Time*'s choice. Looking at *Time*'s best responses, we see that there they would want to choose Budget if they thought *Newsweek* would choose either AIDS or Flood. Looking at *Newsweek*'s best responses, we see that there they would want to choose Flood if they thought *Time* would choose Budget. So, if *Time* picks Budget and *Newsweek* picks Flood, neither magazine would change its cover. This is the combination of covers the magazines will select.

2.   Connoisseurs of fine beer recognize Pilsner Urquell as one of the world's best. This quaffable drink is a fine example of pilsner beer, a form of brewing mastered by residents of the old Czechoslovakia centuries ago. (Budweiser, the self-proclaimed "king of beers," derives from an old Czech brewery.) Suppose that there are literally hundreds of tiny brewmasters in the former Czechoslovakia, all of whom produce superb—and indistinguishable—pilsner beer. These brewers are split between the newly defined countries of Slovakia and the Czech Republic. Their beers are sold mainly in the United States, in large part because the only other major beer drinking countries are either too nationalistic (think Germany) or too fixated on ale (think Britain) to drink Czech or Slovakian pilsner. Owing to the large number of virtually identical sellers, the market for Czechoslovakian pilsner in the United States is perfectly competitive. The supply curves for Czech and Slovak brewers are labeled as S_c and S_s, respectively, in Figure 13.1. The horizontal summation of these supply curves gives the total supply, S_T, of Czechoslovakian beer in the United States. The governments of the Czech Republic and Slovakia can each influence their respective country's supply curve by strategic use of tax or subsidy on their country's sellers. Following their ice hockey triumph in the 1998 Winter Olympics, the

Czech government decides it will place a per-unit tax on Czech pilsner. This tax shifts the Czech supply of pilsner in (from S_c to S_c'' in Figure 13.3, below). Assuming that the Slovakian government does not respond to the Czech tax, what is the effect of this tax on Czech welfare?

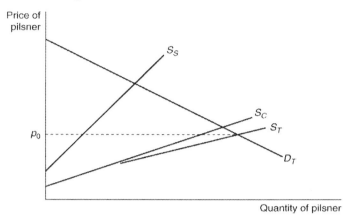

Figure 13.1

Step 1: Calculate the market equilibrium price in the United States before the Czech tax. See Figure 13.1. The market demand for pilsner is D_T, both before and after the Czech tax. Market supply, S_T, is the horizontal sum of the Slovakian supply, S_S, and the initial Czech supply, S_C. The pretax equilibrium price, p_0, is found at the intersection of D_T and S_T.

Step 2: Determine the impact a tax on Czech sellers has on the United States market for pilsner beer. This tax affects neither Slovakian supply nor United States demand, but it does reduce Czech supply (it shifts the Czech supply curve to the left). Correspondingly, market supply is reduced to S_T'. This causes an increase in market price, to p_1. Despite this higher price, Czech brewers sell fewer units of pilsener, and their costs (made up of production costs and taxes) have gone up. See Figure 13.2.

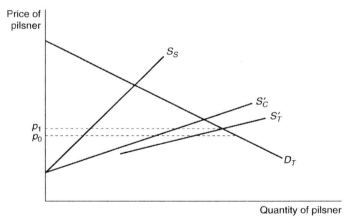

Figure 13.2

Step 3: Determine the effect of the tax on Czech sellers. Referring to Figure 13.3, producer surplus at the original price is the area below price p_0 and above the pre-tax Czech supply curve (S_c), or the sum of areas B, C, and E. After the tax, producer surplus is the area below the new price p_1 and above the post-tax Czech supply curve (S_c'), or the sum of areas A and B. There are two conflicting effects of the tax upon Czech sellers. On the one hand, the tax increases their costs, which lowers producer surplus (areas C and E are removed from producer surplus). On the other hand, the tax leads to a higher price, which tends to raise producer surplus (area A is added to producer surplus). The net effect is a reduction in producer surplus, since the sum of areas C and E exceeds area A.

Step 4: Determine the effect of the tax on Czech welfare. If we think of Czech welfare as the sum of producer surplus, consumer surplus, and government revenue, a one-zlotny loss for sellers (from higher taxes) is a one-zlotny gain for the government (from higher tax revenues). Or perhaps those taxes are redistributed, either to sellers (in the form of a lump-sum cash payment) or to consumers. Again, the gains to one group exactly cancel out the tax payments from brewers. Tax receipts are the sum of areas C and D. Since Czech beer is consumed in the United States, there is no impact on Czech consumer surplus if the price of pilsner beer rises. So the net effect on Czech welfare is the tax revenue, $C + D$, minus the reduction in producer surplus, $C + E - A$, or $A + D - E$. Inspecting Figure 13.3, areas D and E are about the same size, and each is smaller than area A. So Czech welfare is higher with this tax in place. This rather surprising result occurs because the tax allows Czech brewers to collectively commit to smaller outputs. When there is a tax, they set price equal to marginal cost plus the tax, which means that marginal cost is less than price. In other words, the Czech government has concocted a scheme that allows the Czech brewers to form a cartel, though perhaps not a perfect one. Since the tax raises Czech welfare, it is in the country's best interest to impose a tax if the Slovakian government is not expected to react.

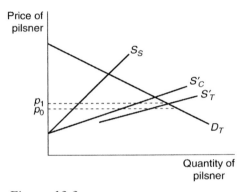

Figure 13.3

■ Practice Problems

Multiple-Choice

1. An important difference between oligopoly and monopoly is that
    a.   there are no entry barriers in oligopoly.
    b.   oligopoly firms' demand curves are not downward sloping.
    c.   oligopoly firms generally do not make positive economic profits.
    d.   None of the above.

2. Frick and Frack are oligopolists in the gibberish industry. Every week on National Public Radio, they each produce an output of gibberish. At the Nash equilibrium, we would expect that each was producing
    a.   an amount of gibberish that maximized the industry's profits.
    b.   an amount of gibberish that was in his own best interests, given the amount the other guy produced.
    c.   an unlimited amount of gibberish.
    d.   the monopoly amount of gibberish.

3. Suppose that the market for essential oils is monopolistically competitive. Which of the following statements is most likely to be *false*?

   a. Each firm selling essential oils is able to convince consumers that their product is different from other firms' oils.

   b. Each firm will charge a price above marginal cost.

   c. Each firm is unlikely to remain in the industry if it bears economic losses over a long period of time.

   d. Each firm will produce an output that minimizes its average costs.

4. If firms engage in a game that has a dominant strategy, then

   a. each firm will achieve its best possible outcome in the game.

   b. once one player picks some strategy; no other players can pick the same strategy.

   c. each player has one best choice, no matter what the other players do.

   d. None of the above is correct.

5. Compared to the Cournot equilibrium, prices in the Bertrand equilibrium tend to be _____ while quantities tend to be ____.

   a. lower; lower.

   b. lower; higher.

   c. higher; lower.

   d. higher; higher.

Fill-in

6. Red Bounty and Green Acreage are the only sellers of gumboots in Yachats. Because it rains almost daily in Yachats, gumboots are in high demand. Indeed, the number of pairs of gumboots purchased each year, Q_t, is related to the price of gumboots, p_t, according to $p_t = 16 - Q_t$ (we'll use "t" to indicate the year). Because Red and Green are the only two sellers of gumboots, market sales equal the sum of their outputs: $Q_t = q_{Rt} + q_{Gt}$, where q_{Rt} is the number of gumboots Red sells and q_{Gt} is the number of gumboots Green sells. It costs each of these guys $4 to produce a pair of gumboots, no matter how many pairs they make. Red and Green each make all the gumboots they plan to sell for the upcoming year on December 31. In deciding how many pairs of gumboots to make, Red guesses that Green will make the same number of gumboot pairs as last year.

   a. If Green made six pairs last year, at what price does Red expect gumboots to sell if he makes three pairs this year? _____.

   b. What if Red sells four pairs? _____.

   c. In fact, the demand curve that Red expects to face this year is _____.

   d. Based on this information, we would expect Red to make ____ pairs of gumboots this year.

   e. If Green made four pairs of gumboots last year, Red would make _____ pairs this year.

True-False-Ambiguous and Explain Why

7. A Cournot oligopolist's demand curve is more elastic than the market demand curve.

8. To deter firms from colluding, it is not important that every cartel be detected and prosecuted. Collusion can be discouraged if some cartels are successfully prosecuted and heavily penalized.

9. In a monopolistically competitive market, new firms will enter if existing firms are making positive accounting profits.

10. Suppose there are two firms engaged in the Cournot model of noncooperative behavior, both of whom have constant marginal costs. However, the firms have different marginal costs. In the Cournot equilibrium the firms will produce different amounts.

Short-Answer

11. Officials in North Dakota and South Dakota are each thinking about building a large industrial park in an attempt to lure expansion by the Out-tel PC company. Building the plant will cost $1 million, and the officials reckon the expansion would be worth $3 million to the local economy (in terms of tax revenues and new jobs). If only one state builds the park, Out-tel will locate there. If both states (or neither) build the park, Out-tel will flip a coin to decide. Which state(s) will build the park?

12. Imagine that there are two sellers of chocolate bars, Willie's and Wonka's. On the last day of each month, Willie's and Wonka's simultaneously choose the number of chocolate bars they will make for sales during the next month. Willie's best-response function is graphed in panel (a) of Figure 13.4, while Wonka's best-response function is graphed in panel (b). Use this information to predict the quantity of chocolate bars each sells, and the resultant price.

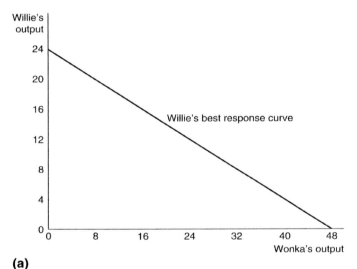

(a)

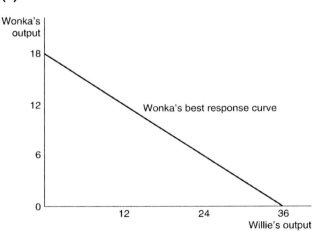

(b)

Figure 13.4

13. Now let's imagine that owing to a peculiar twist of fate, Willie's is able to choose its production of chocolate bars a week before Wonka's. Assume that the market demand for chocolate can be expressed as $p = 58 - Q$, where p is the price of chocolate bars, $Q = q_{\text{Willie}} + q_{\text{Wonka}}$ is total output, q_{Willie} is Willie's output, and q_{Wonka} is Wonka's output. Willie's costs are $TC_{\text{Willie}} = 10q_{\text{Willie}}$. Using this information along with the information on Wonka's best-response curve from Figure 13.4b, predict the quantity of chocolate bars each will sell, and the resultant price.

14. Although Centennial has a population of merely 100, it boasts two of the finest refreshment stands in the West: the Old Corral and the Trading Post. Once a week, the owner of each establishment calls up the local Sam's Club and orders their week's allotment of Sam's Finest Cola. Both stands get their cola from Sam's, and both are charged $1/bottle. Assume there are no other costs. (It's so cold in Centennial that you can chill the drink just by putting it in a snow bank out back.) The market demand for colas is $p = 4 - Q/40$, where p is the price a bottle of cola commands, and Q is the number of bottles sold. Total sales are the sum of the number of bottles sold by the Old Corral and the number of bottles sold by the Trading Post. Predict the number of bottles each bar will sell in a typical week, and the resultant market price.

15. Suppose Claire and Anne are the only producers of sweetheart hugs, a delightful new product guaranteed to put a smile on anyone's face. Claire and Anne use different packages for their sweetheart hugs, so while consumers regard the products as substitutes, they do not regard them as perfect substitutes. In fact, the demand curves for Claire and Anne are

$$q_C = 99 - p_C + 1/2p_A, \quad \text{and}$$
$$q_A = 110 + 1/3p_C - p_A.$$

Because of their innate charm, Claire and Anne are each capable of producing sweetheart hugs at no cost (hence their marginal costs are zero). Determine the Bertrand equilibrium in the sweetheart hugs market.

16. Suppose the bungee jumping market is an oligopoly with N firms. (Bungee jumping is a "recreational" experience where an elastic cord is tied to your feet and you jump off a very high bridge; before you crash on the ground or water below, the cord stops your fall, then pulls you back up into the air. Evidently, this experience is not for everyone.) The market demand for bungee jumps is $p = a - bQ$, where p is the price per jump and Q is the total number of jumps supplied by the industry. Each bungee jumping firm i faces the same costs, $TC_i = cq_i$, where q_i is the firm's output. Express each firm's Cournot equilibrium output of bungee jumps, the Cournot equilibrium price, and the resultant profits earned by each firm, in terms of the parameters a, b, c, and N.

■ Answers to Practice Problems

1. Oligopolists face downward-sloping demand curves if the market demand curve is downward sloping, so answer b is false. Oligopolists typically make positive economic profits, so answer c is incorrect. Unlike monopoly, oligopolies do not benefit from *large* entry barriers. Even so, they are generally protected from some entry. Thus, answer a is also wrong. The best answer is d.

2. In a Nash equilibrium, no player can obtain a higher payoff by choosing a different strategy, holding the other player's strategy fixed. For Frick and Frack, this means selecting that amount of gibberish that is in their own best interests, given the amount the other guy produced. Answer b is correct.

3. Monopolistically competitive markets are characterized by differentiated products—consumers believe that each firm's product is different from other firms' products. So the statement in answer a is correct; it is not false. With this product differentiation, no firm will lose all its sales if it raises its price slightly—every firm faces a downward-sloping demand curve. As with a monopoly, the downward-sloping demand curve here allows monopolistically competitive firms to charge a price greater than marginal cost. Thus, the statement in answer b is also correct; it is not false. Monopolistically competitive markets are also characterized by costless exit and entry. So just like perfectly competitive firms, if monopolistically competitive firms are continually bearing losses, they will exit. Answer c is not false. Ultimately, monopolistically competitive firms make zero economic profits, which means they charge a price that equals average cost. Unlike competitive firms, this price does not equal marginal cost, which means that the output monopolistically competitive firms produce does not equate average cost with marginal cost. Therefore the monopolistically competitive firm's output cannot minimize average costs: Answer d is false.

4. A dominant strategy is one an agent would pick no matter what its rivals do. The correct answer is c. While choosing a dominant strategy gives the best payoff for a fixed choice by the rival, this payoff need not be the largest possible. For example, collusive profits are commonly large relative to Cournot profits. But if firms must choose between equally splitting the monopoly output and producing the Cournot output, the latter is a dominant strategy.

5. As a general rule, we expect more dramatic competition when firms choose price as opposed to quantity. Correspondingly, we expect lower prices to emerge. Since each firm faces a downward-sloping demand curve, the lower prices imply larger outputs. The correct answer is b.

6. Answers and brief explanations follow.
    a. Red expects Green to make six pairs of gumboots, so if he makes three pairs he expects market price to be $16 - (6 + 3) = \$7$.
    b. If Red sells four pairs, he expects price to be $16 - (6 + 4) = \$6$.
    c. As a general rule, he expects price to equal $16 - (6 + q_{Rt}) = 10 - q_{Rt}$ this year.
    d. To maximize his profits, Red balances his marginal cost against the marginal revenue he expects to receive. Since he thinks he will get a price equal to $10 - q_{Rt}$, his anticipated total revenue is $TR = (10 - q_{Rt}) \times q_{Rt}$; his marginal revenue is $MR = dTR/dq_{Rt} = 10 - 2q_{Rt}$. So, Red maximizes his profit by solving $10 - 2q_{Rt} = 4$, or $q_{Rt} = 3$.
    e. Now Red thinks he will get a price equal to $16 - (4 + q_{Rt}) = 12 - q_{Rt}$. Here, Red's marginal revenue is $12 - 2q_{Rt}$, and his profits are maximized by setting $12 - 2q_{Rt} = 4$, or $q_{Rt} = 4$.

7. True. The firm's elasticity of demand is the percentage change in its output divided by the percentage change in price. The market price elasticity of demand is the percentage change in market output divided by the percentage change in price. Each Cournot firm takes all other firms' outputs as given. So for a given market price and market quantity, the Cournot firm believes it will cause a one-unit change in market output for each one-unit change in its own output. Since its production is necessarily less than market output, the percentage change in the firm's output is smaller than the percentage change in market output (associated with a small change in the firm's production). But the change in market price is the same whether market output changes by a given amount or if the firm's output changes by that same amount. For a fixed change in output (be it from the firm or from the market as a whole), the percentage change in price is the same. However, the percentage change in the firm's output is larger than the percentage change in market output. Since the numerator of the firm's price elasticity is larger than the numerator of the market price elasticity, while the two denominators are the same, the ratio is larger for the firm than for the market: The Cournot firm's price elasticity of demand is larger smaller in magnitude than the market price elasticity of demand. In other words, its demand curve is less elastic than market demand.

8. True. In deciding whether to participate in a cartel, each firm compares the flow of profits it can earn by colluding with the flow of profits it can earn if it cheats on the cartel. These latter profits include a one-time gain—when a firm cheats, it steals away a fair bit of business from other members of the cartel, which raises the cheating firm's profits, perhaps dramatically. But the cartel then disintegrates, leaving all firms (including the cheater) with lower profits forever after. Successful cartels must offer member firms large enough profit flows to dissuade cheating. One purpose of antitrust policy is to lower the benefits of sticking with the cartel by threatening large punishments. For antitrust policy to successfully deter firms from forming a cartel it is sufficient that firms believe the collusive profits (netting out the anticipated fines associated with conviction) are small enough to make cheating look attractive. The necessary impact on collusive profits can be accomplished by making the anticipated penalty large, either by convicting everyone (and using a modest penalty) or by convicting a few (and using an enormous penalty).

9. Ambiguous. Since monopolistically competitive markets have free entry, firms will enter if existing firms are making positive *economic* profits. Because economic profits are the difference between accounting profits and the opportunity cost of the owner's time and the money invested in the business, positive accounting profits can yield positive, zero, or negative economic profits. Thus firms could be encouraged to enter if accounting profits are positive, but it is also possible that they would not want to enter.

10. True. In the Cournot model, the firms produce homogeneous products, so that market price depends on the sum of their outputs. For firm 1, marginal revenue can be written as $MR_1 = P + q_1 dP/dQ$; similarly, marginal revenue for firm 2 is $MR_2 = P + q_2 dP/dQ$. Therefore, if the firms produce the same amount they would have the same marginal revenue. At the Cournot equilibrium, $MR_1 = MC_1$ and $MR_2 = MC_2$; for the Cournot equilibrium to entail identical levels of production by the two firms they would have to have identical marginal costs. Since they have different marginal costs their Cournot equilibrium outputs must not be the same.

11. First, let's look at North Dakota's optimal decision. If they think South Dakota won't build an industrial park, North Dakota can be certain of attracting Out-tel by building a park. Since attracting Out-tel is worth $3 million and the park costs $1 million to build, North Dakota will receive a payoff of $2 million. If North Dakota does not build the park, they have a 50 percent chance of attracting Out-tel, which is worth $3 million, and a 50 percent chance of getting nothing. The average of these two values is $1.5 million. Because there are no costs when the park isn't built, North Dakota's net gain is $1.5 million. Because this is less than $2 million, North Dakota is better off building an industrial park if they think South Dakota won't build a park. If North Dakota's thinks South Dakota will build an industrial park, North Dakota will expect a net gain of $0.5 million if they build a park. (There is a 50 percent chance they can attract Out-tel, and so receive $3 million in benefits, and a 50 percent chance they will receive nothing, so the park is expected to bring benefits of $1.5 million. Since building the park costs $1 million, the anticipated gain is $0.5 million.) If North Dakota doesn't build the park they get no benefits (South Dakota will attract Out-tel), but they bear no costs. Hence their payoff is $0. Since something ($0.5 million) is better than nothing, North Dakota will build an industrial park even if they think South Dakota is going to build a park. That is, building is a dominant strategy for North Dakota. South Dakota's incentives are exactly the same as North Dakota's incentives. They stand to gain by building the park whether they expect North Dakota to build or not. If they think North Dakota won't build an industrial park, South Dakota can guarantee a payoff of $2 million by building ($3 million in benefits less $1 million in building costs). If they don't build, they expect a payoff of $1.5 million (the average of $3 million if they get the park and nothing if they don't). They are better off building. If they think North Dakota will build a park, South Dakota expects a payoff of $0.5 million by building (the $1.5 benefits that represent the average of $3 million and nothing), less the $1 million building costs. They get nothing if they don't build. Again they are better off by building. Since deciding to build the industrial park is a dominant strategy for both North Dakota and South Dakota, both states will decide to build a park.

12. To use the information in both panels (a) and (b) of Figure 13.4, we need to use the same value on the x-axis. Either "flip" panel (b) to place Wonka's output on the x-axis for each diagram, or flip panel (a) to place Willie's output on the x-axis for each diagram. Figure 13.5 is constructed by flipping panel (a). The equilibrium combination of chocolate bars is found at the intersection of the two best-response functions, which gives outputs of 20 cases of chocolate bars for Willie's and 8 cases for Wonka's.

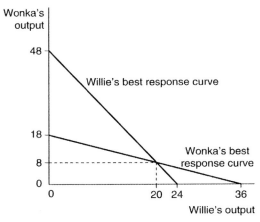

Figure 13.5

13. Because Willie's gets to select their quantity of chocolate bars before Wonka's, Willie's is a Stackelberg leader. To determine the quantity of chocolate bars that each firm will sell in the Stackelberg equilibrium, we need to determine Wonka's best-response curve. Using the information from Figure 13.4b, we see that Wonka would produce 18 if Willie produced 0, and that Wonka would produce 0 if Willie produced 36. Thus, Wonka's best-response curve is $q_{Wonka} = 18 - \frac{1}{2} q_{Willie}$. Combining with the market demand information, we have $p = 58 - q_{Willie} - (18 - \frac{1}{2} q_{Willie})$. Thus, Willie's profits can be expressed as $\pi_{Willie} = (40 - \frac{1}{2} q_{Willie}) q_{Willie} - 10 q_{Willie}$. To maximize his profits, Willie solves $d\pi_{Willie}/dq_{Willie} = 0$, or $40 - q_{Willie} - 10 = 0$. Thus, at the Stackelberg equilibrium, Willie produces 30 cases, and Wonka produces $18 - 1/2 (30) = 3$ cases; market price is $25.

14. Because the two stands select their output for the week at the same time, the appropriate model to apply is the Cournot model. We need two quantities, one for each stand, such that each stand is maximizing its profits given the number of bottles of cola the other stand has decided to sell. Let q_{OC} denote the number of bottles sold by the Old Corral, and q_{TP} denote the number of bottles sold by the Trading Post. As market demand is $p = 4 - Q/40$, the Old Corral thinks it faces the demand curve $p = 4 - q_{TP}/40 - q_{OC}/40$. Since the Old Corral's costs are the wholesale costs of $1/bottle, its costs are so each stand's marginal costs are constant at $1. The Old Corral's costs are q_{OC}. Thus the Old Corral's profit function is $\pi_{OC}(q_{OC}, q_{TP}) = (4 - q_{TP}/40 - q_{OC}/40)q_{OC} - q_{OC}$. To maximize its profits, the Old Corral solves $\partial\pi_{OC}(q_{OC}, q_{TP})/\partial q_{OC} = 0$, or

$$4 - q_{TP}/40 - q_{OC}/40 - q_{OC}/40 - 1 = 0.$$

This expression may be simplified to

$$q_{OC} = 60 - q_{TP}/2,$$

which is the Old Corral's best-response curve. Applying the same reasoning to the Trading Post's decision, we find the amount they will sell, in terms of the number of bottles they predict the Old Corral will sell:

$$q_{TP} = 60 - q_{OC}/2.$$

This relation gives the Trading Post's best-response curve. At the Cournot equilibrium, each of these equations must be satisfied. Upon substituting the expression from the Trading Post's best-response curve into the formula for the Old Corral's best-response curve, we find the Old Corral's Cournot equilibrium output

$$q_{oc} = 60 - [60 - q_{oc}/2]/2,$$

or $q_{oc} = 40$. Inserting the Old Corral's Cournot equilibrium output into the formula for the Trading Post's best-response curve, we find that the Trading Post's Cournot equilibrium output also equals 40. Finally, we determine price by summing these outputs and inserting into the market demand curve. The combined output is 80 bottles of cola, so that the Cournot equilibrium yields a price equal to $2.

15. To determine the Bertrand equilibrium in sweetheart hugs, we first find Claire and Anne's best response functions. Since Claire's marginal cost is zero, the marginal effect on her profits from a small change in price equals

$$d\pi_c/dp_c = q_c + p_c \times dq_c/dp_c$$

Using the formula for Claire's demand curve, and noting that $dq_c/dp_c = -1$, we find that Claire maximizes her profits by solving:

$$99 - 2p_c + 1/2p_A = 0, \quad \text{or}$$
$$p_c = 49.5 + 1/4p_A.$$

As Anne's marginal cost is also zero, the marginal effect on her profits from a small change in price is

$$d\pi_A/dp_A = q_A + p_A dq_A/dp_A.$$

Using the formula for Anne's demand curve, and noting that $dq_A/dp_A = -1$, we find that Anne maximizes her profits by solving:

$$110 - 2p_A + 1/3p_c = 0, \quad \text{or}$$
$$p_A = 55 + 1/6p_c.$$

Combining these two best-response functions, we get: $p_c = 49.5 + 1/4[55 + 1/6p_c]$, or $23p_c/24 = 63.25$. Therefore, Claire's Bertrand equilibrium price is $p_c = \$66$. Insert $p_c = 66$ into Anne's best-response function to find Anne's price: $p_A = 55 + 1/6(66) = \$66$.

16. Since each firm's costs are $TC_i = cq_i$, and $p = a - bQ$, each firm i has profits of $\pi_i = (a - bQ)q_i - cq_i$. To maximize its profits, firm i solves $\partial\pi_i/\partial q_i = 0$. Thus, we have

$$a - bQ - bq_i - c = 0$$

for each firm. Since the firms all have the same marginal cost they also share the same Cournot equilibrium output, q^*, and so $Q = Nq^*$. Accordingly, each firm's Cournot equilibrium output solves

$$a - c - bNq^* - bq^* = 0, \quad \text{or}$$
$$a - c - [b(N + 1)] \times q^* = 0.$$

It follows that the common Cournot equilibrium output is $q^* = (a - c)/[b \times (N + 1)]$. Market price is therefore

$$p^* = a - bQ = a - b \times N \times q^*$$
$$= a - b \times N \times (a - c)/[b \times (N + 1)]$$
$$= (a + N \times c)/(N + 1).$$

Each firm's profit is $p^* q^* - cq^*$, which can be simplified to $(p^* - c) \times q^*$. Subtracting c from the expression for p^* above gives

$$p^* - c = (a + N \times c)/(N + 1) - c$$
$$= (a + N \times c)/(N + 1) - c \times (N + 1)/(N + 1)$$
$$= (a - c)/(N + 1).$$

Thus each firm's Cournot equilibrium profit equals

$$(p^* - c) \times q^* = (a - c)/(N + 1) \times (a - c)/[b \times (N + 1)]$$
$$= (a - c)^2/[b \times (N + 1)^2].$$

■ Exercises

Fill-in

1. Suppose that the market demand for bamboo is given by $p = 70 - Q$, where Q is the total amount supplied by firms in the industry. Each firm in the bamboo industry bears marginal costs of 10 and fixed costs of 125.
   a. If there are three firms in the bamboo industry, each will produce _____ units of bamboo in the Cournot equilibrium and earn profits equal to _____.
   b. If there are four firms in the bamboo industry, each will produce _____ units of bamboo in the Cournot equilibrium and earn profits equal to _____.
   c. If there are five firms in the bamboo industry, each will produce _____ units of bamboo in the Cournot equilibrium and earn profits equal to _____.
   d. If entry and exit were free, how many firms would you expect to sell bamboo? _____.

True-False-Ambiguous and Explain Why

2. Suppose there are only two firms in a market. Since these firms can collectively earn monopoly profits either by colluding or by merging, there is no point in preventing them from merging.

3. We expect monopolistically competitive firms to select outputs that result in excess capacity.

Short-Answer

4. How well do the states fare in the Out-tel problem (Practice Problem 11)? Is there a different outcome that makes both states better off? Why don't they reach that outcome?

5. Let's reconsider the *Time* and *Newsweek* example, from Solved Problem 1. As before, each magazine must select a cover story from the three good stories available: They can discuss a recent minor breakthrough in AIDS research, the debate over current budget impasse, or a major flood that has just ravaged the Midwest. Also as before, the payoff table for *Newsweek* and *Time* is:

		Newsweek's choice		
		AIDS	**Budget**	**Flood**
Time's Choice	AIDS	1, 1	3, 7	2, 6
	Budget	10, 2	1, 1	4, 3
	Flood	8, 3	7, 2	1, 1

Now, assume that *Time* can select their cover story the day before *Newsweek*, and that *Newsweek* will know *Time's* choice when they make their decision. Determine *Time* and *Newsweek's* equilibrium choices.

6. When OPEC decided to substantially raise their annual production quotas in 1997, one group of pundits argued that no member states would change their production levels. How does this argument relate to the stability of cartels?

7. There are two espresso shops in the town of Perkasie, PA: Turtle Rock and Moonbeam's coffee. Each shop claims to have the best cappuccino in town. Each morning, the two shops set their price for the day at exactly 8 AM and then open their doors. Each firm will set one of four prices, as described in the following table. The table describes the profit each seller can earn for the day, at each of the possible combinations of price. Determine the Bertrand equilibrium.

		Moonbeam's price			
		2.10	**2.15**	**2.20**	**2.25**
	1.80	1110,1024	112,1023	1135,1020	1130,1015
Turtle	2.00	1125,1088	1138,1089	1150,1088	1155,1085
Rock's	2.20	1105,1152	1126,1155	1145,1156	1170,1155
price	2.40	1080,1216	1113,1221	1135,1224	1150,1225

8. Now suppose that the owner of Turtle Rock gets up 15 minutes earlier, and so chooses its price before Moonbeam's. What combination of prices do the two sellers charge now? How do their profits change, relative to the Bertrand equilibrium discussed in exercise 7?

9. Once upon a time, there was a "wannabe" football league called the United States Football League (USFL). USFL wanted very much to be successful, but they had a big problem. Most American football fans have a deep emotional attachment to the National Football League (NFL). USFL had to choose between playing their games in the fall or the spring. The fall market is the biggest, so each league does best if it plays in the fall while the other league plays in the spring. If NFL chooses to play in the fall, USFL does better to play in the spring. The worst possible outcome for the USFL would be if both leagues moved to a spring schedule. If USFL plays in the fall, NFL is better off also playing in the fall. Construct a payoff table to describe this interaction, and discuss the likely season choice for each league.

10. Find the Cournot equilibrium in the gumboot market discussed in Practice Problem 6.

11. A popular measure for determining the "concentration" of market power within an oligopoly is the *Herfindahl Index*. The Herfindahl Index equals the sum over all firms in an industry of their market shares squared. (For example, if there are two firms, one producing 60 percent of market output and the other producing 40 percent, the Herfindahl Index is $40^2 + 60^2 = 5200$.)

   a. Give a relation between the profits earned by a firm at the Cournot equilibrium in Practice Problem 16 and the firm's output.

   b. Give a relation between a firm's market share at the Cournot equilibrium, the firm's output, and industry output.

   c. Using your answers to parts a and b, give an expression for the Herfindahl Index.

   d. All else equal, what do you think happens to the Herfindahl Index as the number of firms increases?

12. Cliff and Joe are the only producers of genuine Yellowstone spring water. Yellowstone spring water is fabulously popular, with market demand given by $p = 200 - Q^2$, where Q is the total number of Yellowstone spring water bottles available. Cliff and Joe obtained their enviable position by purchasing the rights to all the water they can bottle from the natural spring in the town of Big Springs. For these rights, Cliff paid $200 and Joe paid $250. To produce one bottle of Yellowstone spring water, all either Cliff or Joe has to do is dip a bottle in the spring. Correspondingly, neither Cliff nor Joe bears any variable costs.

   a. Produce expressions for Cliff's best-response curve and Joe's best-response curve.

   b. Find the Cournot equilibrium outputs for Cliff and Joe, and their resultant profits.

   c. Suppose the town fathers of Big Springs decide to charge Cliff and Joe an extra $175. Does this change the Cournot equilibrium? If so, how?

   d. Suppose the town fathers of Big Springs decide to charge Cliff and Joe an extra $275. Does this change the Cournot equilibrium? If so, how?

   e. Upon further reflection, the town fathers decide not to use a flat tax (of the sort in parts c and d). Instead, they tax Cliff and Joe $72 for each bottle produced. How does this change the Cournot equilibrium?

   f. How does your answer to part e change if the per-unit tax were combined with a $10 flat tax?

Chapter 14
Game Theory

■ Chapter Summary

In many important settings, a small number of individuals interact. In such a setting, it is highly likely that any one individual's outcome is partially influenced by the other participants' actions. When a small number of individuals interact, with any one player's reward depending on other participants' actions, there is strategic interaction. Examples abound in economics, but are also relevant in fields such as political science. Game theory is the study of **strategic behavior**. Game theory can be used to analyze situations where the individuals only interact once, or where they interact repeatedly. The former situation is called a **static game**, while the latter is a **dynamic game**. In static games, individuals take their actions simultaneously—so players cannot base their actions on other players' actions. In this setting, special attention is devoted to a combination of actions where no one player can improve his or her situation by a unilaterally changing behavior. Such a combination of actions is called a **Nash equilibrium**. In dynamic games, actions taken later on in the game are quite likely to be based on observed actions taken earlier. In games with such a sequential structure, later decisions can be influenced by earlier decisions. Understanding this potential, individuals are likely to take actions that are linked to other participants' battle plans, or **strategies**. A strategy involves planned actions for any possible contingency within the dynamic game. If these planned actions would be in the party's best interests were the contingency to actually occur, then the planned action is **credible**. A strategy combination where the planned actions are credible for each of the players is called a **subgame perfect Nash equilibrium**. To ensure that planned actions in a dynamic game are credible, one looks at behavior in the final stage of the game. This behavior is tied to earlier actions in a way that is in the decision maker's best interests. Then, move back one stage and ask how *that* decision maker should behave, in light of the anticipated behavior at the final stage. An implicit assumption that underlies this analysis is that decision makers are *rational*. Not only must agents take actions that are strictly in their best interests, they must all know that *everyone else* acts in a purely self-interested way, too. The process of identifying credible actions in the last stage of a dynamic game, then seeing what implications those actions have for credible play in the next-to-last stage, and then the stage before that, and so on, is called *backwards induction*. Using the technique of backwards induction allows one to derive a subgame perfect Nash equilibrium.

Suppose two firms have independently identified a profitable business opportunity, but that the stakes are small enough that they would each lose money if they both undertook the opportunity. Shuttle commuter service between a small outlying airport and a larger metropolitan airport could be one example; expending money on a speculative new drug might be another. The new opportunity has the characteristics of a natural monopoly—there is only enough room for one firm to make money. If each firm decides to enter, each loses money; if each decides to stay out, each misses out. In this game, there are two possible *pure strategy* Nash equilibria, where one firm enters and one firm does not. Despite the fact that the firms decide whether or not to enter at the same time, one firm is effectively prevented from entering. One difficulty with the pure strategy equilibria in this game is that there is no obvious way for the firms to know who is going to enter and who is going to stay out. Since they have exactly the same motivations, why should either kowtow? One way to resolve this dilemma is to allow each firm to randomly decide its course of action, that is, to play *mixed strategies*. With mixed strategies, each firm stands a chance of becoming the monopolist. On the flip side of the entry issue, if both firms found themselves slugging it out in a natural monopoly, how would they decide which firm should exit? One resolution is for each firm to choose a mixed strategy ("maybe I'll exit, and maybe I'll stay").

Suppose one firm has obtained a foothold in an industry and wishes to keep other firms from entering. Perhaps the incumbent firm can commit today to the output it will produce after entry, or maybe it can influence production costs so as to make entry unpalatable. Either type of action would induce a benefit for the incumbent because of its ability to take an action prior to the potential entrant. This situation is an example of a first-mover advantage. Players who go first in a dynamic game are not always better off, however: imagine you are playing a game of *matching pennies* with a friend. Both of you must show either heads or tails on your coin; if the faces of the two coins match, you get your friend's coin, otherwise he gets yours. If you go first, and he sees your action, you will certainly lose.

A particularly interesting form of strategic interaction, and one where players typically do not know something important about their rival players' motivations, is an **auction**. Auctions come in many types: they can involve repeated, publicly announced bids or sealed bids; they can involve increasing prices or decreasing prices. Many auctions involve increasing, publicly announced bids. Auctions on eBay are an example of this type of institution. If the auction involves an item with the same intrinsic value to everyone, for example a plot of land that may contain a deposit of a valuable mineral, the auction is **common value**. If each bidder places his or her own intrinsic value on the item, the auction is **private value**. An important concern in common value auctions is that the winning bidder is most likely more optimistic about the item's value than all the other bidders. In such a scenario, there is a legitimate concern that the winning bidder may have been too optimistic, and that the true value of the item is smaller than the winning bidder predicted, so that the winner may have paid more than the item was worth. This phenomenon is known as the *winner's curse*.

■ Key Concepts and Formulas

- **Static game:** a strategic interaction where players only act once, and all players move simultaneously.
- **Dynamic game:** a strategic interaction where players only more than once, or where players do not move simultaneously.
- **Nash equilibrium:** a combination of strategies with the property that no one player can make him or herself better off by unilaterally changing strategies.
- **Credible threat:** a threatened response that would be in the agent's best interest, should circumstances call on the agent to follow through.
- **Subgame perfect Nash equilibrium:** a combination of strategies with the property that each player's strategy contains only credible threats.

■ Application: Airline Predation

In April 1998, the U.S. Department of Transportation (DOT) proposed new guidelines regarding "anticompetitive" activities in the airline industry. The principal concern was that incumbent carriers responded to small-scale entrants by radically increasing the number of flights and seating capacity and slashing prices on those lines contested by the entrant. The goal of this behavior was allegedly the destruction of the new firm and the creation of a business environment nonconducive to future entry, as stated in the DOT's proposed policy:

> When small, new-entrant carriers have instituted new low-fare service in major carriers' local hub markets, the major carriers have increasingly responded with strategies of price reductions and capacity increases designed not to maximize their own profits, but rather to deprive the new entrants of vital traffic and revenues.

A leading example of the type of interactions in question is the conflict between United Airlines and Frontier Airlines. Both use Denver as a major hub, so the two carriers compete head-to-head on a number of routes. On two of these routes, between Denver and Phoenix and between Denver and Los Angeles, United sharply increased its seating capacity during the period from mid-1995 to mid-1996 (by 30 percent on the former route, and 24 percent on the latter route).

Question: Why would United increase the number of flights on routes where it competes with Frontier if this lowered its profits? How might this adversely impact Frontier? What are the welfare implications of United's actions?

Answer: One possible motivation for increasing the number of flights out of Denver International Airport (DIA) is to raise marginal costs, both for United and Frontier. All else equal, with more flights going out of an airport, the runways get more crowded, departures are slower, and landing slots are more costly. All these features suggest that flights are more expensive to run out of DIA if the number of flights goes way up. On the other hand, increased traffic can generate some benefits for United, since many of its customers must make connections through Denver. Because it serves many routes to many destinations, the extra service through DIA makes United more appealing and can raise its demand for service between other cities (e.g., flights between San Francisco and Chicago). These benefits are more important to a larger carrier such as United, who can offer greater networking to its customers, than to a smaller carrier like Frontier. As such, the external benefits blunt the impact of higher departure costs for United, but probably not for Frontier. The issue seems to be one of raising a rival's costs. An illustration of this phenomenon is presented in Figure 14.1. Prior to United's actions, its reaction curve is R_U, while Frontier's reaction curve is R_F. These reaction curves are based on a model where firms choose outputs, though the issues are much the same if firms choose prices.

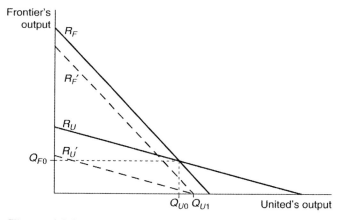

Figure 14.1

Each firm's reaction curve represents its profit-maximizing output, given the output it anticipates the rival firm will choose. These profit-maximizing outputs are based on the firm's demand and cost conditions. Now suppose United increases the number of flights out of DIA, which raises both its costs and Frontier's costs. Because United has many more flights, the increased cost would appear to impact United more dramatically. But the extra flights also raise United's demand on routes where it does not compete with Frontier, generating extra profit. These outside benefits effectively create an incentive for United to increase sales, relative to the initial effect from higher costs. While United's reaction curve shifts in to R'_U, Frontier's reaction curve also shifts in, to R'_F, and the shift in Frontier's reaction curve is more pronounced. If the differential impact on reaction curves is large enough, as in Figure 14.1, the new equilibrium has Frontier dropping out of the market altogether. United trades its earlier dominant position in the DIA market for a monopoly position, albeit with a higher cost.

The welfare implications of United's actions are mixed. On one hand, the reduction in the number of carriers and the artificial increase in costs are both negative effects. On the other hand, the increase in service by the carrier with numerous connecting flights is good. To a large extent, the costs from the elimination of Frontier are likely to be borne by passengers flying between Denver and the small number of cities Frontier used to serve. The benefits from increased connection options are most likely to be realized by passengers traveling through Denver. Weighing these two effects is not simple, so the welfare effects are ambiguous. One important concern is that United might reduce its traffic after Frontier leaves. This seems unlikely, however, since it is the increased flow in and out of DIA that makes competition with United so unappetizing. If United reacted to Frontier's exit by curtailing flights, they would likely be faced with new entry in the near future. To convince any potential entrants that they would lose from entry, United needs a credible commitment, such as locking in a large number of flights in and out of DIA.

■ Solved Problems

1. Back in Centennial, things aren't looking so good for the refreshment stands we visited in Practice Problem 14 of Chapter 13. The Centennial Quilt Guild has convinced the city council to levy a weekly tax of $70 on both stands. Since this tax does not depend on the number of bottles sold, it is a fixed cost; however, either stand could avoid the tax by shutting its doors. As in the earlier analysis, the market demand for cola is $p = 4 - Q/40$, where Q is the number of bottles sold during the week, and marginal cost is constant at $1 for each vendor. What will happen to this industry—how many firms will remain, and how will the vendors decide who remains?

    Step 1: Describe the new duopoly equilibrium.
    Because market demand and firms' marginal costs are the same as in Practice Problem 14 of Chapter 13, so is the Cournot equilibrium. Each firm sells 40 bottles, so that market price is $2. Unlike the earlier analysis, the two stands do not make money in this problem. Their revenues are the same ($80 = $2 × 40 bottles), and their variable costs are the same ($40 = $1 × 40 bottles), but now they also bear fixed costs of $70. So duopoly profits are −$30.

    Step 2: Describe the equilibrium if one firm exits.
    Since the two firms have identical costs, they would make identical profit as monopolists. As market demand is linear with slope −1/40, market marginal revenue is also linear, but with slope −1/20. Hence the monopoly output is 60, where MR (= $4 - Q/20$) equals MC (= 1). The associated monopoly price is $2.50 (= 4 − 60/40), and monopoly profit is $20 (= $2.50 × 60 − $1 × 60 − $70).

    Step 3: Describe the profit matrix for the two stands' choices between staying in the market and exiting.
    Each stand bears losses of $30 if both stay in; each makes no profit if they exit, and a lone remaining firm would make monopoly profit of $20. So the profit matrix is

		Old Corral's Choice	
		Stay In	**Stay Out**
Trading Post's Choice	Stay In	−30, −30	20, 0
	Stay Out	0, 20	0, 0

    where the first number in each cell is the profit earned by the Trading Post and the second number is the Old Corral's profit.

Step 4: Determine the Nash equilibrium actions.

Each bar prefers to be the lone remaining monopolist, so they would stay if the other firm exited. But it is also true that each bar prefers exit to losing money as a duopolist. So we have two pure strategy equilibria: one where the Trading Post stays in while the Old Corral exits, and one where the Trading Post exits while the Old Corral stays in. Plainly, identifying the firm that should exit is problematic here.

Step 5: Determine the mixed strategy Nash equilibrium.

One way to resolve the difficulty of finding the exiting firm when incentives are symmetric is to appeal to a mixed strategy Nash equilibrium. In a mixed strategy equilibrium, both firms are indifferent between each action. So the anticipated profits to be had by staying must equal the certain profit (of $0) that may be had by exiting. If we let ρ represent the probability that the Trading Post will exit, the anticipated profits that the Old Corral can earn by staying are $\rho \times 20 + (1 - \rho) \times (-30) = -30 + 50\rho$. For the Old Corral to be indifferent between staying and exiting, these anticipated profits must equal 0, the certain profit from exit. We conclude that $\rho = 3/5$: The Trading Post must decide it will exit about 60 percent of the time. Next, we look at things from the Trading Post's perspective. Since their incentives are exactly the same as the Old Corral's, we find that the probability the Old Corral will exit is also 3/5. In the mixed strategy equilibrium, neither stand is certain who will remain. There is a chance that both will stay, though this chance ($0.16 = 2/5 \times 2/5$) is fairly small. There is also a chance that both will exit ($0.36 = 3/5 \times 3/5$); this is slightly more likely than both stands staying. About half the time ($0.48 = 1 - [0.16 + 0.36]$), one stand will stay and one will go.

2.   Among the great proliferation of bakeries, you will find some with truly exceptional food, while others bakeries are less impressive. Aside from differences in their chefs' innate skills, one plausible explanation for this difference in quality is experience. Those who have been in business longer are likely to be more efficient. With this extra efficiency comes the ability to serve baked goods at lower cost: it just takes longer for a less experienced baker to get things right. At present, the Medicine Bow Bread Company (MBBC) is the only decent bakery in the small town of Basalt, but rumor has it a second high-class joint (Oil Sludge Baking, or OSB) is thinking about opening up next month. Does it pay MBBC to produce more than its monopoly level this month?

Step 1: Draw the game tree for MBBC's problem.

To this end, we need to lay out the various actions that are available to the two bakeries. This month, MBBC can produce either the monopoly level (Q_M) or the higher level (Q_H). Then OSB can decide to enter or stay out. If they enter, the two bakeries will play a Cournot game next month. If they do not enter, MBBC gets to pick its monopoly output next month. Essentially, there are only four combinations of interest: MBBC picks Q_M and OSB enters; MBBC picks Q_M and OSB stays out; MBBC picks Q_H and OSB enters; and MBBC picks Q_H and OSB stays out. A game tree that captures these combinations is presented in Figure 14.2. At each end node of the game tree, the number after the comma represents OSB's profit, while the sum of numbers before the comma represents MBBC's profit. The first number in the sum is MBBC's profit this month, and the second number is MBBC's profit next month. (Because of the experience MBBC gains this month, their costs are much lower next month, and their profits are correspondingly much larger.)

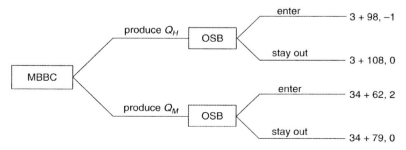

Figure 14.2

Step 2: Determine OSB's optimal entry decision.

Since OSB can ensure itself of zero profit by staying out, it will only enter if it can make positive profits. If MBBC produces high output this month, OSB cannot make positive profit next month and so will not enter. But if MBBC produces the monopoly output this month, OSB can make positive profit (equal to $2) in the Cournot equilibrium, so it will enter.

Step 3: Determine MBBC's best output choice this month.

MBBC's decision this month depends on its current profit and the profit it will earn next month, based on OSB's entry decision. By producing Q_H this month, MBBC assures itself of monopoly profit next month, but it also lowers current profit. By producing Q_M this month, MBBC gets the largest possible current profit but it must accept entry, and it will realize a smaller reduction in next month's costs (associated with the lesser amount of experience). So MBBC's decision to produce Q_H this month is linked to a comparison of the increased profit next month against the decreased profit this month. Based on the game tree in Figure 14.2, MBBC gains more next month (108 vs. 62) than it loses this month (34 vs. 3) if it produces Q_H, so it will raise its current output and deter entry. Had the loss this month been more dramatic, say, from 34 to −15, MBBC would prefer *not* to increase current output above the monopoly level. A more dramatic first period loss might occur if it took a larger increase in current output to lower next month's marginal costs.

■ Practice Problems

Multiple-Choice

1. Two firms (Agnes' and Zelda's) are considering entry into a new market. Early indications are that this market will be a natural monopoly, so that each will lose money if both enter. Which of the following combinations is a Nash equilibrium?
   a. Agnes' enters and Zelda's stays out.
   b. Agnes' stays out and Zelda's enters.
   c. Agnes' and Zelda's each enter with some probability between zero and one.
   d. All of the above can be a Nash equilibrium.

2. The market for gumdrops is currently served by Gumby's, a monopoly. Market demand for gumdrops is given by $p = 48 - Q$, where Q is market output of gumdrops. Licorice Licks, Inc. is considering entering the gumdrop market. Entry entails a one-time cost of $70; there are no other costs for either firm. If Gumby's can set their output prior to Licorice Licks' entry decision, which output will Gumby's select?
   a. 24
   b. 32
   c. 42
   d. Either *a* or *b* could be correct.

3. Suppose Licorice Licks' entry cost was $10, not $70. Which of the following outputs will Gumby's select?
   a. 24
   b. 32
   c. 42
   d. Either a or c could be correct.

4. Here is a third variation on the gumdrop market question. Suppose that Gumby's can't commit to an output prior to Licorice Licks' entry decision; they can, however, select an advertising level prior to entry. If Gumby's uses an advertising blitz before Licorice Licks' entry decision, which of the following is *most* likely?

   a. Advertising by either firm will raise *market* demand for gumdrops.

   b. Gumby's uses this advertising blitz in hopes that Licorice Licks will respond by also advertising heavily.

   c. Advertising by either firm will raise *its* demand for gumdrops, while lowering its rivals' demand.

   d. There is not enough information to determine which of a, b, or c is most likely.

Fill-in

5. At present, Coal Creek Coffee Co. (CCCC) is the only purveyor of espresso drinks in Coffeeville. But the locals' interest in double-mocha-cappuccino-latte-grandes is such that Moonbucks, Inc., that well-known seller of corporate cappuccino, is considering entering the market. Entry into this local market will cost Moonbucks $1,089; moreover, CCCC is able to commit to a price in advance of Moonbucks' entry decision. If Moonbucks enters the Coffeeville market, they will choose a price in response to CCCC's price. Because of differences in name recognition and ambience, the typical caffeine seeker regards these two sellers as imperfect substitutes; the payoff matrix describing the profits that the two sellers will earn for various combinations of prices is given in the table below. (The first number represents CCCC's profit, while the second number is Moonbucks' profit.) However, if Moonbucks does not enter, CCCC will remain a monopolist, with demand curve $Q = 980 - 100p$, where Q is the number of cups of cappuccino sold. CCCC's marginal cost is $.50/cup.

   a. If CCCC sets a price of $1.80, Moonbucks will set a price of _____ if they enter, and earn a profit of _____ (net of the entry cost).

   b. If CCCC sets a price of $2, Moonbucks will set a price of _____ if they enter, and earn a profit of _____ (net of the entry cost).

   c. If CCCC sets a price of $2.20, Moonbucks will set a price of _____ if they enter, and earn a profit of _____ (net of the entry cost).

   d. If CCCC sets a price of $2.40, Moonbucks will set a price of _____ if they enter, and earn a profit of _____ (net of the entry cost).

   e. CCCC's profits at the four prices it can charge are ___, _____, _____, and _____.

   f. CCCC's optimal price is _____, and entry _____ occur.

   g. If the entry cost were $1024, CCCC's optimal price would be _____, and entry _____ occur.

| | **Moonbucks' Price** | | | |
	2.10	2.15	2.20	2.25
1.80	1066, 1024	1079, 1023	1092, 1020	1105, 1015
2.00	1110, 1088	1125, 1089	1140, 1088	1155, 1085
2.20	1122, 1152	1139, 1155	1156, 1156	1173, 1155
2.40	1102, 1216	1121, 1221	1140, 1224	1159, 1225

CCC's Price

True-False-Ambiguous and Explain Why

6. At the start of the semester a professor hands out a syllabus describing her grading policy. A student, realizing he has enough credit to earn a B, refuses to turn in a term paper for the course. The professor threatens to flunk the student unless he writes and submits a term paper. The professor's threat is credible.

7. An incumbent monopolist is earning economic profits of $500. A second firm can enter this market, but entry costs $400. We may conclude that entry will occur.

8. Firms in the cigarette industry rely heavily upon advertising to boost their sales, often promoting specific brands of smokes. If cigarette companies could not sell branded cigarettes—only generic cigarettes—individual companies would still advertise.

Short-Answer

9. Two pharmaceutical firms are considering a research program for a new drug. A successful R&D program will create a monopoly, since there are presently no close substitutes for this potential drug. However, before it can conduct an R&D program, a firm must hire a staff of chemists. The potential monopoly profit that will accrue to the winning firm exceeds the wages associated with hiring this staff, but is less than double these wages. Write out a payoff matrix for the R&D race, and predict the outcome of this game.

10. In the classic film *Rebel Without a Cause,* James Dean's character Jimmy engages in a "Chickie Run" with Buzz. Each drives a car towards a cliff overlooking the Pacific Ocean; whoever leaps out of his car first is the loser. To think about what is going on in this game, let's suppose that each guy has two possible actions: jump or wait. The payoff to waiting if the other guy jumps is large, since you "win;" let's say this payoff is 7. However, the payoff to waiting if the other guy waits is small—you both go over the cliff!—so let's say this payoff is −5. If both jump, nothing is lost and nothing is won, so this payoff is 0. Finally, if you jump while the other guy waits you lose face, so your payoff is small, let's say −3. What are the Nash equilibria to this Chickie Run game?

11. Panel (a) in Figures 14.5 and 14.6 in the text show a potential entrant's best-response curve when the incumbent can precommit to a large output, and entry requires payment of a fixed cost. Suppose instead that the incumbent can precommit to a price, but not an output. Show the effect on the entrant's best-response curve, and discuss the incumbent's pricing decision.

12. The market for corndogs is remarkable: Consumers demand 100 of these meals on a stick and will pay any price up to $1.50 for them. There are two firms currently selling corndogs, Bow-Wow Beef and Corny's Copia. Because of the curious nature of demand, each firm charges $1.50 for each corndog, and their combined sales are 100. Consumers regard these sellers' meals as imperfect substitutes, so that the number of corndogs each firm sells will depend on the amount of money each firm spends on advertising. But the consumers are fickle: They will only buy from the firm that advertises the most. Predict the amount each firm will spend on advertising, the number of corndogs it will sell, and the profit it will make.

13. Imagine there are currently two firms selling fried green tomatoes in Whistle Stop Alabama, Izzy's Best and Green Guys. Izzy's uses a special technique that allows it to salvage more than twice as much of each tomato as Green. The local supermarket provides these two sellers with the necessary green goodies, at a per-unit price of m. Izzy's realizes that she can force the price of green tomatoes up by making a deal with the supermarket. Suppose the demand for fried green tomatoes is linear. Under what conditions would Izzy's wish to see m increase? How would an increase in m impact Green Guys' profits?

14. Suppose the market demand for Baby Barbie dolls is $p = 34 − 2/5Q$. At present, the only manufacturer of these cute toys is Bambi's, but there is a potential entrant: Ken's. Ken's fixed cost of entering is $160. Marginal cost is $7.60 for both Bambi's and Ken's. While Bambi's can't set its output prior to Ken's entry decision, it can adopt a new technology that will lower its marginal cost to $2.80.

    a. Determine the equilibrium number of Baby Barbie dolls each seller will provide when Bambi's marginal cost is $7.60.

b. Determine the equilibrium number of Baby Barbie dolls each seller will provide when Bambi's marginal cost is $2.80.

c. What is the most Bambi's would pay to obtain this new technology?

■ Answers to Practice Problems

1. Since Agnes' and Zelda's cannot both make money if both enter, but they can get zero profit by staying out, each prefers to do the opposite of the other. So it is a Nash equilibrium for Agnes to enter and for Zelda to stay out, but it is also a Nash equilibrium for Agnes to stay out and for Zelda to enter. In addition, there is a third equilibrium, where each plays a mixed strategy, entering with probability between zero and one. At this mixed strategy Nash equilibrium, the anticipated profit from entering must equal the certain payoff from staying out (which is zero). If π_M is the monopoly profit, L_d the duopoly loss, and ρ the probability each will enter, the expected profit from entry is $\rho L_d + (1 - \rho)\pi_M$. Setting this equal to zero we find $\rho = \pi_M/(\pi_M - L_d)$. Since $\pi_M > 0 > L_d$, ρ must be between zero and one. The correct answer is d.

2. Since market demand is $p = 48 - Q$, and Gumby's gets to set its output, q_G, before Licorice Licks enters, Gumby's knows that Licorice Licks will face the residual demand curve $p = (48 - q_G) - q_L$, where q_L is Licorice Licks' output. Because marginal cost is zero, after entry Licorice Licks will produce where its marginal revenue, which is described by $48 - q_G - 2q_L$, equals zero. So Licorice Licks would produce 12 if Gumby's chose 24. Likewise, Licorice Licks would produce 8 if Gumby's chose 32. Finally, Licorice Licks would produce 3 if Gumby's produced 42. The prices that go with these three output combinations are $12 if Gumby's chose 24, $8 if Gumby's chose 32, and $3 if Gumby's chose 42. Licorice Licks' profit after entry would then be $144, $64, and $9, respectively. Because Licorice Licks' entry cost is $70, Gumby's can deter entry by producing either 32 or 42. If entry is deterred, Gumby's gets a price of $16 and profit of $392 if it chose 32, or a price of $6 and profit of $252 if it chose 42. It can also get a profit of $384 by allowing entry. Of these three possible profit levels, $392 is the largest, so Gumby's will produce 32. Answer b is correct.

3. This problem uses most of the data from above; the distinction is that entry costs are much smaller. If Gumby's chooses 24 or 32, Licorice Licks will enter. Of these two outputs, 24 yields the larger profit, so Gumby's won't produce 32. However, Gumby's can deter entry by producing 42, as this will limit Licorice Licks' post-entry profit to $9. Because entry costs $10, Licorice Licks wouldn't enter if Gumby's chose 42. Even so, the profit Gumby's gets by choosing 24 ($384) exceeds the profit it gets by choosing 42 ($252). Hence, Gumby's produces 24: Answer a is correct.

4. If advertising raises market demand, Gumby's is better off not advertising and letting Licorice Licks advertise. It gets the benefits of the ads without paying the cost. In this case, increases in the amount Gumby's advertises will likely lead Licorice Licks to advertise less. So answer *a* is not likely to be correct. On the other hand, if advertising by either firm raises its demand at the expense of the rival firm, the last thing Gumby's wants is for Licorice Licks to advertise heavily. Answer b is wrong. If Gumby's can lower Licorice Licks' demand, through whatever means, it makes entry less appealing. In fact, this is a major reason for precommitting to large outputs in advance of entry to lower the entrant's residual demand. The expansion in the incumbent's demand makes advertising even more appealing. Answer c is best.

5. Answers and brief explanations follow.

   a. If CCCC sets its price at $1.80, then Moonbucks' post-entry profits are $1024 at $2.10, $1023 at $2.15, $1020 at $2.20, and $1015 at $2.25. So Moonbucks' best price is $2.10; its net profit is $1024 – $1089 = –$65. CCCC's profit is $1066.

   b. Using the same approach as in part a, we inspect Moonbucks' profit in the row associated with CCCC's price of $2.00. The best Moonbucks can do is to charge $2.15; its net profit is $0 (= $1089 – $1089). CCCC's profit is $1125.

   c. If CCCC sets a price of $2.20, Moonbucks will respond with a price of $2.20. Moonbucks' post-entry profit is $67; CCCC makes $1156.

   d. If CCCC sets a price of $2.40, Moonbucks will respond with a price of $2.25. Moonbucks' post-entry profit is $136; CCCC makes $1159.

   e. Since Moonbucks does not make a positive profit when CCCC charges either $1.80 or $2.00, it does not enter in either case. Thus, CCCC will sell 800 cups at a price of $1.80, for a profit of $1040. If CCCC charges $2.00, they will sell 780 cups (because Moonbucks doesn't enter), for a profit of $1170. CCCC's profit is $1156 if they charge $2.20, and $1159 if they charge $2.40.

   f. CCCC's optimal price is $2.00; entry does not occur.

   g. With entry costs at $1024, CCCC can only prevent entry by charging $1.80; at $2.00 entry occurs and CCCC's profits become $1125. Hence, the best CCCC can do is to charge $2.40; entry occurs.

6. Ambiguous, but unlikely. A threat is credible if the party that makes the threat would wish to carry it out. Whether the professor would be willing to flunk the student depends on her preferences. However, the syllabus issued at the start of the semester describes the professor's standards, so unless she is vindictive, the student could well believe that his work merited a passing grade. In the event the professor failed the student, one expects the behavior would be viewed as capricious by the university administration, with unpleasant repercussions for the professor. Based on this analysis, would you decline to turn in the term paper?

7. Ambiguous, but unlikely. The entry decision must be linked to the second firm's post-entry profits. To motivate entry, profits larger than $400 must be anticipated. It is possible that the second firm is so much more efficient than the incumbent that it would take over the market, and make profits at least as large as $500. However, a more likely interpretation is that duopoly industry profit is unlikely to be as large as the incumbent's monopoly profit, and that industry profit has to be shared between two firms. So it seems most likely that the second firm's profit would be considerably smaller than $400, and that entry would not occur.

8. Ambiguous, but likely. If generics were the only type of cigarette, any advertising would have to be aimed at raising market demand for cigarettes. Thus each firm benefits from all firms' ads. It is conceivable that each firm chooses to not advertise, hoping that someone else will do it for them. Even though the benefits to the advertising firm from the first advertisement it runs are just a fraction of the benefits received by the industry, the firm will advertise if these benefits exceed the cost.

9. This game is a variation on preventing entry with simultaneous moves. If each firm hires a staff of chemists and engages in R&D, each stands a 50 percent chance of winning the R&D race and obtaining the monopoly. If only one firm hires a staff, it will surely obtain the monopoly while the other firm loses nothing. If we denote the cost of the R&D program (the staff's wages) as W, and the monopoly profit by π_M, the payoff matrix for the R&D game is

		Firm 2's Choice	
		Hire Chemists	**Stay Out**
Firm 1's Choice	Hire Chemists	$\pi_M/2 - W,\ \pi_M/2 - W$	$\pi_M - W,\ 0$
	Stay Out	$0,\ \pi_M - W$	$0,\ 0$

Because the monopoly profit is not twice as large as the wages, $\pi_M/2 - W < 0$. Thus, if Firm 1 hires a staff, Firm 2 would rather stay out. Likewise, if Firm 2 has hired a staff, Firm 1 would prefer to stay out. Each combination is a Nash equilibrium. A third possibility is that each firm hires a staff with some probability; that is, they each play a mixed strategy. With either of the pure strategy Nash equilibria, the drug is produced. With the mixed strategy Nash equilibrium it is possible that both firms hire a staff, in which case one will patent the drug. If only one hires a staff, it will patent the drug. But it is also possible that neither hires the chemists, so that the drug isn't discovered.

10. If Jimmy waits, Buzz's payoff is larger from jumping than from waiting (−3 vs. −5), so Buzz will jump. But if Buzz jumps, Jimmy is better off waiting than jumping (he gets 7 as opposed to 0). So it is a Nash equilibrium for Jimmy to wait and Buzz to jump. Similarly, it is a Nash equilibrium for Jimmy to jump and Buzz to wait. Finally, there is a Nash equilibrium in Chickie Run, where each waits with some probability a (see Appendix 14A in the text). Both Jimmy and Buzz would then receive an expected payoff of $7\alpha + -5(1-\alpha) = 12\alpha - 5$ if they wait, and an expected payoff of $-3\alpha + 0(1-\alpha) = -3\alpha$ if they jump. In the mixed strategy Nash equilibrium, these expected payoffs must be equal, or $12\alpha - 5 = -3\alpha$. Rearranging, we see that $15\alpha = 5$, or $\alpha = 1/3$. Of course, this all assumes that the action you wish to take is carried out—in the movie, Buzz's coat gets stuck on the door handle as he attempts to jump out, so he winds up in the ocean!

11. The key distinction between the quantity-choosing model and the price-choosing model concerns the slope of firms' best-response curves. In the quantity-choosing model, best-response curves are negatively sloped; in the price-choosing model they are *positively* sloped. One important implication of positively sloped best-response curves is that the incumbent must cut her price if she wants to force a reduction in the rival's post-entry profit. At a low enough price, such as p_D in Figure 14.3, the entrant's best response yields a profit that just covers his entry cost. So if the incumbent prices at or below p_D, entry will not occur. On the other hand, if entry is allowed, the incumbent can induce the entrant to charge more than his Bertrand equilibrium price if *she* charges a higher price. The incumbent's optimal price is either the leader price p_L (which allows entry) or p_D, which prevents entry. A comparison of duopoly profit when she charges p_L with monopoly profit when she charges p_D will determine the best option.

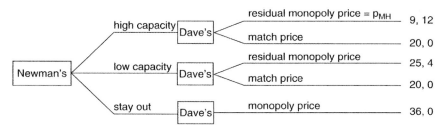

Figure 14.3

12. Because the total number of corndogs purchased is fixed at 100, and price is fixed at $1.50, the only variable that can influence a firm's profit is its level of advertising. Each firm wants to outspend the other firm, so long as they don't spend more than $150 on ads, because the firm that spends the most makes $150 in revenues (100 corndogs at $1.50 each). But if Bow-Wow spends less than $150, Corny's can make positive profit by spending just a tiny bit more than Bow-Wow. So if Bow-Wow is going to spend anything, they'd better spend $150. Likewise, if Corny's spends less than $150, Bow-Wow can steal away all their customers. There are two possible outcomes: one where Bow-Wow spends $150 on ads and Corny's spends nothing, and one where Corny's spends $150 on ads and Bow-Wow spends nothing. In each equilibrium, both firms make zero profit. In either equilibria, the firm spending $150 makes all the sales.

13. Izzy's total costs are mc_Iq_I, where m is the price of price of green tomatoes, c_I is the amount of meat Izzy's uses in each meal produced, and q_I is the number of meals Izzy's produces. Likewise, Green Guys' total costs, are mc_Gq_G, where c_G is the amount of meat Green Guys' uses in each meal produced, and q_G is the number of meals Green Guys' produces. Since Izzy's gets more meat from her tomatoes, $c_I < c_G$ (and hence Izzy's marginal cost per meal is smaller than Green Guys'). Since demand is linear, we can write it as $p = a - bQ$, where p is market price and Q is the sum of the two producers' outputs. In the Cournot equilibrium, Izzy's produces an output q_I^* and Green Guys' produces an output q_G^*; these outputs solve the two producers' first-order conditions:

$$0 = \partial \pi_I(q_I^*, q_G^*)/\partial q_I = a - b(q_I^* + q_G^*) - bq_I^* - mc_I;$$
$$0 = \partial \pi_G(q_I^*, q_G^*)/\partial q_G = a - b(q_I^* + q_G^*) - bq_G^* - mc_G.$$

Summing the two expressions yields $0 = 2a - 3b(q_I^* + q_G^*) - mc_I - mc_G$, or $q_I^* + q_G^* = (2a - mc_I - mc_G)/3b$. Inserting this formula into Izzy's first-order condition, we get

$$0 = a - (2a - mc_I - mc_G)/3 - bq_I^* - mc_I, \quad \text{or}$$
$$q_I^* = (a - 2mc_I + mc_G)/3b.$$

Izzy's profits at the Cournot equilibrium are $\pi_I(q_I^*, q_G^*) = [a - b(q_I^* + q_G^*) - mc_I]q_I^* = [a - (2a - mc_I - mc_G)/3 - mc_I]q_I^* = [a + m(c_G - 2c_I)]^2/9b$. We conclude that Izzy's would like to see m increase if—and only if $- c_G - 2c_I > 0$: that is, if Izzy is able to get at least twice as much meat from each tomato. Using a parallel line of reasoning, one can calculate $\pi_G(q_I^*, q_G^*) = [a + m(c_I - 2c_G)]^2/9b$. Since we know that $c_G > c_I$, this expression is certain to shrink if m increases, so an increase in m lowers Green Guys' profits. Ultimately, by forcing up the price of tomatoes enough, Izzy's could drive Green Guys' out of the market.

14. Let's call Bambi's output q_B, and Ken's output q_K; market price is then determined by $p = 34 - (2/5) \times (q_B + q_K)$. Based on market demand, Bambi's profit is given by $\pi_B(q_B, q_K) = (p - m_B)q_B$, where m is Bambi's marginal cost. Bambi's best-response function is found by choosing that value of q_B that maximizes π_B, taking Ken's output as given, which we find by solving $\partial \pi_B/\partial q_B = 0$. In this problem, $\partial \pi_B/\partial q_B = p - m_B - q_B \times \partial p_B/\partial q_B = 34 - (2/5)q_B - (2/5)q_K - m_B - 2/5q_B$; setting this equal to zero, we find $34 - (2/5)q_K - m_B = 4/5q_B$. Thus, Bambi's best-response function is given by:

$$q_B = (34 - m_B)/(4/5) - 1/2q_K.$$

Ken's best-response function is found in an analogous manner. Since his marginal cost is 7.6, his best-response function is

$$Q_K = (34 - 7.6)/(4/5) - 1/2q_B.$$

The Cournot equilibrium is the pair of outputs q_B^* and q_K^* that simultaneously satisfy the two firms' best-response functions; when marginal cost (m) equals 7.6, these outputs solve:

$$q_B^* = (34 - 7.6)/(4/5) - 1/2q_K^*;$$
$$q_K^* = (34 - 7.6)/(4/5) - 1/2q_B^*.$$

So, we get $q_B^* = 22$ and $q_K^* = 22$ for part a. If Bambi's marginal cost falls to $2.80, and If Ken has entered, the Cournot equilibrium would be the pair of outputs q_B^{**} and q_K^{**} that simultaneously satisfy

$$q_B^{**} = (34 - 2.8)/(4/5) - 1/2q_K^{**};$$
$$q_K^{**} = (34 - 7.6)/(4/5) - 1/2q_B^{**}.$$

In this case, the Cournot equilibrium would be $q_B^{**} = 30$ and $q_K^{**} = 18$, which would yield a market price of \$19.20. But at that price, Ken's profit after entry is only \$129.60, which isn't enough to cover his entry cost. Thus, if Bambi obtains the new technology, Ken won't enter. Bambi's then gets to sell Baby Barbie dolls for \$22 apiece ($34 - 2/5 \times 30$), and her profit would be \$576 ($= 22 - 2.8) \times 30$. If she doesn't get the technology, her profit is \$193.60. Bambi would pay up to \$382.40 (the difference in profits, $576 - 193.60$) to obtain the new technology.

■ Exercises

Fill-in

1. Let's revisit the land of chocolate bars. The market demand is $p = 58 - Q$, Willie's marginal cost is constant at \$10, and Wonka's marginal cost is constant at \$22. Imagine that Willie can select his production of chocolate bars before Wonka can enter the market.

   a. Wonka's best response function is _____.
   b. If Willie produces 24, Wonka will produce _____ and make profits of _____.
   c. If Willie produces 30, Wonka will produce _____ and make profits of _____.
   d. If Willie produces 32, Wonka will produce _____ and make profits of _____.
   e. If it costs Wonka \$4 to enter, Willie will produce ___ and make profits of _____.
   f. If it costs Wonka \$1 to enter, Willie will produce ___ and make profits of _____.

True-False-Ambiguous and Explain Why

2. Fred's Turbo may no longer be a monopolist in the Fast Gas market. There is a potential entrant on the horizon: Phil's Fill-er-up. To enter, Phil will have to pay a certain amount, and Fred knows that Phil will not be able to cover these entry costs if Fred commits to producing 100 units. Fred will deter entry.

3. Imagine that Cliff and Joe, the two sellers of Yellowstone spring water we met in Exercise 10 from Chapter 13, select prices instead of quantities. Suppose also that consumers regard their products as absolutely identical, and so will buy from the cheaper seller. Cliff is already in place; Joe must pay an entry cost of \$F to sell spring water. If Cliff sets his price before Joe decides whether to enter, Cliff will deter entry.

4. Two firms are contemplating advertising levels. As in panel b of Table 14.4 in the text, advertising attracts new customers to the market, but here the firms choose from three possible advertising levels: none, medium, and heavy. Suppose their payoffs are as described in the table below (the first number represents Firm 1's profit; the second number is Firm 2's profit). The firms will choose levels that maximize industry profit.

		Firm 2's Advertising Level		
		None	**Medium**	**Heavy**
	None	\$1, \$1	\$2, \$3	\$3, \$4
Firm 1's Advertising Level	Medium	\$3, \$2	\$6, \$6	\$7, \$5
	Heavy	\$4, \$3	\$5, \$7	\$7, \$7

Short-Answer

5.   Give the game tree for the interaction between CCCC and Moonbucks in Practice Problem 5.

6.   Two duopolists, firm 1 and firm 2, are competing head-to-head in a market that can only support one. Each firm must decide whether to exit or stay in the market; if either firm exits it gets 0, if both firms stay in the market they each lose 50. If one firm stays in while the other exits, the firm remaining in the market gets 100. Find the Nash equilibria for this game.

7.   Dave's and Newman's are the only firms capable of producing fiery hot sauce. Dave's already has a plant that can meet any possible demand. Newman's must decide what size plant to build. It can choose not to build (basically, it decides not to enter), it can choose a small plant, or it can choose a large plant. After Newman's selects a plant size, Dave's selects a price. (For simplicity, we assume that Newman's chooses the same price no matter what size plant it builds, and that this price is smaller than Dave's monopoly price.) If Dave's decides to match Newman's price, Dave's captures the entire market, since hot pepper consumers know that Dave's has an insanely high habanero pepper content (after all, it is called Dave's Insanity Sauce!). If Dave's decides to choose a higher price, it makes fewer sales, with its sales dependent upon Newman's plant size. What size plant should Newman's set?

8.   In a recently reported series of experiments (Mason and Nowell, *Journal of Economic Behavior and Organization,* 1998), human subjects (typically students just like you) played the part of firms. Some subjects were incumbents, while others were potential entrants. Payoffs were based on the demand curve $p = 240 - 10Q$, and there were no variable costs. To enter, the entrant had to pay a cost F; this value was low in one treatment and high in a second. Attempts to deter entry were relatively rare when F was small (30), but common when F was large (180). Let's investigate these results.

   a.   What is the entrant's best response function?
   b.   What is Stackelberg equilibrium, and what are the two firms' profits?
   c.   If entry costs 30 and the incumbent produces 22, what is the entrant's best response and how much profit is earned? Should entry occur? What profit would the incumbent receive?
   d.   If entry costs 220 and the incumbent produces 16, what is the entrant's best response and how much profit is earned? Should entry occur? What profit would the incumbent receive?
   e.   If entry costs 30, does the incumbent prefer to choose the Stackelberg output or to deter entry?
   f.   If entry costs 180, does the incumbent prefer to choose the Stackelberg output or to deter entry?

9.   Suppose those consumers in the market for corndogs have a sudden change of heart (no, not heartburn). Instead of flocking to the firm that advertises the most, some buy from each vendor. If Bow-Wow spends A_B and Corny's spends A_C, then Bow-Wow sells $[A_B/(A_B + A_C)] \times 100$ corndogs (Bow-Wow's share of sales equals its share of total advertising dollars spent). As before, the two firms combine to sell 100 corndogs at $1.40 each, no matter how much money is spent on advertising. Determine how much each firm spends on advertising, the number of corndogs it will sell, and its profit.

Chapter 15
Factor Markets

■ Chapter Summary

Before a firm can produce the output that it will sell, it must obtain and organize a variety of inputs. Of these, the input that is likely to strike you as most significant is labor—after all, one big reason to attend college is to elevate your employment opportunities! But how do firms decide on the level of the various inputs that they will use? And how does this relate to the rule for determining the profit-maximizing output that the firm will sell? A related issue concerns the firm's decision to procure the input, as opposed to making the input itself. The focus of this chapter is on the nature of markets for inputs: What levels of inputs are demanded by firms, how these demands are tied to the market structure in the product market, the effect market power might have if there is only one buyer of the input, and issues related to the firm's decision about producing its own inputs as opposed to purchasing them from others.

If there are many firms in the market for the input, sometimes referred to as the *downstream market*, the price of the input is determined by typical competitive pressures. That is, we are considering a **competitive factor market**. In competitive factor markets, the demand for the input is tied directly to the demand for the final good. On the other hand, if the downstream market is monopolized, then the demand for the input is linked to the marginal revenue for the final good. One important **effect of monopolies on factor markets** has to do with the demand for the input. Since monopolies tend to depress final good production, they have a correspondingly smaller demand for the input. The flip side of this discussion occurs when the downstream market is competitive but there is only one *seller* of the input. Such an input market is called a **monopsony**. Like a monopolist, a monopsonist knows that it has the only game in town. Accordingly, it has the ability to influence the price of the input: The more the monopsony demands, the higher the price it must pay. Because this higher price applies to all units of the input, not just the marginal unit, buying more units of the input raises costs by more than the input's price. Correspondingly, the monopsonist is inclined to hedge its demand downward.

In determining the amount of an input that a typical firm demands, we use one guiding rule: Compare the benefit received from that input with the extra cost associated with purchasing the input. The extra benefit is the extra output produced, multiplied by the impact that increase in output has on revenues. The extra output produced from using an additional unit of the input is the marginal product of the input. The impact of an additional unit of production upon revenues is marginal revenue. The multiple of these two terms is called *marginal revenue product,* or *MRP*. The extra cost is simply the price of the input, unless the firm is a monopsonist. If the downstream firm is a monopsonist, it must offer a higher price if it wishes to purchase an additional unit of the input. Thus the extra cost associated with buying one more unit equals the price of the input *plus* the effect on this increase in input price multiplied by the number of units that were originally demanded. So the extra cost to the monopsonist, its *marginal expenditure,* exceeds the input's price.

A wide range of economic decisions are intertemporal in nature—someone makes a choice today that will have consequences well into the future. This intertemporal environment gives a new dimension to most decisions, both for firms and for consumers. Should you pursue a graduate degree rather than seeking employment immediately after you finish college? In deciding, you make a trade-off between short-term incentives—benefits and costs that are readily identifiable in the near future—and long-term incentives. If you go to graduate school, you are likely to enhance your employment possibilities in two to five years, but in the meantime you forfeit the chance to earn a steady income. Firms also must make decisions that involve both current and future effects. Should they engage in research and development (R&D)? Again, decisions compare immediate effects such as foregone cash flow against future impacts—a successful R&D program will enhance future profitability.

Before we can make much progress in analyzing decisions with effects at different points in time, we need to develop a mechanism for **comparing money today with money in the future**. Since money can be banked, and thereby earn interest, a specified amount of money received today is generally worth more than the same amount of money received in one year. The method by which we compare these two items, say $100 today vs. $100 next year, is to determine the amount of money today that is equally attractive as $100 next year. That amount of money received right now is called the *present value* of the money received in the future. The present value of a future amount is based on an individual's *discount rate,* which is a construct we devise to help in calculating present values. By converting future amounts into their present value, we are able to compare them directly to monies received or forfeited right now. Once we have converted future amounts into their present value, we can analyze **choices over time**.

A particularly important class of intertemporal decision-making problems arises when current decisions influence a variable that evolves over time. The current actions typically involve adjustments to *flows*—for example, investments in capital or R&D. The variable that evolves over time is a *stock*—for example, the amount of capital the firm has available or the knowledge it has accrued from its R&D programs. **Exhaustible resources** are good examples of the interrelation between flows and stocks. The amount of oil a firm extracts this year is a flow; the amount in the ground is a stock. The amount of the resource extracted this period depends on the profit from a unit of the resource today (the resource's *rent*) and the present value of future rent. When the former exceeds the latter, the firm extracts as much as it can right now. Economists predict that rents will rise at the interest rate, so that firms are equally happy to extract now or in the future.

■ Key Concepts and Formulas

- **Short-run factor demand of a firm:** the amount of the input the firm demands, given the price of the input, the price of the final product, and holding some inputs—like capital—fixed.
- **Long-run factor demand of a firm:** the amount of the input the firm demands, given the price of the input, the price of the final product, and adjusting all other inputs to their profit-maximizing levels.
- **Monopsony power:** the ability of a single buyer to profit from paying less than the competitive price for the input.
- **Discount rate:** the value placed upon future consumption, relative to current consumption.
- **Present value:** the amount a specified payment received at a future date is worth today.
- $MRP_L = MR \times MP_L$: the algebraic definition of marginal revenue product for labor.
- $ME_L = w + L(dw/dL)$: the rule for determining marginal expenditure for labor from the labor supply curve; if the downstream firm is not a monopsonist, the second term equals zero.
- $MRP = ME$: the algebraic relation for determining the firm's input demand; if $ME = w$, this relation is equivalent to $MR = w/MP_L = MC$, the rule for determining the profit-maximizing output.
- $PV = f/(1 + i)^t$: the present value of a payment of $\$f$ to be received in t periods.

■ Application: Anadarko Buys into Enhanced Oil Recovery

In early 2002, Anadarko Petroleum Corporation made two acquisitions: First, they bought the rights to extract oil from Salt Creek oil field from Anadarko Corporation. Soon thereafter, they bought the rights to build a pipeline to the field from PetroSource Corporation. This pipeline will be used to transport CO_2, a key ingredient in enhanced oil recovery techniques. These acquisitions were not cheap, but Anadarko seems convinced that they will ultimately pay off in a big way.

Question: Why would Anadarko benefit from purchasing the pipeline?

Answer: Prior to its acquisition by Anadarko, PetroSource (the previous owner of the pipeline) held a monopoly position in the delivery of CO_2 to the Salt Creek field. On the other hand, Anadarko (the previous owner of the Salt Creek field) was the only likely purchaser of transported CO_2, making them a monopsony. The interaction between PetroSource and Anadarko is more complex than either a monopolized market (PetroSource is the only seller of CO_2 transportation services) or a monopsonized market (Anadarko is the only purchaser of CO_2 transportation services). This interaction is sometimes called a bilateral monopoly, since both buyer and seller have substantial market power. To understand the complications that occur with bilateral monopoly, consider each player's motivations in isolation. Since PetroSource has monopoly power, it would like to set the level of CO_2 transportation services so as to maximize its profits. The resultant level of CO_2 to be supplied is Q^*, where marginal revenue equals marginal cost. With this quantity supplied, PetroSource would charge p^* per unit shipped. Figure 15.1 shows these features. On the other side of the market, Anadarko has substantial market power: They do not merely take the transportation tariff as given. Anadarko realizes that if they ask to have a larger quantity of CO_2 shipped, the shipping tariff will be increased. This higher price is paid on all units shipped, not just the additional units, so the extra cost Anadarko bears when it increases its purchases—its marginal expenditure—lies above the supply curve (i.e., PetroSource's marginal cost curve). Anadarko's optimal level of CO_2 purchases balances its demand for CO_2 against this marginal expenditure. This would yield a purchase amount of Q^{**}. The price per unit shipped is then taken from PetroSource's marginal cost curve; it is p^{**} in this application. The heart of the problem is that Anadarko and PetroSource want different levels of CO_2 to be shipped, and they disagree on the tariff. Resolution of such disagreements is no simple feat, depending on such features as the participants' negotiating skills, their willingness to suffer losses in an attempt to convince the other party of their "toughness," their patience, and the accuracy of each party's assessment of the other party's toughness and the deal that they would be just willing to accept. Accordingly, we might expect substantial transactions costs to arise in these negotiations. One simple way to avoid these transactions costs would be for one of the parties to buy out the other—or at least to acquire the relevant line of business from the other party; such an acquisition is an example of vertical integration. In this particular case, Anadarko acquired the rights to the pipeline from PetroSource, thereby eliminating the transactions costs. The acquisition also allowed Anadarko to obtain CO_2 at a lower price, an additional benefit to vertical integration.

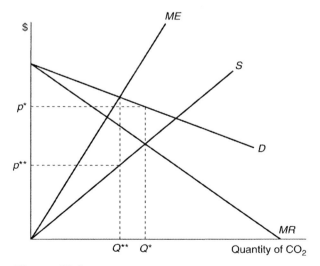

Figure 15.1

■ Solved Problems

1. In the remote village of Leftbehind, Wyoming, there is only one place for people to work: at the local open-pit coal mine. The employer at the coal mine, Snidely's Carbon, Inc., sells its coal in the national market and faces competition from hundreds of other coal mining companies. Suppose there is no difference between all these vendors' coal, so that the market is perfectly competitive. One day the town mayor decides to do something for the unfortunate folks who struggle in the coal mine, and so he proposes that Snidely's be subjected to a minimum wage that exceeds the current wage. What effect will this minimum wage have on the number of people Snidely's employs?

    Step 1: Determine the level of employment and wage paid prior to the mayor's intervention.

    A monopsonist chooses its level of labor to balance marginal revenue product with marginal expenditure; this level is denoted as L^* in Figure 15.2. The wage that Snidely pays is w^*, read off the labor supply curve at L^*. In an unfettered market, marginal expenditure exceeds wage, since the monopsonist typically has to raise every employee's wage when it hires more labor. Thus the wage paid by Snidely's is smaller than w, the value read off the *MRP* curve at L^*.

    Step 2: Determine the level of employment and wage paid after the minimum wage is imposed.

    When Snidely's is forced to pay a minimum wage w_M larger than w^* a slight increase in the amount of labor it uses does not require that a higher wage be paid to any employee—in fact, Snidely's will wind up paying the same wage so long as the amount of labor it uses is no larger than the amount read off the labor supply curve at w_M (the quantity denoted by L_0 in Figure 15.2). Thus Snidely's winds up hiring L^{**} units of labor, where marginal revenue product equals w_M, and paying the minimum wage.

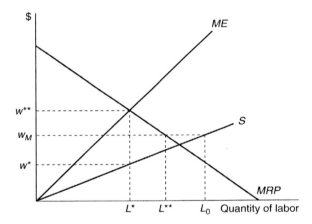

Figure 15.2

    Step 3: Compare the level of labor used before and after the minimum wage is imposed.

    If the minimum wage lies between w^*, the old wage paid by Snidely's, and w^{**}, Snidely's original marginal expenditure, then the minimum wage will lead to an increase in the amount of labor used by Snidely's. However, if the minimum wage is larger than w^{**}, say at w_M', Snidely's would lower the amount of labor it uses. This complication arises because a very large minimum wage will force Snidely's marginal expenditure above w^{**}, causing Snidely's to adjust its labor below L^*.

2. Suppose there is a small island in the Southern hemisphere that is the only place where one can find penguin wool. Sweater knitters all over the world agree that penguin wool is without parallel. Presently, the only purveyor of penguin wool is a firm called Little Blue's. Not only is Little Blue's the only seller of penguin wool, they are the only possible source of demand for penguin wool producers. That is, Little Blue's is both a monopolist in the sale of penguin wool and a monopsonist in the purchase of penguin wool. After they buy the wool from penguin wool producers (who have an upward-sloping supply curve), they repackage it for sale abroad. The repackaging costs Little Blue's a constant amount c per package, no matter what they pay penguin wool producers. How much penguin wool will Little Blue's sell, how much do they pay penguin wool producers, and what price will they charge?

Step 1: Determine Little Blue's demand for penguin wool.

Because Little Blue's is a monopolist in the penguin wool market, they choose an output to equate marginal revenue with marginal cost. Their marginal cost is $c + w$, where w is the price they pay to penguin wool producers. Since Little Blue's sells one unit of penguin wool to the international market for every unit they buy from penguin wool producers, the marginal product of penguin wool is exactly equal to one. So, if Little Blue's decides it wants to sell Q_w units of wool on the international market, it must buy Q_w units of wool from penguin wool producers. Referring to Figure 15.3a, when Little Blue's pays w_1 for penguin wool, they sell Q_1 units of wool abroad. When the price is w_2, they sell Q_2 units, and so on. In Figure 15.3b, we use this information to construct Little Blue's demand curve for penguin wool. At price w_1 they demand Q_1 units of wool, at price w_2 they demand Q_2 units of wool, and so on. In general, a firm demands that amount of input where the input's price equals its marginal revenue product. In this example, each unit of wool procured from wool producers yields one unit of sales: The marginal product is exactly unity. Hence marginal revenue product equals marginal revenue (represented in terms of the input).

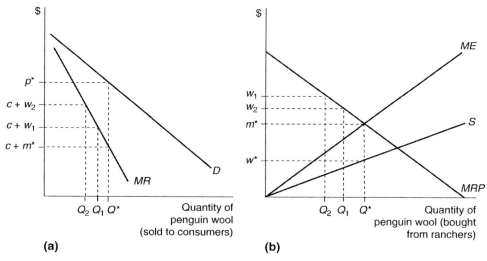

Figure 15.3

Step 2: Determine Little Blue's profit-maximizing usage of penguin wool.

Because Little Blue's is a monopsonist, it maximizes profits by equating its marginal expenditure with its demand curve. Little Blue's marginal expenditure curve is derived from the supply curve for penguin wool producers. At any level of usage, marginal expenditure (ME) equals the price (w) plus the impact of an increase in demand upon price multiplied by the level of usage ($Q \times dw/dQ$). The latter term is usage multiplied by the slope of the supply curve. The profit-maximizing amount of penguin wool for Little Blue's to buy is Q^*. The price Little Blue's pays is then read off the supply curve; it is w^*. At this level, Little Blue's marginal expenditure is m^*.

Step 3: Determine the price Little Blue's will charge for its penguin wool.

Based on the amount of penguin wool that Little Blue's buys from penguin wool producers, it sells Q^* units to the international market. At that quantity, penguin wool users are willing to pay a market price of p_w^*, and that is the price Little Blue's charges.

3. Suppose that the Airhead Corporation is considering three possible investments: build a new factory in South Dakota for $700,000 with an expected rate of return of 8 percent; buy $300,000 worth of government treasury bills (T-bills) with a rate of return of 7.9 percent; or invest $500,000 in an R&D project with an expected rate of return of 8.5 percent. Airhead can borrow up to $1,000,000 at the interest rate offered to a bank's best customers, the prime rate, which is 5 percent. However, if Airhead borrows more than $1,000,000, the bank worries about Airhead's ability to repay the loans, and so will charge a higher rate on the entire loan. Imagine that the bank uses the following formula for determining the interest rate it will charge on loans above $1,000,000: $r = 0.05 + (K - 1,000,000)/50,000,000$, where K is the amount on money loaned. For example, if Airhead borrows $1,500,000, the bank charges 6 percent; if Airhead borrows $2,000,000 the rate is 7 percent, and so on. In which of these projects should Airhead invest?

Step 1: Order the investments in terms of their rates of return.

The rate of return is highest on the R&D project, second highest on the new factory, and lowest on the T-bills.

Step 2: Determine whether Airhead should invest in the R&D project—the program with the highest rate of return.

Airhead makes an investment if the rate of return on that investment is greater than its marginal expenditure, which is Airhead's discount rate. Since the R&D project costs less than $1,000,000, it can be funded with a loan at 5 percent. As the rate of return on the R&D project exceeds 5 percent, Airhead should make this investment.

Step 3: Determine whether Airhead should also build the new factory—the program with the second-highest rate of return.

The rate of return on the new factory is 7 percent. If Airhead invests in this second project, it must borrow $1,200,000 ($500,000 for the R&D project and $700,000 to build the new plant). Accordingly, the bank will charge an interest rate of 0.054 (5.4 percent). From Chapter 15, we know that the marginal expenditure is $r + (\Delta r/\Delta K)K$. The term in parentheses is 1/50,000,000, while $K = 1,200,000$. Thus, Airhead's marginal expenditure is 0.054 + 1,200,000/50,000,000, or 0.078. Since the rate of return on the new factory exceeds the marginal expenditure, Airhead builds the new factory, as well as investing in the R&D project.

Step 4: Determine whether Airhead should also buy the T-bills–the program with the third-highest rate of return.

If Airhead buys the T-bills, it must borrow $1,500,000. The interest rate is then 5.5 percent, and the marginal expenditure is 0.055 + 1,500,000/50,000,000 = 0.085, or 8.5 percent. As the marginal expenditure exceeds the rate of return on the T-bills, Airhead should not invest in this third project.

■ Practice Problems

Multiple-Choice

1. Which of the following best defines marginal revenue product?
   a. $p \times MP$
   b. $MR \times MP$
   c. w/MP
   d. MR/MP

2. Suppose that a certain manufacturer of computer diskettes can sell its product at $20 for a box of 100 diskettes. The labor the firm uses to make boxes of diskettes has a marginal product of $MP = 12 - Q_L/10$. If the manufacturer is a perfectly competitive firm in the market for diskettes, its firm's marginal revenue product of labor is
   a. $240 - 2Q_L$.
   b. $120 - Q_L$.
   c. 20.
   d. 240.

3. Suppose the price of diskettes is $10/box and the wage the firm in Multiple-Choice Question 2 paid its employees is $20/hour. To maximize its profits, how many hours of labor should it use?
   a. 0
   b. 20
   c. 100
   d. 200

4. Kair-Magee has a large coal deposit that it can extract and then sell for $10/ton today. If it waits until next year, it anticipates that the coal will sell for $12/ton. If Kair-Magee's marginal extraction costs are constant at $2/ton, how high would its discount rate have to be for it to be willing to extract the coal today?
   a. At least 10 percent
   b. At least 15 percent
   c. At least 20 percent
   d. At least 25 percent

5. If the present value of an investment is $100, the interest rate is 10%, and interest is compounded twice annually, what is the future value in two years?
   a. $121
   b. $82.64
   c. $82.27
   d. $121.55

Fill-in

6. Let's revisit TCA, the cable monopoly we met in Chapter 11. Suppose that the marginal product of TCA's employees is described by $MP_L = 4 - Q_L$, where Q_L is the amount of labor TCA uses. As before, TCA's demand curve can be described by $p = 18 - Q$, where p is TCA's price and Q the resultant quantity sold. The wage that TCA pays its labor is 12.
   a. In terms of its output, TCA's marginal revenue is _____.
   b. In terms of the amount of labor it uses, TCA's marginal revenue product is _____.

c.   If TCA uses 1 unit of labor, its marginal revenue product is _____.

d.   If TCA uses 2 units of labor, its marginal revenue product is _____.

e.   If TCA uses 3 units of labor, its marginal revenue product is _____.

f.   To maximize its profits, TCA should hire ___ unit(s) of labor.

True-False-Ambiguous and Explain Why

7.   A firm demands more labor if it is a monopolist than if it is a competitive firm.

8.   Imposing a minimum wage will raise the price a monopsonist charges.

9.   A firm is considering two R&D projects. Project A costs more than project B but has a higher internal rate of return. The firm should not invest in project B.

Short-Answer

10.   Suppose that the market for extra-caffeine cappuccinos in Walla Walla, Washington is perfectly competitive, and that there is a large variety of sources for the espresso coffee beans sellers use to produce these high-octane drinks. One day, Moonbuck's buys out all the Walla Walla extra-caffeine coffee shops, and so becomes the only buyer of espresso beans. Owing to a large number of vendors selling lukewarm instant coffee, which many Walla Walla residents consider a perfect substitute for extra-caffeine cappuccinos, Moonbuck's regards the price of extra-caffeine cappuccinos as fixed. (Think of Moonbuck's as a perfectly competitive firm.) Discuss the impact of Moonbuck's acquisition upon sellers of espresso beans and coffee purchasers.

11.   The market for watermelon-seed ice cream is certainly unusual. In Alabama, the only firm that buys watermelon seeds to make this curious concoction is Dagen-Haze. In Mississippi, by contrast, there are several sellers of watermelon-seed ice cream, but watermelon growers have formed a collective, Seeds-R-Us. Seeds-R-Us is the only source of seeds for the Mississippi ice cream market. The demand, supply, marginal revenue, and marginal expenditure curves for the two markets are identical, as depicted in Figure 15.4. Graph the price for watermelon seeds, the amount of seeds traded, and the resultant deadweight social welfare loss in each state. In what way are the graphs similar? In what way(s) do they differ?

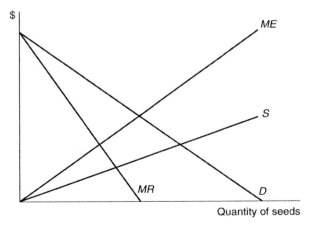

Figure 15.4

12. Continuing on with our analysis of the market for watermelon-seed ice cream, suppose that the sellers of seeds in Alabama form a union, which they decide to call "Chew-on-This." As in Practice Problem 11, there is only one buyer of seeds, Dagen-Haze. What effect will the formation of the Chew-on-This union have upon the price for watermelon seeds, the volume of seeds traded, and the price of watermelon-seed ice cream in Alabama if the relevant demand, supply, marginal revenue, and marginal expenditure curves are as in Figure 15.4?

13. Jack and Jill are both going up to Hill University (Hill U.) at the start of the next school year. Both figure that they can land jobs straight out of high school that would pay them $30,000 each year for the next 47 years. If they go to Hill U., it will cost them $5,000 per year in tuition, room, and board. Both reckon they can land better jobs after matriculation, paying $f per year for 43 years. Jack's discount rate is 8 percent, while Jill's is 6 percent. How large does f have to be to induce Jack to go to Hill? How about Jill? Give an intuitive explanation for this comparison.

14. You have recently taken a position with the Go-bot corporation, which makes plastic alien invaders, and are placed in charge of organizing production. Your superiors inform you that they have recently signed a contract to deliver 1000 invaders to Mal-Wart, a large department store chain. The toys are to be delivered in 60 days. You need to decide how many invaders to produce this month and next month. Marginal production costs are $10x_t$, where x_t is the number of toys produced in month t (let's denote $t = 0$ for this month and $t = 1$ for next month). The company tells you not to worry about discounting (or, if you prefer, use a discount rate of zero) and to neglect any inventory costs. Determine the number of alien invaders to be produced in each month.

15. Because you did so well at Go-bot, you have obtained a consulting job. OPEC wants you to decide how much oil they should extract this year and next year. To assist you in your computations, they have provided the following information: The interest rate is 5 percent, 77 units of oil must be extracted between the two years, and extraction is costless. OPEC believes the demand for their oil is given by $p_t = 100 - Q_t/2$, where Q_t is the amount of oil they sell in period t and p_t is the resulting price they can charge ($t = 0$ for this year and $t = 1$ for next year). How much should be extracted each period?

■ Answers to Practice Problems

1. Marginal revenue product is the multiple of marginal product and marginal revenue. Answers c and d have no relation to the correct definition. For a competitive firm, $MR = p$, so answer a would be correct if the firm was perfectly competitive. But answer b is correct for any type of firm, be it perfectly competitive, an oligopoly, or a monopoly. Answer b is best.

2. Since the firm is perfectly competitive, its MRP is $p \times MP_L$. Since $p = 20$ and $MP_L = 12 - Q_L/10$, $MRP_L = 240 - 2Q_L$: Answer a is correct.

3. If the price of diskettes were $10/box, the firm's MRP_L would be $120 - Q_L$. To maximize its profits, the firm should select that level of labor where $MRP_L = \$20$ (the wage it pays). Thus the firm should use 100 units of labor: Answer c is correct.

4. The profit Kair-Magee makes from a ton of coal is $8 (= 10 − 2) this year and $10 next year. The present value of next year's profit is $10/(1 + r)$; if this present value is larger than 8, Kair-Magee prefers to hold the coal until next year. Only when $8 \geq 10/(1 + r)$ would Kair-Magee be willing to extract today. You can answer this question by plugging in the four values $r = 0.1$ (10 percent), 0.15, 0.2, and 0.25. Or you can manipulate the inequality to obtain $1 + r \geq 10/8$. Either way, you will find that Kair-Magee is unwilling to extract coal today if the discount rate is less than 25 percent: Answer d is correct.

5. The future value of an investment that pays an interest rate of i per year for 2 years is $FV = PV \times (1 + i)^2$; in this case $i = 0.1$ and $PV = 100$, so $FV = \$121$. But interest is compounded twice annually, so $FV = PV \times (1 + i/2)^4$, or $100 \times (1.05)^4 = \$121.55$; answer d is correct. Note that the answer in b is $100 / (1.1)^2$ and answer c is $100 \times (1.05)^4$: each divides, instead of multiplying, by the term involving the interest rate.

6. Answers and brief explanations follow.

   a. $MR = 18 - 2Q$.

   b. To get this part, you first need to determine output in terms of the amount of labor used. Output is the same as total product, the area under the marginal product curve between 0 and an amount Q_L. The geometric figure is a trapezoid, and its area is found by multiplying the base times the average height. The base is the amount of labor to be used, Q_L. If no labor is used, the height is the marginal product with no labor $(4 - 0$, or 4$)$. If Q_L units of labor are used, the height is $MP_L = 4 - Q_L$. Thus total product is

$$Q = Q_L \times [4 + (4 - Q_L)]/2$$
$$= Q_L \times [4 - Q_L/2].$$

   Insert this expression into the formula for marginal revenue to express marginal revenue in terms of the amount of labor used: $MR = 18 - 2Q_L \times [4 - Q_L/2]$. Finally, multiply marginal revenue by marginal product to derive marginal revenue product as $MRP_L = (4 - Q_L) \times (18 - 2Q_L \times [4 - Q_L/2])$.

   c. With $Q_L = 1$, $MRP_L = 3 \times (18 - 2 \times 3.5) = 33$.

   d. With $Q_L = 2$, $MRP_L = 2 \times (18 - 4 \times 3) = 12$.

   e. With $Q_L = 3$, $MRP_L = 1 \times (18 - 6 \times 2.5) = 3$.

   f. To maximize profits, TCA needs to find that level of labor where $MRP_L = 12$ (the wage). From part d, we see that the desired level of labor is 2 units.

7. False. Any firm chooses an amount of labor to equate marginal revenue product—marginal revenue times marginal product—with the wage rate. Marginal revenue for a perfectly competitive firm (market price) exceeds marginal revenue for a monopolist. Thus the marginal revenue product curve for a monopolist (MRP_M) lies below the marginal revenue product curve for a competitive firm (MRP_C). See Figure 15.5. As a result, a firm hires less labor if it is a monopolist (L^{**}) than if it is perfectly competitive (L^*). This is really just the flip side of the usual result that a monopolist restricts output, in which case it will use less labor input.

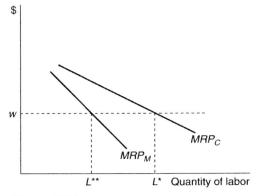

Figure 15.5

8. Ambiguous. As we saw in Solved Problem 1, the minimum wage will often lead a monopsonist to use more labor, but it can lead to a reduction in employment. All else equal, an increase in employment raises production (labor has a positive marginal product). If the monopsonist has any market power in its output market, the increased production will lead to lower prices. But if a monopsonist with market power uses less labor, decreased production results, so that price would rise. Finally, if the monopsonist has no market power in its output market, any changes in its output cannot affect market price. Thus, the minimum wage can lead to an increase, a decrease, or no change in the monopsonist's price.

9. Ambiguous. The firm should only invest in project B if its rate of return exceeds the firm's discount rate. As we saw in the second solved problem, the firm's discount rate is the marginal expenditure it makes when it takes out a loan. If the firm gets a fixed rate for loans at least as large as the amount needed to fund project A, it would invest in project A first. But that doesn't mean it wouldn't invest in both projects. It is also possible that the firm must pay a higher interest rate for larger loans. In this case, project B has a lower rate of return but it also has a lower marginal expenditure. It is possible that the rate of return exceeds the marginal expenditure for project B but not for project A, in which case the firm would invest only in project B. On the other hand, it is possible that the firm pays a fixed interest rate that is smaller than the rate of return for project A but larger than the rate of return for project B, in which case it would not invest in project B.

10. The market for espresso beans has been converted from a perfectly competitive market to a monopsonized market. The price paid for beans and the number of beans purchased will both fall.

11. See Figure 15.6. The Alabama market is a monopsony, since Dagen-Haze is the only buyer of watermelon seeds. The Mississippi market is monopolized, because Seeds-R-Us is the only seller of watermelon seeds. In both markets, there is a participant with substantial market power (Dagen-Haze in Alabama and Seeds-R-Us in Mississippi). Both Dagen-Haze and Seeds-R-Us use their market power to raise their profits. Dagen-Haze restricts the amount of seeds they purchase so as to keep the price of seeds low (the seed price is read off sellers' supply curve as w_A). Seeds-R-Us restricts the amount of seeds they sell so as to keep the price of seeds high (here, the seed price is read off buyers' demand curve as w_M). In this problem, the number of seeds traded is smaller in Mississippi than in Alabama (Q_M vs. Q_A). The resultant deadweight loss is the area between demand and supply curves from the amount traded to Q_C, the volume of seeds where supply and demand curves cross. The deadweight loss in Alabama is area A; the deadweight loss is areas A and B in Mississippi.

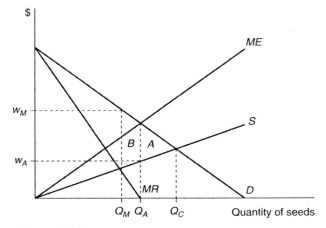

Figure 15.6

12. The market for watermelon seeds has been converted from a monopsony to a bilateral monopoly. While we cannot predict the final price of seeds, we can be relatively certain that Chew-on-This will be able to negotiate a higher price for seeds. What is less certain is the ultimate impact on the number of seeds traded; it could either rise or fall, as the discussion of the Anadarko application makes clear. The ambiguity of the impact upon the number of units of seeds that Dagen-Haze purchases translates into ambiguity concerning the price of watermelon-seed ice cream. If Dagen-Haze purchases more seeds they will make more ice cream, and so the price of ice cream will fall. If Dagen-Haze purchases fewer seeds they will make less ice cream, and so the price of ice cream will rise. Either outcome is possible.

13. For either Jack or Jill to be willing to attend Hill U., the present value of the salary they will earn after graduation must be at least as large as the present value of the salary they can earn right now *plus* the present value of tuition, room, and board over the next 4 years. Because the length of time in employment is so long (43 years after college or 47 years without college), we can get a good approximation by pretending that they will be employed forever. The present value of \$30,000 per year forever is $30,000/0.08 = \$375,000$ for Jack and $30,000/0.06 = \$500,000$ for Jill. The present value of tuition, room, and board is $\$5000 \times [1/1.08 + 1/1.08^2 + 1/1.08^3 + 1/1.08^4] = \$16,560.63$ for Jack and $\$5000 \times [1/1.06 + 1/1.06^2 + 1/1.06^3 + 1/1.06^4] = \$17,325.53$ for Jill. The present value of a salary of \$$f$ per year forever is $f/0.08$ for Jack and $f/0.06$ for Jill. However, they don't get this salary until 4 years from now, so the present value of the salary obtained after graduation is $f/[0.08(1.08^4)]$ for Jack and $f/[0.06(1.06^4)]$ for Jill. For Jack to be willing to go to Hill U., he requires

$$f/[0.08(1.08^4)] \geq \$375,000 + \$16,560.63,$$

or
$$f \geq [0.08(1.08^4)] \times \$391,560.63,$$

or
$$f \geq \$42,617.11.$$

For Jill to be willing to go to Hill U., she requires the salary after college to satisfy

$$f/[0.06(1.06^4)] \geq \$500,000 + \$17,325.53,$$

or
$$f \geq [0.06(1.06^4)] \times \$517,325.53,$$

or $f \geq \$39,186.69$. It takes a smaller future salary to induce Jill to attend Hill U. because she has a smaller discount rate than does Jack. Accordingly, she places a higher value on future rewards than he does, so she is more willing to forfeit current employment opportunities.

14. Your task is to determine two numbers: x_0 (the number of alien invaders to be produced this month) and x_1 (the number produced next month). You know that $x_0 + x_1 = 1000$, so you really only have to figure out how many toys to produce this month. Every additional toy produced this month adds an amount $10x_0$ to this month's costs (the marginal cost of current production). But producing one more alien invader this month means that there is one less to be produced next month, which reduces next month's costs by the amount $10x_1$ (the marginal cost of next month's production). So the net effect on total costs of increasing current production by one unit is $10x_0 - 10x_1$. Because $x_1 = 1000 - x_0$, the net effect on total costs can be simplified to $20x_0 - 10,000$. If x_0 is less than 500, a small increase in current production lowers total cost. On the other hand, if x_0 is larger than 500, a small *decrease* in current production lowers total cost. Either way, you save money by moving current production towards 500 alien invaders. The best you can do is to set $x_0 = 500$. While it looks like the way to answer this question is to split the output between the two months, there is a better way to think about things. A small increase in current production raises the present value of the flow of costs by an amount equal to current marginal cost. But the increase in current output also lowers the present value of the flow of costs by an amount equal to the present value of next period's marginal cost. You have made the present value of the flow of costs as small as possible when this net effect is zero or, in other words, when the current marginal cost is set equal to the present value of next period's marginal cost.

15. If OPEC adds one unit of oil to this year's sales, they will add an amount to profit given by current marginal revenue. However, they will have one less unit to sell next year, which will lower next year's marginal revenue. Because OPEC's demand is given by $p = 100 - Q/2$, its marginal revenue is $MR = 100 - Q$. So the effect on the present value of the flow of OPEC's profit is $100 - Q_0$ (the increment in current revenues) $- (100\, Q_1)/1.05$ (the decrement in next year's discounted marginal revenues). Since $Q_1 = 77 - Q_0$, we may rewrite the net effect as

$$100 - Q_0 - (23 + Q_0)/1.05, \quad \text{or}$$
$$(82 - 2.05Q_0)/1.05.$$

If this expression is positive, a small increase in current extraction will raise OPEC's present value. If the expression is negative, a small decrease in current extraction raises OPEC's present value. To maximize the present value of the flow of OPEC's profits, find that value of Q_0 where the net effect of a one-unit increase in OPEC's current extraction upon its present value is zero. That value sets $82 - 2.05Q_0 = 0$, or $Q_0 = 40$. The remaining 37 units are extracted next year.

■ Exercises

1. Let's take a closer look at Snidely's, the coal baron we met in Solved Problem 1. Assume that the market price for coal is $10/ton, that Snidely's marginal product of labor curve is $MP_L = 6 - Q_L$, and that the labor supply curve in Leftbehind may be described by $Q_L = 2w - 10$, where Q_L is the amount of labor supplied and w is the wage rate Snidely's offers.
   a. In terms of the amount of labor it uses, Snidely's marginal expenditure is _____.
   b. In terms of the amount of labor it uses, Snidely's marginal revenue product is _____.
   c. To maximize its profits, Snidely's should hire _____ unit(s) of labor.
   d. At the level of labor you found for part c, Snidely's must pay a wage of _____.
   e. At the level of labor you found for part c, Snidely's marginal expenditure is _____.

True-False-Ambiguous and Explain Why

2. When a monopolist sells to a monopsonist, we would expect to see a price that is higher than a monopsonist would normally pay.

3. Imposing a minimum wage will *raise* the price charged by a monopsonist.

4. Suppose that the market for gumdrops is monopolized. One of the key ingredients in the making of gumdrops is sugar. The monopoly seller of gumdrops, Goody's, buys its sugar from PureCane, which happens to be a monopolist in the sugar market. If PureCane is forced to sell its sugar at marginal cost, Goody's would lower the price of gumdrops.

5. Chad needs wheels. He is looking at two cars, a Geo Metro and a slightly used Honda Accord. While Chad thinks the Metro will cost him much less to run in a given year, since it gets better gas mileage and is less likely to need repairs, it will cost a lot more to buy. After thinking carefully about his options, Chad decides to buy the Metro. Just then, he hears that the Fed has lowered interest rates. Chad should re-evaluate his decision.

Short-Answer

6. If a monopsonist faces a labor supply with constant elasticity 0.4, what is its marginal expenditure curve?

7. Virtually all of the major airlines' employees are unionized, which suggests that the airline industry is probably characterized by market power at both the final stage (that is, the market for air travel) and the input stage (the market for labor to be used in flying the planes). One carrier, United, makes a big deal about the fact that it is employee owned. Discuss the impact employee ownership is likely to have upon ticket prices.

8. Threatened strikes between labor unions and big business seem commonplace. Explain why such conflicts might naturally arise.

9. You've got your eye on a gorgeous 1965 Mustang. The price is somewhat daunting—the current owner wants $15,000 for it—but you tell yourself it's a classic. Unfortunately, it will cost you $500 each year for the next 5 years in upkeep. After that, you expect to sell it, again for $15,000. But you've always wanted one of these beauties, and so you anticipate $2000 worth of services (enjoyment, envy of your friends, and so on) every year you own it. If your discount rate is zero, would you buy the Mustang? If your discount rate is 10 percent, would you buy the Mustang?

10. Jane loves to sing, so she is planning on majoring in music at college. She knows that she could get a job at a local music store right now that would pay her $25,000 per year. She expects to be able to get a job at a music studio upon graduating, which would pay her $30,000 per year. Jane thinks she will work for 40 years after graduating from college; because she is a somewhat casual student she plans on taking 5 years to graduate. For simplicity, let's assume her wages stay constant over her entire work life. Should she attend college if her discount rate is 2%? 5%?

11. Back at Go-bot (the company we met in Practice Problem 14), your bosses have discovered that holding inventories of N alien invaders next month has an opportunity cost of $1000N$. You are to determine the optimal production of alien invaders this month and next, with 1000 toys produced in total, using a discount rate of zero.

    a. To help you perform this calculation, first determine production costs this month, production costs next month, inventor costs next month, and Go-bots' combined costs (the sum of current production costs and future inventory costs) when (i) 500 invaders are produced this month; (ii) 400 invaders are produced this month.

    b. Give a formula for the implicit contribution from a one-unit increase in this month's production to Go-bots' combined costs.

    c. How many invaders should you produce each month? What are the total production costs and inventory costs? What are Go-bots' combined costs?

12. Suppose a perfectly competitive firm is a monopsonist, with the Cobb-Douglas production function $q = 10L^{1/2}K^{1/2}$, and that it faces a labor supply curve with constant elasticity η. Describe the profit it earns if it hires the profit-maximizing amount of labor.

13. You are the manager of a small Midwestern company that produces shoes and must decide how to run the factory for the next two half-year periods. (While the company is likely to be around longer, let's ignore effects past the next two periods.) The number of pairs of shoes that can be produced in the half-year period, t (let $t = 1$ for the first half of the year and $t = 2$ for the second half), depends on the number of machines in the factory according to $Q_t = AM_t^{1/2}$, where M_t is the number of machines in period t. While the number of machines available in period 1 can't be adjusted, you can add to the

number of machines next period by spending money this period. The number of machines in period 2 is $M_2 = M_1 + I_1$, where I_1 is the amount you invest this period on next period's machines. The price of shoes is p_s in both periods. Find the value of I_1 that maximizes the net present value of the company.

14. The production of rabbit's feet requires hiring rabbit trappers. Each trapper must be paid the same wage, and the price of a rabbit's foot is fixed at p_{RF}. Bugsies is the only firm in town hiring rabbit trappers. The total product of rabbit trappers is

$$TP(Q_L) = AQ_L^{1/2},$$

where Q_L is the number of trappers hired and A is a positive constant. Determine the number of trappers that maximizes Bugsies' profit and the associated wage that Bugsies will pay if

a. the supply of rabbit trappers is perfectly elastic at w_0;

b. the supply of rabbit trappers is given by $w = BQ_L$.

Chapter 16
Uncertainty

■ Chapter Summary

A line in a Lyle Lovett song says, "Life is SO uncertain." Sometimes the uncertainties we face aren't significant, and it doesn't really matter if we pretend they're not there. But in other instances, these uncertainties are truly important. If you skip a lecture, you may miss a key point, one that shows up on the next exam—or the class might be horribly boring. If you go tooling down the highway at 80 miles per hour, you might get where you're going in record time, or you might get nabbed by the state patrol. Uncertainty matters to virtually every economic decision maker at one time or another. Firms gamble on future market conditions when they bring out a new product line, when they run an advertising campaign, or when they hire a new employee. Consumers face risks when they invest in the stock market or when they take out a mortgage with a variable mortgage rate. Not all risks are bad—perhaps while you are walking to class next week you will accidentally bump into someone who becomes your true love. This chapter is devoted to a discussion of uncertainty.

The building blocks for our discussion are possible outcomes, or *states of nature,* and the chance that one of these outcomes will occur, or the *probability* of that state. These two notions allow us to describe the **degree of risk** an individual faces. Armed with a way of describing this risk, we can talk about how people **make decisions under uncertainty**. The fundamental tool we use in analyzing such decision making is *expected utility*. Expected utility places a number on each possible state of nature (the utility arising from that outcome), multiplies this number by the chance the state will occur, and then sums over all the possible states of nature. Expected utility gives us a way of comparing two uncertain scenarios: If the expected utility under one scenario is larger than the expected utility of a second scenario, the decision maker likes the first scenario better. For example, if the expected utility you get from going to class exceeds the expected utility you get from going out to play Frisbee, you should probably go to class. A major ingredient in developing the expected utility framework is the individual's attitudes toward risk. Some folks are willing to play small-stakes gambles, like betting a friend $1 that a tossed coin will come up heads. This sort of behavior indicates a person is *risk neutral*. Most people, however, find that gambling over large stakes makes them nervous. Would you be willing to gamble on the outcome of a tossed coin if the stakes were $1000? Sure, you could win a grand if heads comes up, but think about how bad you're going to feel if it's tails instead.

Two particularly important applications of our decision-making framework have to do with **avoiding risk** and **investing under uncertainty**. Just about everyone has automobile insurance, but how many people do you know who have insured the contents of their apartment against theft or fire? Perhaps such insurance is too expensive, or maybe your apartment-dwelling friend has found a different way to reduce his or her exposure to risk (such as locking doors and windows, or by not having anything worth stealing in the first place). Despite most people's aversion to risk, lots of regular folks put big sums of money in the stock market. Perhaps they think that they have found the sure winner that all the other investors missed. But a more likely explanation is that these investors are lured by the possibility of large returns.

While the framework developed in this chapter is elegant, it is not without controversy. Take the notion of probability, for instance. What's the chance that a democrat will win the next presidential election? Chances are anyone you ask will have an opinion, but it's not likely that they will agree with their neighbor. If we all knew the true probability, there wouldn't be any such disagreement. This example illustrates the distinction between *objective* probability—a probability that we all know to be true—and *subjective* probability—one that we have to guess about. While it is possible to work out a framework with subjective probabilities, that framework is much harder than the one we'll use in this chapter. One point that is worth keeping in the back of your mind, however, is that the models in this chapter are meant to allow a characterization of decision making; they shouldn't be taken too literally. People make mistakes in assessing probabilities, perhaps because they are just throwing out a guess, or perhaps because the problem is just too tough to resolve. When lottery jackpots get very large, lots of people buy lottery tickets. When they buy these tickets, do they think about the chances of winning, or how the massive interest in the lottery impacts their odds of winning? Or do they just think "life as a millionaire would be so much better than my tame existence that it's worth plunking down a buck?"

■ Key Concepts and Formulas

- **Probability:** a way of quantifying risk.
- **Expected value:** the average occurrence; it could be the average outcome or the average utility from the possible outcomes, depending on the context.
- **Variance:** a way of describing the spread of possible outcomes.
- **Risk-averse person:** someone who prefers not to take a fair bet, one with an expected value of zero.
- **Risk-neutral person:** someone who is indifferent between playing and not playing a fair bet.
- **Risk premium:** the amount of money an individual would be willing to pay to avoid a source of risk.
- **Decision tree:** a graphical method for identifying the possible outcomes, the associated consequences, and any possible mitigating actions the decision maker has available.

■ Application: Tax Evasion

Nobody likes paying taxes. Even so, most people are reasonably honest when they fill out their tax forms. Some individuals, however, are less forthright. The United States Internal Revenue Service (IRS) refers to such behavior as tax evasion. While the IRS gets forms from employers that document each employee's annual salary, there are other potential sources of income. Receipts from a garage sale and tips received by waiters or cabdrivers are generally not reported to the IRS by the individual who parts with the cash. Individuals who receive income from such cash transactions may be tempted to not report it. The only way the IRS can find out about these transactions is through a costly audit of the taxpayer. If the IRS catches a tax evader, the penalties are often severe: The unpaid taxes are collected with interest, large fines are levied, and jail time is sometimes imposed. But tax evaders know that there is a positive probability that they won't get caught. To understand the incentives confronting a potential tax evader, let's consider Mark's situation. Mark receives an annual salary of $50,000, which is reported to the IRS by Mark's employer. Mark also takes on occasional work as a handyman. The income from this second source is $10,000. If the IRS audits Mark, they will find out exactly how much income he earned. So, if he does not report the extra $10,000, the IRS will find out about it if they audit Mark, but otherwise they won't know about the extra income. Mark pays 25 percent of any reported income in taxes, which leaves him with 75 percent of his salary as after-tax wealth. Suppose the probability the IRS will audit Mark is 10 percent, and the costs he will bear if he hides the $10,000 and gets caught are $20,000.

Question: If Mark is risk neutral, will he report his income from the handyman jobs?

Answer: Because Mark is risk neutral, he cares only about his expected wealth. To answer the question, we need to determine Mark's expected wealth if he hides the $10,000 and compare it to his expected wealth if he reports all his income. If Mark reports $50,000, he pays $12,500 in taxes (25 percent of his reported income). If the IRS doesn't audit him, Mark has $47,500 after taxes ($60,000 – $12,500). If the IRS does audit him, Mark must pay the IRS an additional $20,000, which leaves him with $27,500. The probability that Mark will be audited is 0.1 (10 percent).

There are just two possible outcomes—either Mark is audited or he isn't audited. The probability that Mark is audited summed with the probability that he isn't audited must equal 1. Since the probability he will be audited is 0.1, the probability he won't be audited must equal 0.9. Mark's expected wealth if he doesn't report the $10,000 is

$$EW = 0.1 \times \$27,500 + 0.9 \times \$47,500$$
$$= \$45,500.$$

If Mark reports his income as $60,000, he pays $15,000 in taxes (25 percent of his reported income), and retains $45,000. His wealth is $45,000 whether the IRS audits him or not. Thus, Mark's expected wealth if he does report the $10,000 is

$$EW = 0.1 \times \$45,000 + 0.9 \times \$45,000,$$

or $45,000. Because Mark's expected wealth is larger if he doesn't report the $10,000, he won't report the income from his handyman jobs.

The IRS is unlikely to be happy with this outcome. To deter tax evaders like Mark, the IRS has to lower the expected wealth from tax evasion. Such a reduction can be accomplished either by making it more likely that cheaters will get caught or by increasing the fines for those who are caught. Solved Problem 2 analyzes these two methods for authorities to deter crime.

■ Solved Problems

1.   Biff is occasionally accident-prone. Some years his medical expenses are $5000, and in other years he has no expenses. Biff thinks that there is a 50 percent chance his expenses in the upcoming year will be $5000 (and a 50 percent chance that they will be $0). Biff's income is $32,000, out of which he must pay any medical expenses. Biff has just heard about an insurance company called State Harm. If Biff pays State Harm a large premium, they promise to pay all his medical expenses. Biff is risk averse, with a utility function over wealth as depicted in Figure 16.1. How much would he be willing to pay for State Harm's insurance?

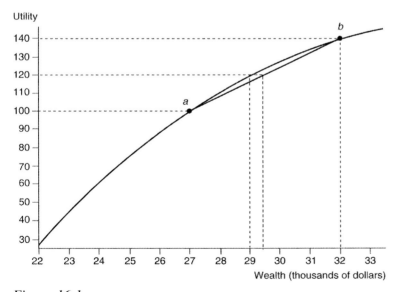

Figure 16.1

Step 1: Determine Biff's expected income if he doesn't buy insurance from State Harm.

If his expenses are $5000, Biff has $27,000 left over (point a on Figure 16.1). If his expenses are $0, Biff's wealth is $32,000, at point b. There is a 50 percent chance that his medical expenses will be $5000, and a 50 percent chance that he won't have any expenses. So, Biff's expected wealth is

$$EW = 1/2 \times 27,000 + 1/2 \times 32,000$$
$$= \$29,500.$$

Step 2: Determine Biff's expected utility if he doesn't buy insurance from State Harm.

If his income is $27,000, Biff's utility is $U(\$27,000) = 100$. If his income is $32,000, Biff's utility is $U(\$32,000) = 140$. His expected utility is thus

$$EU = 1/2 \times 100 + 1/2 \times 140$$
$$= 120.$$

Step 3: Determine Biff's risk premium.

The amount of income that makes Biff's utility 120—the same as the expected utility from Step Two—is $29,000 (point c in Figure 16.1). Biff is indifferent between the risk he faces when he doesn't have medical insurance and having $29,000 but facing no risk. Biff is willing to pay the difference between $29,000 and $29,500, his expected wealth without insurance, to avoid any risk. Biff's risk premium is $500.

Step 4: Determine the amount of money Biff would be willing to pay to State Harm for their insurance.

Biff starts out with $32,000. The uncertainty he faces about his medical expenses lowers his expected wealth by $2500, and his risk premium is $500. He would pay the sum of these two amounts, or $3000, for State Harm's insurance policy. (Another way to get this answer is to compare his initial income, $32,000, with the wealth he would accept if he could avoid any risk, $29,000.)

2. Richard, a dyed-in-the-wool politician, argues that the best way to reduce crime is to spend more on law enforcement. Milton, a preeminent economist, counters that raising the penalties for those who are convicted is likely to be more cost effective. To help them resolve their debate, let's consider this simple tale. A potential robber has $40,000 in wealth. He believes he can pick up an additional $50,000 by breaking into shops after dark. The probability that the potential robber will get caught when there are N police on patrol is $N/15$. (While it is true that the number of police who patrol the area on any given day must be an integer, the average number of police in the area can be a fraction, so we treat N as a continuous variable.) If caught, the robber forfeits the purloined income and an amount F of his wealth. The largest possible sanction would entail confiscating all his wealth, so F can not exceed $40,000. If a potential robber's utility function over wealth is $U(W) = W^{1/2}$, what values of F and N should be chosen to deter the potential robber from breaking into the shops at minimal cost?

Step 1: Determine the potential robber's expected utility if he burgles, as a function of F and N.

If he burgles and doesn't get caught, his wealth is $40,000 + 50,000$, or $90,000. If he gets caught, his wealth is $40,000 - F$. Since the chance he gets caught is $N/10$, his expected utility is

$$EU = (90,000)^{1/2} \times (15 - N)/15 + (40,000 - F)^{1/2} \times N/15$$
$$= 300 \times (15 - N)/15 + (40,000 - F)^{1/2} \times N/15.$$

Step 2: Determine the impact of an increase in the number of patrolmen on the incentive to burgle.

$\partial EU/\partial N = [(40,000 - F)^{1/2} - 300]/15$. Since the smallest possible value of F is 0, the largest possible value of $(40,000 - F)^{1/2}$ is $(40,000)^{1/2}$, or 200. Thus, the largest possible value of $\partial EU/\partial N$ is $[200 - 300]/15$, or $-100/15$. In other words, an increase in N must lower the burglar's expected utility, and so makes burgling relatively less attractive. On this score Richard is correct.

Step 3: Determine the values of N and F that will deter the potential robber from burgling.

To keep the potential robber from burgling, N and F need to be set large enough that the expected utility from burgling is no larger than the certain utility from not burgling, which is $(40,000)^{1/2} = 200$. The required values sets

$$300 \times (15 - N)/15 + (40,000 - F)^{1/2} \times N/15 = 200.$$

Step 4: Determine the values of N and F that deter burgling at the lowest cost to society.

Placing an additional policeman on patrol costs society something—either we have to hire more cops or we have to redirect some away from other law enforcement activities, which has an opportunity cost. On the other hand, an increase in F costs society nothing. So the cheapest way to deter crime is to choose the largest possible value of F, and then determine the necessary value of N. (Milton is correct: the most cost-effective way to deter crime is to increase penalties for those who are convicted.) The largest possible value of F is 40,000; choosing that value of F, the required value of N would solve

$$300 \times (15 - N)/15 = 200, \text{ or } N = 5.$$

■ Practice Problems

Multiple-Choice

1. When is the risk you face by investing in each of two stocks smaller than the risk you would face by investing the same total amount of money in only one stock?
   a. Never.
   b. Always.
   c. Whenever the two stocks are perfectly negatively correlated.
   d. Whenever the two stocks are not perfectly positively correlated.

2. Phil decides to bet on the outcome of a rolled die. If the die shows an even number, then Phil will win $10. If the die shows an odd number, Phil wins nothing. The expected value of Phil's gamble is
   a. $0.
   b. $5.
   c. $10.
   d. There isn't enough information to tell.

3. The variance of Phil's gamble is
   a. 5.
   b. 10.
   c. 25.
   d. There isn't enough information to tell.

4. Bill faces an uncertain outcome. The expected wealth he receives from this outcome is $100. Bill reckons that his expected utility from the uncertainty he faces is 20, while the utility he would obtain from receiving $100 for sure is 25. What can we say about Bill's risk attitudes?
   a. Bill is risk averse.
   b. Bill is risk neutral.
   c. Bill is risk preferring.
   d. There isn't enough information to say anything about Bill's risk attitudes.

Fill-in

5. Joe's Garage is considering sending one of its mechanics to a training program so that he will be able to work on computerized engines. There are two potential programs that Joe is considering. The cost of program A is $182, while program B costs $219. There are two possible outcomes from these programs: The employee's skills will be increased or they will not be increased. Joe thinks the chance that program A will increase his employee's skills is 50 percent, while the probability that program B will enhance the employee's skills is 65 percent. If the employee's skills are increased, Joe will make an extra $340 of profit next year (not including the training cost). If the employee's skills are not noticeably increased, Joe will only make an extra $60 of profit next year (again, not including the training cost). Joe's discount rate is 10 percent.

   a. The expected change in next year's profit from program A is _____.
   b. The expected change in next year's profit from program B is _____.
   c. The present value of the expected change in next year's profit from program A is _____.
   d. The present value of the expected change in next year's profit from program B is _____.
   e. If Joe chooses program A, the expected net present value (including training costs) is _____.
   f. If Joe chooses program B, the expected net present value (including training costs) is _____.
   g. Should Joe choose program A, program B, or neither? ___

True-False-Ambiguous and Explain Why

6. Fred is a contestant on the popular TV game show "Let's Make a Deal." The host of the show, Monty Hall, has offered Fred an interesting choice. Fred may have the item behind the big door or he can take a dream vacation worth $8,000. The prize behind the big door is equally likely to be a goat (a *baaad* prize, worth literally nothing) or a $20,000 car. If Fred takes the dream vacation, he must be risk averse.

7. Every Christmas, Dorothy organizes a "Yankee gift exchange" with her family. Each family member brings a gift that costs $5, and recipients of the gifts are randomly determined. Someone always brings five $1 lottery tickets, and everyone thinks the tickets are the best gift. Members of Dorothy's family are risk preferrers.

8. Frank is thinking about two possible investments. For each option, Frank thinks there is a probability of ½ that the investment will produce a 5 percent return and a probability of ½ that the investment will offer a 15 percent return. However, Frank would have to put more money into the first investment than the second. Since the two investments have the same expected rate of return, and the variance in the rates of return are the same, Frank should be indifferent between the two investments.

Short-Answer

9. In Car-phonia, the government is thinking about putting on tough emission control devices on all cars that would cut the output of a suspected cancer-causing pollutant to (virtually) zero. There are 20,000 cars in Car-phonia. The cost of putting on the device is $100 per car. Currently, estimates range from as high as 0.1% (0.001) to as low as 0.01% (0.0001) of the population will develop cancer in 10 years' time due to exposure to the pollutant. There are 100,000 people who live in Car-phonia. Estimates from studies on the value of life place a range of $200,000 to $2,000,000 per life saved. To simplify the problem, suppose that imposing restrictions this year will cause no change in the cancer rate in any year except year 10 when the cancer rate will fall to zero. The discount rate is 5% per year.

   a. If you took the low estimate for both the value of life and the risk of cancer, what is the net present value of installing emission control devices?
   b. If you took the high estimate for both the value of life and the risk of cancer, what is the net present value of installing emission control devices?

c.   Assume for this part that the cancer risk really is 0.1%. Suppose that you think that there is a 50% probability that the low estimate on the value of life is correct and a 50% probability that the high estimate on the value of life is correct. What is the expected net present value from installing emission control devices?

10.   Mason is an avid collector of antique fishing rods. He hears about a rod that he thinks he might be interested in. The rod is in need of some work, and Mason is not certain how much the work will cost. The repair costs will either be $100 or $400, with equal probability. After it is repaired, the rod will be worth $700. The price of the rod is $500.

a.   Determine Mason's expected gain if he buys the rod.

b.   Suppose that Mason can have an expert look at the rod before he buys it. For a fee of $25, the expert will tell Mason exactly how much the repairs will cost. Now what is Mason's expected gain if he buys the rod?

11.   Write out the decision tree for Joe's decision in Practice Problem 5.

12.   Shale Oil Company is contemplating a $10,000,000 investment today into an advanced production technique. This investment will raise production by 500,000 barrels per year in 5 years (with no other effect on production). However, Shale Oil is not so sure about the future price: price in 5 years will either be $25 per barrel, $30 per barrel, or $40 per barrel. The chance that the price will be $30 is 2/5, the chance that the price will be $35 is 2/5, and the chance that the price will be $40 per barrel is 1/5. Assuming Shale Oil is risk neutral, and that they use a discount rate of 11.1%, should they invest in the project?

13.   Continuing from Practice Problem 5, suppose that Joe remembers that two of his friends have sent their mechanics for training. Amos sent his employee to program A, while Andy sent his employee to program B. Joe won't be able to talk to either Amos or Andy until after he has enrolled his employee, but he can talk to them before the program starts. Each program is willing to return the training cost if Joe decides to cancel before the program starts. Joe decides that he will pick one of the programs and then talk to the friend who used that program. If his friend is pessimistic about the program Joe picked, then Joe will cancel; otherwise, he will send his employee for training. Joe trusts his friends' opinions, and thinks they will be able to tell him if the program they used was worthwhile. Joe thinks there is a 50 percent chance that Amos would tell him that program A will improve his worker's skills, and that there is a 65 percent chance that Andy will tell him that program B will improve his worker's skills. Recalculate the expected present value of each program. Should Joe choose program A, program B, or neither program?

14.   John and Todd are discussing two stocks. One share of stock in the Red House Construction Corporation will cost $100. John and Todd agree that the price of a share of Red House stock will fall to $70 with 20 percent probability, but that there is an 80 percent chance the stock will become worth $120. One share of Blackened Voodoo Chile Beer company stock costs $80. John and Todd agree that the price of a share of Voodoo Chile stock could fall to $70, and that there is a 1/3 chance of this occurrence. They also agree that there is a 2/3 chance that the stock will become worth $100. Todd argues that Red House corporation is the better investment, while John thinks that Voodoo Chile company looks better.

a.   Calculate the expected value and variance of the profit (in dollar terms) from buying one share of Red House stock.

b.   Calculate the expected value and variance of the profit (in dollar terms) from buying one share of Voodoo Chile stock.

c.   What can we tell about Todd's risk attitudes? What about John's risk attitudes?

15. Always on the lookout for a good investment, Shale Oil Company is now thinking about exploring for oil in Alaska. They believe that two outcomes are possible: Either they will find a deposit with 700,000 barrels or they won't find any oil. The probability that they won't find any oil is 9/10. The cost of exploring is $1,000,000. If oil is discovered, it can be extracted and sold next year. Shale Oil's discount rate is 8 percent, and the marginal cost of extraction will be constant at $1. The CEO at Shale Oil thinks next year's price will be around $17, but he worries that it could be higher or lower. He asks you to tell him the expected net present value of the exploration program under two scenarios:

    a. Next year's price is known to be $17.

    b. Next year's price will be $13; $16, or $21, where the chance that price will be $13 is 1/3, the chance that price will be $16 is 4/15, and the chance that the price will be $21 is 2/5.

    c. How do these two expected net present values compare? Give an intuitive explanation of this outcome.

    d. Should Shale Oil explore for oil if it is risk neutral?

16. Write out a decision tree for Shale Oil's exploration problem from Practice Problem 15, part b.

■ Answers to Practice Problems

1. If the two stocks are perfectly correlated—their prices always move in the same direction—then there really is no difference between splitting the money between the two stocks on the one hand or putting it all in one of the stocks on the other hand. Either way, you win if both of the stocks appreciate in value, and you lose if they depreciate. But if the stocks aren't perfectly correlated—they don't always move together—you face less risk by investing in both stocks. Spreading your money between two stocks is one way to diversify, and diversification lowers risk. Answer d is correct.

2. Since the chance the rolled die will come up with an even number is 50 percent and the chance it will come up with an odd number is 50 percent, the expected value of Phil's bet is $1/2 \times 10 + 1/2 \times 0$, or 5. Answer b is correct.

3. The variance of Phil's bet is based on the difference between the outcome and the expected value and the probabilities of each outcome. The expected value is 5 (see the answer for Multiple-Choice Problem 2 above), while the probability for each outcome is 1/2. The variance of Phil's bet is $1/2 \times (10 - 5)^2 + 1/2 \times (0 - 5)^2$. The first term is 1/2 times 5^2, while the second term is 1/2 times $(-5)^2$. So the variance is $1/2 \times 25 + 1/2 \times 25$, or 25. Answer c is correct.

4. Bill prefers to receive $100 rather than face uncertainty that has an expected outcome of $100. Facing the uncertainty instead of receiving $100 for sure is basically a fair bet—Bill gives up $100 to play a gamble that is worth $100. Since Bill really doesn't want to play this fair bet, he must be risk averse. Answer a is correct. If Bill were risk neutral he'd be indifferent between facing the uncertainty and receiving the cash, in which case his expected utility would have to be 25, the same as the utility of receiving $100 for sure. If he were risk preferring, the expected utility from facing the uncertainty would be larger than 25. If you answered d because you were thinking that Bill might be risk averse some of the time and risk preferring some of the time, you get credit for creativity. If you guessed d just because it seemed like a good guess, you should probably study the material some more.

5. Answers and brief explanations follow.

a. With program A, there is a 50 percent chance that next year's profit will go up by $340. In other words, the probability that next year's profit rises by $340 is 1/2. There are just two possible outcomes—profits rise by $340 or by $60. The probability that profits rise by $340 summed with the probability that profits go up by $60 must equal 1. The probability that profit goes up by only $60 is 1 minus the probability that profits rise by $340, which is $1 - 1/2 = 1/2$. The expected gain is thus $1/2 \times \$340 + 1/2 \times \$60 = \$200$.

b. With program B, the probability that next year's profits rise by $340 is 0.65; the probability that they go up by $60 is $1 - 0.65$, or 0.35. The expected gain is then $0.65 \times \$340 + 0.35 \times \$60 = \$242$.

c. Since the expected profits from program A show up one year in the future, we know from the material in Chapter 16 that their present value is the expected gain divided by one plus Joe's discount rate. Joe's discount rate is 10 percent, so the present value is $200/1.1, or $181.82.

d. The present value of the expected profits from program B is $242/1.1, or $220.

e. Subtracting out the program cost of $182, Joe loses $0.18 in present value from program A.

f. Subtracting out the program cost of $219, Joe gains $1 in present value from program B.

g. Program B, since its expected present value exceeds its up-front cost ($219). Joe wouldn't pick program A anyway, since its expected present value does not exceed the up-front cost.

6. True. Think of the big door as a big gamble. Fred either gets something worth $20,000 or he gets something that is worthless. The expected value of this prize is $10,000 ($= 1/2 \times \$20,000 + 1/2 \times \$0$). Since Fred took a prize worth $8000, he must prefer this amount of cash to the gamble. If someone is risk averse, their risk premium (the difference between the expected value of a gamble, like the prize behind the door, and the amount of cash they would take in place of the gamble) is positive. Fred's behavior tells us that his risk premium is at least $2000, which is positive, so Fred must be risk averse.

7. Ambiguous. It is true that a risk preferrer would want the lottery tickets rather than some other prize. But is also true that a risk-averse person who liked to play games for small stakes, purely for the recreational fun, would want the tickets. We can't really say anything about the risk preferences of Dorothy's family members from the information in this problem.

8. False. Frank's decision is tied to the expected utility he gets from the two investments. Although $1 invested in either option is equally attractive, Frank won't be investing the same amount: The first option requires that he put more money at risk. Since the expected return is the same, but the first investment entails a larger amount of money, it yields a larger expected increase in Frank's wealth. On the other hand, with more money at risk, the variance in his wealth is larger with the first investment—it is riskier than the second investment. The higher expected gain in wealth is appealing, but the higher variance is likely to be worrisome. If Frank is risk neutral, he won't care about the extra risk, and he'll choose the first investment. If he is a risk preferrer, then he will like both the larger expected gain in wealth and the larger variance in wealth. If he is risk averse, he will have to weigh the two effects. If he is only mildly risk averse, he will prefer the first investment, but he will prefer the second investment if he is very risk averse.

9. The idea here is to calculate the future expected benefits as the product of population (100,000), cancer risk (0.001 if high or 0.0001 if low), and value of life ($2,000,000 if high or $200,000 if low). This future expected benefit is then divided by 1.05¹⁰ to obtain the present value of benefits, since the discount rate is 5% and the future effects show up in 10 years. Finally, we compare the present value of benefits against the present value of costs. The present value of costs is $100 (the installation cost) multiplied by 20,000 (the number of cars), or $2,000,000.

a. If the health risk is 0.0001 and value of life is $200,000 (the low estimates), we get a future expected benefit of $2,000,000. This gives a present value of benefits equal to $1,227,826.23, so that the net present value is −$772,173.77.

b. If the health risk is 0.001 and value of life is $2,000,000 (the low estimates), we get a future expected benefit of $200,000,000. This gives a present value of benefits equal to $122,782,622.58; the net present value is then $120,782,622.58.

c. If there is a 50% chance that the value of life is $2,000,000 and a 50% chance that the value of life is $200,000, the expected (or average) value of life is [$2,000,000 + $200,000]/2 = $1,100,000. Since the health risk is 0.001, we get a future expected benefit of $110,000,000. This gives a present value of benefits equal to $67,530,442.42, and so the net present value is $65,530,442.42.

10. Mason's expected gain is the price he can get after repairs, less the price he pays and the repair cost.

a. He buys the rod for $500 and sells it for $700, so his expected gain is $200 minus the expected repair cost. The two possible repair costs, $100 and $400, are equally likely. Because the two probabilities add up to one, they must each be 1/2. The expected repair costs are thus 1/2 100 + 1/2 400, or $250. His expected gain is $200 − $250, or −$50: He anticipates losing $50.

b. If the expert tells Mason the repair costs will be $100, he buys the rod for $500, pays the $100 repair costs, and sells the rod for $700, making a profit of $100. If the expert tells Mason the repair costs will be $400, Mason will decide not to buy the rod, making no profit. As in part a, the probability the repair costs will be $100 is 1/2, and the probability the repair costs will be $400 is 1/2. So Mason expects to make 1/2 × $100 + 1/2 × $0 = $50. From this expected profit, Mason has to subtract the expert's $25 fee, so Mason's expected gain is $50 − $25, or $25.

11. See Figure 16.2. To determine the numbers at the end of each branch, you first need to compute the present value of next year's profits. If the employee's skills are increased, next year's profits go up by $340, which gives a present value of $340/1.1 = $309.09. If his skills are not increased, profits only go up by $60, for a present value of $60/1.1 = $54.55. You then need to subtract the program cost ($182 for program A or $219 for program B) from these present values. The expected net present values (ENPV) associated with the two programs are then found by multiplying the net present values at each end node by the associated probabilities listed under the possible outcome. Thus, the ENPV for program A is 0.5 × $127.09 + 0.5 × −$127.45 = −$0.18, and similarly for program B.

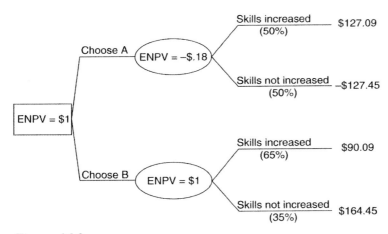

Figure 16.2

12. Shale Oil should invest in the project if doing so will increase Shale's expected utility. As Shale is risk neutral, the project will increase Shale's expected utility if the expected present value of the future payoffs exceed the cost paid today (i.e., if the project has a positive expected net present value). First, we calculate the present value of $1 in 5 years' time as $1/(1 + 0.111)^5 = 1/1.692662 = 0.590785$. Second, we calculate the expected revenues in 5 years. If the price in 5 years is $30, the extra production will be worth $15 million ($30 per barrel × 500,000 barrels). Similarly, if the price in 5 years is $35, the extra production will be worth $17.5 million, and if the price is $40 the extra

production will be worth $20 million. The chances of these three outcomes are 0.4 (= 2/5), 0.4, and 0.2, respectively, so we calculate the expected future revenues (in millions of dollars) as 0.4 × $15 + 0.4 × $17.5 + 0.2 × $20 = 6 + 7 + 4 = $17 million. The present value of the future expected benefits from the investment is therefore $10,043,351 (= $17 million × 0.590785). After subtracting the initial cost of $10,000,000, we calculate the expected net present value of the investment as $43,351; as this is positive and Shale is risk neutral, it should invest in the project.

13. Joe's conversations are likely to change the expected value of each program. Suppose his friend who used program A liked it. Then Joe will be quite certain that the program will increase his employee's skills, and so add $340 to Joe's profit. In this case, it would be well worth the $182 cost. But if his friend thought the program was a bust, so that it only will add $60 to Joe's profit, Joe will know that the program isn't worth the money. In this second case, he will cancel out of the program and get his $182 back. The same holds true for program B: If his other friend recommends the program, Joe will be confident that he stands to add $340 to his profits next year, and so he'll go ahead. But if the friend pans program B, he will cancel out and get the $219 back. The expected present value of using program A is now 1/2 × (340/1.1 − 182) + 1/2 × 0 = $63.55. The expected present value from using program B is now 0.65 × (340/1.1 − 219) + 0.35 × 0 = $58.56. While the expected present value of both programs goes up thanks to Joe's friends' advice, program A now delivers the higher expected present value. Joe should choose program A.

14. If the price of Red House stock rises to $120, one share gives a profit of $20. If the price falls to $70, one share gives a profit of −$30. If the price of Voodoo Chile stock rises to $100, one share gives a profit of $20. If the price of Voodoo Chile stock falls to $70, one share gives a profit of −$10.

   a. The expected value of profit from one share of Red House stock is 0.8 × $20 + 0.2 × (−$30) = $10. The variance in profit is 0.8 × (20 − 10)^2 + 0.2 × (−30 − 10)^2, or 0.8 × 100 + 0.2 × 1600 = 400.

   b. The expected value of profit from one share of Voodoo Chile stock is 2/3 × $20 + 1/3 × (−$10) = $10. The variance in profit is 2/3 × (20 − 10)^2 + 1/3 × (−10 − 10)^2, or 2/3 × 100 + 1/3 × 400 = 200.

   c. The expected profit from a share of either stock is $10, but the variance in profit is larger for Red House stock. Since Todd prefers Red House he must find the larger variance attractive, which suggests he is a risk preferrer. Since John would rather buy Voodoo Chile stock, he must find the smaller variance attractive, which suggests he is risk averse.

15. The expected net present value of exploration is the present value of next year's expected profits less the cost of exploration. To get the present value of next year's expected profits, we first calculate next year's expected profits and then divide by 1 + r, where r is Shale Oil's discount rate. Since r = 8 percent, 1 + r = 1.08.

   a. If oil is discovered, revenues will be $17 × 700,000, or $11,900,000. Costs will be $1 × 700,000, or $700,000. Therefore, profits are $11,200,000. If no oil is discovered, there are no profits from next year. Since the probability that oil is discovered is 0.1, next year's expected profits are 0.1 × $11,200,000 + 0.9 × $0 = $1,120,000. Since Shale Oil's discount rate is 8 percent, the present value of next year's expected profit is $1,120,000/1.08 = $1,037,037.04. Subtracting the $1,000,000 exploration cost, the expected net present value of the exploration program is $37,037.04.

   b. If oil is discovered, costs will be $700,000, just as in part a. If next year's price is $13, revenues will be $9,100,000, so profits would be $8,400,000. If next year's price is $16, revenues will be $11,200,000, so profits would be $10,500,000. If next year's price is $21, revenues will be $14,700,000, so profits would be $14,000,000. The probability that price will be $13 is 1/3, the probability that price will be $16 is 4/15, and the probability that price will be $21 is 2/5, so expected profits are 1/3 × $8,400,000 + 4/15 × $10,500,000 + 2/5 × $14,000,000 = $11,200,000 if oil is found. If oil is not discovered there are no profits from next year, no matter what the price is. Next year's expected profit is thus $0.1 \times \$11,200,000 + 0.9 \times \$0 = \$1,120,000$. The present value of next year's expected profits is $\$1,120,000/1.08 = \$1,037,037.04$; the expected net present value of the exploration program is $\$37,037.04$.

c.   The two expected net present values are the same. To see why we get this outcome, let's calculate the expected value of next year's price in part b. It is $1/3 \times \$13 + 4/15 \times \$16 + 2/5 \times \$21 = \$17$, which is the price in part a. Since the expected price in part b is the same as the price in part a, expected revenues are the same in each part, which means expected profits are the same in each part. With the same expected value for next year's profit in each part, we get identical present values.

d.   Shale Oil should explore for oil if the expected net present value of the operation is positive. Whether next year's price is known to be $17, or uncertain but with an expected value of $17, the present value of next year's expected profits exceed the cost of exploration. Shale Oil should explore.

16. See Figure 16.3. To determine the numbers at the end of each branch, you first need to compute the present value of next year's profits at each possible price. Since the discount rate is 8 percent, the present value of next year's profits is found by dividing profits by $1 + 0.08$. If next year's price is $13, profits will be $8,400,000; the present value is $\$8,400,000/1.08 = \$7,777,777.78$. If next year's price is $16, profits will be $10,500,000, which gives a present value of $9,722,222.22. If next year's price is $21, profits will be $14,700,000, so that the present value is $13,611,111,11. Subtract the initial exploration cost of $1,000,000 from these values to determine net present value at each price.

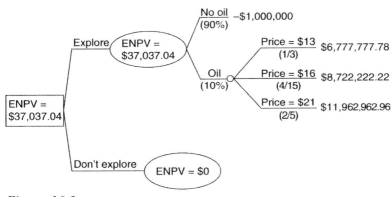

Figure 16.3

■ Exercises

Fill-in

1.   Alison is confronted with two gambles. For each gamble, there are three possible outcomes: She might win nothing, she might win $100, or she might win $500. Suppose that Allison's utility from $0 is 0, her utility from $500 is 1, and her utility from $100 is 3/10. For lottery A, the probability of winning $0 is 2/5, the probability of winning $100 is 0, and the probability of winning $500 is 3/5. For lottery B, the probability of winning $0 is 0, the probability of winning $100 is 1/2, and the probability of winning $500 is 1/2.

a.   The expected value is _____ and the variance is _____ for lottery A.

b.   The expected value is _____ and the variance is _____ for lottery B.

c.   Alison's expected utility from lottery A is _____.

d.   Alison's expected utility from lottery B is _____.

e.   Is Alison risk neutral, risk averse, or risk preferring? _____.

True-False-Ambiguous and Explain Why

2. Back at "Let's Make a Deal," Monty Hall has found a second contestant to tempt with a mystery door. This new contestant, Sherrill, is offered the same gamble that Fred received in Practice Problem 6: The item behind the big door is equally likely to be a goat or a $15,000 car. Sherrill can keep what's behind the door, or he can have a state-of-the-art Bass boat, worth $8000. If Sherrill takes the Bass boat, he must be risk averse.

3. If Shale Oil is risk averse it should not invest in the project described in Practice Problem 12.

4. Jeff is offered two investments. The first investment has both a high expected return and a high variance in potential outcomes. The second investment is less risky in that the variance of potential outcomes is smaller, but it also offers a smaller expected return. Upon reflection, Jeff decides that he is indifferent between the taking the first investment opportunity and taking the second investment opportunity. Jeff must be risk averse.

5. Since mutual funds always entail some risk, anyone who invests in a mutual fund cannot be risk averse.

6. Someone who is risk neutral does not care about the variance of a gamble.

Short-Answer

7. Using the information from Fill-in Exercise 1, graph Alison's utility function for wealth. Is the shape of this function consistent with the answer you gave to part e of Exercise 1?

8. Pete has just graduated from college. He just received a job offer for $37,500 per year. He is also a finalist for a job that he likes better, one that will pay him $50,000. However, the only way he can get the better job is to turn down the job offer that he currently has. If he doesn't get the better job, he can get a job selling used furniture, for $11,000 per year. Pete believes that the probability that he will be offered the $50,000 job is 2/3.
   a. What is Pete's expected wage if he turns down the $37,500 job?
   b. What is the variance of Pete's wage if he turns down the $37,500 job?
   c. What would Pete's risk attitudes have be for him to turn down the job offer he currently has (risk averse, risk neutral, or risk preferring)?

9. It is common to see signs indicating that traffic fines are doubled in construction areas. Will doubling fines be more effective than doubling enforcement levels as a deterrent to speeding?

10. Brian has discovered a new exploration technique for locating oil deposits. There is a 20 percent chance that Brian's technique will find oil, and an 80 percent chance that it will not find oil. If oil is found, the deposit will be worth $15,000,000. Brian is trying to convince the executives at Shale Oil Company, who are risk averse, to use his technique. Draw a graph that shows how much the executives would be willing to pay for Brian's technique.

11. Write out Shale Oil's decision tree for Brian's exploration technique assuming that the technique costs $1,000,000, that the utility they get from −$1,000,000 is −10, the utility they get from $0 is 0, and the utility they get from $14,000,000 is 45. Should they buy the technique?

12. Laura's utility over wealth is $U(w) = w^{1/2}$. Laura's only asset is a valuable violin, which is worth $400. There is a 48 percent chance that the violin will be damaged during the next year. If the violin is damaged, it will only be worth $100. Laura is uncomfortable with this risky situation, so she looks around for a company that will be willing to offer her insurance against the possible damage. The only company she can find that is willing to offer such insurance is Keynote Musical Insurance Corp. If Laura pays Keynote $144, they will pay her $300 if the violin is damaged (i.e., they will fully reimburse her). They are also willing to offer "partial insurance." Under partial insurance, Laura pays a premium of 144s and Keynote pays Laura 300s if the violin is damaged, where s is a number between zero and one. (s Represents the fraction of the potential loss that Laura covers; with $s = 0$ she buys no insurance, while the possible loss is fully insured if $s = 1$.)

   a. Give an expression for Laura's wealth if the violin is not damaged and she buys partial insurance.

   b. Give an expression for Laura's wealth if the violin is damaged and she buys partial insurance.

   c. Write out Laura's expected utility if she buys partial insurance.

   d. Determine the value of s that maximizes Laura's expected utility. How much of the potential loss does Laura insure?

Chapter 17
Externalities, Open Access, and Public Goods

■ Chapter Summary

Imagine this scenario: You are trying to study for your upcoming econ test when the layabout in the next room cranks up his stereo full blast. The noise is so loud you can't hear yourself think, let alone study. You wander down the hall to use the bathroom, only to find all the stalls are in use. Thoroughly frustrated, you head over to the lounge and find that a kind-hearted student has just started watching a video she rented. Just as you are starting to think the evening was a complete waste, you realize that even though you haven't been able to study during the past 5 minutes you have *lived* the material from Chapter 18. When your neighbor drove you from your room with his loud stereo you experienced firsthand an **externality**: You were affected by someone else's actions outside of a market. When you visited the bathroom and couldn't get a stall, you suffered from the sort of crowding that is typical with resources that are **open access**, resources that anyone can use. When your friend started watching the video in the lounge you were also able to watch. Her consumption did not prevent yours—the video is a **public good**.

Examples of externalities are commonplace. The exhaust your car emits, as well as many other sources of pollution, can make people sick or just uncomfortable. These are negative, or bad, externalities. One very important attribute of negative externalities is that free markets typically lead to overproduction of products that are associated with negative externalities. With negative externalities, someone is harmed by another's actions. The implied costs that the first person bears are not considered by the second person. In other words, the direct costs that the second person bears from his or her actions are less than the total costs to society, which also include the external costs borne by the first person. From society's perspective, a comparison of the total costs with total benefits dictates whether or not the correct amount of the action is undertaken. From the perspective of the person engaging in the behavior, however, it is a comparison of the *private* costs and benefits that determines the level of activity. When there are negative externalities, private costs are less than social costs, so the amount selected by the private interests (which we observe produced in the market) is larger than the amount we'd like to see produced. This example illustrates the **inefficiency of competition with externalities**.

While competitive markets will tend to produce too much of a product that is associated with negative externalities, there are conditions where firms will produce an amount closer to the socially desired level. We know that both monopoly and oligopoly markets tend to produce less than is socially desired. Consequently, if the firms that create the negative externality have market power, the incentives to under-produce (to exploit the market power) can partially cancel out the incentives to overproduce (because the firms don't take the externalities into account). Whether an industry produces too much or too little of a good that is tied to an externality depends on the interrelation between **market structure and externalities**.

There are a variety of policy remedies for markets that are plagued by externalities. A regulatory authority can impose taxes on offending firms. While such taxes can be linked to output levels, it is usually more efficient to base taxes on the level of the offending item. For example, if a shoe factory generates air pollution, we could either place a tax on shoes or on the factory's smog. Either approach will induce a reduction in the number of shoes made, and the associated pollution, but the second approach is more flexible. If the factory cuts its output in order to reduce pollution, the cost is the value of the foregone output. If the factory lowers pollution by installing a treatment device in its smokestack, the cost is based on the treatment device expenditures. Taxing output forces the factory to choose the first option; taxing pollution allows it to select the second option. Standards are an alternative to taxes: The factory is informed that it cannot pollute more than some specified amount (or else it will face dire consequences, such as enormous fines). If the regulating agency knows the relevant costs and benefits and can tailor standards to each factory, it can achieve the same result with taxes or standards. If uniform standards must be used, taxes are generally preferred unless firms can trade emissions rights. A third approach is to facilitate negotiation between the factory and the parties harmed by its pollution. Such negotiation requires that **property rights are allocated**, in this case either the right for the factory to pollute or the right for those affected to stop the pollution. It also requires that negotiations have relatively small transactions costs. If both elements are present, the interested parties will negotiate a mutually beneficial settlement.

Externalities are often linked to the lack of property rights. One reason air pollution is such an important issue is that no one "owns" the air, so there is nothing to prevent firms from using it as a dumping ground for smog. In other applications, problems arising from the lack of property rights are subtler. Since nobody owns the right to use the freeway between San Francisco and Sacramento, it is often very crowded. Similarly, lack of property rights to harvest whales is a contributing factor in the near extinction of certain species.

Not all externalities are bad. If a good or service is *non-rivalistic*, then one person's consumption does not prevent someone else from also consuming it, so the second person benefits from the first person's action. Such items are *public goods*. If the consumption of a public good is also not excludable—no one can be prevented from consuming it—then the item is a *public good*. Because the total benefits obtained from the consumption of public goods are generally larger than the benefits to the individual who bought it, public goods are almost always undersupplied from society's perspective.

■ Key Concepts and Formulas

- **Private cost:** the cost to producers, not including any externalities.
- **Social cost:** the sum of private cost and the cost from external damages.
- **Effluent charge:** a tax on discharges into the air or water.
- **Coase Theorem:** a result that shows a resource will be allocated to its most valuable purpose despite an externality, irrespective of initial ownership, so long as property rights are clearly defined and transactions aren't too costly.
- **Free riding:** when someone benefits from another's action without paying.

■ Application: Tradable Emissions Permits

In December 1997, representatives from countries all over the world descended on Kyoto, Japan, to negotiate a treaty aimed at limiting carbon dioxide (CO_2) emissions. The great fear is that these gases will enhance the so-called greenhouse effect, which keeps heat in the atmosphere from escaping back into space. If this enhanced effect is related to current emissions, we may be dooming future generations to a planet with a warmer and more volatile climate. The desire to avoid such potentially dire consequences was the prime motive behind the Kyoto conference. One element of the negotiations that the United States pushed hard for was the inclusion of "joint implementation," which allows countries to meet their obligations by paying other countries to reduce emissions. This program is similar to the U.S. system of tradable emissions permits for sulphur dioxide. Opponents worry that joint implementation will allow richer industrialized countries to avoid their "obligation" to clean up their act, while foisting extra costs off on poorer countries.

Question: Why might joint implementation result in more efficient reductions in CO_2 emissions? Is there any merit to the argument that industrialized countries will avoid their obligations? Are there any other problems with joint implementation?

Answer: While there are many sources of CO_2 emissions, two stand out as most significant: automobile exhaust and emissions from electric power generation. Not all power plants emit the same amount of CO_2, since different power plants use different fuel types. Coal is far and away the dirtiest type of fuel, at least from the perspective of CO_2 emissions. Since different countries have developed a reliance on different fuel bases, abatement costs are likely to vary across countries. Moreover, not all countries are as reliant on automobiles for transportation. All things considered, countries that are more reliant on autos or coal, such as the United States and Australia, will likely have larger costs associated with curtailing emissions. Countries that are more reliant on nuclear power generation, like France, and countries where cars are not as heavily used, such as Britain and Denmark, are likely to have lower abatement costs. If the global community decides that CO_2 emissions need to be reduced by a certain percent, and that all countries must cut emissions by this set amount, we may be very certain that the marginal cost of lowering emissions in the United States will be far larger than the marginal cost elsewhere. Correspondingly, a rearrangement of abatement obligations that lowers the United States's responsibility while raising abatement from a country with lower marginal cost can provide the same total amount of cleanup but at a smaller cost. For concreteness, suppose the last unit of CO_2 cleaned up in the United States costs $100, while the last unit cleaned up in France costs $40. A reduction in U.S. abatement by one unit would save $100; an increase in French abatement will add a bit more than $40 to their cleanup costs (assuming their marginal cost curve for cleanup is upward sloping). The net effect is a reduction in total abatement cost of nearly $60. In fact, so long as different players clean up amounts that yield differing marginal costs, a swap like the one just examined will lower total abatement costs without altering the total reduction in emissions. Now, just because total costs fall doesn't mean the French are happy with this deal. Since their costs rose by around $40, they are surely worse off. To induce the French to lower their CO_2 emissions by one unit, the United States would have to offer a bribe. Tradable emissions permits provide an institutionalized method for such bribes. To reduce CO_2 abatement by one unit, the United States must purchase an additional permit; the French would not sell one extra permit for a price that did not cover their marginal cost, which means the permit will not sell for less than $40. The United States would not pay more than the marginal cost of the unit of abatement they hope to avoid, which means the permit will not sell for more than $100. But there is plenty of room for negotiation here, and we would expect the parties to come to terms. Indeed, were the appropriate numbers $40 and $41, the issues would be the same; the permit would sell for a price between $40 and $41. Ultimately, permits are traded until there are no more mutually beneficial trades available; that is, when all countries' marginal costs are equated. At this point, the price of a permit is just equal to this (common) marginal cost.

Figure 17.1 illustrates an example of the associated cost savings for the United States and France. After trading to the point where marginal costs are equated, the United States pays France $3000 (50 permits at $60 each). U.S. abatement costs fall by an amount equal to the area under the U.S. marginal cost of abatement curve between abatement levels of 125 and 75; the region of interest is a rhombus, so its area is $1/2 \times (\$60 + \$100) \times 50 = \$4000$. At the same time, French costs rise by an amount equal to the area under *their* marginal cost of abatement curve between abatement levels of 100 and 150; this area is $1/2 \times (\$40 + \$60) \times 50 = \$2500$. The net effect on total abatement is a reduction of $1500: France's costs rise by $2500, while U.S. costs fall by $4000.

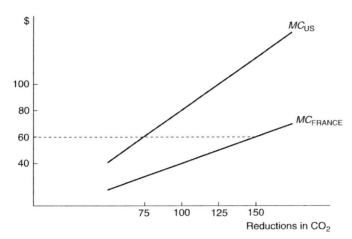

Figure 17.1

What about the claim of avoiding obligations? Well, it is true that the United States lowered its total costs by buying some permits (the United States makes a net gain of $1000). But it is not true that France was taken advantage of; it makes a net gain as well (of $500). If the idea is to be punitive, then we shouldn't allow the United States to buy any permits. But if the idea is to get the most CO_2 reductions for the money, then tradable emissions permits make good economic sense. There is, however, a potential snag. What happens if the United States decides to neither buy permits nor abate? Without some ability to enforce the agreed-upon abatement levels, emissions trading is an empty possibility. Without such enforcement, however, the treaty itself would be meaningless.

■ Application: Should Intel Butt In?

At the Tempe office of the Intel Corporation, employees are not allowed to smoke inside the building. Instead, the company provides an outdoor patio as an area for its employees to smoke. Apparently there is some concern over the accumulation of cigarette butts, to the point where company officials are considering banning smoking on this patio area.

Question: Why might Intel ask that its employees not smoke inside? Is there some way to solve the butt clutter problem without banning smoking on the patio?

Answer: Individuals who smoke inside an office impose an externality on other employees. A company that prohibits smoking indoors eliminates this externality for non-smokers, which can increase their productivity and make them willing to work for a smaller wage. On the other hand, such a ban makes smokers worse off; if they are not compensated for this loss they might seek employment elsewhere. Evidently, Intel came to believe that the externality caused by smokers was reducing the productivity of non-smokers to such an extent that eliminating this loss in productivity would outweigh any deleterious consequences a smoking ban would have on its smoking employees. Providing smokers with a place to smoke, such as an outdoor patio, seems like a reasonable solution. However, the accumulation of cigarette butts in the patio is a different kind of externality—it's an eyesore, and might also have health-related consequences. Rather than prohibiting outdoor smoking as well, Intel could sell employees a pass card that allows them access to the courtyard. This pass card would play the role of an effluent tax. Or, any smoker dropping a cigarette butt in the courtyard could be subjected to a fine. This latter approach would require paying someone to monitor the courtyard.

■ Solved Problems

1. A cattle rancher has his ranch next to a farm. His cattle stray into the farmer's land and trample her crops, which causes $2,000 in damages. If the rancher keeps cattle on his land, he makes a profit of $1,000. The farmer can choose either to farm or not to farm. Her revenue is $3,500 and her cost of production is $2,000, plus any external costs. What will be the outcome if the rancher does not have to pay the farmer for any damages his cattle cause? What if he must compensate the farmer for the damage caused by his cattle?

   Step 1: Determine the farmer's optimal decision, if the rancher owns cattle and does not compensate for damages.
   The costs of farming are $4,000: the sum of production costs ($2,000) and damages ($2,000). Her revenues are $3,5000, less than total costs. Unless the rancher chooses to not own cattle, the farmer chooses to not farm.

   Step 2: Determine the rancher's optimal decision if he does not have to compensate the farmer for damages.
   The rancher makes positive profit (of $1,000) if he owns cattle, and no profit if he does not, so he chooses to own cattle.

   Step 3: Determine the largest amount the farmer would be willing to pay the rancher to not own cattle.
   If the rancher did not own cattle, the farmer would have costs of $2,000. As her revenue is $3,500, she would then make profits of $1,500. Thus if she could convince the rancher to not own cattle, she could raise her profit by $1,500 (from the current level, zero). She would be willing to pay the rancher up to $1,500.

   Step 4: Determine the outcome if the rancher does not have to pay the farmer for any damages his cattle cause.
   There are two possible outcomes: either the rancher owns cattle and makes a profit of $1,000, while the farmer chooses to not farm, or the farmer bribes the rancher some amount B1 to not own cattle, in which case his profits would be B1 while her profits would be $1,500 − B1. So long as the amount of the bribe is larger than $1,000 (the profits the rancher forfeits), and smaller than the profits the farmer could make ($1,500), an amount can be negotiated that satisfies both parties. The farmer will bribe the rancher, who will not own cattle.

   Step 5: Determine the rancher's optimal decision if he must compensate the farmer for any damage.
   If the rancher must compensate for the damage his cattle cause, his costs increase by $2,000. His net profits would then be negative (the original profit of $1,000 less the payment for damages of $2,000). Thus he would choose to not own cattle.

   Step 6: Determine the farmer's optimal decision, if the rancher must compensate for any damages caused by his cattle.
   Whether the rancher owns cattle or not, the farmer does not have to bear the cost of the damages. Her profit is thus $1,500: revenue ($3,500) less production costs ($2,000). She would choose to farm.

   Step 7: Determine the largest amount the rancher would be willing to pay the farmer to induce her to not farm.
   If the farmer chose to not farm, the rancher would bear any damages. Thus if he could convince the farmer to not farm, the rancher's profit would increase by $1,000 (from the current level, zero). He would be willing to pay the farmer up to $1,000.

Step 8: Determine the outcome if the rancher has to pay the farmer for any damages his cattle cause. There are two possible outcomes: either the rancher owns cattle and bribes the farmer some amount, B2, to not farm, or the rancher chooses to not own cattle. In the first case, his profit would be $1,000 – B2, while the farmer chooses to not farm and collects the bribe of B2. In the second case, the rancher makes nothing and the farmer makes profit of $1,500. If the amount of the bribe is larger than $1,500 (the profits the farmer forfeits), and smaller than the profits the rancher could make ($1,000), an amount can be negotiated that satisfies both parties. But there is no amount that is both larger than $1,500 and smaller than $1,000, so the rancher will not bribe the farmer. The outcome is that she will farm and he will not own any cattle—just as in Step 4.

2.   Suppose that Kinky's, a well-known seller of copying services, generates an unappetizing byproduct of its services. This byproduct, which we will call smudge, causes the local citizenry much harm. It has been determined that the marginal benefits these citizens would realize from various levels of smudge reductions are given by the curve MB, in Figure 17.2. Initially, the marginal cost for Kinky's to clean up their smudge is the curve MC_0 in Figure 17.2. The town council is debating between imposing a standard that would require Kinky's to abate Q^* units or setting an effluent charge of t^*. Some council members are absolutely convinced the standard is superior, while others are just as convinced that taxes are the way to go. Just as the mayor is making the point that the two policies would have the same effect, news arrives that Kinky's has found a marvelous new approach to cleaning up smudge, and that their marginal costs have fallen to MC_1. Prior to the reduction in marginal costs, who was correct? What about after the reduction in marginal cost?

Step 1: Determine the impact of the tax t^* when marginal costs are MC_0.

To minimize its costs, Kinky's compares the effluent charge against its marginal cost of abatement. If the tax is larger than marginal cost, Kinky's cleans up more; if the tax is smaller, Kinky's cleans up less. Costs are minimized when the marginal cost of cleanup is exactly equal to the tax. In Figure 17.2, the optimal level of abatement at tax t^* is Q^*.

Step 2: Compare the impact of the tax and the standard when marginal costs are MC_0.

The tax yields precisely the same amount of cleanup as the standard. There is one difference: With the tax, Kinky's costs are larger than with the standard, since it pays t^* for every unit it doesn't get rid of. But in terms of abatement, the tax and the standard are equally efficacious. So the mayor was correct initially.

Step 3: Determine the impact of the tax t^* when marginal costs are MC_1.

After its marginal costs fall, Kinky's will clean up a larger amount. The new level of abatement sets the new marginal cost equal to the tax t^*, at level Q^{**}.

Step 4: Compare the impact of the tax and the standard when marginal costs are MC_1.

The tax no longer yields the same level of clean up as the standard. Kinky's still abates the amount Q^* with the standard, which is now far below the level that balances marginal costs with marginal benefits. On the other hand, Kinky's would clean up the amount Q^{**} with the tax, and this exceeds the level that balances marginal costs and marginal benefits. Of the two policies, the better choice is the one that yields larger net benefits. Net benefits are the area below marginal benefits and above marginal costs. In the context of Figure 17.2, net benefits with the standard are measured by the sum of areas A and B. Net benefits with the tax are measured by the sum of areas A, B, and C, less area D. Thus, determination of the better policy requires a comparison of areas C and D. All else equal, area D is larger and area C smaller the steeper the MB curve (see Exercise 5). Thus there will be situations where the first group is correct (the standard is better) and other situations where the second group is correct (the tax is better). The one certainty is that the mayor is now wrong: The two policies generally do not yield the same result.

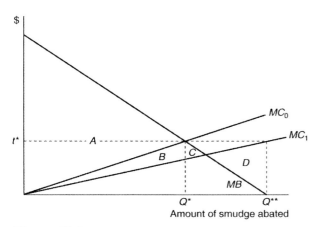

Figure 17.2

3. Imagine there is a firm whose production process generates gunk as a byproduct. Initially, the firm creates 40 units of gunk. Abatement of gunk generates benefits to local citizens (for example, by reductions in illness). The benefits from cleaning up Z units of gunk are $B(Z) = 20Z - Z^2/4$. The firm's costs of abating Z units of gunk are $C(Z) = cZ + Z^2/20$. There are equally likely possible values for the parameter c: It either equals 1 or 3. A regulator is asked to maximize expected net benefits, and is considering two possible policies. She may either set a standard, forcing $Z = Z^*$, or she may set a tax, charging the firm t^* for each unit of gunk it does not clean up. The firm knows its marginal costs (the true value of c) and wishes to minimize its costs (the sum of abatement costs and any taxes it pays). If the regulator does not know the true value of c, which approach should she use, standards or taxes?

Step 1: Determine the level of cleanup that maximizes expected net benefits.

As the only source of uncertainty regards costs, expected net benefits are the difference between (certain) benefits and expected costs: $ENB = B(Z) - EC(Z) = 20Z - Z^2/4 - \frac{1}{2}[Z + Z^2/20] - \frac{1}{2}[3Z + Z^2/20]$; this expression can be simplified to $ENB = 20Z - Z^2/4 - [2Z + Z^2/20]$. The level of cleanup that maximizes expected net benefits, Z^*, solves $dENB(Z^*)/dZ = 0$: $20 - Z^*/2 = 2 + Z^*/10$. (At this level of Z, marginal benefit equals expected marginal cost.) The optimal value of cleanup is then $Z^* = 30$ (at which value $MB = 20 - Z^*/2 = 5$).

Step 2: Determine expected net benefits if a standard is set at Z^*.

Expected net benefits are the difference between expected total benefits and expected total abatement costs, or $20Z - Z^2/4 - [2Z + Z^2/20]$. With $Z = 30$, expected net benefits are $600 - 900/4 - [60 + 900/20] = 270$.

Step 3: Determine the tax that will yield the same expected level of abatement as the standard.

The tax that generates the same expected cleanup as the standard must induce the same marginal benefit. Thus, $t^* = \$5$ (the marginal benefit associated with the standard Z^*). One important point here is that the firm will choose its cleanup level to balance its marginal cost against the tax. If its marginal cost is $1 + Z/10$, it will clean up 40 units (setting $MC = \$5$). If its marginal cost is $3 + Z/10$, it will clean up 20 units (again setting $MC = \$5$). Because these two marginal cost curves are equally likely, the expected level of cleanup is the average of 40 and 20, or 30 units.

Step 4: Determine expected net benefits if a tax is set at $t^* = \$5$.

Because the firm will select different levels of abatement with different marginal costs, we must derive its costs for each value of c and then take the average. If $c = 1$, the firm's total costs are $1 \times 40 + 40^2/20 = \$120$. If $c = 3$, the firm's total costs are $3 \times 20 + 20^2/20 = \$80$. So expected total costs are $(\$120 + \$80)/2 = \$100$. Total benefits also depend on c, since different levels of abatement result. Since the firm would clean up 40 units if $c = 1$, total benefits would be $20 \times 40 - 40^2/4 = \$400$. If $c = 3$, the firm would clean up 20 units, so benefits would be $20 \times 20 - 20^2/4 = \$300$. Expected benefits are thus $(400 + 300)/2$, or $\$350$. Expected net benefits are therefore $\$350 - \$100 = \$250$.

Step 5: Determine the policy that yields the largest value of expected net benefits.

The standard produces expected net benefits of $270 while the tax generates expected net benefits of $250. Hence the standard is preferred for this example.

■ Practice Problems

Multiple-Choice

1. Which of the following is an externality?
   a. A drought lowers yields on crop production.
   b. Your neighbor plants flowers that passersby can see.
   c. Your other neighbor does not install insulation in his mansion, which forces up energy prices.
   d. All of the above are correct.

2. A key difference between a commons and a public good is that
   a. commons have rivalry and public goods do not.
   b. public goods have rivalry and commons do not.
   c. commons have exclusion and public goods do not.
   d. public goods have exclusion and commons do not.

3. If firms that produce tomato sauce create air pollutants as a byproduct, it is most likely that
   a. too high a price is charged for too much total output.
   b. too high a price is charged for too little total output.
   c. too low a price is charged for too much total output.
   d. too low a price is charged for too little total output.

4. The main reason polluting firms do not produce the socially optimal quantity is
   a. pollution makes people sick.
   b. such firms care only about making money.
   c. such firms fail to take private costs into account.
   d. None of the above are correct.

Fill-in

5. Let's reconsider the gunk pollution problem from Solved Problem 3, now assuming that costs are not uncertain. To facilitate a comparison to the solved problem, let abatement costs be $C(Z) = 2Z + Z^2/20$. Benefits from abatement are $B(Z) = AZ - Z^2/4$. For part a, assume that $A = 20$.

   a. The optimal level of abatement is _____. This can be achieved by limiting pollution at _____ units, or by applying an effluent charge of _____. Now suppose that A is unknown; there are two possible values of A, either 18 or 22, which are equally likely.

   b. Marginal benefits are _____.

   c. An algebraic expression for expected marginal benefits is _____.

   d. The value of Z that equates expected marginal benefits to marginal costs is _____.

   e. At this value of Z, expected net benefits are _____.

True-False-Ambiguous and Explain Why

6. Since a main reason externalities exist is a lack of well-defined property rights, there would be no externalities if property rights were completely defined.

7. Imposing an effluent charge on a polluting monopolist will raise welfare.

8. As a general rule, public goods are supplied at lower levels and lower prices than is socially optimal.

Short-Answer

9. Every day, the local Hoboken Hoki fishermen climb onto their Hoki boats and set sail into Hoboken Hoki harbor. There are no entry barriers to fish for Hoki. Anyone living in Hoboken who wants to catch some fish can do so. Each fisherman catches the same number of Hoki. If N fishermen head out, total catch is $Q = 4 \times N \times (50 - N)$; the number of Hoki each fisherman brings home is Q/N. The market price for Hoki is $5, and the opportunity cost of a day out on the harbor is $200 per fisherman.

   a. If N fishermen head out onto the bay, how much profit does each fisherman make?

   b. If N fishermen head out onto the bay, what is the average catch?

   c. How many fishermen will head out onto the bay?

   d. To maximize industry profit, how many fishermen should go out?

10. Using the information for Practice Problem 9, plot total revenue and total industry cost as a function of N.

11. Administrators at Mid America University (MAU) recently began a program in which office paper was recycled from various academic and administrative buildings. Currently, recycled paper is worth $40/ton. If the paper is not recycled it must be disposed of as waste and taken to a landfill or incinerator. These facilities are currently charging $85 per ton. To collect one ton of paper takes an average 15 hours. The prevailing wage rate for student (slave) labor is $5 per hour. It is possible that work-study students can be hired, in which case 2/3 of the wages are paid by the Federal Government. Is it efficient to recycle paper? Assume the recycling coordinator doesn't get any credit for lowering waste disposal costs. Could the recycling venture break even if the coordinator can hire work-study students? What if she can't hire work-study students?

12. The government of Smogville wants to enact new pollution control policies and you are called upon to advise them. You are told that the initial level of pollution is $P_0 = 60$ units, that the costs of abatement are $C(Q_A) = (3/2)Q_A^2$, and that the benefits of abatement are $B(Q_A) = 120Q_A - Q_A^2$, where Q_A is the level of unabated (remaining) pollution.

   a. Find the optimal level of abatement and the resultant amount of unabated pollution.
   b. At what rate should an effluent tax be set in order to achieve the optimal level of abatement?
   c. Determine the total abatement costs at the optimal level of abatement.
   d. What is the opportunity cost of the remaining (unabated) pollution?

13. Chemical factory S and chemical factory G both pollute the environment within a 20-mile radius of their factories with toxic air emissions. Their emissions, prior to any intervention, yield ambient levels of 100 mg per cubic meter. The cost of improving air quality to x mg per cubic meter, for $0 \le x \le 100$, is

$$C(x) = (1000/3)(100 - x)^3.$$

   Factory S is on the outskirts of Sludgedale with a population of 90,000 in the area. Factory G is located near Grimetown, which has a population of 10,000 in the area. Each mg per cubic meter of exposures causes $10 in damage to exposed individuals (in lost work-time and health care costs.)

   a. What is the efficient level of emissions in Sludgedale? In Grimetown?
   b. What tax level would you set to achieve the efficient outcome in Sludgedale? In Grimetown?
   c. Which rate would be higher? Give an intuitive explanation of why it is higher.

14. A cattle rancher has his ranch next to a farm. His cattle stray into the farmer's land and damage her crops. The rancher sells his cattle for $6 apiece. The schedules of his marginal cost (*MPC*) and marginal external cost (*MEC*, the damage caused by each extra cow) are:

# of Cattle	MPC	MEC
1	$4	$1
2	3	2
3	3	3
4	4	4
5	6	5
6	8	6

   The farmer can choose either to farm or not to farm. Her cost of production is $10. Her revenue is $12, less any damages caused by the rancher's cattle.

   a. What will be the outcome if the rancher does not have to pay for any damages his cattle cause?
   b. What will be the outcome if the rancher must compensate the farmer for the damage caused by his cattle?
   c. What outcome maximizes welfare?
   d. Suppose the farmer and rancher can negotiate a settlement as to whether there are any cattle roaming loose. Will the decision depend on liability?
   e. Suppose that it is possible to build a fence to enclose the ranch for a cost of $10. What is the outcome that maximizes welfare?
   f. Suppose the farmer can build a fence around her crops for a cost of $1. What is the outcome that maximizes welfare?

15. The government of East Bitumia wants to enact new pollution control policies and you are called upon to advise them. You are told that the costs of abatement are $C(Q) = 12Q^3$, and that the benefits of abatement are $B(Q) = 3(90 − Q)^3$, where Q is the level of abatement. Initially, there are 90 units of pollution.

    a. Determine the optimal level of abatement, and the resulting level of pollution.
    b. What effluent charge should the government set to achieve the outcome from part a?
    c. Now suppose that the government sets a subsidy for reducing pollution. (That is, instead of taxing pollution the government offers to pay firms for each unit of pollution they abate.) What is the optimal subsidy rate?
    d. How does the subsidy rate you found in part c compare to the tax from part b? Explain.

■ Answers to Practice Problems

1. An externality occurs when one person is affected by someone else's actions outside of a market. When your neighbor decides to not insulate his mansion, you are affected by higher energy prices, but that happened through a market. When a drought lowers crop yields, fruits and vegetables will be more expensive, but again that happened through a market. But when your neighbor plants beautiful flowers, someone is made better off (they just enjoy pretty flowers), and they didn't pay for that pleasure. Here is an effect outside of a market: Answer b is correct.

2. Commons are characterized by rivalry and no exclusion; public goods are characterized by no rivalry. (While some public goods also have no exclusion, public goods can have exclusion; see Table 17.2 in the text.) So answer a is correct.

3. The byproduct of tomato production imposes costs on those who suffer from smog; there is an externality. Because tomato producers have no incentive to take these costs into account they will produce too many tomatoes. With too many tomatoes offered for sale, the market price will be too low: Answer c is correct.

4. The problem with pollution is that it creates external costs. These costs can be aesthetic in nature: Air pollution often obscures the view across the Grand Canyon, and this creates an externality even if nobody gets sick. So answer a is wrong. Whether or not they create externalities, firms generally are interested in making money. It's not the pursuit of profit that is the problem. So answer b is wrong. Polluters neglect external social costs; they almost certainly care about private costs. So answer c is wrong. The correct answer is d.

5. Answers and brief explanations follow.

    a. Optimal abatement equates marginal benefits $(20 − Z/2)$ with marginal cost $(2 + Z/10)$; this level is 30. Since we started with 40 units of pollution, a standard limiting pollution to 10 units will force a cleanup of 30 units. The required effluent charge equals the marginal cost for 30 units abated, or $5.
    b. $MB(Z) = A − Z/2$.
    c. $1/2 \times (18 − Z/2) + 1/2 \times (22 − Z/2)$, or $20 − Z/2$.
    d. $Z^* = 30$ $(20 − Z^*/2 = 2 + Z^*/10$ $[EMB = MC]$, which yields $18 = 6Z^*/10$, or $180/6 = Z^*$).
    e. If $A = 18$, total benefits are $30 \times (18 + 3) \times 1/2 = \$315$. If $A = 22$, total benefits are $30 \times (22 + 7) \times 1/2 = \$435$. Hence expected total benefits are $375. With $Z = 30$, total costs are $30 \times (2 + 5)/2 = \$105$. Expected net benefits are $260.

6. False. If property rights were clearly defined, the Coase Theorem tells us that parties will negotiate a mutually beneficial settlement *so long as transactions costs are small.* Imagine that a factory is disposing of wastes into a river, which then becomes unsafe for swimming. If the town downriver is heavily populated by swimmers, they are most surely made worse off by the water pollution. But the townsfolk suffer to different degrees. Imagine a town meeting that attempts to create a fund with which the polluting firm could be bribed. This meeting would almost certainly be highly contentious, and probably would lead nowhere. While the establishment of property rights can lead to resolution of externalities, it need not resolve the externality. Indeed, in cases where many people are harmed, it is virtually certain that establishing property rights will not solve the externality problem.

7. Ambiguous. While the statement would be true for a competitive firm, which surely produces too much of the product to begin with (as we saw in Multiple-Choice Question 3), there are two opposing effects with a monopolist. On one hand, society is better off if the firm takes any external costs into account, and so lowers its output. On the other hand, society is better off if the monopolist does not take advantage of its market power, and so produces more. In the final analysis, we cannot say with certainty that welfare will increase if the monopolist internalizes its externalities, just as we cannot say with certainty that welfare will increase if the monopolist stops taking advantage of its market power.

8. True. Individuals choose levels of public goods that balance the price with their private marginal benefit. Because the marginal benefits to society include both these private benefits and any external benefits others gain by using the public good without paying for it, price is less than marginal social benefit. Increased production of a public good would raise welfare. To induce firms to sell more of the good, price must also rise. So too small an amount of the public good is supplied at too low a price.

9. Since each fisherman gets an equal share of the catch, each gets an equal share of profit. Revenues are the product of price ($5) and total catch; costs are $200 \times N$. So industry profit with N fishermen is $[20 \times (50 - N) - 200] \times N$.

    a. Each fisherman makes a profit of $20 \times (50 - N) - 200$.

    b. The average catch is $4 \times (50 - N)$.

    c. Since there are no entry barriers, positive profit will induce more fishermen to head out onto the bay, while negative profit will induce fewer fishermen to head out onto the bay. In equilibrium, there can be no incentive for N to change, so profit must be zero. Therefore, $20 \times (50 - N) = 200$, or $N = 40$.

    d. To maximize industry profit, we need the multiple of price and marginal catch ($1000 - 40N$) to equal the opportunity cost of an additional fisherman (200). Rearranging, we obtain $800 - 40N = 0$, or $N = 20$.

10. See Figure 17.3.

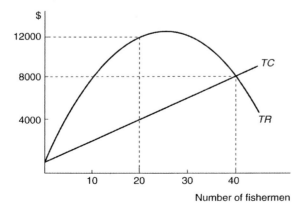

Figure 17.3

11. Efficiency is based on a comparison of costs. The recycling costs are $75/ton (15 hours × $5 per hour), while the disposal costs are $85/ton. Since recycling is cheaper than disposal, it is efficient. But if *MAU* recycling doesn't get to keep the $85 from lowered disposal costs, say, because someone in the administration decided to keep it so they could go to Guatemala on spring break, the only benefits from recycling are the $40/ton received from selling recycled paper. So recycling doesn't break even if costs are $75/ton (no work study), but it does break even if costs are $25/ton (work study).

12. Specifics follow.

   a. The optimal level of abatement, Q_A^*, sets marginal benefit equal to marginal cost: $120 - 2Q_A^* = 3Q_A^*$. Rearranging, we find $120 = 5Q_A^*$, or $Q_A^* = 24$.

   b. Total abatement costs are the area under the *MC* curve. Here, that area equals the area of a triangle with base 24 (the optimal amount of abatement) and height $72 = 3 \times 24$ (*MC* at Q_A^*). As the area of a triangle is ½ × base × height, total abatement costs are ½ × 25 × 72 = 864.

   c. The opportunity cost of the remaining (unabated) pollution corresponds to benefits from abatement not realized. This value equals the area under the marginal benefits curve from the level of abatement chosen to the point where all the initial pollution is abated; here, that is the area from an abatement of 24 (the optimal level of pollution) to an abatement of 60 (the initial level of pollution). The triangle in question therefore has a base of 36 (= 60 − 24) and a height of 72 (marginal benefit at 24), and so its area is ½ × 36 × 72 = 1296.

   d. To achieve the optimal level of abatement, the government can impose an effluent tax equal to the marginal cost at the optimal abatement level. That marginal cost is $72.

13. To find the efficient level of emission reduction, set marginal cost equal to marginal benefit (the damage per person, $10, multiplied by the population).

   a. The marginal benefit of emission control in Sludgedale is 900,000. At the optimal level of emissions, x^*, $MB = MC$ so $900,000 = 1000(100 - x^*)^2$. Thus $900 = (100 - x^*)^2$, or $30 = 100 - x^*$; $x^* = 90$. The marginal benefit of emission control in Grimetown is 100,000. At the optimal level of emissions, $100,000 = 1000(100 - x^*)$, so $x^* = 90$.

   b. The effluent charge should be set equal to marginal benefit at x^*. The appropriate level is $900,000 per unit in Sludgedale and $100,000 per unit in Grimetown.

   c. The tax should be higher in Sludgedale because pollutants cause more damage (there is a larger population affected by air pollution).

14. The rancher would maximize profits by setting his marginal cost equal to price ($6). The farmer will operate so long as her profit is not negative; otherwise she would shut down.

   a. The rancher's marginal costs here are *MPC*, which equals $6 when he owns 5 cattle. The farmer would shut down. Profits are $10 for the rancher and $0 for the farmer.

   b. Now the rancher's marginal costs are *MPC* + *MEC* (= marginal social costs, *MSC*). *MSC* is $6 at 3 cattle; this is the number the rancher would own. While the 3 cattle cause $6 worth of damage, driving the farmer's revenues below her costs, the rancher must compensate her for this damage. Total profit for the rancher will be $2 (revenues − costs − compensation to farmer, $18 − $10 − $6). Total profit for the farmer will be $2 (revenues − costs − damage + compensation from rancher, $12 − $10 − $6 + $6).

   c. The efficient outcome is for the farmer to shut down and for the rancher to own 5 cattle. The efficient solution is found by setting *MB* = *MSC*, where *MB* is the benefit from another cow, or $6 (price). We get a different outcome than in part b because *MEC* equals zero if the farmer is shut down. Alternatively, it is optimal for the farmer to shut down since total profits in this case are $10, versus $4 when the farmer does not shut down.

d. The resource should go to its highest valued use, irrespective of initial property rights. If the farmer initially has the property rights, the rancher will buy them, paying at least $2 (the farmer's forgone profits) and no more than $7 (the rancher's profits in part a less his profits in part b). If the rancher initially has the property rights, he will keep them.

e. The farmer should still shut down as the cost to society is only $2 (the farmer's forgone profits), whereas the fence costs $10.

f. The farmer should build the fence and operate, making a profit of $1 (revenues – costs – the cost of the fence, $12 – $10 – $1); the rancher should own 5 cattle.

15. a. The optimal level of abatement, Q^*, balances marginal costs with marginal benefits. Marginal cost is $36Q^{*2}$ and marginal benefit is $9(90 - Q^*)^2$, so we get $4Q^{*2} = (90 - Q^*)^2$, or $2Q^* = 90 - Q^*$. Thus, $Q^* = 30$. Since there were initially 90 units of pollution, 60 units remain.

b. The requisite effluent charge must equal marginal benefit at Q^*, which is $32,400.

c. If the government set a subsidy of $32,400 for each unit cleaned up, this would also induce an abatement level of 30. The necessary subsidy rate equals the effluent charge because each technique makes an additional unit abated worth $32,400 to the firm. The firm compares the cost it bears to the benefit it receives when it abates an extra unit. The cost of abating an extra unit is its marginal cost.

d. With an effluent charge, the benefit is the tax savings; with a subsidy, the benefit is the payment for cleaning up. Either way, the benefit to the firm is $32,400.

■ Exercises

Fill-in

1. There are three plants located in the city of Lost Airless (LA) that emit SO_2 as part of their production process. Currently, plant A emits 100 units of SO_2, plant B emits 200 units of SO_2, and plant C emits 500 units of SO_2. The cost of cleanup is $C_A(y_A) = 2y_A^2$ at plant A, $C_B(y_B) = y_B^2$ at plant B, and $C_C(y_C) = 2y_C^2$ at plant C, where y_A is the amount cleaned up at plant A, y_B is the amount cleaned up at plant B, and y_C is the amount cleaned up at plant C. The total benefits of cleanup in LA are $B(y) = 1200y - y^2$, where y is the total amount cleaned up $(y_A + y_B + y_C)$.

a. Marginal cost of cleanup _____ at plant A, _____ at plant B, and _____ at plant C.

b. If the firms' abatement levels equate marginal costs, the marginal cost curve for cleanup for the entire LA area is _____.

c. The optimal level of cleanup of SO_2 for LA is _____.

d. The effluent charge that achieves the efficient level of cleanup is _____.

e. At this tax, plant A would clean up _____ units, plant B would clean up _____ units, and plant C would clean up _____ units. _____ percent of the initial amount of SO_2 is cleaned up.

f. Total abatement costs associated with the optimal effluent tax are _____. If standards are imposed that require each firm to reduce pollution by the same percentage, total abatement costs are _____.

True-False-Ambiguous and Explain Why

2. If a rancher's cows trample a farmer's corn on their way to pasture, the rancher is imposing an externality on the farmer.

3. One simple way to alleviate the crowding associated with a common property resource is to levy a user charge, where the fee is set equal to the external costs an individual imposes on others.

4. An *altruistic* individual is one who takes actions for the benefit of others. If society were made up of altruistic folks, there would be no problem with under provision of public goods.

5. Many cities charge water users a flat fee. A change to the billing system that assesses water users a per-unit charge will increase welfare.

Short-Answer

6. Compare an effluent charge and a standard in the framework of Solved Problem 2 when the marginal benefit curve is (i) very flat and (ii) very steep.

7. In the context of the Fill-in Exercise 1, suppose the government auctioned pollution permits that gave firms a right to pollute 1 unit of SO_2. What is the efficient number of permits to sell? What would be the equilibrium price of a permit if the efficient number of permits were sold? How would your analysis change if the government decided to give the permits to firms instead of selling them?

8. Many public radio stations now offer gifts to possible donors, with the value of the gift increasing with the level of the donation. Discuss the effect this is likely to have on donations.

9. Two people work together in a certain office. One of them smokes, and the other cannot stand smoke. The smoker's benefits from smoking yield benefits of $B(x) = 12x - x^2$, where x is the number of cigarettes smoked. The external cost imposed on the non-smoker yields costs of $C(x) = \frac{1}{2}x^2$. Suppose first there are only two ways to govern the office: either the smoker may smoke as much as he likes (in which case he smokes 6), or smoking is not allowed.

   a. Graph these relations, showing the "costs" to society from allowing the smoker to smoke as much as he likes.
   b. Show the "costs" to society from prohibiting smoking on your graph.
   c. Now suppose the office manager can rent a second office for $15 per day, so that each worker can have his or her own room. Of the three options—allow unlimited smoking, prohibit smoking, rent a second office—which is the most socially desirable?

10. Slipshod Plastics Corp. produces both plastic materials and water pollution. Suppose that Slipshod currently produces 40 gallons per minute of polluted water. Company officials estimate that the cost of reducing pollution is $C(Q_A) = 20Q_A + \frac{1}{2}Q_A^2$, where Q_A is measured in gallons of polluted water abated per minute. Health officials estimate that the benefits of reducing emissions from Slipshod are: $B(Q_A) = 80 Q_A - Q_A^2$.

   a. Find the optimal level of abatement, and the level of remaining pollution.
   b. What level of tax per unit on pollution yields an efficient outcome?
   c. Imagine now that Slipshod Plastics can eliminate its pollution entirely by installing a filter. This filter costs $800. Is it efficient to install the filter?

11. Suppose that the production of steel causes the emission of a recently discovered carcinogen, yucka. There are currently several steel plants emitting yucka, and these plants are of differing designs and vintages. Two policies have been proposed to deal with this problem. Proposal A will impose a standard upon the level of yucka that firms may emit. Proposal B will place an effluent tax upon the emitted levels of yucka. A consultant has calculated the requisite tax and standard to reduce yucka pollution to the desired level. Compare these policies in terms of the likely costs of abatement. Which is likely to yield the larger net social benefits?

12. In Solved Problem 3, we compared effluent charges and standards when the regulatory authority knew marginal benefits, but only the firm knew whether marginal costs were really $1 + Z/10$ or $3 + Z/10$. In Practice Problem 5, we compared effluent charges and standards when the regulatory authority knew marginal costs, but marginal benefits could be either $18 - Z/2$ or $22 - Z/2$. Now suppose the regulator knows neither costs nor benefits. There is a 50 percent chance that marginal costs are $1 + Z/10$, and a 50 percent chance that they are $3 + Z/10$. Similarly, there is a 50 percent chance that marginal benefits are $18 - Z/2$ and a 50 percent chance that they are $22 - Z/2$. As in Solved Problem 3, the firm knows its true costs and acts to minimize its costs. Repeat the analysis of Solved Problem 3. Does the uncertainty about benefits change the outcome of the comparison?

13. One extremely important complication associated with global warming is the fact that most of the consequences will not appear for decades, perhaps centuries. Because any costs will be paid today, while benefits arrive well into the future, a complete analysis must pay attention to two features absent in our discussion above. First, CO_2 emissions are a *stock* pollutant: It is not the flow of emissions, but the accumulation of emissions over time that matters. Second, future effects are not worth as much as present effects; they need to be discounted. As a first crack at this more complicated problem, suppose there are two periods, and that damages next period are based on the sum of emissions over the two periods. Abatement costs must be paid today. Discuss the optimal level of abatement in this context. What elements would we need to know in order to determine this level? If the second period is 100 years away, and we use a discount rate of 2.75 percent, what is the present value of $1,000,000 worth of damage next period? Does this seem "fair?"

14. Suppose those Hoboken Hoki fishermen in Practice Problem 9 provide the only source of Hoki to a hungry world. The market demand for Hoki is $p = 23 - Q/168$, where Q is the total catch. As before, $Q = 4 \times N \times (50 - N)$, where N is the number of fishermen, each fisherman's catch is Q/N, and the opportunity cost of to the fisherman is $200. The Hoboken city council decides to limit entry, by requiring fishermen to hold a Hoki license. The first M fishermen who apply receive a license at no cost; all other applicants are out of luck. Determine price, industry catch, profits, and welfare in terms of M. What is the optimal industry size (value of M)?

Chapter 18
Asymmetric Information

■ ## Chapter Summary

In a variety of interactions in modern life, we deal with others who probably know something we don't know. If you go to a garage sale looking for a great deal, you might walk away with a toaster that burns your toast, while the guy who sold you the bad toaster got a bit of cash for an appliance that was virtually worthless. If you are the manager of a late night convenience store, the person you just hired might be a hard worker or he might be a bum. In each of these examples, one participant in the transaction knows something the other party doesn't. The guy selling the toaster knows it will burn toast, but the buyer is not sure how well the toaster will work. The new employee knows his work ethic, while the manager doesn't.

In situations where one party knows something important that the other party does not know, a variety of **problems due to asymmetric information** can emerge. The ignorant party has every reason to be nervous about the transaction, since the asymmetry in knowledge lets the informed person act opportunistically. If you knew the toaster burned toast, you probably wouldn't buy it, and if you did buy it, you wouldn't pay nearly as much for it. The example with the bad toaster is one of *adverse selection,* which occurs when the informed person takes advantage of some unobserved characteristic (like the quality of the toaster). It is also possible that the uninformed person is able to act opportunistically by taking an unobserved action, which we term *moral hazard.* Problems with moral hazard are discussed at length in Chapter 20; for now, it's enough to know the difference between adverse selection and moral hazard. If left unchecked, adverse selection can lead to undesirable outcomes. For instance, if those who go to garage sales know that people selling toasters are likely to act opportunistically, they won't be willing to pay very much for a toaster, which gives potential sellers with functioning toasters less of an incentive to offer them for sale. A potential result is that the great majority—perhaps all—of the toasters at garage sales burn toast, so garage sale toasters sell for very low prices. Ultimately, **ignorance about quality can drive high quality items out of the market**.

While we wouldn't lose much sleep over the inability of those with good toasters to get a fair price, we might be more concerned about the convenience store example. If the manager isn't sure about the new hire's work ethic, she may only be willing to offer a modest wage. If this wage is low enough hard workers could be dissuaded from applying. To counteract this unfortunate outcome, the parties involved can take actions that are **responses to adverse selection**. The convenience store manager might *screen,* by using some technique that allows harder workers to show their true colors. For example, applicants might be asked to fill out a lengthy form. If it is unseemly for slackers to spend much time at this task, the detail of responses can allow the manager to distinguish harder workers from slackers. Alternatively, hard-working applicants might *signal,* by taking an action that convinces the employer of their work ethic. For example, hard workers might spend 4 years at college. A third way to get around the adverse selection problem is to have a *third party provide information.*

Sellers have an incentive to take advantage of consumers who are uninformed about product qualities. For example, a major manufacturer of bleach might sell two brands, one with the company's label and one "generic" brand, which differ only in terms of the label. If consumers think the name-brand bleach is of higher quality, they are likely to be willing to pay more for it than they would pay for the generic, allowing the company to **price discriminate because of false beliefs about quality**. When consumers are well informed about prices, competitive firms have no market power. But if consumers do not know which firm charges which price, firms can charge prices above marginal cost. A good example of such **market power from price ignorance** occurs when consumers are unlikely to participate for a long enough period of time to learn about different firms' pricing policies, as when most customers are tourists. Anyone who has haggled with a street vendor in Mexico will confirm that such sellers try to get you to pay far more than the lowest price they would accept. If you knew that the guy across the street was selling the same curio for 50 pesos less, you wouldn't give the guy in front of you the time of day. But if you don't know where to go to get the best deal, you might wind up overpaying.

Asymmetric information can be particularly troublesome in labor markets. **Problems arising from ignorance when hiring** can take one of two forms. If the firm has a variety of jobs that differ in terms of their skill requirements, it can be in the best interests of all parties to have the correct worker assigned to each job. If a less-skilled worker is assigned a demanding job, the firm's performance will suffer and the worker could wind up miserable. Satisfactory job matching could occur if workers tell the firm what their true talents are. On the other hand, if the less-skilled worker loses nothing from being assigned the difficult job, but is paid a higher wage, then the worker's interests are not aligned with the firm's interests. In this instance, the firm must screen workers, or workers must signal their skills. If the screen or signal is expensive, as with a college degree, it is possible that the individual will take an action in his or her best interests, but that society would be better off if the signal weren't used.

■ Key Concepts and Formulas

- **Adverse selection:** opportunism that occurs because of asymmetric information.
- **Signaling:** actions taken by informed parties with higher-quality items or greater skills that allow uninformed parties to infer quality or skill.
- **Screening:** actions taken by uninformed parties that attempt to separate sellers with higher-quality items from sellers with lower-quality items.
- **Lemons market:** an outcome where low-quality units drive high-quality units from the market; also sometimes known as "Akerlof's lemons model" in honor of the man who first described it.
- **Cheap talk:** claims or promises that can't be verified.
- **Separating equilibrium:** an outcome where agents' actions differ by the quality of their items.
- **Pooling equilibrium:** an outcome where agents' actions do not differ with quality.

■ Application: Used Japanese Vehicles in New Zealand

On the whole, New Zealand is very much like the United States. We speak the same language, have similar cultures, and have similar interests. And while drivers in New Zealand sit in the right seat and drive on the left side of the road, we even drive cars produced by the same corporations, for the most part. (The GM cars in New Zealand are Holdens, which are manufactured in Australia.) But there is one big difference between the Japanese cars in the United States and New Zealand. While virtually all cars imported into the United States are new, the vast majority of Mazdas, Nissans, and Toyotas imported into New Zealand are used. These used vehicles are purchased at auctions in Japan and then shipped across the South Pacific. In May of 1997, New Zealanders (or kiwis, as they are affectionately called) learned that they were buying something else with their cars. Immediately after the sale at the auction is completed, and for the trivial fee of around 50 Yen, a large fraction of used Japanese vehicles bound for New Zealand are "clocked:" They have their odometers rewound. Although it is possible in principle to learn if one's car has been clocked, the process is time-consuming and expensive. Thus the vast majority of used Japanese vehicles in New Zealand are sold with odometer readings in the neighborhood of 50,000 kilometers (km).

Question: Why are so many used Japanese vehicles sold with around 50,000 kilometers on their odometers?

Answer: This is a classic example of Akerlof's lemons model. Lots of cars come into the NZ market, and within a category (compact, family car, pickup truck, etc.) we would expect that vehicle prices would be based on observable features. These features might include the overall condition of the car, the presence or absence of rust, and mileage. All else equal, in comparing two similar cars we would anticipate a lower price for the car with the higher mileage. Dealers have two options upon purchase: Clock the odometer, or play honest. If the dealer plays honest, his car will sell at around the average price for a vehicle with the mileage indicated on the odometer. If he clocks the car, say, to 52,345 kilometers, it will sell for a price around the average price for a vehicle with 50,000 km. The fee for clocking is so small relative to the purchase price that we may as well ignore it. Thus the dealer is likely to base his decision on the difference in price between a car with high km and a car with around 50,000 km. As this price difference can be thousands of NZ dollars, the great majority of dealers have their vehicles clocked.

Now, some vehicles really do have only 50,000 km on them, and these generally aren't clocked. So kiwi car buyers might originally be willing to pay big bucks for such a smart car; for concreteness, let's say they'd pay $18,000. On the other hand, a car with higher kms, perhaps 100,000 km, would sell for much less; say, for $6,000. Suppose these are the only two possible mileages. A dealer buying one of the high mileage cars stands to make a fast $12,000 just by clocking the vehicle. Moreover, since it makes sense for one dealer to change the odometer reading, it makes sense for all dealers to change the odometer reading. If all high mileage cars are clocked, a car buyer can't use the odometer reading to infer value anymore. Instead, the price he or she would be willing to pay ought to be linked to the expected value of the car (perhaps marked down a bit if he or she is risk averse).

Suppose that 80 percent of used Japanese vehicles really do have high mileage. These cars are each worth $6,000 to car buyers. The remaining 20 percent of the available cars, which have low mileage, are worth $18,000 to car buyers. The expected value of a typical kiwi used car is thus

$$0.2 \times \$18,000 + 0.8 \times \$6,000 = \$8,400.$$

Since the price a typical car can fetch is greater than $6,000, the price a high-mileage car would fetch if the odometer weren't adjusted, all dealers who buy high-mileage cars are inclined to clock them. The result is that the kiwi market is flooded with clocked high mileage used vehicles.

■ Solved Problems

1. You have decided to take a drive out across the open plains so you can see the purple mountains' majesty. One evening you find yourself in Outer Podunk, a town renowned for its tourism. Before you head out for your evening meal, you ask the owner of the motel you are staying in about the local eateries. He tells you of six restaurants, and tells you what a typical meal is likely to cost. He also tells you that Joe's Big Boy is popular with tourists, and that they also have "reasonable prices." Upon arriving at Joe's, you notice that their prices are about the same as the price the motel owner mentioned. What quality of meal should you expect to receive at Joe's, and how does this compare to the other restaurants in town?

Step 1: Describe the way a typical customer selects a restaurant.

Since the restaurants in Outer Podunk do a heavy tourist trade, there is an excellent chance that most of their business comes from diners who won't return. Since these diners are unlikely to know much about the quality of meals at various restaurants, chances are they will regard all restaurants as average quality. (Average for Outer Podunk, not necessarily average for the country as a whole.) If tourists think all restaurants serve meals of the same quality, they are most likely to visit the restaurant with the lowest prices.

Step 2: Determine the impact on Joe's profits if it changes the quality of its meals.

Like all the other restaurants in town, the number of diners who visit Joe's is based on the prices Joe's charges. Since Joe's customers think Joe's meals are of average quality for Outer Podunk, Joe's demand won't change if it alters its quality. On the other hand, raising quality is probably costly. So Joe's profits are likely to increase if it lowers the quality of its meals. If Joe's lowers the quality of its meals but doesn't change its prices, it should expect the same volume of business, and hence the same revenues, while saving on costs. Thus Joe's profits rise if they cut their quality.

Step 3: Predict the quality of meals at restaurants in Outer Podunk.

Like Joe's, the other restaurants in town are motivated to cut quality. The result is a version of Akerlof's lemons model: All restaurants in Outer Podunk serve lower-quality meals.

2.   As you continue on the drive you started in Solved Problem 1, you come to a town that has just lost a major employer. Many workers, having been laid off, are planning to move elsewhere to seek employment. All of these former workers, along with a good proportion of those still employed, are holding garage sales the day you arrive in town. Because you are an avid garage-sale shopper, you can't resist the opportunity to look around. After visiting a number of garage sales, you notice an abundance of toasters offered for sale. If you buy one of these toasters, how likely is it that you will get burned?

Step 1: Determine the motives of those who are selling toasters.

Anyone leaving town is probably unwilling to haul an old toaster with them, and so they'll sell at any price, whether the toaster functions properly or burns toast. Anyone who is staying in town is likely to want a price close to the toaster's true value. If the toaster functions properly, they will want a higher price; if the toaster burns toast, they will probably take any price.

Step 2: Determine the motives for a typical garage sale shopper.

Since buyers can't know the true quality of any toaster, they will only be willing to pay a price that reflects the average quality. Suppose a good toaster is worth $5 and a bad toaster is worth nothing. If buyers think that N toasters are offered at garage sales and that M of these toasters are good, then the probability of getting a good toaster is M/N. The average value of a toaster is $5 \times (M/N)$.

Step 3: Determine the incentives for sellers with good toasters.

Since anyone with a bad toaster would be willing to sell it at any price, you can be sure that there are some bread burners out there. Consequently, the total number of toasters N exceeds the number of properly functioning toasters M, which means that M/N is less than one. So the average value of a toaster, $5 \times (M/N)$, is less than the value of a good toaster, $5. Anyone staying in town would require a price near $5 to sell a good toaster, which is greater than the price for a typical toaster. None of these folks would sell a good toaster. However, anyone leaving town would take any price for a good toaster.

Step 4: Describe the equilibrium in the market for used toasters.

Suppose there are L people leaving town who have a good toaster and B people selling bad toasters (counting both those who are leaving town and those who are staying). If consumers think that the chance they will get a good toaster at a garage sale is $L/(B + L)$, they are willing to pay $5 \times L/(B + L)$ for a used toaster. All those with a bad toaster and everyone leaving town who has a good toaster would take any positive price, so they are all willing to sell for $5 \times L/(B + L)$. On the other hand, anyone with a good toaster who is staying in town requires $5, so they wouldn't sell. The result is that all B bad toasters are put up for sale, as are the L good toasters owned by people leaving town.

Thus the total number of toasters is $N = B + L$; the number of good toasters available is $M = L$; and the probability of getting a functioning toaster is $L/(B + L)$. Consumers' expectations of the probability that a used toaster will function properly are correct, so the price they offer is optimal for them. Likewise, nobody holding a garage sale can do any better. Because consumers' expectations are correct and no seller can do better by altering his behavior, we have found the equilibrium.

■ Practice Problems

Multiple-Choice

1. You are thinking about buying a used refrigerator. You find three that are available. One is being sold by a couple that just bought a new refrigerator, one is being sold by a student who just flunked out of school, and the third is being sold by a handyman. They are priced about the same. From whom should you buy?

   a. The flunkout
   b. The married couple
   c. The handyman
   d. None of these guys

2. You are thinking about purchasing an elegant shirt by mail order but aren't sure about the quality of the workmanship. You consult the colorful catalogs for two companies, Shirts Galore and Over the Tops. Shirts Galore offers an unlimited returns policy, while Over the Tops will refund 80 percent of the shirt's value should you decide to return it. Which of the following statements is most likely to be true?

   a. Neither company's shirts are more likely to be high quality.
   b. Shirts Galore's shirts are more likely to be high quality, while Over the Tops's shirts are less likely to be high quality.
   c. Shirts Galore's shirts are less likely to be high quality, while Over the Tops's shirts are more likely to be high quality.
   d. Both companies' shirts are more likely to be high quality.

3. Why can't safe drivers get lower rates by telling insurance companies that they are less likely to have an accident?

   a. Because accidents can happen to anyone.
   b. Because insurance companies don't want to cut rates for anyone.
   c. Because no one can really know if he or she is a safe driver.
   d. Because unsafe drivers would make the same claim.

4. Which is the most likely reason that insurance companies don't monitor their customers' driving habits?

   a. Insurance companies don't care about drivers' habits.
   b. Insurance companies have more accurate ways to tell how careful a driver you are.
   c. Insurance companies have cheaper ways to tell how careful a driver you are.
   d. None of the above are true.

Fill-in

5. Suppose there are 200 people trying to sell used cars. 100 of these cars are "lemons," worth only $2000. The other 100 of the cars are "cherries," worth $5000. Each seller know whether his or her car is a lemon or a cherry, but buyers can't determine a car's quality until after they have driven it for a month.

   a. If all the cherries were placed on the market, buyers would be willing to pay up to _____ for a used car.

   b. If half of the cherries were placed on the market, buyers would be willing to pay up to _____ for a used car.

   c. If none of the cherries were placed on the market, buyers would be willing to pay up to _____ for a used car.

   d. If *C* cherries were placed on the market, buyers would be willing to pay up to _____ for a used car.

True-False-Ambiguous and Explain Why

6. Low-quality used cars drive high-quality used cars out of the used car market because buyers don't know the quality of any car.

7. You may have noticed that there are various grades of gasoline, with fuel labeled as higher octane selling at higher prices. The fact that fuel labeled as higher octane is more expensive means that this fuel will give drivers better performance.

8. Advertising can increase a firm's demand even if the ads don't convey any useful information to potential buyers.

Short-Answer

9. Using the information from Practice Problem 5, plot the relation between the price of a randomly selected used car and the number of cherries on the market. Based on this graph, predict the number of cherries that will be offered for sale under the following scenarios.

   a. Each seller of a cherry will sell for any price at or above $4000.

   b. Each seller of a cherry will sell for any price at or above $3500.

   c. Each seller of a cherry will sell for any price at or above $3000.

   d. Half the sellers of cherries will sell for any price at or above $3000 and the other half will sell for any price at or above $4000.

10. Contrast the answers to parts b and d of Practice Problem 9. Give an intuitive explanation for any differences.

11. Suppose that there are only two types of people, those with high ability and those with low ability. Upon graduating from high school, either type could get a job selling used furniture. The present value of the stream of wages at this job equals $500,000. Alternatively, the individual can go to college. Either type of person can get the college degree, but it takes a low-ability person 5 years to graduate, whereas a high-ability person can graduate in 4 years. After graduating from college the individual can get a job managing people who sell used furniture. The present value of this stream of wages for someone who graduates in 4 years' time is equal to $800,000 today. Suppose the full cost of a year in college (tuition, room and board, books, and so on) is $50,000. Discuss the conditions under which the college degree can serve as a signal of an individual's ability.

12. As in Practice Problem 5, suppose there are 100 sellers with lemons and 100 sellers with cherries, that lemons are worth $2000, and that cherries are worth $5000. Suppose also that the relation between the number of cherries that will be placed on the market and the price for used cars is described in Figure 18.1. Plot the relation between the price consumers are willing to pay for a used car and the number of cherries offered for sale on this graph. Show the equilibrium price for used cars and the number of cherries offered for sale in equilibrium.

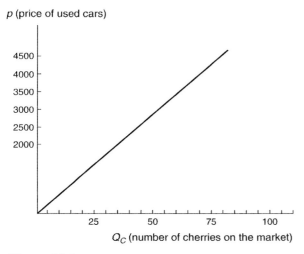

Figure 18.1

13. Three of your fellow students are sitting in a coffee bar, engaged in an animated discussion about problems of asymmetric information. Larry argues adamantly that problems arise when sellers know something that buyers don't know, and that any other details are unimportant. Moe is insistent that it only matters whether buyers are ignorant or fully informed. Curly is trying to convince the others that there is a difference between problems where sellers see an attribute of their product before they decide what to do and problems where buyers don't see how sellers behave. Help these three stooges resolve their debate.

14. Many employers offer health insurance coverage as part of their compensation packages to employees, and often pay lower rates for such insurance than individuals buying health insurance on their own pay for health insurance. Explain this contrast based on the content of this chapter.

15. Owen's Adventure Rafting is the only firm selling personal float trips on the Wild River. Like other monopolists, Owen's can pick an output level to maximize its profits. Unlike customers of other monopolies, however, Owen's clients aren't sure what quality of trip he will offer. If they thought his trips were high quality, their demand would be

$$p = 180 - Q,$$

where p is the price of a float trip and Q is the total number of trips taken. On the other hand, if Owen's clients thought his float trips were of low quality, their demand would be

$$p = 100 - Q.$$

His marginal cost is constant at $40 per trip.

a. How many trips would Owen offer, and what price would he charge, if consumers knew his trips were high quality?

b. How many trips would Owen offer, and what price would he charge, if consumers knew his trips were low quality?

    c.   If consumers think Owen's trips are equally likely to be high or low quality, how many trips will he offer and what price will he charge?

    d.   Why doesn't Owen just tell his customers what quality his trips are?

    e.   Imagine now that a group of 80 customers gets together and offers Owen a package deal. If he books trips with all of them, then they will pay him $100 each. If he won't book them all, then those he does book are only willing to pay $20 apiece. Will this package deal get Owen to reveal his quality? Explain.

    f.   Can Owen offer to refund the clients' fees if they aren't happy with the float trip as a means of signaling the quality of his trips?

16. A firm sells either high- or low-quality appliances in two periods. The demand for high-quality appliances is larger than the demand for low quality appliances in each period. Consumers initially think the firm's appliances are equally likely to be high or low quality. At the start of the first period the firm can claim to sell high-quality appliances or it can say nothing. If the firm claims high-quality, its demand curve is the one for high-quality appliances. After buying the appliance consumers learn the true quality, and they tell all their friends. If the firm lied it makes no sales in the second period; if it told the truth it faces the true demand in the second period. Under what conditions will the firm tell the truth?

■ Answers to Practice Problems

1. You should be wary of dealing with any of these guys, since they know the refrigerator's quality and you do not. Even so, the flunkout is probably selling because he is leaving town. Because the flunkout is leaving town, he will take a lower price for a good refrigerator than he'd require if he weren't leaving town. The other two chose to sell their refrigerators. Unless the proportion of good-quality refrigerators is high, these two sellers are unlikely to be willing to part with a good refrigerator, so you probably should steer clear of them. The best answer is a.

2. The unlimited returns policy is likely to impose extra costs on Shirts Galore. These extra costs could well be a signal of Shirts Galore's quality. An unlimited returns policy is likely to cost more to a firm with lower-quality products, since more of their customers will return their shirts. Therefore, only companies with high-quality shirts are likely to offer an unlimited returns policy. Over the Tops chose a less generous return policy, which suggests that they don't think their shirts are of high quality. Answer b is best.

3. Anyone can say that he or she is a good driver—the claim is cheap talk. Recognizing this fact, insurance companies wouldn't take a driver's claim that he or she was a safe driver seriously. Answer d is best. While it is true that accidents can happen to anyone, insurance companies are interested in distinguishing between drivers who are more likely and drivers who are less likely to get in an accident. So answer a isn't correct. While insurance companies would like to keep their rates high, they particularly like insuring safe drivers. They would rather cut the rates they offer safe drivers than lose them to another insurance company, which is why answer b isn't best. While most drivers might be inclined to overestimate their skills, it seems fair to say that they know more about their driving habits than do insurance companies, which is why answer c isn't best.

4. Insurance companies care very much about drivers' habits. They are worried that good drivers, knowing their acumen, may buy less insurance while bad drivers insure heavily. Moreover, they would like to attract safe drivers by offering low premiums, while at the same time charging higher rates to less careful drivers. So answer a is wrong. While insurance companies might have other ways of determining how careful a driver you are, such as basing your premiums on your age, gender, and past driving record, the use of such indicators doesn't perfectly indicate a driver's habits. Careless people can drive for years without getting in an accident, while a careful driver might have bad luck one day and cause a

crash. So answer b can't be correct. Only by monitoring their customers can insurance companies find out how careful drivers are. But such monitoring is likely to be extremely expensive—imagine hiring one person to follow each of your 5 million customers around for a week just to see what they do behind the wheel. Answer c is most likely to be correct.

5. Answers and brief explanations follow.

    a. Certainly all 100 lemons will be on the market. If all 100 cherries are also on the market, there is a 50 percent probability of getting a cherry and a 50 percent probability of getting a lemon. Hence the expected value of a typical used car is $1/2 \times \$5000 + 1/2 \times \$2000$, or $3500.

    b. If half the cherries are on the market, there are 150 used cars in total (100 lemons plus 50 cherries). The probability of getting a cherry is 50/150, or 1/3. The probability of getting a lemon is 100/150, or 2/3. Hence, the expected value of a typical used car is $1/3 \times \$5000 + 2/3 \times \$2000$, or $3000.

    c. If none of the cherries are on the market, buyers know any car is a lemon. They are only willing to pay $2000, the value of a lemon.

    d. If there are C cherries on the market, then the total number of used cars is $100 + C$. The probability of getting a cherry is $C/(100 + C)$, and the probability of getting a lemon is $100/(100 + C)$. The expected value of a typical used car is $C/(100 + C) \times \$5000 + 100/(100 + C) \times \$2000$, or $5000 \times (C + 40)/(100 + C)$.

6. False. The problem isn't buyers' ignorance per se. If buyers are ignorant of quality then they are only willing to pay the average value of a car on the market. If sellers were also ignorant of quality, they would be willing to take a price equal to average quality, and there wouldn't be any reason to expect high-quality used cars to be removed from the market. The reason bad cars drive out good cars is that there is asymmetric information: Sellers of good cars require a price that is higher than the average value, and so are unwilling to sell. Only lower-quality used cars remain on the market.

7. Ambiguous. The point of this question is not to debate the chemistry of gasoline octane, but rather to consider gasoline sellers' motives. Suppose a gas station gets only high-octane fuel, but they suspect their customers would pay less for low-octane and more for high-octane. Suppose also they think that individuals with expensive cars have larger incomes, and thus greater demands for gas, and that these individuals also are more inclined to buy high-octane fuel. Then it is possible that the gas station will sell some of the fuel as low octane so that they can price discriminate between their two types of customers. (The idea is to use consumers' false beliefs about product quality to price discriminate.)

8. True. Such advertising is probably a signal of product quality. Because advertising is expensive, firms with low-quality products are unwilling to spend large sums to promote their products; they know that consumers will find them out in short order. On the other hand, firms with higher-quality products can expect to develop a solid reputation when consumers try out their wares. Therefore, the benefits from advertising are larger for firms with high-quality products, making them more willing to spend large sums on advertising, whether the ads convey useful information or not.

9. From part d of Practice Problem 5, the price of a used car is $5000 \times (C + 40)/(100 + C)$ when there are C cherries on the market. See Figure 18.2.

    a. Consumers are only willing to pay the expected price of a used car. Since all 100 lemons will be offered for sale, the largest this expected value could possibly be is $3500 (see answer a to Practice Problem 5). But if all sellers of cherries require at least $4000, no seller with a cherry would be willing to offer his or her car for sale. The result is that only lemons are on the market, so cars sell for $2000.

b. If buyers think the chance they will get a cherry equals 1/2, they would be willing to pay $3500 for a used car. All sellers of cherries would be willing to sell at a price of $3500, so all cars would be offered for sale. It is also possible, though perhaps less likely, that consumers are pessimistic. If consumers don't think they will get a cherry, they would only be willing to pay the value of a lemon: $2000. In this case, all sellers of cherries refuse to sell, and we get the same outcome as in part a.

c. If cherry sellers require at least $3000, the same outcomes described in part b are possible. If consumers think the chance a used car is a cherry equals 50 percent, they will pay $3500, and all cherries will be offered for sale. If consumers don't think they will get a cherry, they would only be willing to pay $2000 and all sellers of cherries refuse to sell.

d. As we saw in part a, those sellers who wouldn't sell for less than $4000 aren't going to participate in this market. If half the sellers of cherries would take $3000, there are 50 cherries and 100 lemons offered for sale. The expected value of a used car is thus $1/3 \times \$5000 + 2/3 \times \$2000 = \$3000$. So if consumers anticipated the probability of getting a cherry equaled 1/3, they'd be willing to pay $3000, in which case half the cherries and all the lemons are offered for sale.

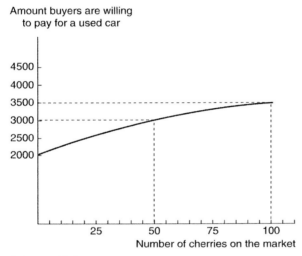

Figure 18.2

10. In part d from Practice Problem 9, half of the sellers would just be willing to sell for $3000, and half would just be willing to sell for $4000. Thus the average price that a seller would just be willing to accept is $3500, which is the price that a seller of a cherry would be willing to accept in part b. Even though the average price a seller would be willing to take is the same in the two parts, the motives of cherry sellers aren't the same. The difference occurs because sellers of cherries can decide to withdraw their car from the market if the price isn't satisfactory, and half the sellers in part d are sure to do so. The number of cherries supplied in part d is depicted as the dashed line in Figure 18.3. By contrast, $3500 is enough to attract all sellers in part b. The number of cherries supplied in part b is the solid line in Figure 18.3 (think of these as supply curves.) The relation between the price buyers would pay and the number of cherries on the market is plotted as the solid curve, taken from Figure 18.2 (think of this as the demand curve). In part b of Problem 9, all 100 cherries are supplied and price is $3500. In part d, half the cherries are supplied, and price is $3000.

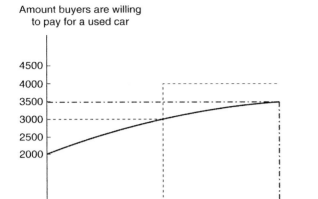

Amount buyers are willing
to pay for a used car

Figure 18.3

11. For a signal to be effective the participants must expect that only the higher-quality participants will use it. In turn, this requires that the gain from signaling is not smaller than the cost of signaling for higher-quality participants (see equation in the text). In this problem, the gain is the increased present value of earnings, or $200,000 (= $700,000 − $500,000). The cost is the present value of the annual costs of attending college over the next 4 years, $PV_4 = 50,000/(1 + r) + 50,000/(1 + r)^2 + 50,000/(1 + r)^3 + 50,000/(1 + r)^4$, where r is the individual's discount rate (Chapter 16). So we require that $PV_4 < 200,000$, which will be true for any positive value of r—i.e., so long as the individual values the present more than the future. In addition, the gain from signaling must be smaller than the cost of signaling for lower quality participants. In this problem, someone with lower ability must spend an extra year in college, which raises the opportunity cost of signaling by an amount equal to the present value of a 5th year in college, or $50,000/(1 + r)^5$; it also lowers the present value of the stream of wages by $w/(1 + r)^5$ (since the lower-ability individual would have to wait an extra year to get the managerial job). For this person to eschew the signal we'd need $200,000 − w/(1 + r)^5 < PV_4 + 50,000/(1 + r)^5$. Rearranging, we get

$$\$200,000 - PV_4 < (50,000 + w)/(1 + r)^5.$$

The left side is the gain to signaling (which must be positive, as discussed above) and the right side is the extra cost of signaling that a lower-ability person would bear if he were to go to college. In other words, for attending college to work as a signal of talent, the net gain to a higher-talent person must be positive (so a higher-ability person would want to signal), but small enough that a lesser-talent person could not gain from signaling.

12. See Figure 18.4. The curve line is taken from Figure 18.2, and the straight line from Figure 18.1. The equilibrium price, $3,000, is found at the intersection. The number of cherries offered for sale is 50, also found at the intersection.

p (price of used cars)

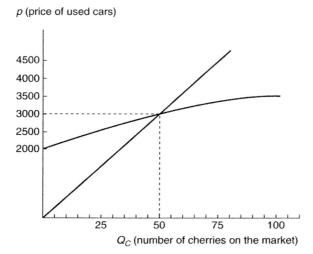

Q_C (number of cherries on the market)

Figure 18.4

13. Moe is sadly confused. The heart of asymmetric information problems is not buyers' ignorance, it is sellers' knowledge. Because sellers know something buyers don't know, they can act opportunistically. Larry is mostly correct, but he has glossed over the distinction between adverse selection, where sellers act opportunistically because they know something about their product that buyers don't know, and moral hazard, where sellers act opportunistically by taking an action that buyers can't see. Curly is apparently the most careful student, as he has picked up on this distinction.

14. Health insurance companies cannot determine whether a customer is a high or a low health risk, which means that premiums must be based on the average clients' health risk. When employers offer group health insurance as part of their compensation packages, all employees are signed up, both those who are high health risks and those who are low health risks. By contrast, when individuals decide whether or not to buy insurance, there is a potential adverse selection problem. The concern is that low-risk clients might be willing to go without health insurance if the price is too high, leaving the company with a larger proportion of high-health-risk customers. While insurance companies raise rates for individuals because of this adverse selection phenomenon, they can offer lower rates for groups when everyone in the group is automatically enrolled in the insurance program.

15. Since Owen is a monopolist, he picks his output to balance marginal revenue and marginal cost and then sets price based on demand (Chapter 11). If Owen's customers don't know the quality of his trips, his choices are based on the demand curve that reflects consumers' expectations of his quality. Since demand is linear, marginal revenue has the same intercept as demand and twice the slope, whether quality is known or not.

    a. If consumers know Owen's quality is high, his marginal revenue is $180 - 2Q$. His profit-maximizing output sets this expression equal to his marginal cost, which is 40. So he would sell 70 trips, and charge $110 per trip.

    b. If Owen were known to be low quality, his marginal revenue would be $100 - 2Q$. Here he would sell 30 trips, which sets $100 - 2Q$ equal to 40, and he would charge $70 per trip.

    c. Since consumers think Owen's trips are equally likely to be high or low quality, the probability that his trips are high quality is 1/2. The probability that his trips are low quality is also 1/2. Owen's demand is the average value consumers place on his trips:

$$p_a = 1/2 \times (180 - Q) + 1/2 \times (100 - Q),$$

    or $p_a = 140 - Q$. (The "a" subscript is for "average.") The marginal revenue associated with this demand is $140 - 2Q$. Equating this marginal revenue to his marginal cost of $40, Owen would sell 50 trips at $90 per trip.

d. If Owen's trips were high quality, he would want customers to know his trips are good, since he can sell more trips at a higher price. Unfortunately, if Owen's trips are low quality, he would also want to tell customers that his trips are high quality. If he didn't tell them his trips were good, they would think his trips were low quality, which means he would lose sales and have to charge a lower price.

e. The customers' package deal is an attempt to screen. To work, a screen has to get the informed agent to behave differently depending on his information. In this case, Owen would accept the deal offered by the customers if his trips were high quality, but he would refuse the deal if his trips were low quality. If Owen did behave this way, the prices the customers offer would be based on the demand curves associated with knowing Owen's quality, so they would make sense. The problem is that Owen is sure to accept the deal whether he has high or low quality. Regardless of the quality of his trips, he sells more trips at a higher price if he takes the deal.

f. To be successful, a signal must be more costly to send when his trips are low quality. For the money-back guarantee to work, Owen's customers must be more likely to ask for a refund if his trip is low quality. The problem here is that once the trip is over, customers have no reason not to ask for a refund no matter what the trip's quality.

16. Since consumers think a randomly drawn appliance is equally likely to be high or low quality, the initial price of an appliance would be the arithmetic mean of the price that would be paid to each type. If we let the price an appliance would receive if it were known to be high quality be P_H and the price an appliance would receive if it were known to be low quality be P_L, then initially the price is $P_0 = \frac{1}{2} \times P_H + \frac{1}{2} \times P_L$. An appliance that is claimed to be of high quality is sold at P_H, so the gain to claiming an appliance is of high quality equals $P_H - P_0 = P_H - (\frac{1}{2} \times P_H + \frac{1}{2} \times P_L) = \frac{1}{2} \times (P_H - P_L)$. Because the demand for high-quality appliances is larger than the demand for low-quality appliances, $P_H > P_L$ and so there is a gain in the first period from claiming to have high-quality appliances. If the vendor has Q appliances for sale, the net gain from claiming they are high quality is then $\frac{1}{2} \times (P_H - P_L) \times Q$. If this guy is lying, he loses the present value of his profits from next period (since he will be found out), $\pi_L/(1 + r)$. For this guy to not lie, the net gain can't be positive, or $\frac{1}{2} \times (P_H - P_L) \times Q < \pi_L/(1 + r)$. On the other hand, for it to make sense for a seller with high-quality appliances to make the claim, he only needs to increase his profits in this period (since buyers will discover he has high-quality stuff anyway at the end of this period). But that only requires he get a higher price, i.e., $P_H > P_0$, and as we saw above that is surely true. Thus truth telling can be an equilibrium if $\frac{1}{2} \times (P_H - P_L) \times Q < \pi_L/(1 + r)$.

■ Exercises

Fill-in

1. ChlorEx Corporation sells bleach under the label "ChlorEx's Best." ChlorEx has two types of customers, but it can't tell them apart so it can't price discriminate. If ChlorEx charges $6 per bottle of ChlorEx's Best, it will sell 600 bottles to type A customers and no bottles to type B customers. If they charge $4.50 per bottle, they sell 750 bottles to type A customers and 150 bottles to type B customers. ChlorEx can also sell bleach in an unlabeled bottle. Both types of customers think ChlorEx's Best is superior to the unlabeled bottle. Type A customers won't buy the unlabeled bottle. Type B customers will only buy unlabeled if they don't buy ChlorEx's Best, in which case their demand for the unlabeled bottle is $p = 5 - Q/100$, where Q is the number of unlabeled bottles sold. ChlorEx's marginal cost for bleach production is zero for both types of bottles.

    a. If ChlorEx only sells ChlorEx's Best, they should sell __ bottles at a price of ___ each.

    b. If ChlorEx sells both ChlorEx's Best and the unlabeled bottle, they should sell __ bottles of ChlorEx's Best at a price of ___ apiece, and ___ bottles of the unlabeled bottle at a price of ___ apiece.

c.   ChlorEx's profits are _____ if they only sell ChlorEx's Best.

d.   If they sell both ChlorEx's Best and the unlabeled bottle, their profits from selling ChlorEx's Best are ___, and their profits from selling the unlabeled bottle are ___.

e.   Should ChlorEx only sell ChlorEx's Best or should they sell both bottles? _____.

True-False-Ambiguous and Explain Why

2.   An increase in the cost of a signal will make it less likely that the signal will be effective.

3.   Suppose there are two types of workers—those that are highly productive and those that are less productive. An employee of XYZ Corporation applies to the ABC Company for a job. While XYZ did not know the worker's productivity when it hired her, it learned her ability after observing her at work. ABC knows that after they make the employee a job offer, she will show the offer to XYZ and demand a raise. In light of this knowledge, ABC should lower the salary they offer XYZ's employee.

4.   Used car dealers often charge more for their vehicles than do individuals selling their cars privately, which is evidence that used car dealers price discriminate.

5.   College graduates earn higher wages than those without a college diploma because higher education provides training that is useful to potential employers.

Short-Answer

6.   An employer knows that he has two types of employees, high skill and low skill. Each worker must be assigned to either an easy job or a hard job. Assigning a high-skill worker to the hard job generates $10 profit, while assigning him to the easy job makes $5 profit. The employer gets $4 profit from a low-skill worker, whether she assigns him to the hard job or the easy job. High-skill workers are happy in either job, but low-skill workers bear a personal cost of $1 when assigned to the hard job. High-skill workers like to read during their free time, while low-skill workers like to lie on the couch in front of the TV after dinner. The employer is considering three options for determining each worker's skills: (1) offer to pay a $5 bonus for accepting the hard job; (2) give any worker who applies for the hard job a trial; and (3) offer to enroll any worker in an evening class to learn a spreadsheet program, and then assign the worker to the hard job and pay him or her a $2 bonus (the spreadsheet class costs the employer $2 per worker; neither job requires the ability to use spreadsheet programs). Which of these options is likely to work? Explain.

7.   Many years ago, salesmen would go door to door hawking vacuum cleaners. These salesmen would ask to be invited in so that they could demonstrate the ability of their product to pick up dirt in the potential customer's home. Explain why potential customers should have been wary of these door-to-door salesmen, and suggest actions that either the customer or the salesman might have taken in response to this nervousness.

8.   A number of consumer products have the potential for differing environmental impacts, and many consumers would prefer to consume products that are more environmentally friendly. In response to this preference, a number of eco-certification schemes have emerged in a variety of countries. Why might these schemes be valuable?

9.   In many rural communities along interstate highways, gas stations situated near the freeway charge substantially more for fuel than stations in town. One explanation for these differences in price is that those passing by are in too much of a hurry to drive into town for cheaper gas. Use the tourist-trap model to suggest an alternative explanation.

10. Suppose that a college education has no impact on potential workers' productivity. There are two kinds of potential employees: those who can figure out how to solve a problem quickly (problem solvers) and those who take forever (sleepyheads). Because employers value the ability to solve problems, problem solvers are worth $60,000 to a firm. By contrast, sleepyheads are only worth $30,000. A typical college costs $20,000 including tuition, room, and board. In addition, sleepyheads find the process of studying so unpleasant that they would have to be paid $12,000 to put up with it. If 80 percent of potential applicants are sleepyheads, who attends college and how much do employers pay college graduates?

11. A firm wishes to distinguish between two types of employees, hard workers and slackers, so that it can put hard workers in a more demanding job. Because the more demanding job generates more profit for the firm, it is willing to offer larger pay to workers assigned to the more demanding job. Workers are equally content to take on any job, so they apply for the job offering them the highest compensation. The firm offers employees their choice of two compensation packages: For either job they can receive their compensation in pay only, or they can receive a lower wage but free health insurance. Discuss the ability of the choice of compensation packages to distinguish between the two types of workers when

   a. hard workers are lower health risks than slackers;

   b. hard workers are greater health risks than slackers;

   c. the health risks for hard workers and slackers are the same, but hard workers are more risk averse than slackers are.

Chapter 19
Contracts and Moral Hazards

■ Chapter Summary

Suppose that you want to get some work done on your house, and you hire a contractor. He promises to complete a high-quality job in short order. Should you trust him? An insurance company wants to sign up lots of clients, but worries about these clients' tendency to take excessive risks. In both of these examples, one party enters into an arrangement with a second party knowing that the second party can do things the first party can't see. Your contractor might work hard and pay close attention to details, or he might cut corners and spend a good part of his time lollygagging around. The insurance company's client could be very cautious or might be quite careless. In examples where one party can take advantage of a second party because their actions can't be seen, we say there is *moral hazard*. In problems with moral hazard, the uninformed person is usually called the *principal,* and the informed person is the *agent*. Interactions between the two are a **principal-agent problem**. The moral hazard that underlies principal-agent problems is commonly addressed by carefully designed contracts, which offer the agent incentives to act in ways the principal desires.

The design of such contracts is often not simple. The principal wants the agent to act in a manner that enhances the principal's final product, but this often requires that the agent bear substantial risk. Unless the agent is risk neutral, the principal often faces a **trade-off between efficiency in production and efficiency in risk bearing**. A contract that does not require the agent to bear as much risk is more appealing to him, but can reduce incentives to act in the principal's best interests. For example, paying a worker an hourly wage means she doesn't bear any risk from variations in the firm's profits, but it doesn't give her an incentive to work hard. Contracts where **payments are linked to production or profit**, say, by paying the worker a percentage of the firm's profits, make her want to work hard so that the firm makes more money. However, such contracts can expose the worker to considerable risk, which will be undesirable to the worker if she is risk averse.

An alternative to profit-based pay is for the principal to use **monitoring**: to devote resources towards determining how hard employees work. If employees know their pay is based on the performance that is observed during the monitoring, they will work harder. While monitoring can induce employees to work harder, it can be quite expensive for the employer.

While moral hazard problems often involve incentives for agents to slack off, there is a second concern. If a contract pays an employee on the basis of the firm's performance it may benefit the employer to underreport the firm's profits. In light of this opportunity for misrepresentation, contracts can include **checks on principals**. If well conceived, such a check will make it in the principal's best interests to truthfully reveal the firm's performance.

A final approach to resolving principal-agent contracts is for the principal to offer the agent a set of contracts, and to then pay attention to the agent's **contract choice**. If this set is cleverly devised, the agent's choice from the set will allow the principal to infer some information about the agent's intended behavior.

It's important that the relation between the principal and the agent involve some source of uncertainty that is beyond either party's control. If the only source of uncertainty is the agent's behavior, so that profits are high if the agent works hard and low if the agent slacks, then the principal can simply tie the agent's compensation to the firm's performance. In this case the agent knows full well that he gets paid more for working harder, because there is no chance that he will work hard and still have the firm perform poorly. By contrast, if the firm's performance depends on the agent's effort and some other source of uncertainty, then the agent can't be sure how well the firm will do if he works hard.

There are many other important applications of the principal-agent model. A regulator wishes to eliminate deadweight loss by instituting a price ceiling that equates demand with a monopolist's marginal cost. Unfortunately, the regulator doesn't know the firm's marginal cost. Knowing what the regulator would do with this information, the firm has no incentive to reveal its costs. In the regulation example, the regulator is the principal and the monopolist is the agent. Similar applications emerge from environmental regulation. Designing good contractual incentives for regulated firms is not easy, but it can be extremely important from a welfare perspective.

■ Key Concepts and Formulas

- **Fixed-fee contract:** a contract that pays the agent the same amount no matter what actions he takes and no matter what the principal's payoffs are.
- **Hire contract:** a contract that pays the agent on the basis of observable effort, such as the amount of time he works or the amount he produces.
- **Contingent contract:** a contract that pays the agent on the basis of the state of nature.
- **Sharing contract:** a contract that pays the agent a fixed portion of the principal's payoff.
- **Efficiency in production:** an outcome that maximizes the sum of the two parties' payoffs.
- **Efficiency in risk bearing:** an outcome in which the party that is less risk averse bears most of the risk.
- **Participation constraint:** the requirement that a contract provides enough compensation to the agent so that he will want to participate, rather than choose some other opportunity.
- **Incentive compatible:** a contract that makes the agent want to behave as promised, rather than act opportunistically.
- **Bonding:** a requirement that the agent leave an amount of money with either the principal or some third party; the agent forfeits this money if his performance is deemed insufficient.
- **Efficiency wages:** wages that exceed the worker's best alternative; they provide an incentive not to shirk.

■ Application: Auto Warranties and After-Sales Service

Many firms that sell consumer durables offer warranties on their products. These warranties typically guarantee that the product will perform well for a specified period, such as a year, and promise to repair or replace any product that has problems during the warranty period. As we saw in the last chapter, firms that sell high-quality products will want to signal the quality to potential customers. A warranty is one way of signaling product quality, since the firm knows that high-quality goods are less likely to be returned for repair or replacement. These warranties also typically include a provision that voids the contract if the consumer has abused the product. For some kinds of products, such as automobiles, the consumer is obliged to follow a specific maintenance schedule if the warranty is to remain in effect.

Question: Why do auto warranties require that the consumer follow a specified maintenance schedule?

Answer: It is conceivable that regular servicing of automobiles lowers the chance that they will need repairs. There would seem to be some disagreement on this point, however. On the National Public Radio show *Car Talk,* that well-known reliable source of information, the hosts have been known to discuss the optimal frequency of oil changes. One view is that it is best to change the oil frequently, say, every 3,000 miles. The other view is that you should change the oil soon after buying the car and just before selling, but not in between. While regular servicing of the car may or may not keep it running well, there is another reason for car companies to insist on regular servicing.

The manufacturer knows that the likelihood of a claim on the warranty is based in part on the care taken by the consumer. Since the car owner's level of care is an unobserved action, car companies face a problem of moral hazard. A consumer who runs the car hard, frequently driving it at high RPMs, grinding gears, and changing oil infrequently is more likely to have problems than a customer who treats the car with tender loving care. On this basis, one might argue that the only vehicles that come in for repair have been abused. But if a car company regularly refused claims for repair under warranty it would soon get a reputation as a firm that reneges on the warranty. Because car companies want consumers to view their warranties as a signal of quality, they have to honor claims.

If car buyers think that any problems that occur during the warranty period will be fixed for free, they have less incentive to take proper care of the vehicle. Such lack of care will increase the cost of offering a warranty, making it harder for manufacturers to offer meaningful protection. So car companies look for ways to ameliorate the moral hazard. One way to lessen the moral hazard problem is to monitor car owners' behavior. Car companies could send out spies to watch how you and I treat our cars, but this would clearly be exorbitantly expensive. A much cheaper alternative is to provide an incentive for the car owner to provide an indication of how well they care for the car. By requiring car owners to change the oil on a regular basis, car companies obtain information on the level of care the car owner exercises. Some drivers will be too busy or too indifferent to get the car serviced, while others fastidiously keep to the service schedule. If the first group is largely made up of those who don't take good care of their cars, then the service requirements screen out some car abusers from the set of possible claimants.

■ Solved Problems

1. Bill has a remarkable smile. All his friends agree his teeth are the brightest, straightest, and cleanest they have ever seen. To keep his teeth so presentable, Bill likes to visit his dentist regularly. Because his dentist charges fairly high rates, Bill would only visit the dentist once in a typical year if he had to pay for his own visits. Some years, however, Bill has problems with his teeth that induce him to visit the dentist four times. Luckily, Bill has a health insurance policy that pays for his visits. Because visits to the dentist are free to Bill under this policy, he wants to visit the dentist every 2 months. Bill's health insurance company will pay for two visits each year; Bill must pay for any additional visits. How does the restriction on the number of Bill's visits affect moral hazard and risk bearing?

    Step 1: Describe Bill's moral hazard and risk bearing if his health insurance policy does not restrict the number of his visits.

    Without any restrictions, Bill visits the dentist six times. Whether he has a good year for teeth (in which case he would only go once if he had to pay for the visit) or a bad year (when he would visit four times), a health insurance policy that pays all of Bill's dental bills and doesn't limit the number of his visits will induce him to go to the dentist more often. These extra visits to the dentist are Bill's moral hazard. At the same time, Bill bears no risk at all with a health insurance policy that doesn't limit his visits. Be it a good year or a bad year, he gets to go to the dentist as often as he likes.

Step 2: Describe Bill's moral hazard and risk bearing if his health insurance policy will only pay for his first two visits to the dentist.

In good years, Bill would only be willing to pay for his first visit. The value he gets from a second or third visit is too small to induce him to visit more often than once. Since the health insurance company will pay for two visits, he goes twice. There is still a moral hazard, since he visits more often than he would if he had to pay for his visits, but it is smaller than with a policy that doesn't limit the number of visits. In bad years, Bill is willing to visit the dentist four times. The insurance company pays for the first two visits and Bill pays for the second two. There is no moral hazard in bad years. Bill faces some risk with this policy. The amount he has to pay for dental visits depends on the state of nature: He pays nothing in good years, and he pays for two visits in bad years.

Step 3: Compare Bill's moral hazard and risk bearing in Steps 1 and 2.

When the insurance company limits the number of visits they will pay for, they sharply reduce Bill's moral hazard. If Bill has a good year, the limit on the number of paid visits reduces his extra visits from five to one. In bad years, the limit on the number of paid visits reduces his extra visits from two to zero. At the same time, the limit on paid visits causes Bill to bear extra risk. If Bill is risk averse and the health insurance company risk neutral, which seems like a probable combination, it is inefficient for him to bear all the risk (as when he is uninsured). However, full insurance—that pays for all of Bill's visits–leads to the largest amount of moral hazard. The cap on paid visits to the dentist strikes a compromise that reduces Bill's risk (relative to no insurance) and lowers the moral hazard (relative to full insurance).

2. An alternative to a traditional health insurance policy that has become relatively popular in the last decade or so is the health management organization (HMO). HMOs are often less expensive than traditional health insurance, but they also typically restrict the physicians that a policyholder may receive care from. They also tend to provide smaller compensation to these physicians than do more traditional policies, which occasionally causes physicians to refuse to do business with the HMO. Why would HMOs limit the amount they will pay for doctor visits, and why are their rates lower?

Step 1: Describe the moral hazard under a traditional policy.

If you are ill and need to see a doctor, and you know that your insurance company will foot the bill, chances are you will seek out the best doctor you can find. Even if this physician charges more than an alternative doctor who would provide adequate care, you will go to the more expensive doctor since you aren't paying for the visit. In addition, you may agree to a battery of expensive tests, even if there are less costly alternative methods for diagnosing your condition. The tendency to visit more expensive physicians and to agree to expensive tests is the moral hazard. Because health insurance companies can't determine whether you had these tests done because they were crucial or just because you wanted to play it safe, they make larger payments than is efficient. In turn, they must pass these costs on to the consumer, through higher premiums.

Step 2: Describe the moral hazard with an HMO.

While an HMO can't eliminate tendencies to test more than is efficient, they can try to set up guidelines for dealing with various potential problems. Not all doctors will agree to these guidelines, but those who do establish a relation with the HMO. This relation gives the doctor an incentive to moderate requests for diagnostic tests so as to keep the HMO happy. In a sense, the doctor serves as a sort of monitor, keeping tabs on the patient's behavior. This monitoring helps to reduce moral hazard, which means that the HMO is less likely to bear larger costs than is efficient. In turn, they can pass these savings on to their customers, through lower rates.

■ Practice Problems

Multiple-Choice

1. A state that institutes mandatory insurance programs will likely be able to limit which of the following problems?
   a. The principal-agent problem.
   b. Moral hazard.
   c. Both a and b.
   d. Neither a nor b.

2. All else equal, which of the following statements regarding types of automobile insurance is most likely to be true?
   a. Collision insurance has a more severe moral hazard problem than comprehensive insurance.
   b. Comprehensive insurance has a more severe moral hazard problem than collision insurance.
   c. Both types of insurance are likely to have severe moral hazard problems.
   d. Neither type of insurance is likely to have severe moral hazard problems.

3. The efficiency wage theory holds that firms will offer abnormally high pay to workers, but threaten to terminate employment if the worker is caught shirking. Such a contract can discourage shirking
   a. if the firm's workers can't easily find a new job.
   b. even if the firm doesn't spend very much time checking up on its workers.
   c. if the firm's workers can find a new job right away, but the new job doesn't pay well.
   d. All of the above are true.

4. Phil wants to hire Tom to go door to door selling Shinola, an obscure product that some think has wonderful curative properties. The amount that Tom sells will depend on how hard he works and various random events, such as the number of potential customers that are home today, the amount of Shinola the potential customers have purchased in the last month, and the amount they have purchased in their life. Before Tom sets off, Phil and Tom are each offered the following bet on the roll of a die. If the die turns up with a 1, 2, or 3, the bet pays off nothing; if the die turns up with a 4 or 5, the bet pays off $6; and if the die turns up with a 6 the bet pays $20. It will cost $5 to play this bet. Phil accepts the bet but Tom does not. Given these facts, which of the following is most likely to be true?
   a. If Phil pays Tom a fixed hourly wage there will be efficiency in risk-bearing.
   b. If Phil pays Tom a fixed hourly wage there will be efficiency in production.
   c. If Phil pays Tom a fixed percentage of the total sales there will be efficiency in production.
   d. If Phil pays Tom a fixed percentage of the total sales there will be efficiency in risk-bearing.

Fill-in

5. Pat, who is risk neutral, hires Angus, who is risk averse, to work for her.
   a. To obtain efficiency in production, the contract Pat offers Angus must _____.
   b. To convince Angus to participate, the contract must pay Angus at least _____.
   c. What type of contract should Pat offer to obtain efficiency in production? _____.

   Now suppose that Pat's profits depend on both how hard Angus works and some other uncertain effect.
   d. To obtain efficiency in risk bearing, who should bear any risk? _____.
   e. What type of contract should Pat offer to obtain efficiency in risk bearing? _____.

True-False-Ambiguous and Explain Why

6. If the principal is risk neutral, it is generally possible to design contracts that achieve both production efficiency and efficiency in risk bearing.

7. Since revenue-sharing contracts neglect opportunity costs, they are not a good type of contract to use in principal-agent relations.

8. Abel (who is risk neutral) wants to hire Tasman (who is risk averse) to work for him. Abel is concerned that if Tasman isn't asked to bear any risk he will slack off. The best way for Abel to prevent such behavior is to constantly monitor Tasman.

9. If a principal's payoffs depend only on the agent's effort, then there is no moral hazard problem.

Short-Answer

10. Chuck is talking to Owen about some electrical work he needs done. Owen recommends an electrician named Jerry, whom Owen says "does good work." Chuck hires Jerry, but is disappointed with the results. Chuck tells Owen about his disappointment, and asks Owen why he thought Jerry was such a great electrician. Owen says that he watched Jerry work, and that Jerry seemed very careful. Suggest a reason Owen was satisfied with Jerry's work but Chuck was not.

11. Once upon a time, a professor at a major university in California gave a final exam. He instructed the students in the class that they were to raise their hands if they saw a classmate cheating, that one of the TAs would come up to them, and that they should then point out the cheating student. The TA would then take the accused student aside and confront him or her. At the TA's discretion, the alleged cheater could then be asked to leave, forfeiting any points from the final. What effect would you expect such a policy to have upon students in the class?

12. Also once upon a time, the Fuller Brush Company hired high school students to sell their products door to door. These students received a fixed hourly wage, and were told that they had to achieve a certain amount of sales each evening. If the student failed to reach this sales level on two consecutive evenings, he would be fired. Discuss this contractual relationship, addressing issues of moral hazard, productive efficiency, efficiency in risk bearing, incentive compatibility, and incentives for the student to participate.

13. In the United States, beer producers are prohibited from listing their products' alcoholic percentage on the container. Discuss the incentives for beer producers and the probable trends in alcohol content of a typical American beer.

14. Robin owns a valuable ring that she wants to insure. Because Robin is risk averse she would like to obtain full insurance on the ring. While some people seeking insurance are careful, Robin's insurance company knows that some clients are careless. All else equal, careless folks are more likely to have their property stolen or damaged. While Robin's insurance company is not willing to fully insure her ring, they are willing to sell her a policy that pays back 95% of the appraised value in the event of theft. Explain why the insurance company is unwilling to offer full insurance, but they are willing to insure 95% of the ring's value.

15. The Old Territorial Prison (OTP) offers tourists a chance to see the old wild west. OTP hires Joe to attract tourists. Joe is to stand out on the street in front of the park, waving a mock six-gun at everyone who passes by. Half of the time, demand is strong, and the number of visitors to OTP equals $a + 4$ where a is the amount of Joe's effort. The other half of the time demand is weak, and the number of visitors to OTP equals a. Standing out front is not pleasant for Joe; the opportunity cost he bears from exerting a units of effort is $c(a) = a^2$. Each visitor pays OTP a $12 admission fee. Both Joe and OTP are risk neutral.

   a. At what level of Joe's effort is there production efficiency?
   b. If OTP pays Joe $12 to stand out front, how hard will he work?
   c. If OTP gives Joe $6 for each visitor, how hard does he work?
   d. Now suppose that OTP pays Joe nothing unless there are at least six visitors. If at least six people visit the park, Joe is paid $68. How hard does Joe work?
   e. Of the three contracts described in parts b, c, and d, which comes closest to achieving production efficiency?
   f. How much risk does Joe bear under each of the three contracts?
   g. Which contract do you think OTP should use, and why?

■ Answers to Practice Problems

1. Relationships between insurance companies and drivers are a form of principal-agent relations where the company is the principal and the driver is the agent. So answer a is incorrect. Car drivers can exercise various levels of care—they can speed, look at the scenery, pay more attention to music than to nearby cars, and so on. Insurance companies can't observe the level of care a driver exerts, which means there is a hidden action. Hence the relation between drivers and insurance companies will have moral hazard. Mandatory insurance does not make it easier for companies to observe drivers' actions, so answer b is also incorrect. Neither a nor b is correct, so answer d is best.

2. Both collision insurance and comprehensive insurance are likely to be marked by moral hazard. Even so, if you get in a car crash you can be seriously hurt or killed. If your car is stolen or damaged by a vandal, you may be inconvenienced, but you don't suffer bodily harm. It is most likely that the potential for serious injury or death limits moral hazard with respect to auto accidents. Chances are, the moral hazard problem is more severe with comprehensive insurance than with collision insurance. Answer b is best.

3. The idea behind the efficiency wage model is that workers know they are receiving high pay at their present job, and that they stand to lose that high pay if they are caught shirking. The extra pay deters them from shirking only to the extent that they will bear real losses if caught shirking. Such losses can emerge if they can't find a new job, or if they can't find a new job that pays as well. It doesn't matter if they think it is likely that they will get caught. What matters is that the expected loss in pay, the probability of getting caught shirking multiplied by the loss in wages, is not smaller than the value they place on shirking. If the loss in pay is large enough, say because the worker can't find a new job, then the probability of getting caught shirking doesn't need to be large to deter shirking. All of a, b, and c are correct, so answer d is best.

4. The bet offered to these two has an expected payoff of $5.33 (= 3/6 × $0 + 2/6 × $6 + 1/6 × $20), which exceeds the cost of playing. Since Phil would play but Tom would not, we can conclude that Tom is more risk averse than Phil. For efficiency in risk bearing, the less risk-averse agent should bear most of the risk. If Tom is paid a percentage of his sales he bears all the risk, so a is incorrect. On the other hand, if Tom is paid a fixed hourly wage he has no incentive to work hard, so there is unlikely to be efficiency in production; b is incorrect as well. Even though Tom is more risk averse than Phil, we can't say that Phil is risk neutral: the bet described above has a positive expected value,

so someone who was a little risk averse might still be willing to play it. Unless Phil is risk neutral, efficiency in risk bearing would probably require Tom to bear a small amount of the risk, so d is not necessarily true. However, if Tom is paid a percentage of sales he will surely work hard so that total sales revenue is as large as possible, and that will usually guarantee efficiency in production. Answer c is best.

5. Answers and brief explanations follow.
    a. Efficiency in production means that Angus's actions maximize the sum of Pat's and Angus's payoffs. To obtain efficiency in production, the contract must make Angus act so as to maximize the sum of their payoffs.
    b. If Angus is to willingly participate in this relation, he must receive at least as much pay as he could get at his best alternative. If the pay is uncertain, as is commonly true, then he must receive the same expected utility from the contract as he can get at his best alternative.
    c. If Pat gives herself a fixed amount and leaves the rest for Angus, he will want to make the sum of payoffs as large as possible, since that maximizes his pay. Similarly, if she gives him a fixed percentage of the sum of their payoffs he wants the sum of payoffs to be as large as possible. So either a contract that pays Pat a fixed fee or a contingent contract that pays Angus a fixed fraction of profit (also known as a profit-sharing contract) will achieve efficiency in production.
    d. Since Pat is risk neutral while Angus is risk averse, efficiency in risk bearing is achieved when Pat bears all the risk and Angus bears no risk.
    e. If Pat can't see how hard Angus works, the two can't write a contract that is based on Angus's effort. They can still agree to give Angus a fixed share of profit, or all of profit minus a fixed payment to Pat, but both of these contracts cause Angus to bear all of the risk. The only form of contract that places all the risk on Pat is one that pays Angus a fixed amount and gives Pat all the residual profit.

6. False. As we saw in Practice Problem 4, efficiency in production generally requires that the agent bear substantial risk, while efficiency in risk bearing requires that the agent bear no risk. The only way to shield the agent from risk is to pay him a fixed amount, in which case he has no incentive to make the principal's profits larger.

7. Ambiguous. As we saw in Practice Problem 5, it is typically not possible to achieve both types of efficiency when the agent is more risk averse than the principal. A revenue-sharing contract gives the agent incentives to make revenues large in comparison to his opportunity costs, which is better than a contract that gives him no incentive to make profits larger (like one that pays him a fixed amount). While it is true that revenue-sharing contracts neglect opportunity costs, they can strike a balance between the goal of efficiency in production and efficiency in risk bearing if there is less risk associated with revenues than with profits. On the other hand, if profits are not riskier than revenues, then the contract is probably not as desirable as a profit-sharing arrangement. As a point of information, revenue-sharing contracts are fairly common. Salesmen, for example, are often paid a commission on their sales, which is a form of revenue sharing.

8. Ambiguous. It is true that monitoring Tasman will ensure he does not slack off, so that moral hazard can be avoided without forcing Tasman to bear any risk. Thus efficiency in risk bearing can be achieved. However, the cost of monitoring must be subtracted from the value of the output Tasman produces. If this net amount is larger than the value that could be produced under any other contractual arrangement, then monitoring Tasman is the best approach as it will yield both efficiency in production and efficiency in risk bearing. On the other hand, other methods that Abel might use won't require costly monitoring. Even though such methods might invite a certain amount of slacking they could still yield a larger net value, in which case monitoring wouldn't yield efficiency in production. In this latter case, some other arrangement could easily be preferable to constant monitoring.

9. Assuming the principal can observe her payoffs, this is true. For there to be a moral hazard problem, the agent's actions must be hidden. If her payoffs depend only on the agent's effort, then the principal can infer the agent's effort from the profit she receives. Since she can determine his effort, there isn't a hidden action, so there is no moral hazard problem.

10. Because Owen watched Jerry work, he could monitor Jerry's effort. If Owen monitored Jerry but Chuck did not, then Jerry will have worked harder for Owen than for Chuck. Owen's satisfaction with Jerry's work is likely to be a result of the monitoring.

11. If one student cheats, then other students are likely to suffer. If the professor grades on a curve and students in the class want to get the largest grade possible, then each student has an incentive to report a cheater. One might argue that reporting a cheater imposes a cost on the person who raises his or her hand, so not everyone will want to report a cheating incident. But the knowledge that a cheater will fail the final could make it more worthwhile to report a classmate. It is also true that the knowledge that others are likely to report you if you cheat could deter a potential cheater.

12. The amount a door-to-door salesman can sell on any given day depends on how hard he tries to sell and on various uncertainties, such as the fraction of homes where someone is home, how recently the potential customer went to the store to buy cleaning products, how much money they've already spent this month, and so on. Since Fuller Brush paid its workers a fixed hourly salary, the worker would bear no risk. Because sales are influenced by uncertainty, the company can legitimately fear the salesman will not try very hard to sell. Requiring a minimum level of sales to keep his job forces the salesman to bear some risk, which is likely to achieve greater efficiency in production. An alternative approach would be to pay salesmen a straight commission, but that forces the individual to bear a larger amount of risk than the minimum sales level would have done. It seems likely that high school students would be more fearful of risk than a large corporation, so a contract that limited the students' risks will likely have achieved greater efficiency in risk bearing. Finally, the hourly wage has to be large enough to induce the salesman to work hard enough that he stands a reasonable chance of meeting the sales quota. If not, the concern is that students will be unwilling to participate, in which case Fuller Brush will have a hard time hiring salesmen.

13. Since beer companies can't list the alcoholic content of their drinks, their choice of alcohol is a hidden action. Breweries can elevate alcohol by using larger amounts of barley malt, but at a larger cost. Since increasing alcohol will raise costs without changing potential buyers' predictions of content, the brewery has an incentive to reduce alcoholic content. The probable industry trend is toward weaker beers.

14. The insurance company is unwilling to offer full insurance because it fears moral hazard. If a client has full insurance, her wealth is the same whether there is a theft or not—even if her property is stolen she will be reimbursed. In selecting a level of care, the insured compares her expected utility if she is careful with her expected utility if she is careless. To the extent that being more careful is costly to the insured, the client will be inclined toward carelessness. While the client has the same amount of wealth with either level of care, she has smaller personal costs when she is careless. But being careless raises the odds that theft will occur, which in turn lowers the insurance company's profits. For a given insurance premium, this reduction in profits lowers the sum of the two parties' expected payoffs, which is a reduction in productive efficiency. The only way to get the insured to exercise care is to force her to bear some risk. Despite the fact that their clients are most likely risk averse, the insurance company forces clients to bear some risk so as to induce them to be more careful. A policy that pays off 95% of the loss when there is a theft forces Robin to bear some risk, since she stands to lose 5% of the value of her ring if it is stolen.

15. If Joe exerts effort level a, OTP's revenues are $12 \times (a + 4)$ if demand is strong and $12 \times a$ if demand is weak. The probability that demand is strong equals 1/2, which is also the probability that demand is weak. So OTP's expected revenues, ER, are

$$ER = 1/2 \times 12 \times (a + 4) + 1/2 \times 12 \times a$$
$$= 12a + 24.$$

Each extra unit of Joe's effort is worth $12 to OTP.

a. The level of Joe's effort that achieves production efficiency maximizes the sum of OTP and Joe's payoffs. OTP's payoffs are the difference between ER and the amount it pays Joe, while Joe's payoffs are the difference between the amount he is paid and the opportunity cost of standing out front, $c(a) = a^2$. So the sum of payoffs equals $ER - c(a) = 12a + 24 - a^2$. To achieve production efficiency, Joe would have to choose a^* such that $dER/da - dc(a)/da = 0$; that is, when $12 - 2a^* = 0$. Thus, productive efficiency is achieved when $a^* = 6$.

b. Joe will choose a to maximize his payoff. If he is paid $12 his payoff is $12 - a^2$, which gets smaller as a gets larger. He has no incentive to exert any effort. He chooses $a = 0$.

c. If the prison pays Joe $6 for each visitor, he collects $6 \times (a + 4)$ if demand is strong and $6 \times a$ if demand is weak. His expected payoff is $E\pi$:

$$E\pi = 1/2 \times 6 \times (a + 4) + 1/2 \times 6 \times a - a^2$$
$$= 6a + 12 - a^2.$$

Joe selects the value of a that maximizes his expected payoff: $dE\pi/da = 0$, or $6 - 2a$. Thus he picks $a = 3$.

d. Since Joe gets paid a fixed amount, he will work no harder than necessary, as in part a. Now, however, he doesn't get paid unless six people show up. To get four people to show up he has to pick $a = 2$ if demand is strong and $a = 6$ if demand is weak. So he either chooses $a = 6$ (to ensure that six people show up), $a = 2$ (so that six people show up when demand is strong), or $a = 0$ (he doesn't participate). If he picks $a = 0$, he gets no pay but bears no costs, so his payoff is zero. If he picks $a = 2$ and demand is strong, he is paid $68. But if demand is weak, he gets no pay, since fewer than six people show up. Whatever the state of demand, he exerts two units of effort and so bears costs of 2^2, or 4. Thus, his expected payoff is

$$1/2 \times 68 + 1/2 \times 0 - 4,$$

or 30. If he picks $a = 6$, he knows that at least six people will come to OTP, regardless of the state of demand. So he gets paid $68 with certainty. His costs are 6^2, or 36, so his payoff is $68 - 36 = 32$. This payoff is larger than both the expected payoff he receives from choosing $a = 2$ (30) and the payoff he gets if he chooses $a = 0$ (0). So, he is best off picking $a = 6$.

e. The contract in part d achieves productive efficiency, while the contracts in b and c do not.

f. Joe bears no risk with the contract in part b, and he bears no risk with the contract in part d when he selects $a = 6$. With the contract in part c, Joe's payoff is 15 if demand is strong and 3 if demand is weak. His average payoff is 9 ($= 1/2 \times 15 + 1/2 \times 3$), so the variance of Joe's payoff is $1/2 \times (15 - 9)^2 + 1/2 \times (3 - 9)^2$, or $1/2 \times 6^2 + 1/2 \times 6^2 = 36$.

g. OTP should use the contract in part d. They achieve efficiency in production. Because both parties are risk neutral, efficiency in risk bearing is not an issue.

■ Exercises

Fill-in

1. Pam runs a coffee shop and wants to be able to spend a little more time at home with her family. She hires Angela to work part time. Pam knows that her profits depend in part on the number of customers who come into the shop, and in part on how good a job Angela does. If Angela is pleasant and carefully prepares every customer's espresso drink, more customers will buy additional coffees. If Angela is surly or careless, most customers will leave after one cup. Because Pam wants to spend more time away from the shop, she can't monitor Angela's effort. Pam considers four types of contracts that she might offer to Angela. The first contract pays Angela $15 for each 2-hour shift Angela puts in. The second gives Angela 10 percent of the store's profit while Angela is working. The third gives Angela $0.25 for each cup Angela sells. The fourth pays Angela $10 for a 2-hour shift, and gives a $0.10 bonus on every cup Angela sells. Pam is risk neutral and Angela is risk averse. Angela has a second job offer that will pay her $14 for a 2-hour job.

   a. Which of these contracts is likely to result in productive efficiency? _____.

   b. Which of these contracts is likely to result in efficiency in risk bearing? _____.

   c. Which of these contracts is likely to be incentive compatible? _____.

   d. Under what conditions will Angela participate in the first contract? _____.

   e. Under what conditions will Angela participate in the second contract? _____.

   f. Under what conditions will Angela participate in the third contract? _____.

   g. Under what conditions will Angela participate in the fourth contract? _____.

True-False-Ambiguous and Explain Why

2. Since nobody wants to get in an automobile crash, there is no moral hazard with automobile insurance.

3. If the agent is risk neutral, it is generally possible to design contracts that achieve both production efficiency and efficiency in risk bearing.

4. They say the only certain things in life are death and taxes. What they don't say, but is nonetheless true, is that nobody wants to die. This desire not to die means that there is no moral hazard problem in life insurance.

5. There is no need for a firm to monitor a risk-neutral employee.

Short-Answer

6. Manufacturers that offer warranties often require the buyer to follow a specific maintenance schedule. Discuss the impact such a requirement has on the efficiency of the relation between manufacturer and purchaser.

7. Brenda and Glenda are talking about some work they had done on their houses. Both women hired Bill to do their work. Brenda paid Bill a fixed fee for her job and is concerned about the quality of Bill's work. Glenda thought Bill's work was okay, but complains that he seemed to take forever. She paid Bill an hourly wage. Explain the outcomes from these two contracts in terms of moral hazard.

8. Summer is a busy season for construction companies that do road improvements. In many parts of the United States, the weather during the autumn and winter is too harsh for repair jobs to be completed satisfactorily. As a result, it is common for road repair contracts to include a clause that penalizes the repair company if the job is not finished by a certain date (often in early to mid-autumn). Relate the use of such clauses to the material from this chapter.

9. Health insurance policies frequently contain both a deductible and a copayment clause. The company does not pay off any claims until a certain level has been reached (the deductible). After the deductible has been met, a fixed percentage of any additional claims are paid off. The remaining fraction of claims is paid by the insured (the copayment). Explain why health insurance companies would use deductibles and copayments.

10. Automobile insurance companies typically offer their clients a range of deductible levels. Why might they use more than one type of contract; what might they hope to learn by observing the customer's choice of contract; and how would you expect such information to be used?